THE JOURNAL OF APPLIED ECOMONY

VOLUME FOUR

"SCALE AND THE BOUNDARIES OF GOVERNANCE"

Contributors

Prof. Michael Faure
University of Pennsylvania

Mr. Clifford Chad Henson
University of Illinois

Prof. Manuel A. Utset
Florida State University

Prof. Robert W. McGee
Florida International University

Prof. Maurice R. Dyson
Columbia University

Dr. George S. Ford
Phoenix Center for Advanced Legal & Economic Public Policy Studies.

Mr. Lawrence J. Spiwak, Esq.
Phoenix Center for Advanced Legal & Economic Public Policy Studies

Design Editor

Mr. Ankit Agrawal
University of Melbourne

Associate Editor

Mr. Karl T. Muth
London School of Economics & Political Science

Mr. Aron Ping D'Souza
The University of Melbourne

Editor

Mr H. Trent Moore
Journal of Applied Economy

SEPTEMBER 2010

PUBLISHED BY THE ELIAS CLARK GROUP

DISTRIBUTED IN CONNECTION WITH THE GALE GROUP,
A PART OF CENGAGE LEARNING

AF798088

The Elias Clark Group
www.elias-clark.com

GPO Box 5001
Melbourne, Victoria 3001
Australia

First Published 2010.

Cataloguing-in-Publication entry

Editors: Moore, H. Trent.
D'Souza, Aron Ping.
Muth, Karl T.

Authors: Muth, Karl T.
Faure, Michael
Henson, Clifford Chad
Utset, Manuel A.
McGee, Robert W.
Dyson, Maurice R.
Ford, George S.
Spiwak, Lawrence J.

Title: The Journal of Applied Economy, Vol. 4, "Scale and the Boundaries of Governance"

ISBN: 978-0-9807318-6-6 (pbk.)
ISSN: 1836-2192

Subjects: Economics – General.

This edition may be cited as
Volume 4 (2010) J. App. Econ.
followed by the page number

ABOUT THE TYPEFACE

The Journal of Applied Economy is typeset in Garamond 12 and the footnotes are set in Garamond 10. The typeface was named for Claude Garamond (c. 1480 - 1561) and are based on the work of Jean Jannon. By 1540, Garamond became a popular choice in the books of the French imperial court, particularly under King Francis I. Garamond was said to be based on the handwriting of Angelo Vergecio, a librarian to the King. The italics of Garamond are credited to Robert Grandjon, an assistant to Claude Garamond. The font was re-popularised in the art deco era and became a mainstay on twentieth-century publication. In the 1970s, the font was redesigned by the International Typeface Corporation, which forms the basis of the variant of Garamond used in this Journal.

TABLE OF CONTENTS

CALL FOR PAPERS

The field of applied economy lies at the nexus of theory and implementation, the practical and the philosophical. We must attempt to link the ivory tower of academia with the glass towers of the City and Wall Street. By understanding the theoretical foundations of global markets and economic decision making, applied economy can inform us about the role of market structures within larger analytical frameworks.

With the support of our varied and distinct community, *The Journal of Applied Economy* has now transformed into a more diverse forum. We will no longer set a question for each issue, but instead will design issues around the articles we receive. Therefore, we invite scholars, economists, institutional investors, philosophers and global citizens alike to tackle any and all of the great questions that lie in the field of applied economics. As ideas appear in all forms, papers can be of any length, although emphasis is placed on readability by the broader economic academy.

Papers may engage with contemporary instances, philosophical arguments or any other method that answers the questions applicable to the field of applied economy. Importantly, articles will be selected based upon quality and the readability of works by non-specialists. The intent of the Journal is to involve non-scholars in the important debates of economic theory and its implementation in contemporary markets.

The Journal also welcomes and encourages submission of articles typically not found in economic journals, including opinionated or personalized insights into the field of applied economy.

We also invite submissions for our Blog at http://appliedeconomy.blogspot.com/ and comments on our Twitter at, http://twitter.com/appliedeconomy.

The Journal of Applied Economy is published four times per year, to coincide with the four terms of the financial year, in an attractive paperback and electronic edition.

All authors who submit to this edition will be provided with a complementary copy of the journal.

Length: Any length is acceptable, although readability is key.

Presentation Style: Papers must comply with Harvard Citation Style Guide.
Example found at http://www.lib.unimelb.edu.au/cite/harvard_dis/

Submission: You must submit electronically in Microsoft Word format to editor@appliedeconomy.com. Extraneous formatting is discouraged. Correspondence can also be sent to this address. If you are considering submitting an article, you are invited to contact the editor to discuss ideas before authoring a work.

SUBSCRIPTION INFORMATION

The Journal is published four times per year in an attractive soft cover book. Subscription to the Journal can be achieved by two methods:

1) Single issues can be purchased on amazon.com. Our publishers, the Elias Clark Group, set a retail price for each edition, typically AU$40. However, due to their agreement with amazon.com, the price may vary for retail customers.

2) A subscription to the Journal can be purchased for AU$150 per year, or AU$280 for two years. This price includes postage throughout the world. Payment can be made by international bank cheque, but not a personal cheque, to:

    The Journal of Applied Economy
    C/o The Elias Clark Group
    GPO Box 5001
    Melbourne, Victoria, Australia.

Alternatively, the Journal is available online at www.appliedeconomy.com and can be read there free of charge.

Introduction

Mr Karl T. Muth, a visionary economist and progressive leader in the field of applied economy, charitably accepted an invitation to guest edit this edition.

As regular readers will know, Mr Muth is a multifaceted scholar who has made many contributions to diverse areas of economic theory. In this fortitude, he has stewarded six prolific articles of this issue of *The Journal of Applied Economy*. He has brought together a diverse profusion of scholars who write articles of such eminence that I have not doubt they will be cited by scholars, practitioners and students for years to come.

The title of the edition, "Scale and Boundaries of Governance," reflects central questions of governance from the economic paradigm. Elegant solutions to the daunting problems of modern economics can be resolved only through scalability. To reduce these problems to their individual parts and philosophical foundations, solutions can be revealed. This issue, I entrust, offers insight into the ways of addressing these prolific obstacles whilst inspiring further discourse.

In the coming year, we have an array of exciting issues addressing global economic application and an opus of theoretics. The coming volumes are shaping up as epics, with many significant contributions.

H. Trent Moore
Editor
Melbourne, Australia
17 September 2010.

Editorial: Scale and the Boundaries of Governance

Central to the questions of effective governance are the questions of scale and bounds.

Changes in scale are quantitative in a finite range; beyond that range they become qualitative and unsuitable for extrapolation. That which works on a small scale will not always work when enlarged and vice versa. The normative governance that works for a small village in the Amazon will not address the teeming hive that is Tokyo or the heterogeneity that is New York City. Meanwhile, volume constraints for an over-the-counter securities market in Africa make as much sense as placing a stoplight in the middle of the Sahara.

Problems can only be solved in context. That which works here may not work there. As with national borders, linguistic enclaves, and budget constraints, there are advantages in including values that are close to the edge. However, like sound, rules become weaker when spread across vast spaces. Rules reduced to a distant whisper are often misheard, or misunderstood even when heard correctly.

This fourth issue of The Journal of Applied Economy includes several authors' efforts to design or critique governance on various scales and within various boundaries, to explore the nuanced question of which rules should apply where and how.

Michael Faure begins at the micro level, quite literally at "street level" with the economic repercussions of a cyclist's collision with a pedestrian and arriving at a broader law and economics analysis in the context of tort law. In examining civil remedies alongside contemporary thinking in the areas of regulation, insurance, and behavioural economics, Faure reminds the reader that the accidental nature of accidents requires a different perspective in conceptualizing efficient dispute resolution.

The accidents Faure describes are, at least initially, dealt with in trial courts. This is where judges must find the applicable law, find a framework within which to apply the law, and utilize this framework to apply the law to the facts. Clifford Chad Henson focuses on the second of these three steps, examining rival methodologies for the decision-making process in parallel and carrying out both process-focused and outcome-focused analyses.

On a larger scale than Faure's discrete accidents and Henson's trial courts, Manuel A. Utset and Robert W. McGee examine, in separate pieces, the links between the mechanical structure of modern corporate governance and the more fluid social fabric of the society within which corporations exist. McGee tackles the challenge of bridging these two worlds – one of corporate legal automatons and one of normative social evolution – by using classical and contemporary ethical constructs. Meanwhile, Utset examines the collective social relationships that coexist alongside corporate entities and can accelerate their success or demise, seemingly with equal ease and puzzlingly similar probability.

The largest scale and the boundless openness in which rules can resonate, echo, and fade is in the abstract. Maurice R. Dyson studies the interaction between concrete legal structures and the observable but unquantifiable structures that form the basis for modern introspective philosophy. The self, the one, is the indivisible basic unit of human civilization. Dyson reminds the reader that to govern corporations, to shape markets, and to build organizations, we must first examine, understand, and take charge of the self.

Lastly, Dr. George S. Ford and Lawrence J. Spiwak examine another, less existential infinite plane: the Internet. As with the other pieces in this fourth issue, Ford and Spiwak examine questions of scale (adoption of Internet access) and governance boundaries (the application and applicability of "net neutrality" rules). However, Ford and Spiwak's boundaries do not exist merely in the ether of the Internet: their research draws physical, geographic boundaries between rural and urban America and raises important questions of economic viability, equity, and policy implementation around an issue that has been obfuscated by political manoeuvring and punditry.

While the scale of many modern economic and policy problems may seem dauntingly large and their bounds so far beyond the horizon as to be wholly out of sight, often the only way to make sense of these problems is to reduce them to their moving parts, their philosophical concepts, their native geography, the economic petri dish in which they first multiplied. Within these boundaries – erected through thought experiments, research, mathematics, statistics, and economics – even the most unruly specimen may reveal its nature and, in turn, the rules needed to contain its behaviour.

Finally, I am honoured to join The Journal of Applied Economy and hope you enjoy reading these excellent articles as much as we have enjoyed selecting them.

Karl T. Muth, Associate Editor, The Journal of Applied Economy

Behavioural Accident Law and Economics

Michael Faure*

1 INTRODUCTION[1]

1.1 Example 1: The Cyclist

Assume a fanatic cyclist rides his race machine through a populated neighbourhood, thereby creating the risk of hitting and hence causing harm to a pedestrian. Traditional economic analysis of tort law assumes that the cyclist will know what the probability is that by adapting his speed and taking other care measures he may hit the pedestrian. The basic idea behind the economic thinking as it has been developed since the early 1970s is that on the basis of his potential exposure to liability our cyclist will be given incentives to reduce his speed in an efficient manner, more particularly to the level where the marginal costs of prevention (reducing his speed) equal the marginal benefits (in reducing the probability that he will hit the pedestrian). Assuming away for a moment some technical differences between various liability rules the bottom line is that the cyclist will, on the basis of the available information, take a rational and moreover efficient decision to take preventive measures.

1.2 Example 2: The Homeowner

Assume someone owns a nice house situated close to a river. This rational house owner knows that these usually nice and romantically looking rivers can, after heavy rains or unexpectedly quick melting of snow and ice in the higher mountains, quickly change into devastating streams which could cause substantial losses to the house owner and his family. The traditional economic theory of insurance assumes that the house owner is willing to maximize his expected utility and will hence, at least in countries where this is available, seek insurance coverage against flooding on a competitive insurance market.

---

* Visiting International Professor of Law, University of Pennsylvania Law School; Professor of Comparative and International Environmental Law, Maastricht University (NL) and Professor of Comparative Private Law and Economics, Erasmus School of Law (NL); faure@frg.eur.nl.

1. I am grateful to Ton Hartlief (Maastricht University), Roger Van den Bergh and Willem van Boom (both Erasmus School of Law, Rotterdam) for helpful comments on an earlier version of this text and to Marina Jodogne (Maastricht University) for editorial assistance.

1.3 Example 3: The Judge

Assume a judge who must decide on an accident caused by the racing cyclist, who drove at reasonable speed but whom, after turning a curve, was confronted with an old lady walking on the bicycle path. The lady, not being visible from before the curve, could unfortunately not be avoided by our cyclist. As a result, an accident is caused which leads to substantial damage to the expensive bicycle and to the lady, of course. The judge is confronted with a liability suit brought by the old lady who claims compensation for her losses. Economic analysis of tort law assumes that the judge will put himself in the *ex ante* position and hence ask whether the costs of additional care by our cyclists could have led to a favourable reduction of the accident risk. Given that the cyclist drove at a reasonable speed and that the lady was an unobservable object who (to complicate things a little) moreover walked on the bicycle path, we may assume that the judge will not find the cyclist liable.

1.4 Reality?

Since the examples are hypothetical, one can of course never be sure, but there is a great likelihood that in reality the results may be different than those just presented, based on the predictions of classic economic analysis of accident law. The cyclist from the first example may or may not take efficient preventive measures, but if he does so it is unlikely that he will only do so on the basis of a rational cost-benefit calculus and out of fear for an expected liability. As to the second example, that of the home owner, there is ample evidence that in fact even in countries where flooding insurance is available home owners often fail to take insurance coverage, even though this would have increased their expected utility *ex ante*.[2] The so called flood of the century of the Elbe in 2002 and a few years later Katrina provided dramatic evidence of this. Also the judge of example 3 may not come to the optimal determination of efficient care by the cyclist, as one had hoped on the basis of the economic model. The mere fact that the accident happened and that the old lady suffered personal injury damage may

2. See for evidence of lacking insurance coverage, for example after hurricane Katrina, inter alia, Howard Kunreuther, Has the Time Come for Comprehensive Natural Disaster Insurance?, in On Risk and Disaster. Lessons from Hurricane Katrina (Daniels, Kettl & Kunreuther (eds.), University of Pennsylvania Press, 2006), 175-201 and see Michael Faure & Véronique Bruggeman, Catastrophic Risks and First-party Insurance, 15 Connecticut Journal of Insurance Law 2009, 1-52.

create a bias against the cyclist as a result of which judges will often hold that the mere fact that the accident occurred, sufficiently proves that the cyclist apparently did not take efficient care. These examples, which could easily be enlarged with many others, show that in reality the parties involved in the accident setting, injurers, victims, potential insurance takers and judges, do not always react in the way in which it was assumed by the economic models.

1.5 Basic assumptions

The examples, which could easily be enlarged with many others, show that in reality, the parties involved in the accident setting, injurers, victims, potential insurance takers and judges, do not always react in the way in which it was assumed by the economic models. The neoclassic models of accident law have always assumed that injurers and victims (in short the participants in an accident setting) are rational individuals, who base their decisions (for example, levels of care and activity upon an objective) whilst weighing of costs and benefits, trying to maximize their utility according to their preferences. On the basis of this assumption the economic analysis of law has, now for a period of more than 40 years,[3] developed extensive models to explain how tort rules can be developed to contribute to a reduction of accident costs. Within this framework it is, moreover, also assumed that rational and well-informed judges will equally apply the applicable tort rules in an effective way, striving towards such a reduction of accident costs. Moreover, based on theories of utility maximization insurance theory has shown that risk-averse individuals may increase their expected utility by taking out insurance coverage. Depending upon the applicable liability rules either victims will have a demand for first party insurance or potential injurers will seek third party liability cover.

1.6 Lessons from cognitive psychology

However, meanwhile (and for an equally long period), a different literature has developed, starting with the seminal work of Kahneman and Tversky, showing that many individuals in fact suffer from a variety of cognitive heuristics and biases as a result of which decision-making may

3. The starting point of the economic analysis of law in general were the publications by Ronald Coase, The Problem of Social Cost, JOURNAL OF LAW & ECONOMICS 1960, 1-44 and Guido Calabresi, Some Thoughts on Risk Distribution and the Law of Torts, YALE LAW JOURNAL 1961, 499-553, which both also dealt with accident law.

take place in a different way than neoclassic economic models assume.[4] Psychological theoretical literature, but moreover convincing empirical evidence, has shown that individuals suffer from so-called heuristics and biases. Heuristics affect our judgement, whereas biases affect our choice.

In recent years law and economics and the insights from behavioural sciences have met into the new domain referred to as '*behavioural law and economics*'. The importance of this encounter is well described by another pioneer of tort law and economics, Richard Epstein:

'There is little doubt that the major new theoretical approach to law and economics in the past two decades does not come from either field, but from the adjacent discipline of cognitive psychology, which has now moored into behavioural economics'.[5]

1.7 Importance of behavioural accident law and economics

Increasingly, the behavioural law and economics literature is also concerned with the consequences of these new insights for traditional economic theories of accident law.[6] However, even though some attention to this behavioural literature is paid, the consequences for existing models of accident law are not that clear yet. It seems interesting to pay more detailed attention to this question since some, especially lawyers, may suppose that this literature has important implications for the traditional model of accident law. For instance when there is indeed a systematic error by individuals both as far as the estimation of probabilities and expected damage is concerned, the question arises what the consequences are of these

4. Amos Tversky and Daniel Kahneman, Judgment under Uncertainty: Heuristics and Biases, 185 Science 1974, 1124-1131; Daniel Kahneman, Paul Slovic & Amos Tversky eds., Judgement under Uncertainty: Heuristics and Biases (Cambridge University Press, 1982).

5. Richard A. Epstein, The Neoclassical Economics of Consumer Contracts, 92 Minnesota Law Review 2008, 803-835.

6. See in this respect more particularly Christine Jolls, Cass R. Sunstein, & Richard Thaler, A Behavioural Approach to Law and Economics, 50 Stanford Law Review 1998, 1471, 1523-1532; Jason S. Johnston, Bayesian Fact-Finding and Efficiency: Towards an Economic Theory of Liability under Uncertainty, Southern California Law Review 1987, 137-181; Christine Jolls, Behavioural Law and Economics, in Economic Institutions and Behavioral Economics (Diamond & Hannu Vartiainen eds., Princeton University Press, 2007, 115-155); Russel B. Korobkin & Thomas S. Ulen, Law and Behavioural Science: Removing the Rationality Assumption from Law and Economics, 88 California Law Review 2000, 1053-1146; Joshua S. Teitelbaum, A Unilateral Accident Model under Ambiguity, 37 Journal of Legal Studies 2007, 431-477; Avishalom Tor, The Methodology of the Behavioural Analysis of Law, 4(1) Haifa Law Review 2008, 237-327.

misperceptions for the economic model of tort law and more particularly for the choice of an efficient liability rule. The question for instance arises whether these misperceptions have a more important effect on the negligence rule than on strict liability or whether they arise under strict liability as well. Moreover, the psychological literature equally indicates that in tort cases there can be misperceptions by judges as well, e.g. leading to a wrong assumption about a high probability of an accident, simply based on recent incidents (availability heuristic). The result may be an inefficiently high care level required from defendants in a tort case (like with the cyclist from example 3). A related important question is of course whether the mentioned misperceptions with participants in the accident setting (and potentially the judiciary) are an argument in favour of regulation. If that would be the case the question equally arises why regulation would be better able to deal with these heuristics and biases than tort law.

Also for the field of insurance behavioural law and economics may have important consequences. The behavioural literature for example shows that for a variety of reasons and differently than assumed by traditional models, individuals do not take out insurance coverage even if it would maximize their expected utility. This hence raises again the question if these cognitive biases could be an argument in favour of a regulatory intervention leading e.g. to mandatory insurance coverage in particular fields such as damage caused by natural disasters.

In this contribution, I would like to examine the potential impact of behavioural law and economics (if any) on the traditional economic models of accident law.[7] By focussing on '*accident law*' I mainly deal with the economics of liability law and insurance and only to some extent briefly with safety regulation as well.[8] Moreover, given the limited scope of this contribution, I can of course only focus on the main results of the meanwhile very rich behavioural literature and its consequences for accident law.[9]

---

7. I hereby build further on an earlier study to honour Guido Calabresi (Michael Faure, Calabresi and Behavioural Tort Law and Economics, 1(4) Erasmus Law Review 2008, 75-102), where I examined to what extent some of the ideas of the behavioural literature are already incorporated into Calabresi's work.

8. I only focus on the relevance of the behavioural literature for accident law, although there is a broad literature dealing with its relevance for other legal domains as well. See for example for the area of criminal law Richard H. MacAdams & Thomas S. Ulen, Behavioural Criminal Law and Economics, in, Criminal Law and Economics (Garoupa ed., Cheltenham, Edward Elgar 2009, forthcoming, chapter 18, available at http://ssrn.com/abstract=129963).

9. The reader interested in further reading can consult the studies concerning behavioural law and economics summarized inter alia supra in note 6.

1.8 Structure

In order to examine the potential impact of the behavioural literature for the economics of accident law I will first briefly review the assumptions underlying the traditional models of accident law (2). Next, some of the most important findings of behavioural law and economics (in as far as relevant for liability and insurance) will be addressed (3). The main questions are of course what the consequences are of this literature for the economic model of tort law (to be addressed in 4) and insurance (5). A few concluding remarks finish this contribution.

2 ASSUMPTIONS OF THE TRADITIONAL ECONOMIC MODELS OF TORT AND INSURANCE

2.1 Tort law: starting points

Classic economic analysis of law starts from the assumption that by exposing parties to the costs of their activities via liability rules they will be given appropriate incentives for taking optimal care to prevent accidents. Taking optimal care would be the way to reduce the total social costs of accidents since it is the level of care where the costs of prevention and the expected damage costs are minimised.[10] The desired incentive effects of course assume that all parties have information about the applicable tort law regime, but equally about the probability that their behaviour may create a certain accident risk, about the magnitude of the damage that may occur in case of an accident and about the optimal preventive measures that could efficiently reduce the accident risk. Moreover, traditional models of tort law equally assume that the parties involved not only have this information available, but that they equally are able to process this information, in other words, to make objective and correct assessments of all of these elements. Economic analysis of tort law hence crucially follows the rationality assumption underlying economic analysis of law. This idea, also referred to as the '*rational choice model*' holds that a rational actor can rank alternatives according to his preferences.[11] In the words of Posner it is assumed that man '*is an rational maximizer of his ends in life*'.[12] Also, economic analysis of tort

10. This optimal care is hence to be found where marginal prevention costs equal the marginal benefits in further reduction of the expected damage. See generally Stephen M. Shavell, Strict Liability versus Negligence, Journal of Legal Studies 1980, 1-25; Stephen M. Shavell, Economic Analysis of Accident Law (Harvard University Press, 1987), 5-32; as well as Stephen M. Shavell, Foundations of Economic Analysis of Law (Harvard University Press, 2004), 175-288.
11. Robert Cooter & Thomas S. Ulen, Law and Economics (Addison Wesley, 4th ed., 2004), 15.
12. Richard Posner, Economics Analysis of Law (Wolters Kluwer, 7th ed., 2007), 3.

is hence based on this rationality assumption, assuming that the decision maker has stable, well-ordered preferences.[13]

Information and the ability to process this information correctly is indeed a crucial assumption of the traditional economic analysis of tort law. The basic assumption is indeed that on the basis of all of this available information parties will adapt their behaviour and thus contribute to reducing accident risks in an efficient manner.[14]

Following upon example 1 from the introduction this means that the cyclist will be assumed to take preventive measures based on information on costs and benefits of these measures, equally taking into account the deterrent effects a liability rule may have.

2.2 Nuances in law and economics

Of course the law and economics literature has clearly indicated that it is by no means necessary that all of this would take place as a cognitive process whereby the cyclist would be aware of this calculus.[15] Many persons will implicitly and without much cost-benefit calculation do the right thing and adapt to a speed by which they can avoid to hit the pedestrian. However, a basic assumption of the economic literature is that it is the exposure to liability law that plays a crucial role in giving the cyclist incentives for taking preventive measures (reducing his speed). Nevertheless, also the economic literature of course recognises that the incentives for speed reduction do not only come from the exposure to tort law: the injurer may fear that in case of an accident he could be hurt himself or he may simply suffer discomfort by the thought of causing harm to a victim. These are in the literature considered as additional but not sufficient motives for the injurer to reduce his speed. In the absence of law (and in situations where private bargaining is not possible)[16] economics assumes that the injurer will not reduce his speed optimally and that thus an internalisation of the externality does not take place.

13. Robert Cooter & Thomas S. Ulen, Law and Economics (Austin, Addison Wesley, 4th ed., 2004), 350-351.

14. Although the idea that tort law can be considered as an incentive mechanism that influences the behaviour of parties potentially involved in an accident setting was originally of North-American origin, it has now largely been accepted by European legal scholars as well: see, for example for Germany, Gerhard Wagner, Prävention und Verhaltenssteuerung des Privatrechts – Annaßung oder legitime Aufgabe?, Archiv für die Civilistische Practicis 2006, Vol. 206, 352-475.

15. In the words of Schäfer and Ott, "rationality does not, however, imply that the agent is conscious of the choices" (Hans-Bernd Schäfer & Claus Ott, The Economic Analysis of Civil Law (Edward Elgar, 2004), 52).

16. Otherwise the Coase Theorem would be applicable and the efficient solution will automatically be reached in this low transaction cost setting (see Coase supra note 3).

2.3 Critics

This traditional economic model of tort law has received a lot of criticism from various strands of literature. Scholars belonging to the so called critical legal studies movement (CLS) have, since the beginning of the economic analysis of law, launched several attacks on law and economics. The main representative of this movement, Duncan Kennedy, launched a serious attack on the use of cost-benefit analysis to determine entitlements and more particularly to internalize externalities.[17] Richard Abel, who also associates himself with CLS, formulates a criticism on '*capitalist tort law*', thereby also criticizing the fact that tort law has turned to the language of economics, replacing moral judgement with concern for the efficient allocation of resources.[18] He also criticized '*the scientific façade of this economic formulation*' (more particularly of the Hand formula) which would conceal '*a number of fundamental theoretical flaws and empirical problems*'.[19] More interesting for the topic of this contribution is that Abel also criticized the fact that economics assumes that tort liability stimulates the potential tortfeasor to the optimum level of safety on the basis of a correct cost-benefit analysis by the judge and an evaluation of all possible safety precautions by potential tortfeasors.[20] In addition, Abel argued that '*the efficacy of tort liability in encouraging safety rests on several dubious assumptions about economic rationality and market conditions. Some actors are not profit maximizers in any simplistic sense*'.[21]

Also tort lawyers have challenged the assumption that potential injurers in an accident setting would change their behaviour on the basis of an exposure to liability. Tort law is not about the rationality of certain precautions (compared to the costs) but about interpersonal reasonableness, so it was held *inter alia* by Keating in an attack on the utilitarian approach to tort law defended by law and economics.[22] A related criticism is that according to some traditional

17. Duncan Kennedy, Cost-benefit Analysis of Entitlement Problems: A Critique, 33 Stanford Law Review 1980-1981, 388-445.
18. Abel 1989-90, A Critique of Torts, 37 UCLA Law Review 1989-1990, 785-831, at 794-795.
19. Ibid., at 808-809.
20. Ibid., at 810.
21. Ibid., at 812.
22. Keating argues that the concept of reasonableness fits the doctrine and rhetoric of due care law better than the rationality concept defended by law and economics scholars such as Robert Cooter, Thomas Ulen and Richard Posner (Gregory C. Keating, Reasonableness and Rationality in Negligence Theory, 48 Stanford Law Review 1995-96, 311-384). Compare this to Rodgers who argues that rational decision-making by an injurer should be an argument in favour of strict liability whereas in case of non-rational decision-making 'risk-creating

lawyers tort law would have as main goal to compensate accident victims, not to provide deterrence, let alone that this were possible. Critics also held that there would be little to no empirical evidence that people would actually change their behaviour as a result of an exposure to liability.[23] The latter point remained an important weakness of the economics of tort law: notwithstanding some modest successes in specific areas it remained generally difficult to find a strong empirical backing for the statement that potential injurers would in all cases change their behaviour as a result of an exposure to liability.[24] In addition, many activities are subjected to extensive safety regulation, which makes it often difficult to distinguish the preventive effects of regulation from the deterrent effect of tort law.[25]

2.4 Strict liability versus negligence

The economic literature moreover makes a distinction between strict liability and negligence. In a case where only one party (usually referred to as the injurer or tortfeasor) influences the accident risk (a so-called unilateral accident case) the literature generally holds that both negligence and strict liability provide incentives for efficient care; strict liability would, however, have a preference if also an efficient activity level needs to be respected.[26] Within the context of

behaviour of psychological origin is unsuited to a social cost-benefit analysis' (William H. Rodgers, Negligence Reconsidered: The Role of Rationality in Tort Theory, 54 Southern California Law Review 1980-81, 1-34).

23. See for an overview of the critics on the law and economics approach to tort the summary in Gary T. Schwartz, Reality in the Economic Analysis of Tort Law: Does Tort Law Really Deter?, 42 UCLA Law Review 1994-95, 377-444, 381-382.

24. Difficulties also arise as far as the measurement of that particular claim is concerned: injurers are often insured (in which case one could only measure the extent to which insurers can control moral hazard; the empirical evidence in that respect was recently summarized by Willem H. Van Boom, Insurance Law and Economics: An Empirical Perspective, in Essays in the Law and Economics of Regulation, In Honour of Anthony Ogus (Intersentia, 2008), 253-276).

25. An early and interesting overview on the effects of tort law with nuanced conclusions was provided by Gary T. Schwartz, Reality in the Economic Analysis of Tort Law: Does Tort Law Really Deter?, UCLA Law Review 1994-95, Vol. 42, 377-444. For an equally interesting overview see Don Dewees, David Duff, & Michael Trebilcock, Exploring the Domain of Accident Law. Taking the Facts Seriously (Oxford University Press, 1996) and Van Velthoven, Empirics of Tort, in Tort Law & Economics (Michael Faure ed., Edward Elgar, 2009), 453-498.

26. See for these criteria for strict liability inter alia Hans-Bernd Schäfer & Andreas Schönenberger, Strict Liability versus Negligence, in Encyclopedia of Law and Economics, II, Civil Law and Economics (Bouckaert & De Geest eds., Edward Elgar, 2000) 597-624 and for a more recent account see Hans-Bernd Schäfer & Frank Müller-Langer, Strict Liability versus Negligence, in, Tort Law and Economics (Michael Faure ed., Edward

this contribution it is, however, important to indicate that there is a difference between strict liability and negligence as far as the necessary information is concerned. In case of strict liability both prevention and damage costs are shifted to the injurer. It is hence the injurer himself who will have to balance these costs and benefits and fix the optimal care standard. All information costs about the elements that underlay the efficient working of tort law, mentioned above, in this case fall on the injurer.[27] In case of negligence there is a division of labour as far as the necessary information is concerned. Under negligence it is the judge who will determine the efficient care standard. Therefore the judge will need information on the costs of preventive measures and will have to weigh these against the probability that additional investments would reduce the expected damage. This will hence be translated in a due care standard to be followed by the potential injurer. Under negligence the injurer only needs information about the due care required by the court on the basis of case law.

In the law and economics literature it is recognised that in this respect problems can arise. The first one to recognise the importance of cognitive biases and bounded rationality for accident law was undoubtedly the founding father of the economic analysis of tort law, Guido Calabresi. In a 1972 article in the Yale Law Journal Calabresi and Hirschoff argue that the choice between different liability regimes should '*depend not on their* theoretical *ability to optimise accident costs given certain assumptions, but on the degree to which the particular assumptions required by each devise actually do obtain*'.[28] This quote is followed by an interesting footnote (17) that holds *inter alia*:

'These assumptions relate, inter alia, to the cost of information to each party, the absence of psychological or other impediments to acting on the basis of available information, the administrative costs of shifting losses, and the extent to which parties actually bear the costs which the particular tests impose upon them'.

Here one notices an explicit reference to psychological impediments that may be decisive in the choice between negligence and strict liability. Even tough Calabresi's work dates from before the behavioural literature, his model for allocating liability seems to allow taking into account the cognitive abilities of all parties involved in the accident setting. Thus Calabresi even holds that account should be taken of the '*likelihood of foolish behaviour by the victim or the unusual sensitivity*

Elgar, 2009), 3-45 and Michael Faure (ed.), Deterrence, Insurability and Compensation in Environmental Liability: Future Developments in the European Union (Springer, 2003), 29-32.

27. Stephen M. Shavell, Foundations of Economic Analysis of Law (Harvard University Press, 2004), 184.
28. Guido Calabresi & Jon T. Hirschoff, Towards a Test for Strict Liability in Torts, 81 Yale Law Journal 1972, 1059.

of some victims'.[29] In these and other publications of Calabresi it becomes clear that the balanced approach he proposes thus provide the scope to incorporate the consequences of human errors – now referred to as cognitive biases – in the decision on the allocation of the accident risk. In that respect Calabresi can even be referred to as a '*behaviouralist avant la lettre*'.[30]

Also Shavell discussed under the heading of '*factors bearing on the determination of negligence*' that there is the danger that either the actual care of the injurer can be too high or too low, since he misperceives the legal standard or the legal standard set by the judge can be either too high or too low because of misperceptions by the judge.[31] The result is of course that the actual care taken by the injurer may not match the due care set by the legal system. This can on the one hand lead to liability cases where the injurer is found negligent (under a perfectly working negligence rule this should normally not be the case since the injurer always has incentives to take due care); on the other hand it may also lead to inefficiencies (also in cases where the injurer is not found negligent).[32]

The consequences of relaxing the rationality assumption in analyzing tort law have been explicitly addressed by Cooter and Ulen. They also suggest a corrective measure when that assumption is violated and more particularly refer to the example of product liability for a defective power tool. If a consumer would err in the probability of an accident and hence take too little precautions, this would make the accident situation unilateral, rather than bilateral and would thus, according to Cooter and Ulen be an argument in favour of strict manufacturer liability.[33] They add:

'*These thoughts raise concerns about whether tort liability induces the appropriate precautionary action by potential injurers and victims. We shall tentatively maintain the rationality assumption but shall be ready to amend our conclusions about efficient tort rules when there is sound evidence that the appropriate decision-makers are not behaving rationally*'.

---

29. Ibid., 1067.
30. So Michael Faure, Calabresi and Behavioural Tort Law and Economics, 1(4) Erasmus Law Review 2008, 96-99.
31. Stephen M. Shavell, Economic Analysis of Accident Law (Harvard University Press, 1987), 73-83. See also Stephen M. Shavell, Foundations of Economic Analysis of Law (Harvard University Press, 2004), 224-241.
32. This may more particularly be the case where the legal standard is set inefficiently low or inefficiently high and followed by the tortfeasor. See on these errors in the determination of the negligence standard also Robert Cooter & Thomas S. Ulen, Law and Economics (Austin, Addison Wesley, 4th ed., 2004), 337-339.
33. Robert Cooter & Thomas S. Ulen, Law and Economics (Austin, Addison Wesley, 4th ed., 2004), 352.

2.5 Liability versus regulation

It should, moreover, be stressed that law and economics scholars have paid attention to particular circumstances under which liability rules may fail to have a deterrent effect. In the so-called public interest theory of safety regulation, again largely developed by Shavell, criteria have been developed indicating that under particular circumstances regulation may provide better results in an efficient reduction of the accident risk than tort law.[34] One relevant criterion in this respect is precisely the availability of information. It is held that when public authorities can better obtain information on the probability of the accident, the expected damage and the efficient preventive measures to reduce the accident, regulation would be preferred over liability. Another argument in favour of regulation is generally that when (for a variety of reasons) liability suits can be expected to have no deterrent effect it is better to rely upon regulation. The latter can for example be the case when there is a long time lapse between the tort and the emergence of the damage (so-called latency) or when causation problems exist.

One could hence argue that when behavioural studies would show that potential parties in an accident setting (injurer, victim or judge) lack appropriate information or when there are other reasons to believe that tort law may lack a deterrent effect, alternative solutions to provide incentives for care should be examined. However, public choice scholars have powerfully presented the private interest theory of regulation, arguing that regulatory failure may cause serious inefficiencies in safety regulation as well.[35]

2.6 Insurance

Traditional economic theory of insurance starts from the assumption of risk aversion and holds that individuals suffer disutility as a result of being exposed to risk. The theory holds that the expected utility can be increased when risk is removed from individuals and traded for

---

34. Stephen M. Shavell, Economic Analysis of Accident Law (Harvard University Press, 1987), 357-374.
35. See James M. Buchanan & Gordon Tullock, The Calculus of Consent: Logical Foundations of Constitutional Democracy (University of Michigan Press, 1962); Mancur Olson, The Logic of Collective Action: Public Goods and the Theory of Groups (Harvard University Press, 1965) and Richard A. Posner, Theories of economic regulation, 5 Bell Journal of Economics and Management 1974, 335. The possibilities of inefficiencies in safety regulation have especially been stressed by Michael T. Maloney & Robert McCormick, A Positive Economic Theory of Environmental Quality Regulation, 25 Journal of Law and Economics 1982, 99-123.

certainty.[36] The basis for this 'expected utility' hypothesis in explaining insurance is therefore that individuals can increase their utility by trading an uncertain risk (being e.g. exposed to the risk of flooding) for a certain loss (the payment of a premium).

Basic assumptions of this expected utility hypothesis (relevant for this topic) are that individuals are aware of the risks they are exposed to, being both of the probability that the event may occur and of the magnitude of the damage and that they are aware of the availability of insurance.[37] The expected utility hypothesis assumes that based on this information (and the availability to process it) individuals will rationally decide to purchase insurance when it increases their utility[38] and if insurance companies are willing to supply cover on a competitive insurance market.

Of course traditional insurance theory also requires that other conditions of insurability are met. In this respect it is for example necessary that both the dangers of moral hazard and adverse selection can be controlled. One of the remedies proposed in the literature is exposing the insured partially to risk (thus providing incentives for care); another remedy is an adaptation of premium conditions in accordance to the behaviour of the insured.[39] This type of risk differentiation of course assumes that the insured is aware of the policy conditions and is able to process this information and react appropriately to it with a behavioural change. In other words: also the expected utility hypothesis as a starting point for insurance theory assumes the ability of individuals to adapt their behaviour to different incentives given to them via the insurance policy.

There are alternative explanations for insurance, *inter alia* based on transaction costs,[40] but they can remain undiscussed, since they are less relevant for this topic.[41]

---

36. See Henri Loubergé, Developments in risk and insurance economics: the past 25 years, in Handbook of Insurance (Georges Dionne ed., Kluwer Academic, 2000) 3-33 (providing an overview of the developments in risk and insurance theory).

37. See for the basic theory of Insurance inter alia Kenneth Arrow, Uncertainty and the Welfare Econmics of Medical Care, American Economic Review 1963, 941-973 and Kenneth Arrow, The economics of moral hazard: further comment, 58 American Economic Review 1968, 537-539.

38. The latter will of course depend upon the specific attitude towards risk of the individual, their degree of risk aversion and the price that ultimately needs to be paid (the premium) to have the risk removed.

39. Stephen M. Shavell, On Moral Hazard and Insurance, 93 Quarterly Journal of Economics 1979, 541-562.

40. Göran Skogh, The Transaction Cost Theory of Insurance, Contract Impingements and Costs, 65 Journal of Risk and Insurance 1989, 726-732.

41. For an overview of insurance theory based on the "non-expected utility analysis" See Loubergé, supra note 36 at 11-12 and Mark J. Machina, Non-expected utility and the robusness of the classical insurance paradyme, in

3 BEHAVIOURAL LAW AND ECONOMICS: MAIN FINDINGS

3.1 General

Since the early writings of Kahneman and Tversky a rich behavioural literature has emerged challenging the assumptions of neo-classic economics.[42] To some extent the limits of the traditional assumptions (availability of and capacity to process information, rationality) were well-known to law and economics scholars.[43] Ulen even notices that it is striking that the behavioural literature seems to be better known to lawyers than to economists.[44] For example, some concepts, such as bounded rationality, pointing at the limits of individuals to make rational choices, have been well-known and were earlier documented in the law and economics literature. However, increasingly also psychological experiments, both in laboratory and in real life have challenged some of the assumptions underlying the economic analysis of accident law. Behavioural law and economics has been the subject of a lot of controversy. Hence, already the previous statement, that behavioural studies would constitute a challenge to the assumptions underlying classic law and economics, has been the subject of controversy. Cass Sunstein, in his well-known provocative style, indeed argues in the many papers he devoted to behavioural law and economics that '*economic analysis of law has proceeded on the basis of inaccurate understandings of decision and choice*'.[45] His co-author Christine Jolls, also well-known for her writings in this domain, however clearly argues that '*behavioural law and economics is not a critique of law and*

Handbook of Insurance (Georges Dionne ed., Kluwer, 2000), 37-96 as well as Christian Gaullier, Optimal Insurance Design: what can we do with and without expected utility?, in Handbook of Insurance (Georges Dionne ed., Kluwer, 2000), 97-115.

42. See Daniel Kahneman, Paul Slovic & Amos Tversky (eds.), Judgement under Uncertainty: Heuristics and Biases (Cambridge University Press, 1982).
43. It is more particularly through the work of Simon that the limits of rational choice theory have been made clear, also to the law and economics community. See, for example, Herbert A. Simon, A Behavioural Model of Rational Choice, 69 Quarterly Journal of Economics 1955, 99-118. For a summary of the work of Simon, see Gerd Gigerenzer, Is the Mind Irrational or Ecologically Rational?, in The Law and Economics of Irrational Behaviour (Parisi & Smith eds., Stanford University Press, 2005), 37-67.
44. Thomas S. Ulen, The Growing Pains of Behavioural Law and Economics, 51 Vanderbilt Law Review 1998, 1747, 1748.
45. Cass R. Sunstein, Behavioural Analysis of Law, 64 The University of Chicago Law Review 1997, 1176, 1194.

economics'.[46] Tom Ulen, also a prolific writer in this domain, seems to agree with Jolls that '*behavioural law and economics does not attempt to undo any of the remarkable accomplishments of law and economics. Rather, it is an attempt to refine*'.[47] The founding father of law and economics, Richard Posner, is not surprisingly critical of the behavioural approach, at least in the way it is presented in a paper by Jolls, Sunstein and Thaler[48] to which Posner reacts. His point of view, to which I will come back in more detail below, is that some insights that are ascribed to behavioural economics are already a part of economic analysis of law and that the problem moreover is that no definition is provided of what behavioural law and economics exactly means. Posner criticizes the fact that the behavioural approach is only defined negatively like: it is law and economics '*minus the assumption that people are rational maximizers of their satisfactions*'.[49] It is not my intention to pronounce a final judgement on the usefulness of behavioural law and economics. However, these quotes already show that it has been subject of controversy and this will of course also affect the central question of this article, being to what extent its findings have implications for the economic analysis of accident law.

Meanwhile, the entire body of literature in this domain has become so rich that it is impossible to review it entirely within the scope of this contribution.[50] Many scholars distinguish a variety

46. Christine Jolls, Behavioural Economic Analysis of Redistributive Legal Rules, 51 Vanderbilt Law Review 1998, 1653, 1654.

47. Ulen, supra note 44, 1748.

48. See Christine Jolls, Cass R. Sunstein, & Richard Thaler, A Behavioural Approach to Law and Economics, 50 Stanford Law Review 1998, 1471-1550.

49. Richard A. Posner, Rational Choice, Behavioural Economics, and the Law, 50 Stanford Law Review 1998, 1551, 1552. Posner refers actually to 'behavioural economics' but his criticism applies as well to behavioural law and economics.

50. For recent summaries see in addition to the studies quoted supra note 6 for example the contributions to Paul Slovic. (ed.), The Perception of Risk (Earthscan Publications, 2000) and to Cass R. Sunstein, Cognition and Cost-benefit Analysis, 29 Journal of Legal Studies 2000, 1065-1073, but also a useful summary provided by Anthony I. Ogus, Regulatory Paternalism: When is it Justified?, in Corporate Governance in Context. Corporations, States and Markets in Europe, Japan and the US (Hopt, Wymeersch, Kanda & Baum eds., Oxford University Press, 2005), 303-320 and Anthony I. Ogus, Costs and Cautionary Tales. Economic Insights for the Law (Hart Publishing, 2006), 219-252 as well as M.R.A.G. Wibisana, Law and Economic Analysis of the Precautionary Principle, Maastricht: Universitaire Pers Maastricht 2008 and Thomas S. Ulen, Rational Choice Theory in Law and Economics, in Encyclopedia of Law and Economics, Vol. I, The History and Methodology of Law and Economics, (Bouckaert & De Geest eds., Edward Elgar, 2000), 790-818.

of possible cognitive problems, sometimes under different names and headings.[51] I will now briefly address some of the main cognitive issues in as far as they can potentially be relevant for accident law.

3.2 Bounds to human behaviour

In contrast to the standard economic theory, which assumes that people will maximize their utility, behavioural economics argues that people's behaviour often violates such an assumption. Behavioural economics tries to explore the actual human behaviour, by stressing the importance of 'bounds' on human behaviour.[52] The notion 'bounded rationality' is of course not new to behavioural (law and) economics but was introduced by Herbert Simon to show that actors often take shortcuts in making decisions that frequently result in choices that fail to satisfy the utility maximization prediction.[53]

In addition to bounded rationality Jolls, Sunstein and Thaler also identify bounded willpower and bounded self-interest as other 'bounds' to human behaviour. According to Jolls *et al.*, bounded willpower occurs because people often make decisions that they know to be in conflict with their long-term interests. On the other hand, the authors state that bounded self-interest occurs because people are willing to be treated fairly; hence they will treat others fairly

---

51. For example Sunstein mentions the following problems: 1. The availability heuristic; 2. Informational and reputational cascades; 3. Loss aversion; 4. Systemic effects; 5. Emotions and alarmist bias; 6. Separate evaluation and incoherence (Cass R. Sunstein, Cognition and Cost-benefit Analysis, 29 Journal of Legal Studies 2000, 1065-1073). Ogus mentions the following: 1. Status quo bias; 2. Availability heuristic; 3. Excessive discounting; 4. Selective optimism and control; 5. Social pressure (see Anthony I. Ogus, Regulatory Paternalism: When is it Justified?, in Corporate Governance in Context. Corporations, States and Markets in Europe, Japan and the US (Hopt, Wymeersch, Kanda & Baum eds., Oxford University Press, 2005), 307-310 and Anthony I. Ogus, Costs and Cautionary Tales. Economic Insights for the Law (Hart Publishing, 2006), 219-252).
52. See further M.R.A.G. Wibisana, Law and Economic Analysis of the Precautionary Principle, Maastricht: Universitaire Pers Maastricht 2008, 229-230.
53. See Russel B. Korobkin & Thomas S. Ulen, Law and Behavioural Science: Removing the Rationality Assumption from Law and Economics, 88 California Law Review 2000, 1075. See on this issue also Siegwart Lindenbergh, Social Rationality as a Unified Model of Man (Including Bounded Rationality), in Roundtable 'Cognition, Rationality and Governance, 5 Journal of Management & Governance 2001, 239-251 and D. M. Krebs, Bounded rationality, in, The New Palgrave Dictionary of Economics and the Law (Newman ed., MacMillan, 1998), 168-173.

as long as these others treat them fairly. As a result, in some situations, people care about others, even strangers, or act as if they care.[54]

In the literature two main reasons are indicated for a decision-making that does not maximize expected utility, being complexity and ambiguity. The limits of human cognitive abilities make it in some (rather complex) situations impossible to follow a utility maximizing strategy. This is the process that Simon refers to as 'satisficing', namely that people's decisions do not choose the option that maximizes their utility, but rather they choose one that satisfies their aspiration.[55] In addition to complexity also ambiguity concerning the consequences of various alternatives can lead to suboptimal decision-making from the perspective of maximization of expected utility. This ambiguity problem plays more particularly a role when decisions concern the estimation of various likelihoods, e.g. that one's house will be damaged as a result of an earthquake.[56]

3.3 Probability neglect

Another deviation from the standard model identified in behavioural studies refers to the fact that people tend to pay more attention to the absolute outcomes than to the probability that this adverse event may occur. The impact of the probability on people's feeling depends strongly on the characteristic of the particular outcome. As a result small probabilities can be largely over-estimated, resulting from the strong feelings about fears for negative outcomes or hopes for a positive outcome. People tend therefore to focus more on the absolute outcomes rather than on the probability that this may occur.[57]

In a broader example, the probability neglect is also indicated by societal concerns about hazards, such as nuclear power and exposure to extremely small amounts of toxic chemicals,

54. Christine Jolls, Cass R. Sunstein, & Richard Thaler, A Behavioural Approach to Law and Economics, 50 Stanford Law Review 1998, 1479.
55. Herbert A. Simon, Rational Decision Making in Business Organizations, 69(4) The American Economic Review 1979, 493-415; see also M.R.A.G. Wibisana, Law and Economic Analysis of the Precautionary Principle, Maastricht: Universitaire Pers Maastricht 2008, 230.
56. Russel B. Korobkin & Thomas S. Ulen, Law and Behavioural Science: Removing the Rationality Assumption from Law and Economics, 88 California Law Review 2000, 1083.
57. M.R.A.G. Wibisana, Law and Economic Analysis of the Precautionary Principle, Maastricht: Universitaire Pers Maastricht 2008, 241-242.

which still fail to recede even after the society is provided with the information showing that the probabilities of such hazards to occur are very small.[58]

3.4 Availability heuristic

People usually do not use statistics to judge the likelihood of a future event. Instead, they use their memory to judge the likelihood of a similar accident to recur. In this case, rather than evaluating the likelihood based on how often the accident has occurred in the past, people usually think an accident is about to happen because a similar accident that occurred in the past is readily available in people's memory, enabling them to easily remember such an accident. The easier this memory comes to the people's mind, the more likely the accident seems to occur. This phenomenon is referred to as the 'availability heuristic'. It is a mental shortcut that individuals use on the basis of which they assume that memorable events are memorable precisely because they are common or have recently occurred. However, these estimates based on 'availability' can be biased and be largely unrelated to the objective statistical probability of certain events occurring.[59] As a result of availability heuristic errors will occur whereby the likelikhood of some incidents (like a nuclear accident) is (wrongly) perceived as high, whereas others (like a stroke) as relatively low.[60]

The availability heuristic is not only affected by the distance of the past events, but also by the imaginability of the future events. Moreover, several studies have shown that risks from dramatic or sensational causes of death tend to be greatly overestimated.[61] The availability heuristic could explain why judged frequencies of highly publicised causes of death (e.g., accidents, homicides, fires, tornadoes, and cancer) were relatively overestimated and underpublicised causes (e.g., diabetes, stroke, asthma, and tuberculosis) were underestimated.[62]

---

58. So M.R.A.G. Wibisana, Law and Economic Analysis of the Precautionary Principle, Maastricht: Universitaire Pers Maastricht 2008, 242.
59. See Russel B. Korobkin & Thomas S. Ulen, Law and Behavioural Science: Removing the Rationality Assumption from Law and Economics, 88 California Law Review 2000, 1087-1090 and Timur Kuran & Cass R. Sunstein, Availability Cascades and Risk Regulation, 51 Stanford Law Review 1999, 683-768.
60. Cass R. Sunstein, Behavioural Analysis of Law, 64 The University of Chicago Law Review 1997, 1188.
61. Paul Slovic, Informing and Educating the Public about Risk, in The Perception of Risk (Paul Slovic ed., Earthscan Publications 2000), 184.
62. M.R.A.G. Wibisana, Law and Economic Analysis of the Precautionary Principle, Maastricht: Universitaire Pers Maastricht 2008, 243.

Thus, if media coverage has given prominence to a particular event individuals may attribute a greater probability to the event recurring than is objectively justified.[63]

One factor contributing to the formation of the availability heuristic is the social amplification risk. Kasperson, *et al.* argue: '*Social amplification of risk denotes the phenomenon by which information process, institutional structures, social-group behaviour and individual responses shape the social experience of risk, thereby contributing to risk consequences*'.[64] Thus, the experience of risk is not only related to the physical harm, but is also a product of a social process by which groups or individuals learn to create the interpretations of risk.[65] This phenomenon is referred to as a 'ripple' effect, because of its analogy of dropping a stone into a pond. The ripple effect can illustrate how a risk event can first affect the directly concerned victims and then spread outward to other levels and potentially even future generations.[66]

One should, however, notice that the term 'availability' has been used to explain quite different reasons for distorted perceptions concerning probability judgements. Gigerenzer therefore argues that first the empirical evidence has to be examined carefully to establish what the term 'availability' exactly refers to before any conclusions are drawn upon it.[67]

3.5 Status quo bias

This bias, related to the so called 'endowment effect' relates to the fact that individuals often place a higher monetary value on items they own than on those they do not own yet. Many experiments have provided evidence of this phenomenon.[68] Experiments also show that, all

63. See Anthony I. Ogus, Costs and Cautionary Tales. Economic Insights for the Law (Hart Publishing, 2006), 236 and M.R.A.G. Wibisana, Law and Economic Analysis of the Precautionary Principle, Maastricht: Universitaire Pers Maastricht 2008, 224 and Christine Jolls, Behavioural Economic Analysis of Redistributive Legal Rules, 51 Vanderbilt Law Review 1998, 1662.
64. Roger E. Kasperson, The Social Amplification of Risk: A Conceptual Framework, in The Perception of Risk (Paul Slovic ed., Earthscan Publications 2002), 237.
65. J. X. Kasperson, The Social Amplification of Risk: Assessing Fifteen Years of Research and Theory, in The Social Amplification of Risk, (Pidgeon, Kasperson & Slovic eds., Cambridge University Press 2003), 15.
66. Ibid.
67. Gerd Gigerenzer, Is the Mind Irrational or Ecologically Rational?, in The Law and Economics of Irrational Behaviour (Parisi & Smith eds., Stanford University Press, 2005), 45.
68. For a summary of the literature see Russel B. Korobkin & Thomas S. Ulen, Law and Behavioural Science: Removing the Rationality Assumption from Law and Economics, 88 California Law Review 2000, 1107-1112.

things being equal, individuals will prefer a status quo outcome.[69] This for example explains continued risky behaviour such as smoking in which individuals have engaged in for a number of years apparently without significant adverse effects.[70] As a result of the status quo bias individuals may disregard objective information (e.g. on the riskiness of their behaviour) but may also not be willing to explore alternatives to familiar choices.[71]

A related point is the phenomenon of so called 'loss aversion', meaning that persons are more displeased with losses than they are pleased with equivalent gains. An implication is, according to Sunstein, that the allocation of legal entitlements does matter since those who are initially allocated an entitlement are likely to value it more than those without the entitlement.[72] Not everyone is, however, convinced that this endowment effect shows an empirical failure of rational-choice economics. Posner for example argues that anyone who owns a good, will value it above the market price. If they did not, they would sell it to non-owners. Hence, he argues that the endowment effect makes perfect sense from a straightforward rational-choice perspective. The fact that you value something more because you possessed it for a long time may, according to Posner illustrate the operation of habit and is not irrational at all.[73]

---

69. See Thomas S. Ulen, Rational Choice Theory in Law and Economics, in Encyclopedia of Law and Economics, Vol. I, The History and Methodology of Law and Economics, (Bouckaert & De Geest eds., Edward Elgar, 2000), 804-806. Recent literature, however, criticizes earlier findings concerning this endowment effect. See in this respect more particularly Charles R. Plott & Kathryn Zeiler, The Willingness to Pay/Willingness to Accept Gap, 'Endowment Effect', Subject Misconceptions and Experimental procedures for Eliciting Valuations, 95 American Economic Review 2005, 530-545.
70. Anthony I. Ogus, Costs and Cautionary Tales. Economic Insights for the Law (Hart Publishing, 2006), 235.
71. This explains for example that default rules in contract law are more difficult to contract around than rational choice theory has suggested. The status quo bias leads individuals to prefer the default rules to alternatives (Russel B. Korobkin, The Status Quo Bias and Contract Default Rules, 83 Cornell Law Review 1998, 608-647 and Russel B. Korobkin, Inertia and Preference in Contract Negotiation: The Psychological Power of Default Rules and Form Terms, 51 Vanderbilt Law Review 1998, 1583).
72. Cass R. Sunstein, Behavioural Analysis of Law, 64 The University of Chicago Law Review 1997, 1179-1181. On this basis Sunstein criticizes the Coase theorem (Ronald Coase, supra note 3). I will come back to that point below. See on loss aversion also Cass R. Sunstein, Behavioural law and economics: a progress report, 1 American Law and Economics Review 1999, 131-135.
73. See these powerful arguments in Richard A. Posner, Rational Choice, Behavioural Economics, and the Law, 50 Stanford Law Review 1998, 1564-1567.

3.6 Selective optimism and overconfidence

Many experiments also provide evidence of selective optimism of individuals: they tend to generalize information based on highly selective examples that suit them well.[74] Jolls reports that nearly 200 studies have shown that individuals believe that good things are more likely than average to happen to them. Bad things are more likely than average to happen to the others.[75] Many experiments have provided evidence of this selective optimism.[76] This optimism seems to be stronger when the individual has a degree of control over the event like in the case of a car driver: a study showed that 90% of drivers thought that they drove more safely than the average driver.[77] Unrealistic optimism leads to an underestimation of the probability that unpleasant events will happen to oneself.[78]

This selective optimism is, so many studies show, not weaker with laymen than with experts. Experiments have for example shown that there is a strong so called self-serving bias in the analysis of the chances of winning a law suit by lawyers. As a result lawyers systematically anticipate their trial prospects as being better than they objectively are.[79] Slovic, Fischoff and Liechtenstein also discuss many examples of overconfidence by experts. They refer for example to studies showing that the reactor safety experts had greatly overestimated the precision with which the probability of a core meltdown could be assessed. Another case discusses the

74. Anthony I. Ogus, Costs and Cautionary Tales. Economic Insights for the Law (Hart Publishing, 2006), 237.

75. Christine Jolls, Behavioural Economic Analysis of Redistributive Legal Rules, 51 Vanderbilt Law Review 1998, 1653, 1659.

76. A nice example is provided in a study concerning Virginia residents who applied for a marriage licence: even though the respondents knew that almost half of all marriages ended in divorce, when they had to predict the likelihood that their marriage would end in divorce the model response was zero (L.A. Baker & R.E. Emery, When Every Relationship is Above Average: Perceptions and Expectations of Divorce at the Time of Marriage, 17 Law and Human Behaviour 1993, 439 and following. For a discussion of this and other studies see Russel B. Korobkin & Thomas S. Ulen, Law and Behavioural Science: Removing the Rationality Assumption from Law and Economics, 88 California Law Review 2000, 1091-1093).

77. See the study by Svenson quoted by Anthony I. Ogus, Costs and Cautionary Tales. Economic Insights for the Law (Hart Publishing, 2006), 237-238.

78. See also the many studies quoted by Christine Jolls, Behavioural Economic Analysis of Redistributive Legal Rules, 51 Vanderbilt Law Review 1998, 1658-1663. See also Cass R. Sunstein, Behavioural Analysis of Law, 64 The University of Chicago Law Review 1997, 1182-1184, and Cass R. Sunstein, Behavioural law and economics: a progress report, 1 American Law and Economics Review 1999, 136-137.

79. Russel B. Korobkin & Thomas S. Ulen, Law and Behavioural Science: Removing the Rationality Assumption from Law and Economics, 88 California Law Review 2000, 1093-1094. This is one explanation for the fact that many more cases than one would expect to go to trial instead of being settled.

unwarranted confidence of engineers who were certain to have solved many serious problems during the construction of the Teton dam which eventually collapsed in 1976.[80] In another paper the same authors summarize several other studies identifying common ways in which experts may overlook pathways to disaster.[81]

Many other studies show so called 'calibration errors', being mistakes in estimating probabilities. These especially occur when experts have to assess risks in the absence of precise data. Moreover, the errors do not seem to diminish once the experts have become familiar with the problem. The 'learn ability' of risk assessment seems therefore to be low.[82]

A particular type of judgement error in probabilistic assessment (also of experts) is the so called 'hindsight bias'. This is the simple tendency of individuals to overestimate the *ex ante* prediction of an event on the basis of the knowledge that the event actually occurred. The hindsight bias plays a role with physicians[83] but also with judges and more particularly in tort cases as well. Experiments showed that the knowledge that an accident actually occurred has a dramatic influence on the appraisal of whether (on the basis of the Learned Hand formula) the accident could have been prevented by taking additional precautionary measures.[84]

---

80. Slovic, Fischhoff, & Lichtenstein, Rating the Risks, in The Perception of Risk (Paul Slovic ed., Earthscan Publications, 2000), 104-120.

81. Slovic, Fischhoff, & Lichtenstein, Facts versus Fears: Understanding Perceived Risk, in Judgement under Uncertainty: Heuristics and Biases (Kahneman, Slovic & Tversky eds., Cambridge University Press, 2001), 477.

82. For a summary of these studies see M.R.A.G. Wibisana, Law and Economic Analysis of the Precautionary Principle, Maastricht: Universitaire Pers Maastricht 2008, 264-268. For that reason Posner is critical of Christine Jolls, Cass R. Sunstein, & Richard Thaler, A Behavioural Approach to Law and Economics, 50 Stanford Law Review 1998 arguing that they put too much trust in expert judgement whereas it is not clear why they would be less subject to 'cognitive quirks' or 'weakness of will' as ordinary people (Richard A. Posner, Rational Choice, Behavioural Economics, and the Law, 50 Stanford Law Review 1998, 1575).

83. See Christine Jolls, Behavioural Law and Economics, in Economic Institutions and Behavioral Economics (Diamond & Hannu Vartiainen eds., Princeton University Press, 2007), 124.

84. See Jeffrey J. Rachlinski, A Positive Psychological Theory of Judging in Hindsight, 65 The University of Chicago Law Review 1998, 571-625 and See also other studies discussed by Russel B. Korobkin & Thomas S. Ulen, Law and Behavioural Science: Removing the Rationality Assumption from Law and Economics, 88 California Law Review 2000, 1095-1096.

3.7 Criticisms

The brief introduction to a few cognitive problems which have been identified in the behavioural literature (and which could easily be extended by discussing many others) shows that individuals may behave differently than what is assumed on the basis of the utility maximization hypothesis. However, not all scholars are to the same extent enthusiastic about this literature, especially when it comes to the central question of the implications of the mentioned studies for traditional law and economics.[85]

First, Posner argues that many of the behavioural findings are based on experimental settings. Selection effects suggest that the real-world environment could be systematically different than the experimental one.[86] Many of the findings of behavioural studies are based on experiments with students, as a result of which Posner argues that the empirical evidence for the claim of the behaviouralists is weaker than is often held.[87] He suggestively adds: '*An interesting study would be to compare the subsequent career paths, and earnings, of students who score high in rationality in experiments conducted by behavioural economists with those who score low*'.

Second, Posner equally argues that much of the empirical evidence which is presented as proof of criticism of rational choice theory in fact is proof of rational behaviour of individuals. Sunstein and co-authors had, in various publications, criticized the fact that the highly publicized rash of illnesses of people living near Love Canal gave rise to the superfund law. It made according to Sunstein *et al.* a legislative response nearly inevitable, irrespective of the actual facts.[88] The example is provided as anecdotal evidence of the above mentioned 'availability heuristic'. Posner to the contrary argues that it is entirely rational for people to rely on anecdotal evidence in the absence of better evidence. '*Limited information must not be confused with irrationality*', so he continues. The fact that people sometimes overreact to highly publicised

85. For a discussion of the criticisms on behavioural law and economics (and a reply to the critics) see Cass R. Sunstein, Behavioural law and economics: a progress report, 1 American Law and Economics Review 1999, 147-150.

86. Richard A. Posner, Rational Choice, Behavioural Economics, and the Law, 50 Stanford Law Review 1998, 1570.

87. Ibid., 1571.

88. See Christine Jolls, Cass R. Sunstein, & Richard Thaler, A Behavioural Approach to Law and Economics, 50 Stanford Law Review 1998, 1521 and Timur Kuran & Cass R. Sunstein, Availability Cascades and Risk Regulation, 51 Stanford Law Review 1999, 691-698.

events may be the result of lacking information to form a correct assessment of the risk, not of irrationality.[89]

Third, another problem with the broad behavioural literature is that the findings do not always clearly point in one direction as far as the deviation from the objective standard of cost-benefit analysis is concerned. Some elements of the behavioural literature may point in one direction (systematic underestimation of risks) whereas others may point in the opposite direction (overestimation of risks). For example due to bounded rationality and limited capacity to process information some risks may be systematically underestimated (probability of being victim of a hurricane or earthquake) whereas other research shows that for example because of high publicity concerning the same risks the availability heuristic could point in the direction of an overestimation of the same risks due to 'social amplification'. Also: probability neglect and availability heuristic may lead to overpessimism and thus overprecaution, whereas selective optimism and overconfidence could lead to overoptimism and thus underprecaution. It is, in other words, not always clear whether the behavioural literature points in the direction of systematic over- or underestimation of risks.[90] Jolls, however, argues that it would be wrong to infer from this that behavioural deviations could go either way. Underestimations of the general probability of an accident tend to be more frequent when individuals are injurers, like car drivers. Highly available events which to the contrary lead to overestimation of the risk tend to involve firms, not individual liability.[91] If one were thus to draw conclusions on the basis of the behavioural studies it is certainly possible to differentiate between these (and other) situations, even though it obviously makes the analysis more complicated as well.

A fourth problem is that the many studies in social psychology can provide evidence that individuals may act differently than assumed in traditional economic models, they do not yet

89. Richard A. Posner, Rational Choice, Behavioural Economics, and the Law, 50 Stanford Law Review 1998, 1572-1573.

90. See also Cass R. Sunstein, Behavioural Analysis of Law, 64 The University of Chicago Law Review 1997, 1184: 'While people may sometimes think that low-probability events have higher probability than they in fact do, many individual agents think that they personally are peculiarly less susceptible to such events, which may lead them to underestimate rather than overestimate probabilities'. See also the interesting study by Eric Posner (to which I will come back below) arguing that errors may both lead to too little care and to too high care (Eric A. Posner, Probability Errors: Some Positive and Normative Implications for Tort and Contract Law, 11 Supreme Court Economic Review 2004, 125-141).

91. Christine Jolls, Behavioural Economic Analysis of Redistributive Legal Rules, 51 Vanderbilt Law Review 1998, 1663.

offer an alternative integrated theory which would replace traditional law and economics.[92] Korobkin and Ulen therefore rightly hold that since 'law and behavioural science' still lacks a single, coherent theory of behaviour there is no reason to replace the rational choice theory through an alternative paradigm.[93] Gigerenzer also points at the fact that behavioural (law and) economics has been criticized *'for merely listing anomalies without providing a theory'*[94] and – not surprisingly – also Posner holds that behavioural (law and) economics is undertheorized *'because of its residual, and in consequence purely empirical, character'*.[95] Posner moreover holds that behavioural economics does not invite to formulate a theory. *'Faced with anomalous behaviour, the rational-choice economist, unlike the behavioural economist, does not respond, 'of course, what do you expect?', but would rather be challenged and would rather 'wrack his brains for some theoretical extension or modification that will accommodate the seeming anomaly to the assumption of rationality'*.[96]

Fifth, again others have held that behavioural economics may point at a variety of human errors but that these should not necessarily lead to regulatory interventions (through aggressive regulation) but to examine how individuals are themselves capable to remedy (partially) these errors by learning in order to improve their situation.[97] For example John List has on the basis of various experiments shown that as participants gain experience in market transactions some of the cognitive biases disappear.[98] More generally some have held that debiasing can counteract

92. See Avishalom Tor, The Methodology of the Behavioural Analysis of Law, 4(1) Haifa Law Review 2008, 237 and ff. See also the suggestive title of the paper by Gregory Mitchell, Why Law and Economics' Perfect Rationality should not be traded for Behavioural Law and Economics' Equal in Competence, 91 Georgetown Law Journal 2002, 67.

93. Russel B. Korobkin & Thomas S. Ulen, Law and Behavioural Science: Removing the Rationality Assumption from Law and Economics, 88 CALIFORNIA LAW REVIEW 2000, 1057.

94. Gerd Gigerenzer, Is the Mind Irrational or Ecologically Rational?, in The Law and Economics of Irrational Behaviour (Parisi & Smith eds., Stanford University Press, 2005), 61.

95. Richard A. Posner, Rational Choice, Behavioural Economics, and the Law, 50 Stanford Law Review 1998, 1559. He adds: 'Behavioural economics is defined by its subject rather than by its method and its subject is merely the set of phenomena that rational-choice models (or at least the simplest of them) do not explain'.

96. Ibid., 1567. Posner there foresees the major fruit of behavioural economics as 'The stimulus it provides to new and better rational-choice theorizing'.

97. Richard A. Epstein, Behavioural Economics: Human Errors and Market Corrections, 73 University of Chicago Law Review 2006, 111-132, 130: 'The real challenge is not to deny the experimental findings, but to explain the full range of personal and market mechanisms that make them disappear without a trace'.

98. John A. List, Does Market Experience Eliminate Market Anomalies, 118 Quarterly Journal of Economics 2003, 41-71 and John A. List, The Behaviourlist Meets the Market: Measuring Social Preferences and Reputation Effects in Actual Transactions, 114 Journal of Political Economy 2006, 1.

cognitive and motivational distortions although many of those debiasing strategies have their own disadvantages and limitations as well.[99]

This literature therefore does not deny the findings of the behavioural economics, but is rather critical of the normative implication that regulation would be necessary to correct for these human errors. This raises more generally the question to the implication of the behavioural literature discussed in this section for the traditional economic analysis of tort and insurance as presented in section 2.

4 IMPLICATIONS FOR LIABILITY LAW

4.1 Relevance of the behavioural literature

4.1.1 Increased integration of behavioural into traditional law and economics

First of all it should be repeated[100] that even traditional economic analysis of accident law never took a completely naïve view of potential parties in the accident setting assuming e.g. that they would be consciously calculating individuals constantly making decisions on the basis of a weighing of prevention costs versus the expected damage. Take the first example mentioned in the introduction of the cyclist deciding on what measures to take to avoid running over the pedestrian. Even tough law and economics scholars would generally assume that this decision-making takes into account the fact that there may be an exposure to liability, no scholar ever held that the cyclist would actually make a conscious calculation of costs and benefits taking into account the existence of liability rules. That is not what traditional law and economics claims and also not necessary for the predictions of the economic model to work. In the words of Posner: '*rational choice need not be conscious choice*'.[101]

However, it can not be denied that the behavioural law and economics literature presented in Section 3 showed that potentially both individuals in an accident setting and judges, having to examine *ex post* an accident situation, may be exposed to a variety of heuristics and biases which may affect the assumptions underlying the traditional economic model, especially concerning

99. See Christine Jolls & Cass R. Sunstein, Debiasing through law, 35 Journal of Legal Studies 2006, 199-241; Cass R. Sunstein, Behavioural law and economics: a progress report, 1 American Law and Economics Review 1999, 150-151 and Avishalom Tor, The Methodology of the Behavioural Analysis of Law, 4(1) Haifa Law Review 2008, 292-300.

100. See supra section 2.2.

101. Richard A. Posner, Rational Choice, Behavioural Economics, and the Law, 50 Stanford Law Review 1998, 1551.

the way in which these individuals are expected to behave. However, since the early work of Herbert Simon, Tversky and Kahneman, these insights have, perhaps slowly, but still increasingly been incorporated into the law and economics literature as well. Sunstein still held in 1997 that '*economic analysis of law has proceeded on the basis of inaccurate understandings of decision and choice*'.[102] That seems, however, no longer correct. Major handbooks of law and economics now take the behavioural literature seriously and include the results in the economic analysis, even though admittedly some authors seem to be more convinced of its relevance[103] than others.[104] Posner himself could therefore rightly argue that some of the insights that are ascribed to behavioural economics are already a part of economic analysis of law '*which long ago abandoned the model of hyperrational, emotionless, unsocial, supremely egoistic, non-strategic man or woman*' that some appear to ascribe to it.[105] It can therefore certainly not be held that a pure rational choice theory would still be the mainstream paradigm of law and economics.[106]

4.1.2 Prescriptive and predictive analysis

The importance of the behavioural literature for the economic analysis of liability law and accident law more generally could be analysed from different angles. A first question that could arise is whether the behavioural literature is better able to prescribe more actually how parties in an accident setting will behave and whether it also allows to make better predictions about how parties will react e.g. to an exposure to liability rules. If that were the case the use of the results of the behavioural literature would certainly be useful since it could improve the prescriptive and predictive value of economic models of accident law. This is the way in which for example Jolls tries to present the behavioural literature to seduce law and economic scholars. Behavioural law and economics, so she argues '*is not a critique of law and economics*', '*its goal is to offer*

102. Cass R. Sunstein, Behavioural Analysis of Law, 64 The University of Chicago Law Review 1997, 1194.

103. See, for example, Robert Cooter & Thomas S. Ulen, Law and Economics (Austin, Addison Wesley, 4th ed., 2004) who spent substantial attention to behavioural law and economics, also in their discussion of accident law (Robert Cooter & Thomas S. Ulen, Law and Economics (Austin, Addison Wesley, 4th ed., 2004), 350-352) as well as Schäfer and Ott, who provide a detailed discussion of the various cognitive biases (Schäfer & Ott, supra note 15).

104. Posner also spends some attention to the behavioural literature in his famous handbook Economic Analysis of Law even though it obtained a less prominent place than in the other just mentioned monographs (Richard Posner, Economics Analysis of Law (Wolters Kluwer, 7th ed., 2007), 17-20).

105. Richard A. Posner, Rational Choice, Behavioural Economics, and the Law, 50 Stanford Law Review 1998, 1552.

106. So A. Arcuri, An Eclecticism in Law and Economics, 1(3) Erasmus Law Review 2008, 59-81, 79.

better predictions and prescriptions about law based on improved accounts of how people actually behave'.[107] If this is what behavioural literature does, no law and economic scholar could object against its, use since it would allow to make prescriptions and predictions about the functioning of accident law which are closer to reality. However, here again Posner would react that many of the insights presented under behavioural economics in fact already are part of law and economics and moreover, '*need not derail rational-choice economics*'.[108] Taking again the cyclist from the introduction: one does not need cognitive psychology to know that the cyclist will not make conscious calculations of costs and benefits of preventive actions taking into account the applicable liability law. However, an advantage of the behavioural studies is that they undoubtedly provide possibilities to come to a further refinement of existing models of accident law, thus allowing better predictions e.g. on reactions of potential injurers or victims taking into account the biases that may affect their behaviour. However, as I will argue below, one can question to what extent these insights were not already largely present in traditional models of accident law as they were e.g. developed by Shavell, or at least to what extent the existing models allow to incorporate these new behavioural insights, without fundamentally changing them.

To the extent behavioural studies allow to improve the predictive and prescriptive economic analysis of law its use will hardly be disputed. One problem is, however, as Posner indicated, that the more one takes the behavioural literature into account and the more the description of actual behaviour becomes more accurate, the less economic models become predictive. In the words of Posner '*descriptive accuracy is purchased at a price, the price being loss of predictive power*'.[109] The rational choice model may irrealistically assume rational behaviour, but by relying on what rational men would do in a given situation, economic models have at least a higher predictive value.[110]

107. Christine Jolls, Behavioural Economic Analysis of Redistributive Legal Rules, 51 Vanderbilt Law Review 1998, 1654.

108. Richard A. Posner, Rational Choice, Behavioural Economics, and the Law, 50 Stanford Law Review 1998, 1557.

109. Ibid., 1559.

110. Ibid.

4.1.3 Normative implications?

The enthusiasm for the behavioural literature, however, disappears when at the normative level behavioural literature is used to formulate policy recommendations.[111] Ogus rightly pointed at the fact that one should be careful with paternalistic interventions based on cognitive biases since notwithstanding the biases there may still be welfare maximization and hence no need for regulatory intervention. Moreover, if such an intervention takes place the question still arises whether the benefits outweigh the costs.[112] Second, Korobkin and Ulen rightly pointed at the fact that in some cases more empirical research is needed for policymakers to be able to make effective use of the insights provided by behavioural literature[113] and that in some other cases the legal implications of a particular behavioural phenomenon may not be that clear cut.[114] That is why warnings are especially formulated at the normative use of behavioural law and economics.[115]

4.1.4 Various consequences

With these limitations in mind, I will simply examine how relaxing the behavioural assumptions of rational choice based on the behavioural literature may affect the traditional economic model of tort law.[116] In this respect we can meanwhile refer to a large body of literature where these

111. For a summary of the critics see Avishalom Tor, The Methodology of the Behavioural Analysis of Law, 4(1) Haifa Law Review 2008, 318-325.

112. Anthony I. Ogus, Costs and Cautionary Tales. Economic Insights for the Law (Hart Publishing, 2006), 250-252.

113. E.g., concerning the overconfidence bias (Russel B. Korobkin & Thomas S. Ulen, Law and Behavioural Science: Removing the Rationality Assumption from Law and Economics, 88 California Law Review 2000, 1092).

114. More particularly of the so called hindsight bias (Russel B. Korobkin & Thomas S. Ulen, Law and Behavioural Science: Removing the Rationality Assumption from Law and Economics, 88 California Law Review 2000, 1097).

115. See Richard A. Posner, Rational Choice, Behavioural Economics, and the Law, 50 Stanford Law Review 1998, 1553, 1575. Also Sunstein argues that normative accounts should not be confused with descriptive accounts (Cass R. Sunstein, Behavioural Analysis of Law, 64 The University of Chicago Law Review 1997, 1175).

116. Given the limits of this study I will only address a few possible effects of the behavioural literature for accident law. However, many other could be examined as well. For example loss aversion could have consequences for the way in which damages are calculated as well as for the choice between specific performance and damages. See on these issues, Jeffrey J. Rachlinski, Gains, Losses and the Psychology of Litigation, Southern California Law Review 1996, 113-185 and Cass R. Sunstein, Behavioural law and economics: a progress report, 1 AMERICAN LAW AND ECONOMICS REVIEW 1999, 133.

consequences have also been examined.[117] There are in fact many more potential consequences of behavioural literature for the economics of accident law which go beyond the scope of this study. Sunstein for example claims that one important consequence of loss aversion and the endowment effect is that the Coase theorem is in one respect quite wrong for the simple reason that the allocation of the initial entitlement may well matter.[118] As I, however, mentioned above this endowment effect is highly criticised by Posner.[119]

I will first address the importance of the behavioural literature for the efficient care by injurers (4.2), then address the possibility of errors with the judiciary (4.3) and analyse the consequences for the choice between negligence and strict liability (4.4). I then discuss whether the cognitive problems addressed in section 3 can be interpreted as a case for regulation (4.5).

4.2 Efficient care by injurers

A question which of course arises as a result of the behavioural literature is how these findings affect a crucial assumption of the standard economics of tort law, being that injurers will react with efficient care to efficient standards set by judges (under negligence) or will find themselves the efficient care-level on the basis of a weighing of costs of prevention and benefits in reducing the accident risk (under strict liability).[120] The question therefore arises how human errors by

117. Again, given limited space I will only address a few consequences. The reader interested in further details can be referred to e.g. Jason S. Johnston, Bayesian Fact-Finding and Efficiency: Towards an Economic Theory of Liability under Uncertainty, SOUTHERN CALIFORNIA LAW REVIEW 1987, 137-181; Russel B. Korobkin & Thomas S. Ulen, Law and Behavioural Science: Removing the Rationality Assumption from Law and Economics, 88 California Law Review 2000, 1053-1146; Eric A. Posner, Probability Errors: Some Positive and Normative Implications for Tort and Contract Law, 11 Supreme Court Economic Review 2004, 125-141; Schäfer & Müller-Langer, Strict Liability versus Negligence, in Tort Law and Economics (Michael Faure ed., Edward Elgar, 2009), 3-45 and Joshua S. Teitelbaum, A Unilateral Accident Model under Ambiguity, 37 Journal of Legal Studies 2007, 431-477.

118. Cass R. Sunstein, Behavioural Analysis of Law, 64 The University of Chicago Law Review 1997, 1179.

119. Richard A. Posner, Rational Choice, Behavioural Economics, and the Law, 50 Stanford Law Review 1998, 1564-1567. See for a behavioural criticism on the Coase theorem also Thomas S. Ulen, Rational Choice Theory in Law and Economics, in Encyclopedia of Law and Economics, Vol. I, The History and Methodology of Law and Economics, (Bouckaert & De Geest eds., Edward Elgar, 2000), 810-811.

120. I disregard situations where also victims can affect the accident risk (so-called bilateral accidents) and thus focus merely on unilateral accidents. It may be clear, however, that equally victims may suffer from similar cognitive limitations. For a discussion of the influence of cognitive problems on the victim's side (and hence

potential injurers and judges may affect the economics of tort law. The question arises what can go wrong, in the sense of what the deviations are from the standard model and what the implications may be.

4.2.1 Underdeterrence

Many of the cognitive limitations described in section 3 can influence the care taken by injurers. It is remarkable that some of these limitations point in the direction of injurers taking higher care (overprecaution) whereas others point in the direction of injurers taking lower care (underdeterrence). Starting with the latter, some have indicated that bounded rationality will lead to systematic misperception of individuals in the probability of accidents. One reason is the well-known affect heuristic: if an individual considers a certain activity as useful and pleasant, the likelihood that he will realise that the consequences of the activity are damaging will be lower than when he dislikes or disapproves of the activity.[121] Also the presentation of the facts and social acceptance may have an influence on the estimation that the activity will lead to damage.[122] Jolls, Sunstein and Thaler also point to overoptimism as a source for miscalculations of the probability of a bad outcome of certain events. Such overoptimism may lead to underdeterrence of potential tortfeasors.[123] Especially with respect to car accidents there is overwhelming evidence of the so called optimism bias as a result of which drivers underestimate their absolute as well as their relative (to other individuals) probability of being involved in a car crash.[124]

the bilateral case) See Eric A. Posner, Probability Errors: Some Positive and Normative Implications for Tort and Contract Law, 11 Supreme Court Economic Review 2004, 137-138, 140-141.

121. See, for example, with respect to smoking Paul Slovic ed., Smoking – Risk, Perception and Policy (Thousand Oaks, CA: Sage, 2001).

122. A summary of this literature is also provided in the inauguration address of Willem H. Van Boom, Structurele fouten in het aansprakelijkheidsrecht (inauguration address University of Tilburg, 14 March 2003), The Hague: Boom., 9-11.

123. Christine Jolls, Cass R. Sunstein, & Richard Thaler, A Behavioural Approach to Law and Economics, 50 Stanford Law Review 1998, 1524-1525. They, however, equally indicate that the role of overoptimism can vary significantly with context, since there is equally a tendency to overestimate the likelihood of being sanctioned (for example concerning superfund litigation).

124. Christine Jolls, Behavioural Law and Economics, in Economic Institutions and Behavioral Economics (Diamond & Hannu Vartiainen eds., Princeton University Press, 2007), 123. See also an empirical study showing evidence of this so called self-favouring bias with drivers by Guppy 1993, p. 375-382. See also Christine Jolls, Behavioural Economic Analysis of Redistributive Legal Rules, 51 Vanderbilt Law Review 1998, 1658-1660.

4.2.2 Overprecaution

Other cognitive limitations (or even the same) may lead to injurers taking higher care than would be efficient (overdeterrence). A typical problem leading to a potential overdeterrence is the so-called probability neglect: overweighing of small probabilities because of fear of negative outcomes.[125] Focussing more on the outcome than on the probability of such an outcome potential injurers may take excessive care against low probability high damage events.[126]

The same danger exists with the so-called availability heuristic. When a danger has materialised and thus is 'available' the probability of that negative outcome may be overestimated. This availability heuristic can be strengthened by negative publicity concerning particular types of accidents.[127] Excessive care can thus be the result.[128]

Moreover, bounded willpower can also explain why in some situations people care about others, even strangers, or act as if they care. The importance of this bounded willpower for accident law is clear: it may explain why potential tortfeasors (e.g. the cyclist from the example in the introduction) may simply whish to avoid inflicting harm on the pedestrian.[129]

4.2.3 Various directions

So far a problem with the consequences of this literature for injurer behaviour is that, of course depending upon the circumstance, the results go in various directions: some problems like

---

125. M.R.A.G. Wibisana, Law and Economic Analysis of the Precautionary Principle, Maastricht: Universitaire Pers Maastricht 2008, 241-242.

126. Eric Posner argues also that a person who discounts remote risks might take too much care, which would equally lead to overdeterrence (Eric Posner, supra note 117, 126).

127. In the words of Ogus: 'If media coverage has given prominence to a given contingency, say an accident, individuals will attribute a greater probability to the contingency recurring than is objectively justified' (Anthony I. Ogus, Regulatory Paternalism: When is it Justified?, in Corporate Governance in Context. Corporations, States and Markets in Europe, Japan and the US (Hopt, Wymeersch, Kanda & Baum eds., Oxford University Press, 2005), 308).

128. See Christine Jolls, Behavioural Economic Analysis of Redistributive Legal Rules, 51 Vanderbilt Law Review 1998, 1558-1663 and Eric A. Posner, Probability Errors: Some Positive and Normative Implications for Tort and Contract Law, 11 Supreme Court Economic Review 2004, 125-141.

129. This can also be related to notions of fairness people have: most people care about being fair and about being treated fairly, so Cass R. Sunstein, Behavioural law and economics: a progress report, 1 American Law and Economics Review 1999, 121 and 125.

overoptimism may lead to underdeterrence, whereas others such as the availability heuristic may lead to precisely the opposite result.

The interesting question is of course to which conclusions this leads as far as the economic analysis of liability rules is concerned. Ulen rightly notes that cognitive limitations should not necessarily affect liability rules. If it for example appears that as a result of limitations drivers take insufficient care one solution may be the installation of passive restrains like airbags which operate independently of a judgment made by the driver.[130]

Cognitive problems may not only affect potential injurers, but can also have an influence on the judiciary.

4.3 Errors with the judiciary?

Given that errors with injurers are multidirectional the question arises whether similar problems arise when the judge has to fix the standard of due care in the context of the determination of negligence. There seems to be no evidence that judges systematically do better than laymen.[131] First of all it is not clear whether judges in fixing a standard of care in a negligence case are really 'experts'. They deal with a lot of different cases and compared especially to corporate defendants, it is not difficult to argue that the likelihood that judges misinterpret the efficient care standard is larger than that defendants do so. There is overwhelming evidence that also judges are subject to cognitive limitations which influence their judgement. Biases that played a role in the assessment of probabilities and risks for laymen can equally play a role when similar assessments are undertaken by judges. Hence, the judges may also overweigh small probabilities and hence fix a too high standard of care for activities which, if they result in an accident, cause high damage. Also the availability heuristic can influence the judiciary: highly publicised causes of death (through particular accidents) could thus lead to higher estimations concerning the danger of those activities by the judiciary. In the literature various methods have been proposed to educate the judges e.g. by developing guidelines for communicating statistical information in

130. Thomas S. Ulen, The Growing Pains of Behavioural Law and Economics, 51 Vanderbilt Law Review 1998, 1753.

131. Also Posner argues that there is no reason to assume that 'experts' would not be subject to the same cognitive limitations as ordinary people (Richard A. Posner, Rational Choice, Behavioural Economics, and the Law, 50 Stanford Law Review 1998, 1575: 'The expert, too, is behavioural man… Dare we vest responsibility for curing irrationality in the irrational?').

court.[132] These remedies may of course help, but may not completely remove cognitive limitations of the judiciary in dealing with accident cases. As a consequence the due care level set through case-law could be either higher or lower than the efficient one and under- or overdeterrence could follow.

Judges may also suffer under the representativeness heuristic, which considers a previous performance as typical for a future performance. Willem van Boom provides an interesting example of this based on a case before the Netherlands Supreme Court. The case concerned the following facts: Wendy Jansen helps her sister Monique Jansen moving a cupboard up the staircase to Monique's apartment. It considers two cupboards of each 180 cm height and 60 cm breadth. Moving the first cupboard nothing goes wrong. However, when the second cupboard is brought up the staircase Monique loses her balance, is in danger of falling down with the cupboard and in a reflex she pushes the cupboard up. As a result of that Wendy's arm is squeezed between the cupboard and a door and suffers serious injury. Wendy files a claim against her sister based on tort. The *Hoge Raad* refuses to accept liability *inter alia* based on the argument that the sisters had just before brought a similar cupboard up the staircase without apparent problem.[133] Van Boom rightly argues that this reasoning of the *Hoge Raad* provides a good example of a representativeness heuristic: the mere fact that the first act did not cause any damage does not say anything at all about the dangerousness of the particular activity as such. Van Boom argues that from a statistical point of view staircases are an important source of death and personal injury: 70% of all accidents in the house take place on staircases, many of which have a fatal outcome.[134] The *Hoge Raad* apparently assumes that the previous performance (nothing happened on the staircase) was typical for the future performance and

132. See Gerd Gigerenzer, Is the Mind Irrational or Ecologically Rational?, in The Law and Economics of Irrational Behaviour (Parisi & Smith eds., Stanford University Press, 2005), 52, 56.

133. Hoge Raad, 12 May 2000, NJ 2001, 300, Aansprakelijkheid en Verzekering, 2000, 106-107, with case note by Tom Hartlief, Aansprakelijkheid met terugwerkende kracht, Ars Aequi 2005, Vol. 54, 553-563. For a discussion of this case see also Michael Faure & Tom Hartlief, The Netherlands, in Tort and Insurance Law Yearbook European Tort Law 2001 (Koziol & Steininger eds, Springer, 2002), 358-359.

134. Susan P. Baker et al (eds.), The Injury Fact Book (Oxford, 1992, 2nd ed., 135 ff).. Viscusi even argues that staircases are on number one in the top ten of 'products most involved in injuries' (W. Kip Viscusi, Consumer Behaviour and the Safety Effects of Product Safety Regulation, 28 Journal of Law and Economics 1985, 530. See also W. Kip Viscusi & Richard J. Zeckhauser, The Denominator Blindness Effect: Accident Frequencies and the Misjudgement of Recklessness, 6(1) American Law and Economics Review 2004, 74).

made the methodological mistake of ignoring the objective probability that during this type of activity personal injury would emerge.[135]

A well documented problem, which may play a role in case of decision making by the judiciary, is the so called hindsight bias, being the tendency of decision-makers to attach an excessively high probability to an event simply because it ended up occurring.[136] It is related to the fact that judges will *ex post* always take their decision on the basis of the information that the accident happened and that therefore the particular activity was apparently risky. The result of this hindsight bias is that the decision on whether the defendant took appropriate care to avoid the accident will always be biased against the defendant: the fact that the accident occurred apparently shows that he did not take sufficient care, whereby a debate on the objective question whether from *an ex ante* perspective the defendant took efficient care is not asked anymore: '*hindsight bias will lead juries making negligence determinations to find defendants liable more frequently than if cost-benefit analysis were done correctly – that is, on ex ante basis. Thus plaintiffs win cases they deserve to lose*'.[137]

In a lengthy study Rachlinski, however, shows that the situation should not necessarily be as negative as sketched at first sight. Many judicial opinions explicitly recognise the prejudicial aspects of judging in hindsight and judges have developed specific tools to avoid the hindsight bias. For example when a reliable *ex ante* assessment of reasonable care is available, such as custom in a medical malpractice case, courts will rely on that rather than on their own independent assessment of reasonable care.[138] This implies that judges being aware of the

135. Willem H. Van Boom, Structurele fouten in het aansprakelijkheidsrecht (inauguration address University of Tilburg, 14 March 2003), The Hague: Boom., 11-13.

136. Christine Jolls, Cass R. Sunstein, & Richard Thaler, A Behavioural Approach to Law and Economics, 50 Stanford Law Review 1998, 1471; Willem H. Van Boom, Structurele fouten in het aansprakelijkheidsrecht (inauguration address University of Tilburg, 14 March 2003), The Hague: Boom., 14-15; Christine Jolls, Behavioural Law and Economics, in Economic Institutions and Behavioral Economics (Diamond & Hannu Vartiainen eds., Princeton University Press, 2007), 124 and Russel B. Korobkin & Thomas S. Ulen, Law and Behavioural Science: Removing the Rationality Assumption from Law and Economics, 88 California Law Review 2000, 1095-1100 and W. Kip Viscusi & Richard J. Zeckhauser, The Denominator Blindness Effect: Accident Frequencies and the Misjudgement of Recklessness, 6(1) American Law and Economics Review 2004, 72-94.

137. Christine Jolls, Cass R. Sunstein, & Richard Thaler, A Behavioural Approach to Law and Economics, 50 Stanford Law Review 1998, 1524.

138. Jeffrey J. Rachlinski, A Positive Psychological Theory of Judging in Hindsight, 65 The University of Chicago Law Review 1998, 571, 574.

hindsight bias should for example in negligence cases suppress evidence of subsequent remedial measures because it reflects the defendant's understanding after an accident, not before.[139]

Also in the Netherlands the Hoge Raad has repeatedly held that the lawfulness of particular behaviour of a defendant in a tort case should be judged according to the standards applicable at the time of the behaviour. The Hoge Raad applies this for example in employer's liability cases for asbestoses[140] but also on the domain of professional liability of notaries.[141]

These examples show that even though some biased judgements may still be unavoidable courts are often aware of the problem, have responded to concerns about the hindsight bias by suppressing post-event information and may thus to some extent be able to mitigate the adverse consequences.[142]

4.4 Strict liability versus negligence

After having established that according to this literature human errors may affect the judgement of potential injurers in a tort case the next question is of course what the consequences may be for the economic model of tort law (and more particularly for the choice of the optimal liability rule). One way of approaching this problem is to return to the classic distinction in tort cases, mentioned above,[143] between unilateral and bilateral accidents. Ulen suggests that cognitive problems related to dealing with uncertain outcomes may be a factor in determining whether precaution was unilateral or bilateral. For example in product related accidents one could argue that if it is more likely that consumers err as far as their abilities in taking care are concerned and assuming that producers remain reliably rational, the situation is in fact one of unilateral precaution which would be an argument in favour of a strict liability rule.[144]

However, the choice between strict liability and negligence is not only related to the question whether care is unilateral or bilateral. An important difference also relates to whether cognitive problems are more serious with potential injurers than with judges. If that were indeed the case

139. Ibid., 624.

140. Hoge Raad, 2 October 1998, NJ 1998, 683 with case note by J.B.M. Vranken and Hoge Raad, 17 December 2004, Rechtspraak van de Week 2005, 4.

141. Hoge Raad, 15 September 1995, NJ 1996, 629.

142. See supra note 139, 624.

143. See supra note 120.

144. Thomas S. Ulen, Rational Choice Theory in Law and Economics, in Encyclopedia of Law and Economics, Vol. I, The History and Methodology of Law and Economics, (Bouckaert & De Geest eds., Edward Elgar, 2000), 815-816.

it would be an argument in favour of a negligence rule and against strict liability. Indeed, strict liability assumes that injurers weigh costs and benefits and thus apply efficient care, whereas negligence assumes that the judge determines the due care standard. There are, however, a number of problems with this reasoning: first, the behavioural evidence showed that there are both problems with potential injurers and with judges that can lead to misperceptions and thus to inefficient care standards. There is no *a priori* reason to argue that judges would in that respect do better than injurers. Second, even if one would move to a negligence rule, judging that the judiciary is better able to fix a due care standard, problems can still arise under negligence since potential injurers may still have various misperceptions either concerning the actual care they should take or concerning the due care required by the judiciary, which can lead to inefficiencies. Third, it might be dangerous to move to a negligence rule simply on the basis of behavioural arguments (even though it is not clear in which direction they go), thereby neglecting that an overwhelming economic literature has pointed at other advantages of strict liability with respect to internalisation of risks.[145]

Problems of course arise in the negligence determination as well. The consequences can go in various directions and depend on whether the judiciary alone, the potential injurer or both err. However, these imperfections of the negligence standard are well-known in the traditional doctrine and have been described in detail by Shavell.[146]

The consequences of the various cognitive limitations for the economic model of liability law have recently also been analysed in detail in papers by respectively Eric Posner[147] and Teitelbaum.[148]

Teitelbaum explicitly analyses the unilateral accident model under ambiguity (explicitly referring to the behavioural literature). He argues that neither strict liability nor negligence is generally efficient in the presence of ambiguity and that the injurers level of care decreases with ambiguity when he is optimistic and increases when he is pessimistic. Teitelbaum argues that in case of optimism negligence leads to better results than strict liability in some cases and that in case of pessimism negligence leads to better results than strict liability in all cases. On the basis of this

145. Stephen M. Shavell, Strict Liability versus Negligence, Journal of Legal Studies 1980, 1-25 and Stephen M. Shavell, Economic Analysis of Accident Law (Harvard University Press, 1987), 8.

146. See Stephen M. Shavell, Economic Analysis of Accident Law (Harvard University Press, 1987), 73-83.

147. Eric A. Posner, Probability Errors: Some Positive and Normative Implications for Tort and Contract Law, 11 Supreme Court Economic Review 2004, 125-141.

148. Joshua S. Teitelbaum, A Unilateral Accident Model under Ambiguity, 37 Journal of Legal Studies 2007, 431-477.

study it could therefore be concluded that in case of ambiguity the negligence rule should be preferred. However, in his study Teitelbaum merely focuses on ambiguity on the side of the injurer and therefore assumes that the judge is able to set an efficient level of care (essential for the efficiency of the negligence rule). The result may be different when also biases on the side of the judiciary are taken into account such as the hindsight bias, which I discussed before. Korobkin and Ulen argue that the hindsight bias casts doubt on the ability of juries (and the judges) to reach a proper negligence determination because they are likely to believe that precautions that could have been taken would have been more cost-effective than they actually appeared *ex ante*. Since this bias does not occur under a strict liability regime they argue that the hindsight bias points towards favouring strict liability.[149]

Eric Posner also comes to differentiated conclusions on the optimal liability rule depending on whether injurers are either overoptimistic or pessimistic which is again related to their exposure to various cognitive limitations.[150] Posner comes to the counter intuitive conclusion that under specific conditions optimism concerning the probabilities of an accident could lead to higher levels of care both under strict liability and negligence. Posner hence argues that optimism could result in too little care because of an underestimation of the expected liability, but that under strict conditions the individual could also think that little extra care will have a dramatic effect on the probability of a bad event occurring as a result of which too high care would follow.[151] He therefore argues that the optimism with the potential injurer can lead to various effects depending '*on the relationship between the probability distribution, the level of harm and the care function*'.[152]

The least one can say looking briefly at the way the results of behavioural studies have been incorporated into the literature on tort law and economics and more particularly as far as the choice between strict liability and negligence is concerned, is that it has certainly not become easier to identify an efficient liability rule. In that respect the finding of Jason Scott Johnston is also rather compelling, being that the behavioural problems do not have a clear direction and

149. Russel B. Korobkin & Thomas S. Ulen, Law and Behavioural Science: Removing the Rationality Assumption from Law and Economics, 88 California Law Review 2000, 1098-1099.

150. Eric A. Posner, Probability Errors: Some Positive and Normative Implications for Tort and Contract Law, 11 Supreme Court Economic Review 2004, 125-141.

151. Ibid., 127-128.

152. Ibid., 127.

that both under- or overdeterrence relative to the correct application of the cost-benefit standard is possible.[153]

Teitelbaum equally argues that ambiguity leads to the result that neither strict liability nor negligence is generally efficient, but shows, focussing on injurers care, a slight preference for the negligence rule. When, however, the hindsight bias is taken into account as well, like Korobkin and Ulen do, a strict liability rule seems to be preferred. If one were therefore to take into account the result of this literature in the economic models of tort law, it would lead to a highly elaborated and differentiated system whereby the efficient liability rule would depend upon the nature of the biases (pessimism or optimism) with either the injurer or the judiciary. It may be clear that, as Korobkin and Ulen indicated, one can wonder whether sufficient empirical evidence is already available to provide clear guidance as far as the choice of an efficient liability rule is concerned. The available studies so far point towards a highly differentiated system of which the administrative costs may substantially outweigh the benefits in differentiation.[154]

It was a point already made by Calabresi. As far as the choice between strict liability and negligence is concerned he argued in his 1975 paper 'On optimal deterrence and accidents',[155] that the relevant question is '*who is best suited to make the cost-benefit analysis between accident costs and accident avoidance costs? In other words, it would ask who would bear the incentive to decide correctly*'.[156] He adds that this decision '*is a matter of empirical judgements, not theory*'.[157] However, Calabresi equally recognised that a detailed differentiation on the basis of the (cognitive) abilities of the potential parties involved in an accident setting has the clear disadvantage that '*the administrative costs of making such individualised judgements would presumably be too great*'.[158] In other words, the costs of

153. Jason S. Johnston, Bayesian Fact-Finding and Efficiency: Towards an Economic Theory of Liability under Uncertainty, Southern California Law Review 1987, 154-164. Johnston does not explicitly deal with implications of the behavioural literature, but the findings of his paper (from 1987) which deal with optimal liability rules under ambiguity, uncertainty and possibilities of error, also apply to the cognitive biases identified in the behavioural literature.

154. Confirming the worry of Ogus that an intervention based on behavioural studies should only take place when the benefits exceed the costs (Anthony I. Ogus, Costs and Cautionary Tales. Economic Insights for the Law (Hart Publishing, 2006), 250-252).

155. Guido Calabresi, Optimal Deterrence and Accidents, 84 The Yale Law Journal 1975, 660-662.

156. Ibid., 666.

157. Ibid., 667.

158. Guido Calabresi & Jon T. Hirschoff, Towards a Test for Strict Liability in Torts, 81 Yale Law Journal 1972, 1068.

taking the refinements, offered by the behavioural literature, into account, may simply be too high.

4.5 A case for regulation?

A general finding of the behavioural literature is of course that potential tortfeasors may react less appropriately to incentives given by the tort system than expected by the economic model and also judges may not always be able to set the standards correctly. These errors of course raise the question whether, within Shavell's criteria for safety regulation[159] these constitute arguments for a stronger reliance on regulation than on liability rules.

Many have been critical of using human errors as a reason for regulatory intervention.[160] For example Glaeser argues that bounded rationality will often increase the costs of government decision making relative to private decision making.[161] However, this criticism largely applies in a context where there is consumer choice. Even Glaeser argues '*after all there have always existed plenty of grounds, like market failures and externalities, for government intervention in the economy*'.[162] In the cases discussed here third parties suffer harm and externalities are hence real. A regulatory intervention should thus not necessarily be classified as paternalism, suggesting that it would be an unnecessary intervention. If it could be argued that government is better able to assess specific risks than individuals (potential tortfeasors or judges) there is a simple case in favour of safety regulation based on the superior information of the regulatory authority.[163] A distinction in this respect is of course to be made between on the one hand the question whether the individual has adequate information on certain risks and on the other hand the question whether, even if adequately informed, the individual is able to respond rationally to adequate information. The human errors we discussed in section 3 of course belong more to the second

159. Stephen Shavell, Liability for Harm versus Regulation of Safety, Journal of Legal Studies 1984, 357-374.

160. See, for example, Jonathan Klick & Gregory Mitchell, Government Regulation of Irrationality: Moral and Cognitive Hazards, 90 Minnisota Law Review 2006, 1620; Jeffrey J. Rachlinski, Cognitive Errors, Individual Differences, and Paternalism, 73 University of Chicago Law Review 2006, 207-229.; Jefrey J. Rachlinski, The Uncertain Psychological Case for Paternalism, 97 Northwestern University Law Review 2003, 1165 and Avishalom Tor, The Methodology of the Behavioural Analysis of Law, 4(1) Haifa Law Review 2008, 314-317.

161. Edward L. Glaeser, Paternalism and Psychology, 73 University of Chicago Law Review 2006,. 133.

162. Ibid., 142.

163. See also Anthony I. Ogus, Costs and Cautionary Tales. Economic Insights for the Law (Hart Publishing, 2006), 219-252, 305.

category.[164] In that case Ogus argued that a paternalist goal of increasing social welfare can justify regulation on the basis that the regulator assumes what would have been the preferences of individuals if they had responded rationally to full information.[165] Ogus provides the following criteria to evaluate paternalistic regulation:

'- *are there plausible traditional justifications (externalities, information failure, inadequate competition) for the measure, operating independently of paternalism?*

- *if not, and taking account of the insights of social psychology, is the regulated activity one with regard to which a significant proportion of the agents make decisions that are unlikely to reflect their real preferences?*

- *if so, are the likely costs of the regulatory measure proportionate to the likely benefits and/or could the same be reached at lower cost by an alternative instrument?'.*[166]

Many scholars argue indeed that some of the behavioural biases can be considered as arguments in favour of regulation.[167] For example Korobkin and Ulen argue that the hindsight problem with the judiciary can be an argument in favour of broader *ex ante* regulation of safety by administrative agencies.[168] They also defend the mandatory use of seat belts or the instalment of airbags in cars as a rational decision by government to remove safety decisions from individual actors, given cognitive biases.[169] Camerer *et al.* defend regulation as 'asymmetric paternalism' since e.g. a device which would disable a car

164. Ibid., 306.

165. Ibid.

166. Ibid, 312.

167. Sunstein has a nuanced position on this point: behavioural economics does not necessarily lead to a general sympathy for paternalism. However, regulation may, at least in principle, ensure that judgements will be based on facts rather than intuitions in such a way as to reduce the problems introduced by biases and heuristics (Cass R. Sunstein, Behavioural law and economics: a progress report, 1 American Law and Economics Review 1999, 145-146).

168. Russel B. Korobkin & Thomas S. Ulen, Law and Behavioural Science: Removing the Rationality Assumption from Law and Economics, 88 California Law Review 2000, 1099.

169. Russel B. Korobkin & Thomas S. Ulen, Law and Behavioural Science: Removing the Rationality Assumption from Law and Economics, 88 California Law Review 2000, 1107. See also Thomas S. Ulen, Rational Choice Theory in Law and Economics, in Encyclopedia of Law and Economics, Vol. I, The History and Methodology of Law and Economics, (Bouckaert & De Geest eds., Edward Elgar, 2000), 813 who argues 'that cognitive limitations 'might lead to principled justifications for far more paternalistic policies than those that rational choice theory typically recommends'.

in case the driver would have a too high alcohol level would regulate behaviour of those whose driving and decision making is assumed to be undermined, whereas it would be completely unobtrusive for those who don't need it (the drivers who are not drunk).[170] [171] However, many may question whether standards set by government are necessarily a superior reaction to the tort system, even under bounded rationality. Public errors are as realistic a problem as private errors[172] and moreover public choice scholars have powerfully shown that public regulation always runs the risk of inefficiencies caused by private interests. '*Paternalism has been abused by governments responding to special interests or seeking to aggrandize their own authority*'.[173] It is well-known that thus regulatory interventions can often have effects that are counterproductive for the goals they aim to achieve.

To counter *inter alia* these risks economists have proposed the use of cost-benefit analysis for risk regulation precisely since also regulation runs a serious risk of providing merely a response to irrational social fears.[174] This is also related to the debate on whether the well-known precautionary principle can be a useful tool in risk regulation, an issue which goes beyond the scope of this contribution.[175]

In sum safety regulation can be advanced if there are reasons to believe that the regulator will be better able to make an adequate risk assessment and hence to set standards closer to the efficient care levels than that private parties (under strict liability) or the judiciary (under

170. Camerer, Issacharoff, Loewenstein, O'Donoghue & Rabin, Regulation for Conservatives: Behavioural Economics and the Case for 'Asymmetric Paternalism', 151 University of Pennsylvania Law Review 2003, 1211-1254. This is what Thaler and Sunstein referred to as 'libertarian paternalism' (Richard H.Thaler & Caas R. Sunstein, Nudge. Improving Decisions about Health, Wealth and Happiness (Yale University Press, 2008), 72).

171. Also Thaler and Sunstein provide many examples how through a more careful 'choice architecture' individuals can be 'nudged' in beneficial directions. see Richard H.Thaler & Caas R. Sunstein, Nudge. Improving Decisions about Health, Wealth and Happiness (Yale University Press, 2008).

172. Edward L. Glaeser, Paternalism and Psychology, 73 University of Chicago Law Review 2006,. 134.

173. Ibid., 135.

174. See the eight propositions suggested as remedies by Christine Jolls, Cass R. Sunstein, & Richard Thaler, A Behavioural Approach to Law and Economics, 50 Stanford Law Review 1998.

175. See in that respect inter alia Dana 2003, p. 1322 ff. For a critical appraisal of the precautionary principle see Anthony I. Ogus, Costs and Cautionary Tales. Economic Insights for the Law (Hart Publishing, 2006), 158-161.

negligence) would. Cost-benefit analysis can be used to guarantee that regulators will not be subject to the same cognitive problems as individuals.[176]

5 IMPLICATIONS FOR INSURANCE

5.1 Criticism of 'expected utility' theory

Behavioural experiments have first of all been critical of the descriptive adequacy of the traditional expected utility theory to explain insurance. Many experiments showed preferences which run counter to utility theory. One such problem which is hard to explain by traditional utility theory is the preference which appeared from an experiment for low-deductible insurance policies, notwithstanding the proportionality high premiums; another one refers to the failure of individuals to purchase insurance even when the premiums have been highly subsidised.[177] Some 30-40% of insurance decisions of many residents of hazard-prone areas were inconsistent with predictions from the theory.[178] Jolls also discusses experiments suggesting that under particular circumstances people are risk seeking rather than risk averse towards probabilistic losses of moderate size.[179] Again this is not what is usually assumed in insurance theory.

Hence, Slovic, Kunreuther and White offer an alternative, 'description decision theory' based on bounded rationality which takes into account the cognitive limitations that the decision maker is exposed to as alternative to the expected utility hypothesis.[180] The cognitive limitations discussed in section 3 may indeed also seriously limit the possibility of an individual to take an

176. See Anthony I. Ogus, Costs and Cautionary Tales. Economic Insights for the Law (Hart Publishing, 2006), 250-252 and Cass R. Sunstein, Cognition and Cost-benefit Analysis, 29 Journal of Legal Studies 2000, 1065-1073. Sunstein argues that cost benefit analysis could be used as a sensible response both to interest-group power and to the problems in the public demand for regulation caused by cognitive limitations.

177. See Slovic, Fischoff, Lichtenstein, Corrigan, & Combs, Preference for Insuring against Probable Small Losses: Insurance Implications, in The Perception of Risk (Paul Slovic ed., Earthscan Publications, 2000), 53.

178. Ibid.

179. Christine Jolls, Behavioural Economic Analysis of Redistributive Legal Rules, 51 Vanderbilt Law Review 1998, 1668.

180. See Slovic, Kunreuther & White, Decision Processes, Rationality and Adjustment to Natural Hazards, in The Perception of Risk (Paul Slovic ed., Earthscan Publications, 2000), 1-31.

efficient insurance decision based on his ability to judge his probability of being exposed to a risk, the potential damage and the corresponding premium.[181]

Some of the problems become especially clear when it concerns the ability of individuals to make a decision to take insurance protection against natural hazards. One problem is the status quo bias and the closely related problem of inertia. Individuals may not be prepared to incur even trivial costs of exploring beneficial alternatives to customary choices.[182] Behavioural experiments also have shown that low probability events like the risks of natural hazards are systematically misjudged.[183] Experiments show evidence of the mentioned probability neglect: individuals systematically ignore low probability, high damage events.[184] Occupants of flood prone areas reduce uncertainty by various means of denial.[185] It is related to the inability of individuals to conceptualise floods that have never occurred.[186] The result of these phenomena is that individuals will often take an 'it will not happen to me' attitude.[187]

Jolls indicates that the fact that many people still take insurance is in fact surprising. Given the fact that many people often underestimate the probability of negative events, why would they then take insurance against them? She argues that one reason may be a high level of risk aversion toward large losses, despite their underestimation of the probability that such losses

181. Many more cognitive biases affecting insurance decisions are discussed in Michael Faure & Véronique Bruggeman, Catastrophic Risks and First-party Insurance, Connecticut Journal of Insurance Law 2009 (forthcoming).

182. See Anthony I. Ogus, Regulatory Paternalism: When is it Justified?, in Corporate Governance in Context. Corporations, States and Markets in Europe, Japan and the US (Hopt, Wymeersch, Kanda & Baum eds., Oxford University Press, 2005), 307.

183. Slovic, Kunreuther & White, Decision Processes, Rationality and Adjustment to Natural Hazards, in The Perception of Risk (Paul Slovic ed., Earthscan Publications, 2000), 7.

184. See Cass R. Sunstein, Risk and Reason: Safety, Law and the Environment (Cambridge University Press, 2002), 50-52.

185. Slovic, Kunreuther & White, Decision Processes, Rationality and Adjustment to Natural Hazards, in The Perception of Risk (Paul Slovic ed., Earthscan Publications, 2000), 7.

186. Ibid, 14.

187. See Howard Kunreuther, Mitigating disaster losses through insurance, 12 Journal of Risk and Uncertainty 1996, 175; Richard A. Epstein, Catastrophic Responses to Catastrophic Risks, 12 Journal of Risk and Uncertainty 1996, 287, 293 and Richard Zeckhauser, The Economics of Catastrophes, 12 Journal of Risk and Uncertainty 1996, 113, 115.

will occur. Jolls concludes that in fact we simply do not know why people on the one hand appear to be unrealisticly optimistic but on the other hand often purchase insurance.[188]

Moreover, other psychological experiments have shown that *ex ante* people may prefer uncertain losses rather than the certain loss of having to pay a premium. Kunreuther showed that because insurance is considered as an investment, some people will refuse to insure against low probability, high damage events (such as flooding) because there is a likelihood of never receiving any return during a lifetime.[189] These types insurances provide a low expectation of a return on the 'investment' and hence there is a corresponding low demand. The fact that insurance is seen as an investment again is at odds with the expected utility hypothesis.[190]

To be clear: many of the deviations found from standard theory do not necessarily constitute evidence that the rational choice theory would be wrong. Underestimation of e.g. the risks of natural hazards may be the result of a lack of information and is in that sense not irrational. Perhaps more interesting than examining whether the experiments falsify the rational choice theory or not is what their influence may be for actual behaviour of both insured and insurers.

5.2 Result 1: underinsurance

An obvious result of the underestimation of low probability events is that individuals will purchase too little insurance.[191] As a result also in countries where voluntary first-party insurances for catastrophic losses (such as the ones caused by e.g. flooding) are available,[192] victims apparently do not insure, or only to a limited extent. The evidence in that respect is

188. Christine Jolls, Behavioural Economic Analysis of Redistributive Legal Rules, 51 Vanderbilt Law Review 1998, 1665-1667.

189. See Howard Kunreuther et al., Disaster Insurance Protection: Public Policy Lessons (John Wiley & Sons Inc., 1978), 248 and Paul J. H. Schoenmaker & Howard Kunreuther, An Experimental Study of Insurance Decisions, 46 Journal of Risk and Insurance 1979, 612.

190. Slovic, Fischoff, Lichtenstein, Corrigan, & Combs, Preference for Insuring against Probable Small Losses: Insurance Implications, in The Perception of Risk (Paul Slovic ed., Earthscan Publications, 2000), 62, 70.

191. See Eric A. Posner, Probability Errors: Some Positive and Normative Implications for Tort and Contract Law, 11 Supreme Court Economic Review 2004, 138.

192. In some countries insurances against natural hazards were not available or only to a limited extent. This was for instance the case in the Netherlands where insurance for flooding and earthquake risks was for a long time excluded as a result of a cartel agreement between insurers who agreed not to cover the particular risks. As a result of intervention from the European competition authorities these so called (binding decisions) were abrogated. For details see Michael Faure & Tom Hartlief, The Netherlands, in Financial Compensation for Victims of Catastrophes. A Comparative and Legal Approach (Faure & Hartlief eds., Springer 2006), 202-206.

overwhelming. Kunreuther and others already pointed at the low demand for earthquake insurance, even in areas which are vulnerable to earthquake risks.[193] Well-known is the example that after the Northridge earthquake in California in 1994 a high number of citizens decided to buy first-party disaster insurance as a reaction against the suffered damages. This may be the result of the affect or availability heuristic according to which the past experience shows the individual that the probability of the unpleasant event is apparently that high that it is a problem worthy of attention. However, after daily life had taken over again a large quantity of those new insurance policies was cancelled again.[194] Eight years after the creation of the California Earthquake Authority the coverage went down from 30 tot 17%.[195]

The underinsurance for flooding risks has also already been described in the literature.[196] Recently the experience with Katrina showed once more that only a low percentage of house owners had flood insurance.[197] Similar evidence comes from Europe. For instance after the flooding of the river Elbe in 2002, referred to as the 'flood of the century'[198] it appeared that only a very small percentage of victims had insurance coverage.[199]

Jolls again provides a behavioural explanation for the fact that people fail to buy insurance against negative events such as floods and earthquakes (despite massive federal subsidies): an

193. Kunreuther, Doherty & Klefner, Should Society Deal with the Earthquake Problem?, 15(2) Regulation 1992, 60-68.

194. For details see Rabin and Bratis 2006, p. 303-360 and Slovic, Kunreuther & White, Decision Processes, Rationality and Adjustment to Natural Hazards, in The Perception of Risk (Paul Slovic ed., Earthscan Publications, 2000), 14.

195. Risk Management Solutions, the North Ridge California Earthquake: a 10-year retrospective, May 2004.

196. See, e.g., Howard Kunreuther, Mitigating disaster losses through insurance, 12 Journal of Risk and Uncertainty 1996, 171-187 and Richard Zeckhauser, The Economics of Catastrophes, 12 Journal of Risk and Uncertainty 1996, 135.

197. In Louisiana the percentage of house owners with insurance ranged from 57,7% in St. Bernard's to 7,3%, in Tangipahoa. In Orleans only 40% had flood insurance (see Howard Kunreuther, Has the Time Come for Comprehensive Natural Disaster Insurance?, in On Risk and Disaster. Lessons from Hurricane Katrina (Daniels, Kettl & Kunreuther eds., University of Pennsylvania Press, 2006), 175-201).

198. In Germany referred to as the 'Jahrhundertflut'.

199. Ulrich Magnus, Germany, in Financial Compensation for Victims of Catastrophes (Faure & Hartlief eds., Springer, 2006), 130 and Schwarze & Wagner, In the Aftermath of Dresdon. New Directions in German Flood Insurance, Geneva Papers on Risk and Insurance 2004, 156-160. See also Gerd Gigerenzer, Is the Mind Irrational or Ecologically Rational?, in The Law and Economics of Irrational Behaviour (Parisi & Smith eds., Stanford University Press, 2005), 45.

unrealistic optimism leads to an underestimation of the probability that these events will happen to them.[200]

5.3 Result 2: mixed evidence of moral hazard and adverse selection

Not only does the behavioural research cast doubt on the ability of individuals to choose an appropriate insurance coverage that will maximise their utility. Empirical research equally indicates that the well-known problems of moral hazard and adverse selection may play less of a problem than is assumed on the basis of classic insurance economic literature. A recent overview of the various available empirical studies in this respect shows that the extent of adverse selection depends on the insurance market at hand.[201] For example no evidence of adverse selection was found as far as motor vehicle insurance in France is concerned[202] nor as far as health insurance in the US is concerned.[203] The extent of adverse selection thus seems to depend on the insurance market at hand. Moreover, there is also evidence of an opposite phenomenon: it would more particularly be the serious law abiding citizens (and hence the good risks) that would have a demand for insurance. There is indeed some evidence of this phenomenon of so-called 'propitious selection' for example in motor vehicle insurance[204] but also as far as life insurance is concerned: those individuals purchasing life insurance would have a longer life expectancy than those who don't.[205]

---

200. Christine Jolls, Behavioural Economic Analysis of Redistributive Legal Rules, 51 Vanderbilt Law Review 1998, 1660-1661.

201. Willem H. Van Boom, Insurance Law and Economics: An Empirical Perspective, in Essays in the Law and Economics of Regulation, In Honour of Anthony Ogus (Intersentia, 2008), 253-276. That paper builds further on Faure &Van Boom, Hoe houdbaar zijn gedragsveronderstellingen in verzekeringsrecht en –economie?, in Gedrag en privaatrecht – over gedragspresumpties and gedragseffecten bij privaatrechtelijke leerstukken (van Boom, Giesen & Verheij eds., Boom Juridische uitgevers, 2008), 305-340.

202. Chiappori & Salani, Testing for Asymetric Information in Insurance Markets, 108 The Journal of Political Economy 2000, 56-78.

203. Cardon & Haendel, Asymetric Information in Health Insurance: Evidence from the National Medical Expenditure Survey, 32 The RAND Journal of Economics 2001, 408-427.

204. See again Chiappori & Salani, Testing for Asymetric Information in Insurance Markets, 108 The Journal of Political Economy 2000, 56-78 and see generally on propitious selection David Hemenway, Propitious Selection, 105 The Quarterly Journal of Economics 1990, 1063-1069.

205. John Cawley & Thomas Philipson, An Empirical Examination of Information Barriers to Trade in Insurance, 89 American Economic Review 1999, 827-846.

There is similar evidence as far as the problem of moral hazard is concerned. The empirical evidence seems to suggest that moral hazard is more likely to occur in some insurance markets than others.[206] For example as far as hospital admissions is concerned (probably not surprisingly) moral hazard did not seem to be a major issue.[207]

In sum, also as far as moral hazard and adverse selection is concerned empirical evidence seems to indicate that these problems play (at least in particular cases) less of a problem than one would expect on the basis of the economic model of insurance.[208] Let us return to the finding that psychological research shows that as a result of cognitive problems there may be substantial underinsurance. The question obviously arises whether that should at the normative level give rise to some remedy at the legislative level.

5.4 Towards mandatory (disaster) coverage?

5.4.1 Mandatory liability insurance?

Above I mentioned behavioural research showing that as a result of overoptimism people and more particularly car drivers overestimate their own (driving) capabilities and underestimate the probability of being engaged in an accident. The result would be that those car drivers who could potentially be injurers in an accident setting would also have a too low demand for insurance coverage given their underestimation of the risk.[209] These cognitive limitations could be considered as an argument in favour of mandatory liability insurance. This is a result from behavioural studies that will probably not be shocking to most scholars familiar with the law and economics of accident law. Indeed, information problems, together with the potential underdeterrence resulting from the insolvency of the average car driver have always been

206. See Willem H. Van Boom, Insurance Law and Economics: An Empirical Perspective, in Essays in the Law and Economics of Regulation, In Honour of Anthony Ogus (Intersentia, 2008), 260.

207. Willem H. Van Boom, Insurance Law and Economics: An Empirical Perspective, in Essays in the Law and Economics of Regulation, In Honour of Anthony Ogus (Intersentia, 2008), 260, note 45.

208. The empirical evidence on this point is, however, very mixed. For a much more detailed discussion, see again Willem H. Van Boom, Insurance Law and Economics: An Empirical Perspective, in Essays in the Law and Economics of Regulation, In Honour of Anthony Ogus (Intersentia, 2008).

209. See Christine Jolls, Behavioural Economic Analysis of Redistributive Legal Rules, 51 Vanderbilt Law Review 1998, 1165.

advanced as the main reasons in favour of mandatory liability insurance e.g. for motor vehicles.[210]

5.4.2 *Mandatory disaster insurance?*

One could go one step further and not only argue in favour of the well-known mandatory liability insurance but also in favour of mandatory insurance against low probability events where there is a systematic underestimation of the risk such as disasters. At the policy level behavioural scholars argue that one way to get people to insure low probability high damage risk is to sell disaster insurance along with insurances against likely losses at reasonable costs. Tests confirmed that this compounding with other risks, as a result of which a so-called 'comprehensive insurance policy' was offered was preferred: subjects were willing to spend 30% more for compound insurance than the sum of their expenditures for the two single earn policies. Slovic *et al.* conclude: '*if it is in society's best interest for people to insure themselves against unlikely calamites then adding protection against a small but likely loss might help them accomplish this purpose*'.[211] A consequence from this behavioural literature is thus that they suggest compulsory insurance as an example of a policy that can play a role in improving hazards perception.[212] Compulsory insurance also has the advantage that risks can be spread and that risk based premiums can provide adequate incentives e.g. not to develop in high-risk areas.[213]

5.4.3 *Information remedies?*

However, if lacking information would be the reason for a duty to insure, one could hold that regulation aiming at providing information might to some extent be a less interventionist remedy than mandatory insurance. Showing people the consequences of e.g. flooding with

---

210. See Peter J. Jost, Limited Liability and the Requirement to Purchase Insurance, 16 International Review of Law and Economics 1996, 259-276 and Michael Faure, Economic Criteria for Compulsory Insurance, 31 The Geneva Papers on Risk and Insurance 2006, 149-168.
211. Slovic, Fischoff, Lichtenstein, Corrigan, & Combs, Preference for Insuring against Probable Small Losses: Insurance Implications, in The Perception of Risk (Paul Slovic ed., Earthscan Publications, 2000), 60-61, 70-71, suggesting to combine low probability hazards with high probability threats in one insurance 'package'.
212. Slovic, Kunreuther & White, Decision Processes, Rationality and Adjustment to Natural Hazards, in The Perception of Risk (Paul Slovic ed., Earthscan Publications, 2000), 25 and Anthony I. Ogus, Regulatory Paternalism: When is it Justified?, in Corporate Governance in Context. Corporations, States and Markets in Europe, Japan and the US (Hopt, Wymeersch, Kanda & Baum eds., Oxford University Press, 2005), 303-320, 304.
213. Louis Kaplow, An Economic Analysis of Legal Transitions, 99 Harvard Law Review 1986, 548-550.

visual displays may help to pursue the public to view insurance as a potential remedy.[214] However, a weakness in this argument is that behavioural experiments have shown that it is only to a limited extent possible to cure the information asymmetry through regulation.[215]

The problem is indeed that the behavioural literature not only shows a lack of information (in which case the information asymmetry could constitute a reason for a regulatory duty to purchase insurance), but also that even when potential victims are well informed about the risks, they prefer not to purchase insurance. The reason is that insurance is apparently perceived as an investment. In case of low probability, high loss events there is a great likelihood that people will be paying a lot of premium without ever having any return during a lifetime.[216] This research hence shows that it is not primarily poor information of potential victims which would cause the low demand, but rather the unwillingness of victims (even if well informed) to purchase coverage against low probability high loss events. If this were the case, there is always a danger that the mandatory insurance in fact amounts to paternalism.[217]

5.4.4 Potential dangers

There are, however, also several potential dangers of introducing mandatory disaster insurance.[218] When introducing mandatory disaster coverage, there is always a danger that the legislator in fact forces potential victims to purchase an insurance policy even if there would be no demand.[219]

---

214. See Slovic, Fischoff, Lichtenstein, Corrigan, & Combs, Preference for Insuring against Probable Small Losses: Insurance Implications, in The Perception of Risk (Paul Slovic ed., Earthscan Publications, 2000), 71.

215. See Slovic, Kunreuther & White, Decision Processes, Rationality and Adjustment to Natural Hazards, in The Perception of Risk (Paul Slovic ed., Earthscan Publications, 2000), 15.

216. See Slovic, Kunreuther & White, Decision Processes, Rationality and Adjustment to Natural Hazards, in The Perception of Risk (Paul Slovic ed., Earthscan Publications, 2000), 1-31, and Slovic, Fischoff, Lichtenstein, Corrigan, & Combs, Preference for Insuring against Probable Small Losses: Insurance Implications, in The Perception of Risk (Paul Slovic ed., Earthscan Publications, 2000), 51-72.

217. See Anthony I. Ogus, Regulatory Paternalism: When is it Justified?, in Corporate Governance in Context. Corporations, States and Markets in Europe, Japan and the US (Hopt, Wymeersch, Kanda & Baum eds., Oxford University Press, 2005), 303-320.

218. Slovic, Kunreuther & White, Decision Processes, Rationality and Adjustment to Natural Hazards, in The Perception of Risk (Paul Slovic ed., Earthscan Publications, 2000), 1-31 and Slovic Slovic, Fischoff, Lichtenstein, Corrigan, & Combs, Preference for Insuring against Probable Small Losses: Insurance Implications, in The Perception of Risk (Paul Slovic ed., Earthscan Publications, 2000), 53.

219. See for a discussion of pros and cons of mandatory disaster insurance also Michael Faure, Financial Compensation for Victims of Catastrophes: A Law and Economics Perspective, 29(3) Law & Policy 2007, 339-

There is, moreover, a recent study by Sandroni and Squintani showing that there is some danger with introducing compulsory insurance based on behavioural biases.[220] They argue that compulsory insurance is more particularly problematic when the market has a significant fraction of overconfident agents in which case compulsory insurance could result in a transfer of wealth from low risk to high risk individuals. The reasoning is simple: the higher the fraction of overconfident agents in the economy, the higher is also the average risk of the pool of low-risk and overconfident agents and the higher thus the price that insurance firms will charge. At high prices low risk individuals would be better off with purchasing small amounts of insurance and are in fact hurt by compulsory insurance. This paper therefore shows that basing paternalistic policies on behavioural biases is not totally unproblematic since it may not make all agents better off, more particularly the low risk individuals. Compulsory insurance based on behavioural biases then effectively leads to cross-subsidisation.

A generalized duty to purchase e.g. flooding coverage always entails the risk that the duty is also imposed on those who constitute no risk at all: the well-known owner of an apartment on the tenth floor. This problem plays less[221] when a generalized duty to provide cover is imposed (for all type of risks) such as in the French case: if one cannot be a victim of flooding, there can at least be other risks (such as heavy rainfall, winds or tornados) to which one can be exposed. This problem is more serious if the duty is limited to a specific risk such as e.g. flooding. In that particular case it might be more indicated to limit the duty to specific risk areas, but the administrative (and more particularly political) costs of identifying those areas may be high. This was shown in the case of Belgium: a new act of May 2003 introduced additional mandatory coverage on voluntary insurance policies, but proposed to apply this new solution only to persons living in specified risk areas. These risk areas were to be identified through regulation. However, the attempt to identify the risk areas led to political disagreement and a subsequent impossibility to apply the Act. The result is that in 2005 a new system was introduced with a generalized duty to purchase additional coverage for natural hazards in addition to the fire insurance. It seemed impossible to pursue the idea of limiting the mandatory coverage, given

367 and Michael Faure & Véronique Bruggeman, Catastrophic Risks and First-party Insurance, Connecticut Journal of Insurance Law 2009 (forthcoming).

220. Alvaro Sandroni & Francesco Squintani, Overconfidence, Insurance and Paternalism, 97(5) American Economic Review 2007, 1994-2004.

221. As also indicated by Schwarze & Wagner, In the Aftermath of Dresdon. New Directions in German Flood Insurance, Geneva Papers on Risk and Insurance 2004, 156-160.

the high political costs of identifying the special 'risk areas' where the duty to insure would apply.[222]

The duty to purchase mandatory disaster coverage in addition to voluntarily purchased property damage contracts may cause problems from the angle of competition law. It is a so-called tie-in agreement forcing a consumer to buy a specific service or product together with another product, which may restrict competition.[223]

Mandatory coverage is of course only a solution where insurance markets are available. In many, more particularly developing, countries a large part of the losses is not covered under insurance at all. Where insurance markets are not available to a large part of the population, imposing mandatory disaster insurance will of course not be the miracle solution.

5.4.5 *Advantage: risk differentiation and avoidance of ex post government relief*

Although there are thus several disadvantages of this suggestion a clear advantage is, that through the compulsory insurance solution suggested by behavioural law and economics an adequate risk differentiation through insurance is possible: individuals and communities might better adapt their risk levels if they are forced to do so through insurance premiums rather than when they can rely on *ex post* government relief.[224] Law and economics scholars and more particularly Howard Kunreuther have therefore already since 1968 strongly argued in favour of mandatory disaster insurance;[225] he repeated this plea, supported by behavioural studies, many times. Also after Katrina had again shown large underinsurance in specific neighbourhoods, Kunreuther concluded once more that the time has come for comprehensive disaster insurance.[226]

222. For a detailed discussion of disaster insurance coverage in Belgium see Bruggeman, Faure & Haritz, Schadenersatz für Opfer von Naturkatastrophen – Ein Vergleich zwischen Belgien und den Niederlanden, Vierteljahrshefte zur Wirtschaftsforschung 2008, 18-43.

223. See on this issue further Roger Van den Bergh & Michael Faure, Compulsory Insurance of Loss to Property Caused by Natural Disasters: Competition or Solidarity?, 29 World Competition 2005, 25-54.

224. Slovic, Kunreuther & White, Decision Processes, Rationality and Adjustment to Natural Hazards, in The Perception of Risk (Paul Slovic ed., Earthscan Publications, 2000), and George L. Priest, The Government, the Market and the Problem of Catastrophic Loss, 12 Journal of Risk and Uncertainty 1996, 219.

225. Howard Kunreuther, The Case for Comprehensive Disaster Insurance, 11 Journal of Law and Economics 1968, 133-163.

226. See Kunreuther 2006b, p. 208-227 and Howard Kunreuther, Has the Time Come for Comprehensive Natural Disaster Insurance?, in On Risk and Disaster. Lessons from Hurricane Katrina (Daniels, Kettl & Kunreuther eds., University of Pennsylvania Press, 2006), 175-201.

6 CONCLUDING REMARKS

6.1 Increasing evidence of heuristics and biases

In a publication by leading scholars in the area of behavioural law and economics it was held '*the experimental work described in this chapter documents man's difficulties in weighing information and judging uncertainty. Yet, this work is quite recent in origin and still very much in the exploratory stage. In addition its implication does not fit with the high level of confidence that we typically accord our higher mental processes*'.[227] Notwithstanding this caveat the same authors conclude '*the laboratory conclusions are congruent with many observations of non-optimal decision-making outside the laboratory – in business, governmental policy setting and adjustment to natural hazards. The belief that people can behave optimally when it is worthwhile for them to do so gains little support from these studies. The sources of judgemental bias appear to be cognitive, not motivational*'.[228]

Indeed, notwithstanding the modesty of some of the authors in this domain there is now a wide literature of which just a small summary was presented in section 3, showing that some of the traditional assumptions underlying economic models do not comply with how people behave in real world situations.

It may at first sight seem rather worrisome, at least to law and economics scholars, that many of us apparently do not completely act in the way predicted by the rational actor model. However, we should remember that in a way the heuristics and biases from which we suffer are nothing else than shortcuts to handle a lot of complex situations and thus make our life a lot easier. There is as such nothing wrong with e.g. the overoptimism from which many of us 'suffer' since it tends to correlate with happiness, contentment and the ability to engage in productive, creative work. Jolls indicates that there is also evidence that individuals with accurate as opposed to excessively favourable impressions of their own personal abilities tend to be clinically depressed.[229]

227. Slovic, Kunreuther & White, Decision Processes, Rationality and Adjustment to Natural Hazards, in The Perception of Risk (Paul Slovic ed., Earthscan Publications, 2000), 22.
228. Slovic, Kunreuther & White, Decision Processes, Rationality and Adjustment to Natural Hazards, in The Perception of Risk (Paul Slovic ed., Earthscan Publications, 2000), 23.
229. Christine Jolls, Behavioural Economic Analysis of Redistributive Legal Rules, 51 Vanderbilt Law Review 1998, 1661. See also Cass R. Sunstein, Behavioural law and economics: a progress report, 1 American Law and Economics Review 1999, 136.

6.2 Implications for accident law

Notwithstanding this positive note the relevant question today is of course what the implications are of the behavioural studies for the economics of accident law. Is there a 'Behavioural Accident Law and Economics'? Generally some authors like Jolls hasten to say that behavioural law and economics is not a critique of law and economics.[230] Arcuri holds that other theories may well enrich the analytical apparatus of law and economics and she suggests an 'eclectic' approach to law and economics which would entail a selection of what appears to be best in various doctrines, methods or styles.[231] Posner is, not surprisingly, more critical of such a fishing expedition for ideas and fears that enriching the rational choice model in this way '*runs a risk similar to that of behavioural economics, of explaining nothing by explaining everything*'.[232]

When addressing the potential consequences of the behavioural literature for the economic analysis of accident law one has again to distinguish between the descriptive, prescriptive and normative economic analysis of law.[233] Most relevant and least threatening is of course the relevance of behavioural studies for descriptive and prescriptive law and economics. If behavioural models were better able to explain what happens in real life situations this could certainly add to the explanatory power of the models. There is generally much more criticism on behavioural law and economics when it concerns its implications for normative law and economics. Some have even doubted whether there should be any change at all to the main rules of the common law on the basis of the findings in the behavioural literature.[234]

What are the main consequences of the behavioural literature for traditional economic models of tort and insurance? The implications of the behavioural literature are not as clear cut as it seems. As far as the economics of tort law is concerned at first blush the findings of the behavioural literature suggest important changes. Indeed, the assumptions underlying the economics of tort law assume that potential injurers as rational decision makers have the ability to process information concerning the probability of an accident and expected damage in

230. Christine Jolls, Behavioural Economic Analysis of Redistributive Legal Rules, 51 Vanderbilt Law Review 1998, 1645.

231. A. Arcuri, An Eclecticism in Law and Economics, 1(3) Erasmus Law Review 2008, 59-81, 59 and 79.

232. Richard A. Posner, Rational Choice, Behavioural Economics, and the Law, 50 Stanford Law Review 1998, 1567.

233. Christine Jolls, Cass R. Sunstein, & Richard Thaler, A Behavioural Approach to Law and Economics, 50 Stanford Law Review 1998, 1471-1476.

234. See Richard A. Epstein, Behavioural Economics: Human Errors and Market Corrections, 73 University of Chicago Law Review 2006, 118.

relation to the costs of preventing the accident. Behavioural literature suggests that a lot can go wrong in the way potential injurers process this information, being subject to a variety of heuristics and biases. Not taking into account these cognitive limitations may jeopardize an efficacious enforcement of tort law.[235]

6.3 Behavioural literature multi-directional

However, as has already been shown earlier in the literature, a problem with this strand of the behavioural literature is that the direction of the biases is not always very clear. Some biases point in the direction of injurers being overcautious (and thus being inefficiently overdeterred), whereas others point in the direction of injurers systematically neglecting specific risks and thus spending too little care (leading to underdeterrence). I showed above that, for example as far as the choice between strict liability and negligence is concerned some authors (more particularly Teitelbaum) seem to favour the negligence rule (on the basis of an analysis of certain biases) whereas others (Korobkin and Ulen) seem to favour the strict liability rule (more particularly to counter the hindsight bias with the judiciary). The result therefore is that the findings of the behavioural literature present a very nuanced and differentiated picture, whereby the liability rule would depend upon the type of biases and whether they occur with the parties in the accident setting (injurer or victim) or with the judge. Even if one would already assume that the findings of the behavioural literature are that clear cut that they warrant an adaptation of traditional models, it is hence not that clear in which direction that adaptation goes.

Moreover some of the shortcomings of the negligence standard (errors in factual or efficient care on the side of potential injurers or judges) have been identified earlier by Shavell and have been incorporated into the economic analysis of tort law. Moreover, also mainstream economists had generally acknowledged the problem of 'bounded rationality', although mainly as an indicator of the parameters beyond which traditional analysis could not go.[236]

This does not lead to the conclusion that the behavioural findings are irrelevant for the economic analysis of tort law, but rather that first, it seems too early to replace traditional economic analysis of accidents of which the validity has to some extent also been proven in empirical research[237] by a behavioural approach since that still lacks a coherent theory and

235. See Wilem H. Van Boom, Efficacious Enforcement in Contract and Tort 9Boom Juridische uitgevers, 2006).

236. Anthony I. Ogus, Costs and Cautionary Tales. Economic Insights for the Law (Hart Publishing, 2006), 233.

237. For on overview of the empirical findings, see Dewees, Duff & Trebilcock, Exploring the Domain of Accident Law. Taking the Facts Seriously (Oxford University Press, 1996) and Van Velthoven, supra note 25 and see

second, that given the multidirectional nature of the lessons provided by the behavioural studies, it may be difficult to apply these results in legal practice.

6.4 Regulation?

The behavioural literature only seems to present a strong case in favour of safety regulation where indeed individuals are not able to adequately assess information on risks and thus not able to set efficient care levels. Assuming that government agencies are less vulnerable to these cognitive limitations (although there is doubt that it is really the case) there may be reasons for increased safety regulation. However, again some may argue that this fits into the traditional criteria for safety regulation as advanced by Shavell, although others could argue that in this case regulation does not merely cure a lack of information, but bounded rationality as well and therefore amounts to a justified type of 'regulatory paternalism'.[238] This paternalistic call on government interventions based on cognitive limitations is, however, highly debated. As a reaction to these calls for paternalism some have held that bounded rationality may increase the cost of government decision making relative to private decision making.[239]

6.5 Mandatory insurance?

A much stronger policy conclusion is – at first blush – formulated in the behavioural literature with respect to insurance. Not only do the experiments cast serious doubt on the validity of the expected utility hypothesis to explain the demand for insurance; the literature equally suggests that a type of compulsory coverage for natural hazards, whereby comprehensive insurance is offered would be welfare improving. Individuals would then be forced to purchase mandatory insurance against low probability high damage events (like natural hazards) in addition to higher probability low damage events (e.g. housing insurance). The behavioural literature can thus provide an important support for a tendency in many legal systems to replace the traditional *ex*

Frank Sloan, Automobile accidents, insurance and tort liability, in The New Palgrave Dictionary of Economics and the Law (Newman ed., MacMillan, 19980, 140-144.and Daniel P. Kessler & Daniel L. Rubinfeld, Empirical study of the civil justice system, in Handbook of Law & Economics, Vol. 1 (Polinsky & Shavell eds., Elsevier, 20070, 342-402.

238. See Anthony I. Ogus, Regulatory Paternalism: When is it Justified?, in Corporate Governance in Context. Corporations, States and Markets in Europe, Japan and the US (Hopt, Wymeersch, Kanda & Baum eds., Oxford University Press, 2005), 306.

239. Edward L. Glaeser, Paternalism and Psychology, 73 University of Chicago Law Review 2006,. 133-156.

post government relief for natural hazards by compulsory first party insurance policies. The latter have, moreover, the advantage that some type of risk differentiation can be applied whereby individuals may have incentives for risk reduction under differentiated premiums, incentives which would be absent in government relief programs.[240] However, although a mandatory insurance e.g. for natural hazards may be defended as 'libertarian paternalism'[241] there are many potential dangers and disadvantages as well. One well-known issue, recently again stressed by Sandroni and Squintani[242] is that mandatory insurance could always lead to cross-subsidisation to the disadvantage of low risk individuals.

6.6 Modest, but important

Of course some lawyers could argue that my perception of the implications of the behavioural literature for the traditional economic analysis of accident law is simply too modest: it may not substantially change the economics of tort law and only leads to an argument in favour of compulsory disaster insurance. The suggestions formulated by Shavell to deal with uncertainties in the application of the negligence rule can equally be used to handle human errors of the type suggested by the behavioural literature. Moreover, the literature seems divided on the consequences of behavioural studies for the traditional test between negligence and strict liability. Perhaps, as was also suggested by Korobkin and Ulen, further empirical research is necessary before one could conclude to adaptation of traditional models. Moreover, in that case there is of course no need to abandon the economic analysis of tort law (based on the rational choice model) completely, but rather to refine the models on the basis of the findings from social psychology.

That conclusion would, however, overlook the importance of this literature. Even though there is no need (yet) to fundamentally change the economics of tort law, the knowledge about specific heuristics and biases can provide useful insights in the actual behaviour of potential parties in an accident setting. Moreover, it can, have important consequences for example for

240. See also Louis Kaplow, Incentives and Government Relief or Risk, 4 Journal of Risk and Uncertainty 1991, 167-175.

241. See Camerer, Issacharoff, Loewenstein, O'Donoghue & Rabin, Regulation for Conservatives: Behavioural Economics and the Case for 'Asymmetric Paternalism', 151 University of Pennsylvania Law Review 2003, 1211-1254 and Richard H. Thaler & Cass R. Sunstein, Nudge. Improving Decisions about Health, Wealth and Happiness (Yale University Press, 2008), 72.

242. Sandroni & Squintani, supra note 220.

the way in which judges should be behave in deciding negligence cases. For example the awareness of the existence of the hindsight bias should lead the judiciary to be far more careful in judging 'sins of the past' on the basis of norms of today. Already a good insight with the judiciary in their own exposure to heuristics and biases might increase the accuracy of their decision making. Also, the importance of the behavioural findings for the compensation of victims of catastrophes should not be underestimated given the importance of this topic today. Many countries are increasingly confronted with a variety of natural and technological disasters and governments have increasing difficulties meeting the calls on them to provide relief via the public budget. Hence the behavioural literature can provide an important support for tendencies in some legal systems (notably France) to solve compensation for victims of catastrophes through the type of comprehensive disaster insurance suggested by the behavioural literature rather than through *ex post* government relief.

Finally it should be noticed that some of the implications discussed in this contribution of the behavioural literature for accident law (more particularly the question whether the literature provides arguments in favour of paternalistic regulation and limits individual autonomy) may just play a modest role in the area of tort law (where party autonomy is essentially limited). The importance may, however, be much greater in other areas like consumer regulation, regulation of financial markets and securities. There are in other words many reasons to pay a lot of attention to the implications of this important domain of behavioural economics for the traditional economic analysis of law, also in other fields than accident law.

Judging CERCLA: an Empirical Analysis of Circuit Court Decision-Making

Clifford Chad Henson*

Abstract: Political scientists, and increasingly legal scholars, have become skeptical of judges' attempts to explain decisions based exclusively on applying fact to law, and have attempted to identify factors that influence judicial decision-making. This study isolates a set of cases dealing with the Comprehensive Environmental Response, Compensation, and Liability Act of 1980 and identifies variable sets corresponding to factors one would expect to be significant under competing models of judicial decision-making. While both the legal and extra-legal model independently explain some judicial decision-making, the legal model has more explanatory power and adds significantly to the explanatory power of the extra-legal model, while the extra-legal model does not add significantly to the explanatory power of the legal model. Further, some significant factors in judicial decisions may be open to manipulation by litigants.

I. INTRODUCTION

Theories of judicial decision-making attempt to explain judicial decisions and the factors that play important roles in those decisions. Some legal scholars and political scientists have argued that empirical analysis of judicial opinions reveals more than self-disclosed legal reasoning and stated jurisprudential philosophies.[1] While some studies have tested a single model[2] or the effects of modifying a particular model of judicial decision-making,[3] little research has been done to test the relative predictive and explanatory power of multiple models of judicial decision-making except those studies that have focused on applying constraints to the attitudinal model.[4]

---

* The Property and Environment Research Center made this research possible though their generous fellowship program. In particular, I would like to thank Andrew Morriss, Roger Meiners, Walter Thurman, Dan Benjamin, Jonathan Adler, Sarah Anderson, Dhammika Dharmapala, Hon. Harry T. Edwards III, Corbett Grainger, P.J. Hill, Jonathan Klick, Larry Ribstein, Kurt Schneir, Tom Ulen, and Reed Watson for their valuable suggestions, guidance, insight, and support. All errors are my own

1 See, e.g., Emerson H. Tiller & Frank B. Cross, A Modest Proposal for Improving American Justice, 99 Colum. L. Rev. 215 (1999). Jeffrey A. Segal and Harold J. Spaeth, The Supreme Court and the Attitudinal Model Revisited (Cambridge 2002). Stephen J. Choi and G. Mitu Gulati, Bias in Judicial Citations: A New Window into the Behavior of Judges?, 37 J. Legal Stud. forthcoming 2009. Thomas J. Miles and Cass R. Sunstein, The Real World of Arbitrariness Review, 75 U. Chi. L. Rev. 761 (2008). Max M. Schanzenbach and Emerson H. Tiller, Reviewing the Sentencing Guidelines: Judicial Politics, Empirical Evidence, and Reform, 75 U. Chi. L. Rev. 715 (2008).

2 See, e.g., Theodore W. Ruger, Pauline T. Kim, Andrew D. Martin & Kevin M. Quinn, The Supreme Court Forecasting Project: Legal and Political Science Approaches to Predicting Supreme Court Decisionmaking, 104 Colum. L. Rev. 1150 (2004) (finding that a predictive model was better-able to forecast U.S. Supreme Court decisions than a panel of experts).

3 Thomas J. Miles & Cass R. Sunstein, The New Legal Realism, 75 U. Chi. L. Rev. 831, 838 (2008) (noting that the "standard pattern" of empirical courts scholarship is some variation of Republican appointees preferring more conservative outcomes than Democrat appointees, tempered by other effects).

4 See, e.g. Tracey E. George, Developing a Positive Theory of Decisionmaking on U.S. Courts of Appeals, 58 Ohio St. L.J. 1635 (1998)

This study identifies factors that influence appellate court decision-making in cases involving the Comprehensive Environmental Response, Compensation, and Liability Act of 1980 (CERCLA)[5] and investigates if the results correspond to or differ from the expectations of legal and extra-legal theories of judicial decision-making. To identify these factors, I isolate CERCLA cases resulting in federal appellate opinions, and collect factors on these cases, and use multivariate regression analysis to compare the marginal effect of each decision-making model.

II. CERCLA

CERCLA imposes joint and several liability for the release or potential release of any hazardous substances. Under CERCLA, the Environmental Protection Agency (EPA) can undertake or order others to undertake removal or remedial actions.[6] A removal action is short-term action to address an immediate environmental problem.[7] A remedial action involves longer-term solutions for serious environmental hazards, often including decontamination.[8] To order a remedial action, the EPA must place a contaminated site on the National Priorities List (NPL).[9] After the site is listed, the EPA either undertakes the remedial action and sues any potentially responsible party (PRP) for the costs or orders the private party to clean up the site. PRPs can sue each other to force a determination of how much each PRP will contribute.[10]

CERCLA liability can cost hundreds of millions of dollars.[11] Because of this, many PRPs choose to litigate, and both PRPs and the EPA may appeal adverse trial court decisions.[12] Parties can argue that their property should never have been listed on the NPL,[13] that the appropriate action is a removal rather than a remedial action[14] (removal actions are generally less expensive), that they are not responsible for the damage,[15] that damage should be imposed upon other parties,[16] that the site in question is divisible,[17] or otherwise challenge agency decisions. Some have

5 42 U.S.C. § 9601 et seq.

6 42 U.S.C. § 9604

7 42 U.S.C. § 9601(23), 42 U.S.C. § 9604

8 42 U.S.C. § 9601(24), 42 U.S.C. § 9604

9 47 FR 31180-01, 1982 WL 143362 (F.R.)

10 For a discussion of this remedy, see William D. Evans, Jr., The "Cape Fear" Features of Superfund Contribution Litigation: the Available Remedies and Extent of Liability, 75 Mich. B.J. 1170 (1996)

11 See, e.g. U.S. v. Vertac Chemical Corp. 364 F.Supp.2d 941, 965 (E.D. Ark., 2005), holding parties joint and severally liable for over $100 million in damages.

12 While this study did not track individual cases from the trial court to the appellate level, an identical database search that looked at all federal courts yielded roughly four times as many results as those looking only at state appellate courts. This is a high level of appeals, similar to products liability appeals in state courts and vastly higher than more typical civil litigation. See Bureau of Justice Statistics, Appeals from General Civil Trials in 46 Large Counties, 2001–2005 1-2 (June 2006), available at http://bjs.ojp.usdoj.gov/content/pub/pdf/agctlc05.pdf.

13 See, e.g. Montrose Chem. Corp. v. United States EPA, 1999 U.S. App. LEXIS 2456 (D.C. Cir. Jan. 21, 1999).

14 Colorado v. Sunoco, Inc., 337 F.3d 1233 (10th Cir. Colo. 2003)

15 United States v. Shell Oil Co., 294 F.3d 1045 (9th Cir. Cal. 2002)

16 United States v. Burlington N. & Santa Fe Ry. Co., 520 F.3d 918 (9th Cir. 2008)

17 New Jersey Turnpike Auth. v. PPG Indus., 197 F.3d 96, 99 (3d Cir. N.J. 1999)

challenged the constitutionality of the law as a whole[18] (unsuccessfully), made procedural objections to the case proceeding,[19] or engaged in other litigation strategies.

III. JUDICIAL DECISION-MAKING MODELS

III.A. THE SAMPLE AND DEPENDENT VARIABLES

To test the relationship between predictive factors and outcomes, I obtained information for 44 CERCLA cases.[20] After designating the cases as appropriate for analysis, each significant issue

18 See, e.g. United States v. Monsanto Co., 858 F.2d 160, 173 (4th Cir. S.C. 1988). The court found that the CERCLA liability scheme generally did not constitute an ex post facto law or bill of attainder.

19 Plaskett v. Esso Standard Oil S.A. (In re Tutu Water Wells CERCLA Litig.), 2003 U.S. App. LEXIS 6734 (3d Cir. 2003)

20 To determine which factors influence appellate courts to vote for or against private parties in CERCLA litigation, it was necessary to find cases appropriate cases. Only cases where the United States or an agency thereof and a single or multiple private parties took opposing stances on an issue concerning CERCLA would yield a vote by an appellate court panel clearly classifiable as for/against private parties. To identify appropriate cases for analysis, Lexis-Nexis and Westlaw databases of all federal circuit court decisions for terms (CERCLA or SUPERFUND) in the Overview (Westlaw) or Summary (Lexis) of the case and (U.S. or United States or Environmental Protection Agency or EPA) in the title of the case were searched. Variations on this search consistently yielded the same 201 cases from 1980 to 2009. Certain cases were excluded because there was no issue of contention focused on CERCLA, because the case was brought by a party seeking to force the government to comply with CERCLA rather than the government seeking recovery under CERCLA, or because there was no government party (e.g. cases involving private companies with "U.S." in the name). Subsequently, cases prior to November of 1996 were excluded. The examined cases included: A & W Smelter & Refiners v. Clinton, 146 F.3d 1107 (9th Cir. Cal. 1998). Andrews v. United States, 122 F.3d 1367 (11th Cir. Fla. 1997). Aztec Minerals Corp. v. United States EPA, 1999 U.S. App. LEXIS 26916 (10th Cir. Colo. 1999). B.F. Goodrich v. Betkoski, 99 F.3d 505 (2d Cir. Conn. 1996). Berrey v. Asarco Inc., 439 F.3d 636 (10th Cir. 2006). California v. Montrose Chem. Corp., 104 F.3d 1507 (9th Cir. Cal. 1997). Colorado v. Sunoco, Inc., 337 F.3d 1233 (10th Cir. Colo. 2003). E.I. du Pont de Nemours & Co. v. United States, 365 F.3d 1367 (Fed. Cir. 2004). East Bay Mun. Util. Dist. v. United States DOC, 142 F.3d 479 (D.C. Cir. 1998). Franklin County Convention Facilities Auth. v. American Premier Underwriters, Inc., 240 F.3d 534 (6th Cir. Ohio 2001). GE v. EPA, 360 F.3d 188 (D.C. Cir. 2004). In re Reading Co., 115 F.3d 1111 (3d Cir. Pa. 1997). McKay v. United States, 199 F.3d 1376 (Fed. Cir. 1999). Mead Corp. v. Browner, 100 F.3d 152 (D.C. Cir. 1996). Montrose Chem. Corp. v. United States EPA, 1999 U.S. App. LEXIS 2456 (D.C. Cir. Jan. 21, 1999). National Ass'n of Mfrs. v. United States DOI, 134 F.3d 1095 (D.C. Cir. 1998). New Jersey Turnpike Auth. v. PPG Indus., 197 F.3d 96 (3d Cir. N.J. 1999). OSI, Inc. v. United States, 285 F.3d 947 (11th Cir. Ala. 2002). Plaskett v. Esso Standard Oil S.A. (In re Tutu Water Wells CERCLA Litig.), 2003 U.S. App. LEXIS 6734 (3d Cir. 2003). RSR Corp. v. EPA, 102 F.3d 1266 (D.C. Cir. 1997). U.S. Bank Nat'l Ass'n v. U.S. EPA, 563 F.3d 199 (6th Cir. 2009). United States v. Asarco Inc., 214 F.3d 1104 (9th Cir. Idaho 2000). United States v. Asarco Inc., 430 F.3d 972 (9th Cir. 2005). United States v. Burlington N. & Santa Fe Ry. Co., 520 F.3d 918 (9th Cir. 2008). United States v. Burlington Northern R.R., 200 F.3d 679 (10th Cir. Colo. 1999). United States v. Chromalloy Am. Corp., 158 F.3d 345 (5th Cir. Tex. 1998). United States v. Consolidation Coal Co., 345 F.3d 409 (6th Cir. Ohio 2003). United States v. Davis, 261 F.3d 1 (1st Cir. R.I. 2001). United States v. Dico, Inc., 136 F.3d 572 (8th Cir. Iowa 1998). United States v. Dico, Inc., 266 F.3d 864 (8th Cir. Iowa 2001). United States v. Gen. Battery Corp., 423 F.3d 294 (3d Cir. 2005). United States v. Gurley, 384 F.3d 316 (6th Cir. 2004).

within each case was separately analyzed. Each significant issue is a separate observation, with each case yielding between one and eight observations.[21] For each observation, dependent and independent variables identifiable from the text of the opinion were coded. Independent variables are related to a model of judicial decision-making, explained below.

The dependent variables for each reference are outcomes. Table 1 reports the descriptive statistics for the sample. The dependent variables for each reference are votes for private parties on each issue, outcome for private party on each issue, votes for private party on each case, and outcome for private party on each case. The variables are explained next.

Table 1: Descriptive Statistics for the Sample

	Mean	Median	Min	Max
VotIss	0.7920	0	0	3
VicIss	0.2673	0	0	1
VotCas	0.6138	0	0	3
VicCas	0.2079	0	0	1
ln(Courtclog)	6.2746	6.3421	5.2882	7.0967
ln(Days)	6.7738	7.3914	0	8.4237
CirOvr8	0.7623	1	0	1
LowCtDec	0.3267	0	0	1

United States v. Hercules, Inc., 247 F.3d 706 (8th Cir. Ark. 2001). United States v. JG-24, Inc., 478 F.3d 28 (1st Cir. 2007). United States v. Kayser-Roth Corp., 272 F.3d 89 (1st Cir. R.I. 2001). United States v. Navistar Int'l Transp. Corp. 152 F.3d 702 (7th Cir. Ind. 1998). United States v. Occidental Chem. Corp., 200 F.3d 143 (3d Cir. Pa. 1999). United States v. Olin Corp., 107 F.3d 1506 (11th Cir. Ala. 1997). United States v. Omega Chem. Corp., 156 F.3d 994 (9th Cir. Cal. 1998). United States v. Shell Oil Co., 294 F.3d 1045 (9th Cir. Cal. 2002). United States v. Shell Oil Co., 294 F.3d 1045 (9th Cir. Cal. 2002). United States v. Tarkowski, 248 F.3d 596 (7th Cir. Ill. 2001). United States v. Vertac Chem. Corp. 453 F.3d 1031 (8th Cir. 2006). United States v. W.R. Grace & Co., 429 F.3d 1224 (9th Cir. 2005).

21 Issue designations were distinguished based on (1) the Overview or Summary of the case listing the issue specifically, (2) the opinion specifically affirming or reversing a particular decision, or (3) the organization of the opinion treating the issue separately from other distinguishable issues. For example, one case raised three questions that were each decided separately: did appellant assume predecessor liability, were two locations discrete sites within the meaning of CERCLA, and should the lower court have permitted the plaintiff to present certain evidence related to damages. The court found for the government on all three issues. U.S. Bank Nat'l Ass'n v. U.S. EPA, 563 F.3d 199 (6th Cir. 2009). This methodology is not uncommon, and accounts for the nuance of a particular court decision in a more fine-tuned way than the Liberal-Conservative binary. See Harry T. Edwards and Michael A. Livermore, Pitfalls of Empirical Studies that Attempt to Understand the Factors Affecting Appellate Decisionmaking, 58 Duke L.J. 1895, 1924-1927 (critiquing the standard methods used to code appellate decisions). For example, one previous study has relied on authors' agreement on the philosophy of constitutional interpretation used by a judge. Gregory C. Sisk, Michael Heise, and Andrew P. Morriss, Charting the Influences on the Judicial Mind: an Empirical Study of Judicial Reasoning, 73 N.Y.U. L. Rev. 1434 (1998). One study went further, coding tools of analysis used in judicial opinions, such as reliance on dictionaries, rules of plain meaning, etc. Jason J. Czarnezki & William K. Ford, The Phantom Philosophy? An Empirical Investigation of Legal Interpretation, 65 Md. L. Rev. 841, (2006).

Defer	0.5049	1	0	1
Remedial	0.8712	1	0	1
Cites	38.0396	30	4	107
Constit	0.1683	0	0	1
GovCont?	0.6931	0	0	1
Proced	0.1289	0	0	1
OpinGOP?	0.5544	1	0	1
%GOP	0.5775	0.67	0	1
G-Circ	0.0891	0	0	1
G-Dist	0.3366	0	0	1
SupCtAtt	0.2986	0.302	0.275	0.31
CongAtt	0.0367	0.0359	0.0137	0.0555
Observations	101			

VoteIss takes the value of the number of judges favoring the private party for the issue coded in the observation. A vote for reversal was coded as favoring the private party on any issue where the appellate court outcome was superior to the lower court ruling from the private party's perspective.[22] A vote for affirmance was coded as favoring the private party on any issue where the lower court favored the private party and the government sought review.[23]

VoteCase takes the value of the number of judges favoring the private party in the case coded in the observation. A vote on a case was coded if the outcome favored by the appellate judge was superior to the lower court ruling from the private party's perspective on the case as a whole or, if the government was the appealing party, affirmed the lower court decision in its entirety.

WinIssue takes the value of 1 if the outcome indicated by the appellate decision on the issue coded in the observation was favorable to the private party, 0 otherwise. A victory on an issue was coded if the opinion of the court produced an outcome superior to the lower court ruling from the private party's perspective or, if the government was the appealing party, affirmed the lower court decision.[24]

WinCase takes the value of 1 if the outcome indicated by the appellate decision on the case coded in the observation was favorable to the private party, 0 otherwise. A victory on a case was coded if the opinion of the court produced an outcome superior to the lower court ruling from the private party's perspective or, if the government was the appealing party, affirmed the lower court decision in its entirety. In most cases, decisions were unanimous.[25]

22 E.g. E.I. du Pont de Nemours & Co. v. United States, supra fn 20.
23 E.g. United States v. Tarkowski, supra fn 20.
24 Presumably, the reversal and/or remand of an appealed decision is favorable to the party seeking it.
25 United States v. Navistar Int'l Transp. Corp., supra fn 20 included a dissent; New Jersey Turnpike Auth. v. PPG Indus., United States v. Tarkowski, and United States v. W.R. Grace & Co., supra fn 20, all included concurrences. This low rate of separate opinion-writing in cases that typically involve large sums of money and complicated fact situations may be indicative of "Going-along voting," and thus indicate that more work is being done by utility-

III.B. THE UTILITY-MAXIMIZATION MODEL

Judges are humans, and thus, a standard utility-maximization model would predict, have a desire to get the highest gain for the least cost.[26] Judges do have the ability to act in ways to maximize their own utility.[27] While judges cannot increase their salary, they can reduce the cost of handling their case load, and thereby increase their leisure time. For this reason, as judges' case loads increase, one can reasonably expect that they will want to dispose of cases quickly so they have more time for other activities.[28] To account for this, the restricted model uses *ln(Courtclog)* as an independent variable. It takes the value of the natural log of the average number of cases each judge in the circuit, where the observation took place, decided during that year.[29] I hypothesize a negative parameter estimate on this variable because it would presumably be easier to defer to agency determination of fact and law than exercise a more rigorous review

.

The marginal effect of court clog on outcome is estimated by the following equation:

$\text{Outcome}_i = \beta_0 + \beta_1(\ln \textit{Courtclog}_i) + \varepsilon_i$

where the dependent variable is the outcome, the independent variable is the natural log of the average number of cases each judge in the circuit where the observation took place decided, ε is a zero-mean error term. and $\text{Outcome}_i = V_i, W_i, V_c, W_c$ indicates alternatively *VoteIssue*, *WinIssue*, *VoteCase*, and *WinCase*. The model includes one explanatory variable.[30] 'The null hypothesis cannot be rejected at the $p < 0.5$ level for any of the dependent variables.[31] This means there is no evidence that the level of activity in any judicial circuit, by itself, alters the decision-making of judges. This utility-maximization model serves as the base model. All subsequent tests account for the case load of judges as a factor.[32] No test in any of the future models found it to be significant at the $p < .25$ level for case outcomes. This should not be taken to mean that judges don't maximize utility, however.[33] The influence of court clog on citations was significant and negative, meaning

maximization than I test for here. See Richard Posner, What Do Judges and Justices Maximize? (The Same Thing Everybody Else Does), 3 Sup. Ct. Econ. Rev. 1, 20 (1993)

26 Jeremy Bentham, The Principles of Morals and Legislation 1, Amherst: Prometheus Books (1988)

27 See, e.g. Richard A. Posner, Overcoming Law 109-44 (1995) and Richard S. Higgins & Paul H. Rubin, Judicial Discretion, 9 J. Legal Stud. 129 (1980).

28 Richard A. Posner, What Do Judges and Justices Maximize? (The Same Thing Everybody Else Does), 3 Sup. Ct. Econ. Rev. 1 (1993); William M. Landes & Richard A. Posner, Rational Judicial Behavior: A Statistical Study (Univ. of Chi. Law & Econ., Olin Working Paper No. 404, 2008), available at http://papers.ssrn.com/abstract=1126403.

29 Natural logs were used rather than raw case totals because this method permits a greater degree of distinction among the circuits.

30 This model tests the variable most likely associated with the utility maximization model on its own for two reasons. First, the joint significance of other models is tested using the F-Tests infra at IV.C. Second, Courtclog is tested in conjunction with the other variables in three future models, so its effect when placeholder variables are present is tested elsewhere.

31 The results of these four bivariate regressions are not reported, but are available upon request.

32 This is included in all future models, despite the lack of evidence that it affects case outcomes, for two reasons. First, there is evidence that case load does affect judge (or clerk) behavior regarding average case citations, which are significant. Second, because the coefficient has consistent signs across outcomes, it is preferable to continue to control for any possible effect this variable may have.

33 Indeed, seeking one's preferred policy outcome is a form of utility maximization, but one treated separately for the purpose of this analysis. Further, judges may genuinely derive utility from fulfilling their proscribed roles. Harry T. Edwards and Michael A. Livermore, supra at fn 21, 58 Duke L.J. at 1944 ("Most members of the bench care about

that as judges were required to decide more cases, they included fewer unique citations in the opinion even though this does not appear to alter the final outcome of the case.[34] The implication, that judges accommodate their opinion-writing to case load but do not decide arbitrarily despite case pressures, tends to corroborate the assertion that, ". . .backlog pressure keeps [the judge] working hard, and reversal threat keeps him working carefully.[35]"

III.C. THE LEGAL MODEL

While scholars disagree on the margin about what is appropriate for judges to consider as part of the law, one commonality among variations of the legal model is that the personal outcome preferences of the judge have no significant role to play: law is to remain separate from politics.[36] Proponents of the legal model argue that judges ought to (normatively) and do (positively) follow the law without preferred outcomes exerting substantial influence on judicial decisions.

While the legal model has been criticized for its failure to deal with indeterminacy in the law, proponents argue that judges make a good faith effort to reach the best legal conclusion and that even absent such an effort, the law sets important constraints on the pursuit of policy preferences.[37] Another criticism leveled at the legal model is the lack of empirical verification thus far. Empirically verifying the legal model is a Herculean task.[38] Since most variants of the legal model argue that precedent matters, most studies focus on determining the extent to which cases with high precedential value (e.g. Chevron[39]) altered the decision-making of the courts that made the decision or subordinate courts. As applying precedent is an issue of judgment, efforts to use precedent frequently collapse into an exercise in armchair judging by academics.[40] This is, scholars seeking to test a judge's use of precedent must identify an expected result if a precedent is used properly, and that a departure from that result is a departure from precedent. It is thus difficult to design an objective empirical model. Any model that does not focus on precedent may not be testing a legal model and any model that does may only reflect the substitution of an academic's judgment that that of the judge.

To try to avoid the pitfalls of using adherence to specific decisions to verify the legal model, I identify proxies for the cumulative effect of binding and non-binding precedent as well as other factors one might expect to be important to a judge attempting to use legal reasoning to reach a

the law, about acting responsibly towards the litigants before them, and about discharging their duty to the American people according to the highest professional standards.").

34 This contrasts with previous studies finding that at the District Court level, caseload does not affect the opinion writing practices of federal judges. David A. Hoffman, Alan J. Izenman & Jeffrey R. Lidicker, Docketology, District Courts, and Doctrine, 85 Wash. U. L. Rev. 681 (2007).

35 Richard A. Posner, Judicial Behavior and Performance: An Economic Approach, 32 Fla. St. U. L. Rev. 1259 (2005).

36 Kathleen M. Sullivan, The Supreme Court, 1991 Term--Foreword:The Justices of Rules and Standards, 106 Harv. L. Rev. 22, 64-65 (1992). Anthony T. Kronman, The Lost Lawyer: Failing Ideals of the Legal Profession 250 (1993).

37 Terri Jennings Peretti, In Defense of a Political Court 38 (1999).

38 One study attempted to accomplish the task of categorizing judges on a single Circuit Court according to interpretative methodology. It involved a large coding team and devoted several pages plus two appendices to explaining how this coding worked and why it was (somewhat) reliable. Jason J. Czarnezki & William K. Ford, The Phantom Philosophy? An Empirical Investigation of Legal Interpretation, 65 Md. L. Rev. 841 (2006).

39 See, e.g., Cohen & Matthew L. Spitzer, Judicial Deference to Agency Action: A Rational Choice Theory and an Empirical Test, 69 S. Cal. L. Rev. 431 (1996); Peter H. Schuck & E. Donald Elliott, To the Chevron Station: An Empirical Study of Federal Administrative Law, 1990 Duke L.J. 984; Sidney A. Shapiro & Richard E. Levy, Judicial Incentives and Indeterminacy in Substantive Review of Administrative Decisions, 44 Duke L.J. 1051.

40 William N. Eskridge, Jr. & Lauren E. Baer, The Continuum of Deference: Supreme Court Treatment of Agency Statutory Interpretations from Chevron to Hamdan, 96 Geo. L.J. 1083 (2008).

conclusion. I identify three sets of independent variables that one would expect to significantly explain CERCLA decisions if judges adhere to the legal model.

The first set of independent variables functions as a proxy for precedent. Two variables comprise this set. First, *ln(Days)* is a variable that takes the value of the natural log of the number of days since the day before the first case in the sample.[41] This variable is included in the model because it is a proxy for non-binding precedent that would guide a judge's decision. I hypothesize that this has a negative parameter estimate for all dependent variables because the government usually wins on appeal.[42] For this reason, the trend in pro-government decisions yields non-binding precedent adverse to the interest of private parties, and this increases over time. A judge guided by non-binding precedent would thus be guided toward voting against private parties as precedent accumulates. Second, *CirOvr8,* is a dummy variable that takes the value of 1 if the circuit court contains more than eight observations in the sample, 0 otherwise.[43] Eight observations is the cut-off because a circuit with eight observations is responsible for more observations than the average circuit.[44] This variable is included in the model because it is a proxy for binding precedent that would constrain a judge's decision. I hypothesize that this has a negative parameter estimate for all dependent variables because the government usually wins on appeal. For this reason, the trend in pro-government decisions yields binding precedent adverse to the interest of private parties, and this increases as the number of rulings in a circuit increases. A judge constrained by binding precedent would thus be increasingly prevented from voting for private parties as precedent accumulates.[45] For this assumption to be relevant for early cases in the sample, I assume that the quantity of litigation in each circuit is homogeneous over time, so that circuits deciding a large number of issues during the sample period also decided issues prior to the sample period.[46]

The second set of independent variables relates to the legal and fact situation before the court that is not controlled by the parties to the litigation. Four variables comprise this set. The first independent variable is *LowCtDec*, a dummy variable that takes the value of 1 if the lower court decided the issue for the private party, 0 otherwise. I predict a positive parameter estimate on *LowCtDec* for outcomes on any issue, but a negative parameter estimate for outcomes related to the

41 Thus, ln(Days) for the first case of the sample would be ln(1).

42 Donald R. Songer and Reginald S. Sheehan, Who Wins on Appeal? Upperdogs and Underdogs in the United States Courts of Appeals, 36 American Journal of Political Science 235 (1992). Finding that the U.S. Federal Government has a higher success rate than any other type of party in appeals. Possible reasons for this include expertise, superior resources, a judicial bias toward government, and others. Stanton Wheeler, Bliss Cartwright, Robert Kagan, and Lawrence Friedman, Do the haves come out ahead? Winning and losing in state supreme courts. 21 Law and Society Review 403 (1987).

43 A variable taking the value of the precise number of observations yielded no significant results but did not generate substantial changes to any other variables.

44 The average number of observations/circuit was 7.769.

45 This is known as the "Chain Novel Hypothesis" based on Ronald Dworkin's famous metaphor. Ronald Dworkin, Law's Empire 228-38 (1986).

46 The same Westlaw search that generated the cases in this sample was run restricted to cases prior to the first case in this sample, individualized to each circuit. Using bivariate regression analysis to ascertain the predictive effect of cases prior to 11/1996 on cases after 11/1996, there was a significant and positive relationship ($p < .01$, R-Squared = .49). The overall ratio of post- to pre-sample cases was 1.00:1.08, with results for individual circuits falling between 1.00:0.55 (9th Circuit, which was still above-average for cases in each time period) and 1.00:1.73 (D.C. Circuit, which was still below-average for cases in each time period). A further investigation into the doctrinal development of precedent within and across circuits could certainly inform this analysis and shed some light on the viability of the proxies for precedent used here, but is beyond the scope of this work.

overall case. This variable is included because lower courts applying legal rules would generally be correct, and thus circuit courts applying the law would find similarly to district courts applying the law. If political preferences dominate law, there would be little relationship because the district court judge's party and the circuit court judges' parties need not match. Further, affirmances are generally more common than reversals across appellate decisions,[47] meaning that on any issue where the lower court decided for a private party, the appellate court is more likely to decide for that party (and vice versa). The parameter estimate for the case outcomes is negative, however, because every issue decided for the private party at the trial level increases the likelihood that the net effect of an appeal is to leave the party who won at the lower court worse off than they were prior to the appeal; in short, there are more opportunities to fail.

Second, *Defer,* is a dummy variable that takes the value of 1 if the appellate court indicates that it is deferring to the lower court, 0 otherwise.[48] This is included because a court that accurately claims it is deferring to another court would review cases differently than a court reviewing the case *de novo.* I predict a parameter estimate consistent with the trend of lower court decisions. If private parties win most cases at the district court level, one would expect deference to exacerbate that result at the appellate level (and vice versa). Absent empirical data on that exact point, no a priori expectation of the direction of the parameter estimate is indicated.

Third, *Cites,* takes the value of the number of unique citations in the opinion of the court. This variable is included because, while imperfect, unique citations are a proxy for complexity. To avoid attributing excessive weight to differences in writing style, cases and statutes were only cited the first time they appeared, and a number of citations were excluded.[49] I predict a negative parameter estimate, as increasing complexity would indicate that executive deference is appropriate, resulting in decisions less friendly to private parties opposing executive action.[50]

Fourth, *Remedial,* is a dummy variable taking the value of 1 if the action taken or demanded by the EPA is considered a remedial action under CERCLA, 0 if it is a removal action.[51] This variable is included because removal and remedial actions are subject to different legal standards in some issues. I am agnostic as to the expected parameter estimate.

47 Donald R. Songer and Reginald S. Sheehan, supra at fn 42 (finding that businesses have only a 22.6% rate of success on appeal, while the U.S. government has a 58.2% success rate. Businesses appealed more than four times as often over the sample period as the U.S. government.)

48 Deference to an agency did not necessarily result in a value of 1. If the observation involved an appeal from an agency decision directly, such as was typical for the D.C. Circuit cases, then agency deference resulted in a value of 1 because the appellate court was deferring specifically to the lower tribunal. If the appellate court reviewed the decision of an Article III court, however, plenary or de novo review of the lower court's decision combined with a determination that agency deference was appropriate yielded a value of 0. There is a possible endogeneity issue here if courts use deference to signal that they are going to affirm, but one would then expect an interaction term between deference and lower court decision (i.e. a dummy variable taking the value of 1 if the appellate court signaled deference and the lower court decided for the government, 0 otherwise) to be significant. It is not. This indicates that deference is doing work independent of the lower court decision.

49 Citations to CERCLA were excluded; pinpoint citations in cases and citations to multiple sections of the USC, CFR, or FRCP dealing with the same law, regulation, or rule were only counted the first time they appeared. Because of the ad hoc nature of some exclusions, the number of unique citations should be considered an approximation rather than exact count.

50 Chevron U.S.A., Inc. v. Natural Resources Defense Council, Inc., 467 U.S. 837 (1984).

51 Where the classification of the site was at issue, the eventual decision of the court determined the code for this independent variable.

The third set of independent variables consists of dummy variables indicating the issue before the court. These are important because the legal standards for evaluation of arguments and the controlling precedent differ for each issue before the court. Issues were divided into four mutually exclusive, all-encompassing categories. Three of the issues are represented as dummy variables. The fourth, as required to generate valid results, is excluded.[52] The first, *Constit,* takes a value of 1 if the lower court's decision is challenged on constitutional grounds, 0 otherwise. I predict a negative parameter estimate, though the rarity of constitutional challenges may preclude statistical significance. Because a constitutional challenge to the statute in its entirety would not be upheld except as a last resort, and CERCLA litigation is still ongoing, any challenge to the constitutionality of CERCLA as a whole has obviously failed. Similarly, due process issues would presumably be resolved first as procedural issues or statutory interpretation issues. Thus, it is unlikely that courts would rule for private parties on constitutional grounds. Second, *GovCont,* takes a value of 1 if a private party was seeking contribution from the government or an agency thereof, 0 otherwise. I predict a positive parameter estimate, as *GovCont* is the only non-procedural issue where the government is held to the same standard as a private party. Third, *Proced,* takes a value of 1 if the lower court's decision regarding an issue of civil procedure, evidence, or jurisdiction[53] was addressed[54] by the appellate court, 0 otherwise. The parameter estimate for *Proced* is ambiguous: the sheer range of issues covered under the heading of procedural concerns and the varying standards for evaluating each of them makes it difficult to predict the marginal effect of this argument. The excluded category is all issues related to the private party's responsibility to pay damages. Issues in this category include challenges to site designation, challenges to apportionment, and challenges to the identification of a PRP. Because all these issues are reviewed with deference, the net effect of the exclusion of this variable is likely a reduction in the coefficient of the intercept.

The marginal effect of legal variables and court clog on outcome is estimated by the following equation:

$$\text{Outcome}_i = \beta_0 + \beta_1(\mathit{Courtclog}_i) + \beta_2(\ln \mathit{Days}_i) + \beta_3(\mathit{CirOvr8}_i) + \beta_4(\mathit{LowCtDec}_i) + \beta_5(\mathit{Defer}_i) + \beta_6(\mathit{Remedial}_i) + \beta_7(\mathit{Cites}_i) + \beta_8(\mathit{Constit}_i) + \beta_9(\mathit{GovCont}_i) + \beta_{10}(\mathit{Proced}_i) + \varepsilon_i$$

where the dependent variable is the outcome, the ß's are parameters to be estimated, ε is a zero-mean error term, and outcome = V_i, W_i, V_c, W_c indicates *VoteIssue*, *WinIssue*, *VoteCase*, and *WinCase*. The model includes ten explanatory variables.

III.D. THE EXTRA-LEGAL MODEL

While judges generally claim to adhere to the legal model, a body of literature suggests that judges decide cases based on their political preferences. The political ideology of judges is generally measured along a conservative-liberal spectrum.[55] This theory is grounded in the view of Legal Realists that law is indeterminate and that the individual characteristics of a judge, from their political preferences to their breakfast choices, ultimately drives outcomes.[56] This view has retained

52 Originally, Proced was dropped from the sample because it was the most heterogeneous class. As cases related to damages comprised more than half the sample, however, those cases were dropped to strengthen the intercept.

53 These issues are lumped together because they deal with law (mostly) external to CERCLA.

54 While sua sponte adjudication is ordinarily frowned upon, judges are free to raise questions of subject matter jurisdiction sua sponte.

55 See generally, Jeffrey A. Segal & Harold J. Spaeth, The Supreme Court and the Attitudinal Model Revisited (2002).

56 Alex Kozinski, What I Ate for Breakfast and Other Mysteries of Judicial Decision Making, 26 Loy. L. A. L. Rev. 993, 993 (1992-1993)

currency largely because there are a number of very close cases or cases where no law has been established where a judge's political preferences seem intuitively likely to play a large role. Empirical studies almost unanimously find that some differences in appellate decision-making can be explained by the political ideology of the judge,[57] using appointing President as proxy for the judge's ideology.[58]

While the extra-legal model holds that judges do pursue their political preferences, not all variations of the model hold that judges must do so crudely. Judges who wish for their decisions to have staying power must avoid having those decisions overturned by a higher court or by Congress. Further, at the appellate level, judges must make decisions as part of a three-judge panel, and the preferences of colleagues may constrain any individual judge's pursuit of personal preferences. To capture judges' preferences and their non-legal constraints in pursuing them, I identity five independent variables that theory suggests would predict judges' decisions.

The first independent variable is *OpinGOP*, a variable that takes the value of 1 if the judge writing the majority opinion was appointed[59] by a Republican President, 0 otherwise.[60] This variable is included in the model because it is necessary to identify whether the ideology of all three judges explains decision-making or if the opinion-writer's ideology is most predictive. I hypothesize that this has a positive parameter estimate for all dependent variables because Republicans are disinclined to favor environmental regulations. For this reason, Republican judges might resist writing opinions that would lead to a result they find distasteful, encouraging Democratic appointees with whom they share a panel to take on the burden of writing these decisions, and vice versa.

Second, *%GOP,* takes the value of the percentage of Republican-appointees on the 3-judge panel. The possible values are 0 (3 Democrats), 0.33 (1 Republican, 2 Democrats), 0.67 (2 Republicans, 1 Democrat), or 1 (3 Democrats).[61] I predict a positive parameter estimate on the variable because Republicans are traditionally considered more hostile to environmental legislation and would presumably prefer to limit the scope of CERCLA. This variable is included in the model because decisions are made by majority vote, so the more judges of one party present on a panel, the more

57 See infra at part V.B. For an excellent literature review and an example of such a study, see Frank B. Cross, Decisionmaking in the U.S. Circuit Courts of Appeals, 91 Cal. L. Rev. 1457 (2003).

58 Andrew P. Morriss, Charting the Influences on the Judicial Mind: an Empirical Study of Judicial Reasoning, 73 N.Y.U. L. Rev. 1434, 1465 (1998).

59 See C. K. Rowland & Robert A. Carp, Politics and Judgment in Federal District Courts, 183-84 (1996) (finding the party of the appointing President to reflect judicial political leanings); Stuart S. Nagel, Political Party Affiliation and Judges' Decisions, 55 Am. Pol. Sci. Rev. 843 (1961); S. Sidney Ulmer, The Political Party Variable in the Michigan Supreme Court, 11 J. Pub. L. 352 (1962); Kenneth N. Vines, Federal District Judges and Race Relations Cases in the South, 26 J. Pol. 337 (1964).

60 Two cases did not have signed opinions. In one, all three panelists were Republican appointees. Montrose Chem. Corp. v. United States EPA, 1999 U.S. App. LEXIS 2456 (D.C. Cir. Jan. 21, 1999). In the other, a Republican appointee (Chief Judge Ginsburg) sat with two Democratic appointees. GE v. EPA, 360 F.3d 188 (D.C. Cir. 2004). Each case was responsible for a single observation. The opinion-writing judge in these cases was designated as Republican – in the former case because there was no other possibility and in the latter case because the senior judge on the panel was Republican. Switching the designation of that variable has the effect of causing OpinGop to approach significance at $p < .15$. Nothing else substantially changes. Given the ultimate findings of this paper, some generosity to the Extra-Legal Model seems prudent. Excluding the variable entirely substantially reduces the viability of that model.

61 Altering the model to include three dummy variables for 1-Republican, 2-Republican, and 3-Republican panels did not substantially affect the results.

likely it is that the policy preferences associated with the dominant party will be outcome-determinative. Further, it is a reliable indicator of panel effects because conservatives on a panel tend to moderate the leftward leanings of liberals on that same panel according to the collegial model, and vice versa.[62] I hypothesize that this has a positive parameter estimate for all dependent variables because Republicans are typically hostile to expansive CERCLA liability.[63]

Third, *G-Circ,* is a dummy variable taking the value of 1 if the panel includes a guest judge from another circuit. Fourth, *G-Dist* is a dummy variable taking the value of 1 if the panel includes a guest judge from a U.S. District Court.[64] These are included because judges who do not normally sit with the Court of Appeals may have different incentive structures than the judges who do normally sit on that Court. For example, they may need to worry less about social exclusion or retaliation from other members of that circuit in response to a dissent. Alternatively, they may be more inclined to go along as the immediate cost of disagreement is higher without an established relationship. I am agnostic as to the parameter estimate for these variables.

Fifth, *SupCtAtt,* takes a value equal to the mean Segal-Cover score of the Supreme Court Justices sitting at the time of decision.[65] Each Justice is scored from 0 (most conservative) to 1 (most liberal). Because of the relative stability of the Court over the period studied, scores remained in a narrow band. This variable is included in the model because judges on the Court of Appeals presumably seek to avoid reversal. I predict a negative parameter estimate because Justices that are more conservative seem intuitively likely to prefer pro-business outcomes to those outcomes that would force businesses to pay for environmental harms. A more liberal Court would presumably prefer pro-government rulings in environmental cases.

Sixth, *CongAtt,* takes a value equal to the mean NOMINATE Common Space First-Dimension score[66] for all members of the Congress in power at the time of decision.[67] Each Congressperson is scored from 1 (most conservative) to -1 (most liberal). This is included in the model because judges on the Court of Appeals presumably seek to avoid reversal. I predict a positive parameter estimate because conservatives have historically been hostile to expansive CERCLA liability and

62 Cass R. Sunstein, David Schkade & Lisa Michelle Ellman, Ideological Voting on Federal Courts of Appeals: A Preliminary Investigation, 90 Va. L. Rev. 301, 340 (2004).

63 Rebecca Adams, Superfund at 25: Time for a Makeover?, CQ. Wkly., Nov. 11, 2005, available at 2005 WLNR 18674745.

64 Two alternative tests for guest judges generated substantially similar results: a dummy variable taking the value of 1 if there was any guest judge and a variable taking the value of 1 if a guest circuit court judge and 2 if a guest district court judge.

65 For methodology, see Lee Epstein & Jeffrey Segal, Advice and Consent 109-111 (Oxford 2005); Jeffrey Segal, Lee Epstein, Charles Cameron, & Harold Spaeth, Ideological Values and the Votes of U.S. Supreme Court Justices Revisited, 57 Journal of Politics 812-823 (1995); Jeffrey Segal & Albert Cover, Ideological Values and the Votes of U.S. Supreme Court Justices, 83 American Political Science Review 557-565 (1989).

66 See Keith T. Poole & Howard Rosenthal, Congress: A Political-Economic History of Roll Call Voting 229, 233-249 (1997).

67 Because these scores are not available for the 111th Congress, I used the score for the 110th Congress for the three observations that would otherwise be excluded. While imperfect, the 110th Congress is the most liberal in the sample (though it would presumably be eclipsed by the 111th Congress), and it is used for a small portion of the sample, so any skew is minimal. A more liberal Congress combined with 100% pro-government decisions means that the correlation reported in this paper may be weaker than the correlation that would likely exist with full data. Lower numbers for NOMINATE are more liberal.

judges would be more inclined to rule for private parties to avoid having their interpretations "corrected" by a more conservative Congress.

The marginal effect of extra-legal variables on outcome is estimated by the following equation:
$Outcome_i = \beta_0 + \beta_1(Courtclog_i) + \beta_{11}(OpinGOP_i) + \beta_{12}(\%GOP_i) + \beta_{13}(G\text{-}Circ_i) + \beta_{14}(G\text{-}Dist_i) + \beta_{15}(SupCtAtt_i) + \beta_{16}(CongAtt_i) + \varepsilon_i$
where the dependent variable is the outcome *i*, the ß's are parameters to be estimated, ε is a zero-mean error term, and $i = V_i, W_i, V_c, W_c$ indicates *VoteIssue*, *WinIssue*, *VoteCase*, and *WinCase*. The model includes seven explanatory variables.

III.E. SUMMARY

According to the legal model, judges apply objective external rules of law to the facts of the case in order to reach correct decisions. Under the extra-legal model, judges vote in accord with their policy preferences. Effectively, the debate comes down to the Legal Model's adherents claiming that judges do what they say they do and the Extra-Legal Model's adherents claiming that judges act to maximize preferred policy outcomes, with varying constraints. If the traditional Legal Model is right, then much of a judge's decision-making can be explained by factors such as standards of review, lower court decisions, arguments made, citations to precedent, and similar factors. If the Extra-Legal Model is correct, then one would expect the party of the President who appoints the judges to explain and predict judicial decisions, along with the perceived ideology of the Supreme Court and Congress.

To test the relative power of each model, I run a series of tests to examine the joint significance of the variables in each model and the degree of explanatory power each model adds to the other. The marginal effect of all independent variables ("Combined Model") on outcome is estimated by the following equation:
$Outcome_i = \beta_0 + \beta_1(Courtclog_i) + \beta_2(Days_i) + \beta_3(CirOvr8_i) + \beta_4(LowCtDec_i) + \beta_5(Defer_i) + \beta_6(Remedial_i) + \beta_7(Cites_i) + \beta_8(Constit_i) + \beta_9(GovCont_i) + \beta_{10}(Proced_i) + \beta_{11}(OpinGOP_i) + \beta_{12}(\%GOP_i) + \beta_{13}(G\text{-}Circ_i) + \beta_{14}(G\text{-}Dist_i) + \beta_{15}(SupCtAtt_i) + \beta_{16}(CongAtt_i) + \varepsilon_i$
where the dependent variable is the outcome *i*, the ß's are parameters to be estimated, ε is a zero-mean error term, and $i = V_i, W_i, V_c, W_c$ indicates *VoteIssue*, *WinIssue*, *VoteCase*, and *WinCase*, respectively. The model includes fifteen explanatory variables, previously discussed

After completing the regression analysis for the Utility-Maximization Model, Legal Model, Extra-Legal Model, and Combined Model, I perform a series of F-Tests to test the joint significance of all variables in the model. Using the Utility-Maximization Model as a baseline, I perform an F-Test for the Legal Model and Attitudinal Model. This functions to test the joint significance of the variables other than Courtclog in each of these two models. Subsequently, I perform an F-Test for the Combined Model using the Legal Model as a baseline (to test the added significance of the Extra-Legal Model) and using the Extra-Legal Model as a baseline (to test the added significance of the Legal Model).[68] Because of the prevalence of substantial literature

68 The F-Statistic is estimated by the following equation:
$F = [(RSS1 - RSS2) / (p2 - p1)] / [RSS2 / (n - p2)]$

indicating that political factors can or should influence judicial decision-making,[69] I predict that the Extra-Legal Model will have more explanatory power and that adding legal variables to the extra-legal variables in the Combined Model will have no significant effect.

Where RSS1 is the residual sum of squares of the base model, RSS2 is the residual sum of squares of the model being tested, p1 is the number of parameters in the base model, p2 is the number of parameters in the model being tested, and n is the number of observations. For the test of the Legal Model and Extra-Legal Model, the Utility-Maximization Model forms the base model. The test of the Combined Model is run twice, once with the Legal Model as the base model and once with the Extra-Legal Model as the base model. For these F-Tests, the DV in all analyses was Wc, as this was the outcome each model predicted best and is presumably the most important outcome for a party deciding whether or not to appeal.

69 See supra at part III.D. and infra at V.B.

IV. RESULTS

IV.A. LEGAL MODEL RESULTS

Taken together, the variables in the Legal Model explain just under one-third of the variance in victories and votes for cases and just over one-fifth of the variance in victories and votes on individual issues within those cases. Table 2 reports the parameter estimates for the four outcome models.

Table 2: Legal Variable Parameter Estimates & Results

Legal Model[70]	WinCase	VoteCase	WinIssue	VoteIssue	Predict	Confirm
Intercept	0.9090^	2.4323	1.3991*	3.9027*	N/A	N/A
ln(Courtclog)	-0.0275	-0.0456	-0.1458	-0.4006	N/A	N/A
ln(Days)	0.0190	0.0533	0.0350^	0.1011^	Neg	*No*
CirOvr8	-0.3004***	-0.8312***	-0.2681**	-0.7343**	Neg	**Yes**
LowCtDec	-0.2229**	-0.6425**	0.0455	0.1626	Mix	**Yes**
Defer	-0.3567***	-1.0497***	-0.2019**	-0.5854**	N/A	N/A
Remedial	-0.0971	-0.2912	-0.1768^	-0.5304^	N/A	N/A
Cites	-0.0026*	-0.0074*	-0.0022^	-0.0061	Neg	**Yes**
Constit	-0.0544	-0.1272	0.0979	0.3297	Neg	*No*
GovCont?	0.0803	0.2361	0.4182***	1.2500***	Pos	**Yes**
Proced	0.0078	-0.0389	0.0797	0.1768	Neg	*No*
R Square	0.3165	0.3044	0.2445	0.2386		
Adjusted R Square	0.2405	0.2272	0.1606	0.1540		
Standard Error	0.3554	1.0620	0.4075	1.2155		

Notes: ^p < 0.25,*p < 0.15, **p < 0.05, ***p < 0.01

The first set of independent variables functioned as a proxy for precedent. Two variables comprised this set. The first, *ln(Days)*, takes the value of the natural log of the number of days since the day before the first case in the sample. Originally, I hypothesized that *ln(Days)* would have a negative parameter estimate for all dependent variables. That hypothesis is not confirmed. Rather,

70 The practical significance of the independent variables that are not dummy variables is computed by multiplying the coefficient by the interquartile range, which calculates the effect of the variable moving from its 25th percentile position to its 75th percentile position. Those are:

Practical Significance	WinCase	VoteCase	WinIssue	VoteIssue
Courtclog	-0.0110	-0.0182	-0.0582	-0.1598
ln(Days)	0.0230	0.0647	0.0425^	0.1226^

Thus, for example, in the emboldened results that approach significance, as we move from the 25th percentile time period to the 75th percentile time period, the likelihood that the private party would win the case increases by 4.25% and the private party can expect to obtain 0.1226 additional votes. These findings approach significance at the p < 0.25 level, as reported in Table 2. Other reported outcomes did not approach statistical significance.

the parameter estimates are positive but not significant for all dependent variables. Thus, this study finds no evidence that non-binding precedent, with pro-government decisions accumulating over time and disfavoring private parties, is substantially influencing judicial decisions. Also, since cases in the latter part of the sample occurred during a time of war while the earlier cases in the sample did not, it cautions against extending the tendency of courts to extend deference to government actors in rights and liberties situations[71] to a general governmental deference. It is possible that given the effect of binding precedent, discussed below, persuasive precedent from other circuits has diminishing returns for the government and the accumulation of persuasive precedent benefits the private party, who would otherwise have less to rely upon.

Second, *CirOvr8,* is a dummy variable that takes the value of 1 if the circuit court contained more than the average number of observations in the sample. This variable is included in the model because it is a proxy for binding precedent that would constrain a judge's decision. I hypothesized that *CirOvr8*, a proxy for binding precedent that would constrain a judge's decision, would have a negative parameter estimate for all dependent variables. This hypothesis is confirmed. Circuits that decide more CERCLA issues than average are significantly less-inclined to vote for private parties in CERCLA litigation than circuits that rarely encounter those issues. This would tend to provide some weak confirmation for Dworkin's Chain Novel Hypothesis[72] and contrasts with previous empirical tests finding that as precedent increases, discretion docs as well.[73]

The second set of independent variables relates to the legal and fact situation before the court outside the control of parties to the litigation. Four variables comprise this set. The first of these independent variables is *LowCtDec*, which is included to control for the trial court's decision. I predicted a mixed parameter estimate (positive for issue, negative for case), and this hypothesis was confirmed. This indicates that district courts are generally applying law in ways similar as circuit courts on any particular issue; the negative parameter estimate on cases is simply a function of a party who wins an issue having more opportunities to end up in a worse position following appeal if they lose an issue there. Given the strong and significant correlation between decisions of the district courts and the circuit courts, it seems unlikely that the preferred outcomes of the trial judge just happen to coincide with those of three appellate judges.

Second, *Defer,* is significant and negative for all four dependent variables. Originally, I was agnostic regarding the direction of the predicted parameter estimate, knowing only that courts engaging in deferential analysis are likely to behave differently than courts reviewing cases *de novo.* The

71 Lee Epstein, Daniel E. Ho, Gary King & Jeffrey A. Segal, The Supreme Court During Crisis: How War Affects Only Non-War Cases, 80 N.Y.U. L. Rev. 1 (2005)

72 Ronald Dworkin, Law's Empire 228-38 (1986).

73 Stefanie A. Lindquist & Frank B. Cross, Empirically Testing Dworkin's Chain Novel Theory: Studying the Path of Precedent, 80 N.Y.U. L. Rev. 1156, 1200 (2005). The cited study did not distinguish between binding and persuasive authority for the empirical test. Note that I find persuasive authority to be insignificant as a predictor of decisions, also. It is possible that the Chain Novel Hypothesis only functions for binding precedent. It is also possible, given that the Lindquist & Cross data covers a much longer period of time, that there was no chance of reaching similar results in this study.

prediction that the parameter estimate would be consistent with the trend of lower court decisions was borne out, however.[74]

Third, *Cites,* is a proxy for the legal or factual complexity of the case. I originally predicted a negative parameter estimate, as increasing complexity would indicate that executive deference is appropriate, resulting in decisions less friendly to private parties opposing executive action. This hypothesis was confirmed, with parameter estimates negative and approaching significance across all outcomes. This complexity may provide a legal justification for the varying levels of deference agencies do (or do not) receive: judges increase deference when cases are factually or legally complex.[75]

Fourth, *Remedial,* is included because removal and remedial actions are subject to different legal standards in some issues. Originally, I was agnostic as to the expected parameter estimate. The parameter estimate is universally negative, but only approaches significance at the $p < .25$ level for issue outcomes and is not significant for case outcomes.

The third set of independent variables relates to fact and legal situations within the control of the litigants – the arguments pursued. This set is comprised of three dummy variables, with cases related to the appropriateness of damage awards dropped. The first argument tested *Constit,* a dummy variable taking the value of 1 if a constitutional argument was made. My model predicts a negative parameter estimate on this variable because constitutional challenged to the CERCLA regime as a whole had failed early on, as indicated by the continuation of CERCLA litigation. Surprisingly, this was not confirmed. While the parameter estimate on case outcomes was negative, the results were insignificant. For issue outcomes, where one would expect the result to be strongest, the parameter estimate was positive, though it failed to approach significance as well. One possible reason for this is the small number observations that involved constitutional claims.

GovCont, as predicted, has a large positive and significant parameter estimate for issue outcomes. This likely reflects the specific waiver of sovereign immunity[76] for purposes of CERCLA litigation, forcing the government into the same litigation position as private parties, subject to all the adverse precedent. The model's predicted parameter estimate on *Proced* was ambiguous; so is the outcome. Given the relatively small number of samples and the wide array of issues, it is possible that this variable is insignificant because of an insufficient unifying theme among the coded observations. The excluded argument category was all issues related to the private party's responsibility to pay damages: challenges to site designation, apportionment, and the identification of a PRP. The coefficient on issue outcomes for all three argument variables is positive, confirming my hypothesis that the effect of this exclusion was to reduce the coefficient of the intercept. This is likely due to the deference afforded agency determinations in all of these cases. Interestingly, parameter estimates for case outcomes are mixed and insignificant for issues, indicating that judges appear to make judge issues within cases separately. This provides some reason to suspect that the

74 Per Table 1, private parties won trial court judgments just under one-third of the time. Interestingly, however, the interaction term Defer*LowCtDec was not significant and positive when used to replace those two variables, indicating that perhaps more deference is granted to pro-government decisions than pro-private party decisions.

75 William N. Eskridge, Jr. & Lauren E. Baer, The Continuum of Deference: Supreme Court Treatment of Agency Statutory Interpretations from Chevron to Hamdan, 96 Geo. L.J. 1083 (2008).

76 United States v. Shell Oil Co., supra fn 20.

judicial reasoning in an opinion is driven by something other than desire to reach a particular overall result.

In sum, according to the Legal Model, private parties are significantly more likely to come out ahead in circuits where there is little precedent, they are appealing a range of adverse decisions, and are engaging issues where there is little deference afforded the lower court decision. On any given issue, however, it is marginally beneficial to a private party to have the lower court decide the issue in their favor and to pursue a strategy of seeking government contribution where the government must meet the same standards as a private litigant to avoid liability. Seeking holistic challenges to the statute, trial procedure, or outcome is unlikely to be successful. Courts seem especially reluctant to rule that cost estimates, site definitions, and other administrative aspects of the EPA's enforcement of CERCLA do not meet the requirements and thus preclude full liability on the part of private parties. This is consistent with the expectations of traditional legal analysis, where doctrinal analysis indicates that appellate courts would defer to the determinations of agencies within their areas of competence.[77]

IV.B. EXTRA-LEGAL MODEL RESULTS

Taken together, the variables in the Extra-Legal Model explain just under one-fifth of the variance in victories and votes for cases and just over one-tenth of the variance in victories and votes on individual issues within those cases. Table 3 reports the parameter estimates for the four outcome models.

Table 3: Extra-Legal Variable Parameter Estimates & Results

Extra-Legal Model[78]	WinCase	VoteCase	WinIssue	VoteIssue	Predict	Confirm
Intercept	-1.6645	-5.0387^	-2.6935*	-8.1260*	N/A	N/A
ln(Courtclog)	0.1245	0.3914	0.1020	0.3242	N/A	N/A
OpinGOP	0.2265**	0.6465**	0.0998	0.2663	Pos	Yes
%GOP	-0.0184	-0.0244	0.1191	0.3880	Pos	No

77 Frank B. Cross & Emerson H. Tiller, Judicial Partisanship and Obedience to Legal Doctrine: Whistleblowing on the Federal Courts of Appeals, 107 Yale L.J. 2155, 2163-65 (1998)

78 The practical significance of the independent variables that are not dummy variables is computed by multiplying the coefficient by the interquartile range, which calculates the effect of the variable moving from its 25th percentile position to its 75th percentile position. Those are:

Practical Significance	WinCase	VoteCase	WinIssue	VoteIssue
Courtclog	0.0497	0.1561	0.0407	0.1293
%GOP	-0.0063	-0.0083	0.0405	0.1319
SupCtAtt	0.1627	0.4749	0.2835*	0.8373*
CongAtt	-0.0396*	-0.1154*	-0.0224	-0.0637

Because SupCtAtt had identical 25th and 75th percentile numbers, the practical significance of this variable reflects its movement from the minimum to maximum values in the sample. Thus, as the Supreme Court moved from its most conservative position to its most liberal position, private parties had a 28.35% greater chance of winning any issue and could generally expect 0.8373 more votes on any issue, with this result approaching significance at the $p < 0.15$ level. As Congress moved from its most conservative position to its most liberal position,

G-Circ	-0.4112**	-1.2113**	-0.0991	-0.2753	N/A	N/A
G-Dist	-0.2974***	-0.8631***	-0.1741*	-0.4934*	N/A	N/A
SupCtAtt	4.6484	13.5675	8.1004*	23.9235*	Neg	No
CongAtt	-7.4754*	-21.7779*	-4.2202	-12.0123	Pos	No
R Square	0.1784	0.1746	0.0816	0.0793		
Adjusted R Square	0.1165	0.1125	0.0125	0.0100		
Standard Error	0.3833	1.1381	0.4420	1.3149		

Notes: ^$p < 0.25$, *$p < 0.15$, **$p < 0.05$, ***$p < 0.01$

The first two unique variables in the Extra-Legal Model, *OpinGOP* and *%GOP*, are measures for ideology. The expected parameter for each is positive. While the parameter estimate for *OpinGOP* is positive and significant for case outcomes, it does not approach significance for issue outcomes. The parameter estimate for *%GOP* does not approach significance for any outcome, and the coefficient is negative for case outcomes. Thus, there is no evidence here that the panel composition and the raw ideologies of the judges are substantially altering outcomes. Rather, there is a strong correlation between the opinion-writer and outcomes. Assuming that judges do not just "go along to get along," as a utility-maximizing mechanism,[79] and do vote their views as some judges assert is the case,[80] this means that opinion-writing may be a function of the decision more than the decision is a function of opinion-writing. Thus, judges may use strategies available to them to ensure that they write opinions they want to write (those consistent with their preferred ideological outcomes) and avoiding writing those they would find distasteful (those inconsistent with preferred outcome).

This finding contrasts with studies finding that there are substantial panel effects whereby panels comprised of three judges vote differently based on the number of Republican-appointees in regulatory cases involving deference to agencies.[81] This also contrasts with studies finding both ideological bias in the degree of deference granted to agencies and significant alterations in judicial behavior based on the precise mix of judicial ideologies on a panel.[82] In particular, it does not confirm that panel composition for CERCLA litigation across circuits has as large an impact as it does for environmental challenges generally in the D.C. Circuit,[83] tending to corroborate

79 Richard A. Posner, What Do Judges and Justices Maximize? (The Same Thing Everybody Else Does), 3 Sup. Ct. Econ. Rev. 1 (1993)

80 Harry T. Edwards, Collegiality and Decision Making on the D.C. Circuit, 84 Va. L. Rev. 1335, 1338 (1998).

81 Frank B. Cross & Emerson H. Tiller, Judicial Partisanship and Obedience to Legal Doctrine: Whistleblowing on the Federal Courts of Appeals, 107 Yale L.J. 2155, 2173 (1998)

82 Thomas J. Miles & Cass R. Sunstein, Do Judges Make Regulatory Policy? An Empirical Investigation of Chevron, 73 U. Chi. L. Rev. 823, 864 (2006). Though not included in the final model, I did test for panel effects for 1-, 2-, and 3-Republican panels. This did not generate statistically significant results, though all had positive coefficients. Further, the coefficient for 2-Republican panels was larger than the coefficient for 1-Republican panels. When I attempted to explain results using only the dummy variables, [$Outcome_i = \beta_0 + \beta_1(1GOP_i) + \beta_2(2GOP_i) + \beta_3(3GOP_i) + \varepsilon_i$], no variable was significant and the adjusted R-squared for the model was below .01. Also see, e.g., Thomas J. Miles & Cass R. Sunstein, The Real World of Arbitrariness Review, 75 U. Chi. L. Rev. 761 (2008); J. P. Kastellec, Panel Composition and Voting on the U.S. Courts of Appeals, Paper presented at the annual meeting of the American Political Science Association, Hyatt Regency Chicago and the Sheraton Chicago Hotel and Towers (2007); Cass R. Sunstein, et al, Are Judges Political?: An Empirical Analysis of the Federal Judiciary 8-9.

83 Richard L. Revesz, Environmental Regulation, Ideology, and the D.C. Circuit, 83 Va. L. Rev. 1751-1756 (1997).

supposition that something individual to that circuit may be driving results in previous studies.[84] This study finds no evidence that judges' may be less willing to broadly apply laws that may be adverse to their political predilections in areas such as labor.[85] It also fails to support claims that judges are more sympathetic to litigants coming from groups that are largely comprised of political allies.[86]

The next two variables, *G-Circ* and *G-Dist*, are collegial variables. The predicted parameter estimates on each are ambiguous. The results, however, indicate a negative and significant parameter estimate for all case outcomes. This indicates that guest judges, regardless of whether they normally practice on another circuit or on a district court, are less inclined to vote for private parties than their counterparts who are judging on the circuit for which they normally judge. This may be the result of guest judges (especially district court judges[87]), having an affinity for deferring to their colleagues and taking less active roles in deliberations,[88] also tending to defer to administrative agencies and other government offices. This offers some support for the proposition that judges maximize utility, but this particular version of utility maximization has a political bent because it involves supporting the executive branch. The head of the executive branch gets to appoint judges to federal courts.

The next two variables, *CongAtt* and *SupCtAtt*, are strategic variables. The hypothesized parameter on *SupCtAtt* is negative (meaning that there would be more favorable outcomes for private parties as the Supreme Court became more conservative) and the hypothesized parameter on *CongAtt* is positive (meaning that there would be more favorable outcomes for private parties as Congress became more conservative), due to the different scales. The results indicate the opposite. A more liberal Supreme Court and Congress is associated with outcomes more friendly to private parties. These results approach significance for issue outcomes (for the Supreme Court) or case outcomes (for Congress), but not both for either. One possible explanation for this finding is that conservative politicians may dislike activist judiciaries[89] while Supreme Court conservatives have strong preferences for agency deference.[90] Because this is a small-n sample and the results only approach significance, it is entirely possible that it is just coincidence. A finding of no substantial relationship is consistent with the empirical findings that fear of reversal is not a significant factor affecting judicial behavior on circuit courts,[91] likely due to the low probability that appellate decisions will be reviewed by the Supreme Court.[92] This study also did not evaluate the overall ideology of the circuit to see if judges were voting to avoid potential en banc review – a factor that

84 Id. at 1720-1721.

85 James J. Brudney, Sara Schiavoni & Deborah J. Merritt, Judicial Hostility Toward Labor Unions? Applying the Social Background Model to a Celebrated Concern, 60 Ohio St. L.J. 1675, 137-38 (1999)

86 Adam B. Cox & Thomas J. Miles, Judging the Voting Rights Act, 108 Colum. L. Rev. 1 (2008)

87 James J. Brudney and Corey Ditslear, Designated Diffidence: District Court Judges on the Courts of Appeals, 35 Law and Society Review 565 (2001).

88 Owens, Ryan J. and Black, Ryan C., Strategic Bargaining on the United States Courts of Appeals (September 05, 2009). APSA 2009 Toronto Meeting Paper. Available at SSRN: http://ssrn.com/abstract=1452354

89 Edwin Meese III, The Law of the Constitution, 61 Tul. L. Rev. 979 (1987)

90 Lettie M. Wenner & Cynthia Ostberg, Restraint in Environmental Cases by Reagan-Bush Judicial Appointees, 77 Judicature 217, 219-20 (1994).

91 Richard S. Higgins and Paul H. Rubin, Judicial Discretion, 9 J.Legal Stud 129

92 Frank B. Cross & Emerson H. Tiller, Judicial Partisanship and Obedience to Legal Doctrine: Whistleblowing on the Federal Courts of Appeals, 107 Yale L.J. 2155, 2174 (1998)

might play some role.[93] This ambiguity reflects mixed findings in the literature on the influence of Congressional ideology on court action. Previous studies found that court decision-making trends towards legislative preferences.[94] Others, however, find that judicial challenges to agency action are not strongly affected by the composition of Congress.[95]

In sum, there is some evidence indicating that the political policy outcomes of judges influence decisions in appellate CERCLA litigation when only extra-legal variables are tested. Very little of this influence is based on the ideological composition of the panel, however. The most influential factors include whether there are guests on the panel (which is harmful to private parties) and whether a Republican appointee writes the opinion (which is helpful to private parties).

IV.C. SUMMARY OF RESULTS

Taken together, the variables in the Combined Model explain just over one-third of the variance in victories and votes for cases and just over one-fourth of the variance in victories and votes on individual issues within those cases. Table 4 reports the parameter estimates for the four outcome models.

Table 4: Combined Variable Parameter Estimates & Results

Combined Model[96]	WinCase	VoteCase	WinIssue	VoteIssue	Signif Change
Intercept	-0.3848	-1.5773	-0.5398	-2.0423	N/A
ln(Courtclog)	-0.0203	-0.0251	-0.1722^	-0.4807	Increase
ln(Days)	0.0378^	0.1097^	0.0557*	0.1633*	Increase
CirOvr8	-0.2152*	-0.5751*	-0.2067*	-0.5495^	Decrease
LowCtDec	-0.1815*	-0.5133*	0.0828	0.2796	Decrease

93 Tracey E. George, The Dynamics and Determinants of the Decision to Grant En Banc Review, 74 Wash. L. Rev. 213 (1999).

94 See, e.g. Pablo T. Spiller & Rafael Gely, Congressional Control or Judicial Independence: The Determinants of U.S. Supreme Court Labor-Relations Decisions, 1949-1988, 23 RAND J. Econ. 463 (1990) (finding that Supreme Court decisions become more labor-friendly as Congress becomes increasingly liberal).

95 Richard L. Revesz, Congressional Influence on Judicial Behavior? An Empirical Examination of Challenges to Agency Action in the D.C. Circuit, 76 N.Y.U. L. Rev. 1100 (2001).

96 The practical significance of the independent variables that are not dummy variables is computed by multiplying the coefficient by the interquartile range, which calculates the effect of the variable moving from its 25th percentile position to its 75th percentile position. Those are:

Practical Significance	WinCase	VoteCase	WinIssue	VoteIssue
Courtclog	-0.0110	-0.0182	-0.0582^	-0.1598
ln(Days)	0.0459	0.1331	0.0676*	0.1981*
%GOP	0.0387	-0.0083	-0.0128	-0.0128
SupCtAtt	0.1291	0.4001	0.2258^	0.6903^
CongAtt	-0.0280^	-0.0821	-0.0202	-0.0588

Thus, as the case load of judges in a circuit increases from the 25th to 75th percentile, private parties are 5.28% less likely to win any given issue. As time passes from the 25th to 75th percentile period, private parties are 6.76% more likely to win on any given issue and can expect to receive 0.1981 additional votes on any issue. Because SupCtAtt had identical 25th and 75th percentile numbers, the practical significance of this variable reflects its movement from the minimum to maximum values in the sample. As the Supreme Court moves from its most conservative to most liberal position, private parties are 22.58% more likely to win on an issue and can expect to receive 0.6903 more votes for an issue. As Congress becomes more conservative, from the 25th to 75th percentile, private parties can expect to win 2.8% less often.

Defer	- 0.3176***	- 0.9367***	-0.1776*	-0.5167*	Decrease
Remedial	-0.0324	-0.1002	-0.1269	-0.3834	Decrease
Cites	-0.0017	-0.0049	-0.0018	-0.0051	Decrease
Constit	-0.0768	-0.1983	0.0712	0.2458	None
GovCont?	0.0808	0.2289	0.4236***	1.2572***	None
Proced	-0.0018	-0.0729	0.0170	-0.0164	None
OpinGOP?	0.1560^	0.4538^	0.1850^	0.5406^	Decrease
%GOP	0.0262	0.1138	-0.0243	-0.0377	None
G-Circ	-0.1556	-0.4585	-0.0190	-0.0488	Decrease
G-Dist	-0.1736*	-0.4959*	-0.0783	-0.2099	Decrease
SupCtAtt	3.6881	11.4311	6.4518^	19.7222^	Decrease
CongAtt	-5.2769^	-15.5017	-3.8062	-11.0896	Decrease
R Square	0.3608	0.3488	0.2809	0.2757	**See F-Test**
Adjusted R Square	0.2390	0.2248	0.1439	0.1377	**See F-Test**
Standard Error	0.3558	1.0636	0.4115	1.2272	

Because the previous sections have addressed each independent variable individually, this section briefly focuses on some important changes between the results for independent variables reported in the Legal or Extra-Legal Models and the parameter estimates for those variables in the Combined Model.

Two variables see slight increases in significance. The Utility-Maximization model approaches significance at the $p < .25$ level for one issue outcome. Also, *ln(Days)*, the proxy for non-binding precedent, approaches significance at the $p < .25$ level for case outcomes and the $p < .15$ level for issue outcomes relative to its parameter estimate for outcomes in the Legal Model. This increase in significance may increase the plausibility of the earlier supposition that persuasive authority has diminishing returns for the government, but has not yet reached that point for private parties.

The set of dummy variables indicating the issue before the court does not change in significance. *GovCont?* has the largest coefficient of any dummy variable in the model and remains highly significant for issue outcomes. *%GOP*, the variable identifying ideological composition of the panel, remains insignificant and does not approach significance for any outcome model.

All other independent variables had parameter estimates decreasing in significance when placed in the Combined Model. *CirOvr8* changed from being significant for all outcomes to approaching significance for all outcomes. *LowCtDec* changed from being significant for case outcomes to approaching significance, and no longer approaches significance for issue outcomes. *Defer* remained highly significant for case outcomes but only approaches significance for issue outcomes. Neither *Remedial* nor *Cites* approach significance for any outcome in the Combined Model. Of the independent variables originally in the Extra-Legal Model, none retain significance in the Combined Model. *OpinGOP?* approaches significance at the $p < .25$ level for all outcomes, showing a slight increase in relative importance for issue outcomes but a substantial decrease for case outcomes. The only relationship approaching significance at $p < .15$ is a negative parameter estimate on G-Dist. This seems to indicate that the explanatory power of each variable set is substantially reduced when combined with other variable sets, and further testing is necessary to ascertain which sets of variables are driving the explanatory power of the Combined Model.

Overall, the Combined Model explains more than any of the embedded models, and both the Legal Model and Extra-Legal Model explain more than the embedded Utility-Maximization Model. To ascertain whether or not additional variables are providing some unique explanation within the larger models, a series of F-tests is required. Table 5 reports the results of a series of F-Tests,[97] testing the joint significance of the additional variables to each model.

Table 5: Reported Results of an F-Test

	F-Stat	Cum Prob	Sig-F	Degrees of Freedom
1. F-Test (Util -> Legal)[98]	41.3187	1.0000	p<.01	9
2. F-Test (Util -> Extra)[99]	19.8857	1.0000	p<.01	6
3. F-Test (Extra -> Combined)[100]	2.3972	1.0000	p<.01	9
4. F-Test (Legal -> Combined)[101]	0.8317	0.1900	p>.75	6

As indicated by the first and second F-Test, both the Legal Model and Extra-Legal Model are independently significant. This means that the Legal Model explains some judge behavior beyond that which is explained by the Utility-Maximization Model. Likewise, the Extra-Legal Model explains some judge behavior beyond that which is explained by the Utility-Maximization Model. This is consistent with the Chief Judge of the D.C. Circuit's assertion that "A researcher who assumes the existence of ideological bias or strategic behavior may 'find' that these exist, while a

97 See supra part IV.C.

98 F-Test (Util->Legal) is a 9-degree-of freedom test of the restriction that all the coefficients on the Legal variables are zero, in a model that includes all of the Utility Maximization variables as well. The null hypothesis can be rejected at $p < .01$.

99 F-Test (Util->Extra) is a 6-degree-of freedom test of the restriction that all the coefficients on the Extra-Legal variables are zero, in a model that includes all of the Utility Maximization variables as well. The null hypothesis can be rejected at $p < .01$.

100 F-Test (Extra->Combined) is a 9-degree-of freedom test of the restriction that all the coefficients on the Legal variables are zero, in a model that includes all of the Extra-Legal and Utility Maximization variables as well. The null hypothesis can be rejected at $p < .01$.

101 F-Test (Legal->Combined) is a 6-degree-of freedom test of the restriction that all the coefficients on the Extra-Legal variables are zero, in a model that includes all of the Legal and Utility Maximization variables as well. The null hypothesis cannot be rejected at $p < .75$.

researcher who considers alternative explanations may find that what exists is rather different.[102]" This study adds to the literature by doing both, then comparing the findings.

The comparison comes from the third and fourth F-Test, reported above. The third F-Test uses the Extra-Legal Model as a base model, then adds the additional Legal Model variables to generate the Combined Model. This test indicates that using the Extra-Legal Model as the base model, addition of the unique Legal Model variables adds explanatory power with significance of $p < .01$. This means that it is highly likely that Extra-Legal Model does not fully explain judicial decision-making and that the Legal Model explains some portion of outcomes the Extra-Legal Model does not. This conclusion is intuitively validated by a cursory look at Table 3 and Table 4, where the Adjusted R-Squared more than doubles when moving from the Extra-Legal Model to the Combined Model. The fourth F-Test uses the Legal Model as a base model, then adds the additional Extra-Legal Model variables to generate the Combined Model. This test indicates that using the Legal Model as the base model, addition of the unique Extra-Legal Model variables was not shown to add explanatory power, with $p > 0.75$. This means that it is highly unlikely that the Extra-Legal Model explains some portion of outcomes that the Legal Model does not. This conclusion is intuitively validated by a look at Table 2 and Table 4, where the Adjusted R-Squared slightly decreases when moving from the Legal Model to the Combined Model. This finding validates the finding by empirical researchers[103] and assertions by judges that legal factors are highly important to judicial decision-making.

There are many reasons this study might not confirm ideological voting of the sorts typically found. First, many of the Republican appellate judges in the sample had been sitting judges for some time by the latter portion of the sample, and ideological drift could account for deviation from political preferences.[104] Further, judges could be shaping precedent in accord with their ideology in other ways. One suggestion is that judges selectively publish opinions to avoid generating precedent contrary to ideology.[105] Less than 4% of the sample consisted of unpublished opinions, so it does not appear likely that judges are using that particular strategy to generate ideologically-preferable long-term outcomes in these cases.

V. CONCLUSION

When confined to appellate CERCLA litigation from 1996-2009, judges' self-reports indicating that they decide cases based on law are corroborated by empirical evidence. While there is some evidence that judges do respond to incentives and constraints, the results do not indicate that this is made manifest in outcomes. The Legal Model has the most explanatory power of the three models independently tested. While the Legal Model and Extra-Legal Model are each independently significant, the Legal Model does add explanatory power to the Extra-Legal Model while the Extra-Legal Model has not been shown to add explanatory power to the Legal Model. Specifically, the Adjusted R-Squared of Legal Model is slightly decreased with the Combined Model, while the Adjusted R-Squared of the Extra-Legal Model more than doubles with the

102 Harry T. Edwards, Collegiality and Decision Making on the D.C. Circuit, 84 Va. L. Rev. 1335 (1998).

103 Frank B. Cross, Decisionmaking in the U.S. Circuit Courts of Appeals, 91 Cal. L. Rev. 1457 (2003)

104 Lee Epstein, Andrew D. Martin, Kevin M. Quinn & Jeffrey A. Segal, Ideological Drift Among Supreme Court Justices: Who, When, and How Important?, 101 Nw. U. L. Rev. 1483, 1540-41 (2007).

105 David S. Law, Strategic Judicial Lawmaking: Ideology, Publication, and Asylum Law in the Ninth Circuit, 73 U. Cin. L. Rev. 817 (2005)

Combined Model. Most interestingly, the percentage of Republican appointees on an appellate panel was not shown to be significant at even the $p < .25$ level in any model, indicating that raw political preferences may be irrelevant to outcomes. While the political affiliation of the opinion-writer is significant for case outcomes in the Extra-Legal Model and approaches significance Combined Model, the opinion-writer may be a function of outcome as plausibly as the reverse. Thus, when the conclusion is confined properly to the limits of the cases tested, it appears likely that the Legal Model is the most accurate and parsimonious model for judicial decision-making.

Designing Corporate Governance Regimes

Manuel A. Utset[1]

> "Time is a device that was invented to keep everything from happening at once"[2]

Introduction

If survival is a measure of success, then the public corporation has to be considered a highly successful institution. Notwithstanding the periodic prophesies of its imminent demise,[3] the public corporation has not only survived, but proven to be a highly effective mechanism for coordinating the intertemporal decisions[4] of thousands of actors—employees, customers, suppliers, lenders, shareholders, board members, and managers. At this atomic level, the public corporation can be seen as a system and as such bears a resemblance to another system comprising large number of participants—the market.[5] But unlike fully competitive markets, in which each participant has little power to tilt the scales in its favor, the corporation is all about power—about who has it and the consequences that ensue when it is brought to bear. In fact ever since Berle and Means[6] underlined the power asymmetry between shareholders and managers, the governance gap produced by this "separation of ownership and control" has been the "problem" that corporate governance has sought to address, at least in the context of public corporations. After each new round of corporate

---

1 Charles W. Ehrhardt Professor, Florida State University College of Law.

2 See Harold Abelson & Gerald Jay Sussman, Structure and Interpretation of Computer Programs 298, n.35 (2nd ed. 1996).

3 *See, e.g.*, Michael C. Jensen, *Eclipse of the Public Corporation*, 89 HARV. BUS. REV. 61(1989)

4 Intertemporal decisions are those that have deferred consequences; they involve the general problem of how to choose between outcomes that are distributed over time. *See* George F. Lowenstein & Drazen Prelec, *Preferences for Sequences of Outcomes*, *in* CHOICES, VALUES, AND FRAMES 565, 565 (Daniel Kahneman & Amos Tversky eds., 2000); George F. Lowenstein & Richard H. Thaler, *Intertemporal Choice*, 3 J. ECON. PERSP. 181, 181 (defining intertemporal choices as "decisions in which the timing of costs and benefits are spread over time"). For a general discussion of various roles played by time in decision-making, see Dan Ariely & Dan Kakay, *A Timely Account of the Role of Duration in Decision Making*, 108 ACTA PCYH. 187 (2001).

5 A market can be seen as a web of relationships in which actors can cooperate and compete, produce and divide, without knowing the preferences or identities of other participants. *See* Friedrich A. Hayek, *The Use of Knowledge in Society*, *in* INDIVIDUALISM AND ECONOMIC ORDER 77, 86 (1948) (arguing that the price system allows individuals to make the right decisions by merely acting on the price, through which "only the most essential information is passed on and passed on only to those concerned").

6 *See* ADOLF A. BERLE, JR. & GARDINER C. MEANS, THE MODERN CORPORATION AND PRIVATE PROPERTY (1932).

scandals or wholesale market failures, policymakers identify the sources of governance failures and adjust legal rules to make them more robust and reliable, and shareholders and creditors that answer to their own owners promise then greater vigilance and accountability. The two most recent examples of wholesale governance failures, the Enron/WorldCom scandals in 2001 and financial crisis of 2007-2009, led to myriad blue ribbon panels and Congressional hearings and yielded the Sarbanes-Oxley and the Dodd-Frank Acts.

A corporate governance regime can be seen as a set of formal and informal rules to help actors coordinate their behavior and anticipate and deal with conflicts produced by differences in their expectations and preferences. While each corporation is a system to itself, individual corporations cooperate and compete with each other, and thus form a larger system, governed by a broader set of rules. One can further expand the system to which corporate governance applies by including financial intermediaries, which help corporations raise capital and hedge risks, and households, which provide funds to corporations and financial intermediaries and interact with both of them in myriad other contexts. It follows that the first step in designing a governance regime is to specify the system being governed. For example, the governance rules in the Sarbanes-Oxley Act are primarily aimed at individual corporations; on the other hand, those in the Dodd-Frank Act have a broader scope given that the Act casts a regulatory net that extends to corporations, financial intermediaries, and households. Congress cast this wider net in order to identify and address system-wide problems—systemic risk—in a timely fashion, a task made difficult by the web of interconnections between intermediaries, corporations, and households.

This paper approaches the problem of corporate governance from an engineering perspective. It argues that one should design and test corporate governance regimes using formal techniques similar to those developed by engineers to design, test, and update complex concurrent systems.[7] These are systems that are composed of multiple agents or components that interact over time and must synchronize their individual and joint activities to properly share resources, avoid conflicts, and

[7] Although there has been sporadic interest in the role of corporate lawyers as "transaction costs engineers," very little attention has been given to studying the actual mechanics of specification and designs, and particularly the role played by design innovation in the implementation of governance structures. For the seminal piece on transaction cost engineering, Ronald J. Gilson, *Value Creation by Business Lawyers: Legal Skills and Asset Pricing*, 94 YALE L.J. 239 (1984). The role of corporate lawyers is not limited to coming up with mechanisms to reduce transaction costs, but also in dealing with non-strategic coordination problems and reducing internal corporate production costs that have nothing to do with standard notions of transaction costs. *See* Manuel A. Utset, *Producing Information: Initial Public Offerings, Production Costs, and the Producing Lawyer*, 74 OREGON L. REV. 275 (1995) (arguing that lawyers help reduce both transaction and production costs, which arise outside the standard transactional contexts studied by transaction costs economists).

produce the desired system behavior.[8] Corporations are concurrent systems; in fact, computer scientists sometimes refer to business organizations[9] and contract relations[10] when illustrating characteristics of concurrent systems. Engineers have given close attention to the general problem of how to specify and design concurrent systems for the very reason that costly, even catastrophic, system failures are difficult to detect, particularly when system components or actors are able to engage in behavior that cannot be fully observed by others. This can lead to incongruous behavior that can increase the costs of undertaking planned joint activity (or forecloses it altogether).[11] As a result, a designer of a concurrent system has to anticipate, as best as possible, how these different components will interact and extent to which coordination failure can affect the behavior of the system as a whole.[12]

By using a set of "governance rules" to govern the design and testing of concurrent systems, engineers have been able to build large, extremely complex, safety critical systems that are robust and reliable. As a general matter, a system is robust if it behaves reasonably well even when it encounters unforeseen contingencies.[13] A system's reliability is in turn a function of how well it meets its specifications—i.e., it's stated goals or intended behavior.[14] A designers ability to prove a

[8] These formal methods, which we will refer to generally as process algebras, were developed precisely to deal with the problem of designing systems in which the joint activities of actors mattered and can lead to implementation errors and indeterminacy. Importantly the actors modeled included both artificial computer processes and the human being who interact with them, particularly in contexts in which there is a low tolerance for erroneous results or system deadlocks. *See* C.A.R. HOARE, COMMUNICATING SEQUENTIAL PROCESSES (2004) (setting forth formal methods used to specify, implement, and test concurrent systems to deal with indeterminacy and system deadlocks; ROBIN MILNER, COMMUNICATION AND CONCURRENCY (1989) (introducing calculus of communicating systems which models interactions between agents as a series of synchronization activities); STEVE SCHNEIDER, CONCURRENT AND REAL-TIME SYSTEMS: THE CSP APPROACH (2000) (discussing theory of real-time concurrent systems).

[9] *See* Milner, COMMUNICATION, *supra* note __, at 11 (referring to companies as networks of departments, which in turn are networks of people).

[10] *See, e.g.*, Roscoe *supra* note __, at 9 (describing approach to modeling a transaction between a customer and store as either a single sale event or as composed of independent parts, such as "offer, acceptance, money, change").

[11] *See* HOARE, *supra* note __ (goal of process algebra is to provide formal methods that can be used to identify errors in indeterminate concurrent systems that are not open to standard testing techniques used in systems that execute sequentially).

[12] *See* Schneider, *supra* note __, at v (stating that system complexity due to components that execute in parallel and interact in non-obvious ways, and that one goal of designers is to understand the extent and result of these interactions, in order to keep them under control).

[13] Carlo Ghezzi et. al., *Software Qualities and Principles*, *in* THE COMPUTER SCIENCE AND ENGINEERING HANDBOOK 2278, 2282 (Allen B. Tucker, ed., 1997) (defining robustness of systems).

[14] A "specification" is a description of the desired properties or behavior of the system being built. A "design" is a blueprint or abstract plan of a system meeting the specifications. Finally, an "implementation" is the actual instantiation of the system. There will often be more than one way to implement a system; but the goal is to achieve an implementation that can be verified to meet the specification, and thus behave correctly. One may then choose between different equivalent specification using other metrics, such as cost-effectiveness, robustness, or amenability to future

system's correctness—that it is guaranteed to meet its specifications—can be important where system errors can produce significant harm—e.g., railway crossings, hospital equipment, and nuclear power plants.[15] However, formally proving that a system will meet its specification—i.e., showing correctness—is extremely difficult, except in relatively simple systems.[16] The best that system implementers can hope for is to show that the system is reliable, in that its behavior stays within a specified interval of acceptable error.

As we have seen, concurrent systems are highly complex because the interconnections between the various components change over time in an indeterminate fashion. The goals of this paper are to introduce some of the formal tools that engineers use to pierce through the complexity of concurrent systems and address their inherent indeterminacy, and to provide some examples of how these tools can be used for making sense of the complexity of corporations and governance regimes. It is not my intention in this paper to develop a complete theory of the design of governance regimes.

Part I argues that the standard conception of corporate complexity fails to take into account the important role played by the multi-dimensional "social dependence" of corporate participants, and intertemporal nature of their relationships. Part II first describes the general problem of designing corporate governance regimes, in light of the inherent complexity of public corporations. It then describes the relevant aspects of the tools used by engineers to design and test concurrent systems. After that, it shows how one can extend the general insights from the concurrency approach to the problem of specifying, designing, and verifying the reliability of corporate governance regimes. Part III develops some additional implications of the approach discussed in Part II. Part IV provides a conclusion.

I. Complexity Matters: Social and Intertemporal Dependence

This Part begins by providing an overview of corporate complexity and then describes two sources of complexity that have not received adequate attention in corporate law theories: the social

modifications. *See, e.g.,* Ghezzi et. al., supra note __, at 2281-82 (describing the often iterative process from specification to implementation).

15 This is often done either by showing that the specification can be transformed into an implementation by carrying out a series of logical steps or functional transformations of the specification. *See* RICHARD BIRD, INTRODUCTION TO FUNCTIONAL PROGRAMMING USING HASKELL (1998) (describing use of functional composition to transform specification into correct implementation, within the pure functional language Haskell).

16 In fact, software designers know that it is virtually impossible to produce software that can be guaranteed to be correct; nonetheless, computer scientists have developed a number of formal methods to prove correctness of at least *parts* of systems in which real-time errors can be costly. *See* Ghezzi et. al., supra note __, at 2282.

dependence of corporate actors and the intertemporal nature of their relationships.[17] The last section argues that complexity matters only when decision-makers have limited time and resources to make sense of it; that is, only if they have bounded rationality.

A. Corporate Complexity

What does it mean to say that an organization, a bureaucracy, or set of legal rules, such as the tax code, is complex?[18] The complexity of an object or system[19] is a function of the number of parts that it has and the ways in which they interact.[20] What does it mean for the components of a system to interact with each other? We will say that two objects interact, when the behavior of each influences the other, and where some coordination is required. Human interactions differ in a variety of ways: they can be consensual or imposed by a third party and require different levels of coordination, cooperation,[21] planning,[22] and intersection of intentions.[23] A competitive market, by definition, has many components in the form of buyers and sellers; however, market participants

[17] It should not be assumed that increasing the complexity of a system is necessarily bad, since complexity can be used to achieve other goals. A person who wants to stop smoking, but has trouble committing to it may prefer a system for acquiring cigarettes that is complex—i.e., that imposes a high immediate deliberation cost, since the same pull of immediate gratification that can lead her to override a long-term preference to stop smoking can cause her to procrastinate purchasing cigarettes. Complexity in short can act as a commitment device to overcome self-control problems. See Manuel A. Utset, *Hyperbolic Criminals and Repeated Time-Inconsistent Misconduct*, 44 HOUSTON L. REV. 609, 662-63 (2007) (discussing use of legal rules as "off-the-rack" or default commitment devices).

[18] For an early exposition of the importance of organizational and administrative complexity see HERBERT A. SIMON, ADMINISTRATIVE BEHAVIOR (3d ed. 1976). For a discussion of complexity of legal rules and contracts see Louis Kaplow, *A Model of the Optimal Complexity of Legal Rules*, 11 J. L. ECON. & ORG. 150 (1995).

[19] I will use the term "system" in a non-technical sense of a group of related objects that interact with each other in some regular way. While some of the general discussion below regarding systems and recursive governance can be applied to complex or dynamic systems—those, whose complexity is due to the manner in which system outputs feed back upon themselves—I am concerned with more basic issues of static and dynamic complexity within organizations.

[20] Herbert Simon, defined a complex system as "one made up of a large number of parts that have many interactions," where its complexity will increase whenever, given "the properties of the parts and the laws of their interaction, it is not a trivial matter to infer the properties of the whole" *See* HERBERT A. SIMON, THE SCIENCES OF THE ARTIFICIAL 183–84, 207 (3d ed. 1996).

[21] There are well-known obstacles to achieving cooperation within large groups. These collective action problems have been widely studies and help explain why shareholder voting is a relatively weak governance device. *See* MANCUR OLSON, THE LOGIC OF COLLECTIVE ACTION.

[22] *See* MICHAEL E. BRATMAN, INTENTIONS, PLANS, AND PRACTICAL REASON 10-11 (1987) (discussing the problem of decision-making by individuals given bounded rationality, and the role of planning in reducing the bounded rationality constraint).

[23] The concept of "shared intentions" developed by analytic philosophers can valuably apply to many areas of law, as it helps clarify a number of difficult questions regarding what it means to be a part of a group and the relationship between interpersonal and intrapersonal coordination in groups. *See* Michael E. Bratman, *Shared Intention*, *in* FACES OF INTENTION: SELECTED ESSAYS ON INTENTION AND AGENCY 110–13 (1999) (developing the theory of shared intentions that emphasizes the role of such intentions in intra and interpersonal coordination, as well as in intragroup bargaining and conflict resolution); John R. Searle, *Collective Intentions and Actions*, *in* CONSCIOUSNESS AND LANGUAGE 90 (2002) (developing an account of collective intentions that draws sharp distinction between individual and collective intentions).

interact along a well-defined interface—in the form of prices—which transfers information about the aggregate behavior of all participants.[24] On the other hand, a system with few parts may be complex, if the interface between them is not well-calibrated or involves multiple points of contact—i.e., it requires a greater amount of communication or coordination. For example, when two English-speaking individuals communicate they do so via a more reliable interface than that used by two individuals who do not share the same language and thus have to resort to the much more under-specified syntax and semantics of hand gestures.[25]

Public corporations are highly complex systems, given that they are composed of a large number of actors who, over time, interact with each other in a variety of ways, with incomplete information, and in the shadow of legal rules, contracts, and markets, which are themselves complex. People are also extremely complex along multiple dimensions: their DNA, bodies, minds, as well as their plans, interests, and emotions, and all the other things affecting their behavior. And yet when we interact with each other and corporations, we seem to manage quite well; moreover, when we set out in these transactions between obviously complex entities, we give relatively little attention to their myriad parts and way that they are brought together to form a whole.[26] Paradoxically, the fact that we can proceed in our daily lives oblivious to much of the complexity around and within us only underlines the importance of thinking about the general problem. There is obvious value to well-worn solutions, whose operation becomes automatic or second-nature; but their very invisibility in our deliberation process can also create costs. For example, people transacting in complex

---

[24] The classic exposition of this view is by Hayek:

The problem which we pretend to solve is how the spontaneous interaction of a number of people, each possessing only bits of knowledge, brings about a state of affairs in which prices correspond to costs, etc. and which could be brought about by deliberate direction only by somebody who possessed the combined knowledge of all those individuals.

See Frederick Hayek, *The Use of Knowledge in Society*, 35 AM. ECON. REV. 519, 521 (1945).

[25] The complexity is due in part to the indeterminacy of communicating by pointing and through hand gestures. In fact early work on coordination problems by the philosopher David Lewis developed out of the problem of indeterminacy of translation introduced by the logician Quine. *See* WILLARD VAN ORMAND QUINE, WORD & OBJECt 29-30 (1960) (describing indeterminacy of translation); DAVID K. LEWIS, CONVENTION: A PHILOSOPHICAL STUDY 24-36 (1969). *See also* KENNETH ARROW, THE LIMITS OF ORGANIZATION 55-59 (1974) (discussing importance of communication channels and shared codes, or formal and informal understandings of way information will be transmitted within organizations).

[26] While evolutionary forces have provided us with senses that automatically transform complex environments into pared-down streams of data, it does not follow that we should necessarily rely on the "evolutionary forces" of competitive markets to make our experience of complex corporate institutions or legal rules manageable. *See* SAMUEL BOWLES, MICROECONOMICS: BEHAVIOR, INSTITUTIONS, AND EVOLUTION 344-49 (2004).

environments often resort to decisional short-cuts; using heuristics helps economize on deliberation costs, but they can also lead to systematic deviations from full rationality.[27]

B. Social Dependence

Social dependence relations are ubiquitous across settings touched by law,[28] economics,[29] and ethics.[30] For example, Robert Nozick argued that these mutual connections between people's actions provide the "background that gives rise to ethics."[31] At the same time, social dependence within particular legal contexts can be pervasive, multi-dimensional, and thus complex; as a result, when they are acknowledged in legal analyses it is usually, as the first step in abstracting away from them to focus on more tractable aspects of problems, or alternatively as part of arguments regarding legal indeterminacy.

I will say that a person X is *socially dependent* to Y if two conditions are met: (1) X has a goal that can be brought about if someone takes an action; and (2) X cannot carry out that action alone, but Y can.[32] When two individuals have the same or different goals that can only be brought about by the participation of the other person, they are mutually dependent.[33] For example, if Joe's goal is to marry Sally, Joe is socially dependent on Sally saying "I do," and if Sally's goal is to marry Joe, they

---

[27] *See* Amos Tversky & Daniel Kahneman, *Judgment Under Uncertainty: Heuristics and Biases*, *in* JUDGMENT UNDER UNCERTAINTY: HEURISTICS AND BIASES 3 (Daniel Kahneman, Paul Slovic, Amos Tversky eds., 1982) (arguing that heuristics have benefits and costs, and can lead to systematic—i.e., non-random—deviations from rational behavior).

[28] *See, e.g.,* JOHN RAWLS, A THEORY OF JUSTICE (1970) (developing theory of justice based on choices made behind veil of ignorance in which actors know that they are in social context, but are unaware of the set of social dependent relations in which they are involved).

[29] *See e.g.*, Gerard Debreu, THEORY OF VALUE: AN AXIOMATIC ANALYSIS OF ECONOMIC EQUILIBRIUM 90-97 (1959) (describing theory of general equilibrium in economics).

[30] *See* R. JAY WALLACE, *Reason and Responsibility*, *in* NORMATIVITY AND THE WILL: SELECTED PAPERS ON MORAL PSYCHOLOGY AND PRACTICAL REASON, 123, 123–24 (2006) (describing expectations of behavior in moral communities as reactive sentiments and judgments).

[31] *See* ROBERT NOZICK, INVARIANCES 240-41 (2001) (discussing mutual dependence where the actions of individuals are connected in nontrivial ways and require ethical coordination).

[32] *See* Michael N. Huhns & Larry M, Stephens, *Multiagent Systems and Societies of Agents*, *in* MULTIAGENT SYSTEMS: A MODERN APPROACH TO DISTRIBUTED ARTIFICIAL INTELLIGENCE 83, 113 (Gerhard Weiss ed., 2000) (discussing concept of socially dependent autonomous agents) (stating that person X is socially dependent on person Y whenever the following two conditions hold: (1) person X has a goal, G, that can be brought about (completely or in part) about is someone takes action, A; and (2) person X cannot do A herself but person Y can).

[33] That is, individuals are in a state of mutual dependence whenever: (1) person X has goal G1, which requires actionA1, and person Y has goal G2, which requires actions A2; and (2) person X cannot take action A1, but person Y can, and person Y cannot take action A2, but person X can; where, actions A1 and A2 are necessarily distinct, but goals G1 and G2 can be the same or different goals. *Id.* Dependence relationships may be symmetric or asymmetric in nature.

are in a mutual dependence relationship.[34] Additionally, they cannot marry unless a third party with the proper authority performs the ceremony; that third party will in turn depend on an agent of the state—e.g., the legislature—to grant it the authority to perform the marriage. The legislature depends on others, the voters who elected them, the judges that interpret relevant constitutional provisions, regarding the legislature's own authority, and so on. There are three important points here. First, a web of socially dependent relationships can be extensive and complex, even in relatively simple transactions such as this one, let alone those within large public corporations. Second, social dependence may arise through voluntary or autonomous acts—e.g., entering into a contract—but it does not have to. A person who has a heart attack in a restaurant is socially dependent on other present to perform CPR. Third, people may voluntarily put themselves in socially dependent relationships only to find out later that the costs of terminating them is too costly, as in cases in which transaction-specific investments makes a party vulnerable to opportunistic behavior.[35]

Agency relationships are one example of social dependence, given that a principal hires an agent to act on her behalf to achieve some goal, and does so because of a belief that she can maximize her net returns if the agent is the one who takes the required actions.[36] However, the agency approach is concerned with the basic issue of how to realign the incentives of self-interested agents so that they coincide with those of their principals. Social dependence is a more general concept—for example two individuals can be in a socially dependent situation even if neither of them knows of the existence of the other.[37] In other words, a necessary condition of an agency relationship is the parties' awareness of the agency roles that they are playing.

Finally, when we govern our bodies, corporations, and societies, we resort to one set of dependence relations to manage a second; this is the case whether we are involved in self-governance or delegate

---

34 Some statements, like saying "I do" or "I promise" within well-specified contexts are actions in the sense that they produce a result other than merely transferring information, and are referred to as performatives. *See* J. L. AUSTIN, HOW TO DO THING WITH WORDS 7-11 (J.O. Urmson & Marina Sbisa ed., 2nd Edition 1975).

35 *See* OLIVER WILLIAMSON, MARKETS AND HIERARCHIES 52-56 (1975) (discussing bilateral monopolies and opportunistic renegotiations due to transaction-specific investments).

36 *See* John W. Pratt & Richard J. Zeckhauser, *Principals and Agents: An Overview*, *in* PRINCIPALS AND AGENTS: THE STRUCTURE OF BUSINESS 1, 2 (John W. Pratt & Richard J. Zeckhauser eds., 1985) (stating that agency problem can arise when one individual depends on the actions or behavior of another).

37 *See* CHESTER I. BARNARD, THE FUNCTIONS OF THE EXECUTIVE 91-92 (1938) (discussing "observational feeling"—decisions in groups "arrived at, and acted upon without having ever been formulated by anybody"). The environment in which actors transact is "objective" in the sense that it exists and affect their behavior whether or not they fully understand or are even aware of all the constraints imposed on their actions. For example, we go through most of our lives without giving much thought to the fact that we are constrained by gravity or about the nature of the oxygen that we are breathing in; a person climbing Mt. Everest on the other hand will be keenly aware of the effect of both. *See* ROBERT NOZICK, supra note __ (providing such a definition of "objective").

the task to lawmakers and markets. This second-order social dependence increases the complexity of the governance task, and thus limits the extent to which a group of actors can resort to a set of governance rules to reduce the risks created by their first-order social dependence. As a result, in order to design effective governance regimes, those designing it have to address this second-order, governance complexity.

C. Social Dependence in Corporations

Corporate participants pool capital, labor, and expertise, and repeatedly interact over time, sharing those resources in order to produce and distribute surpluses that they then divide among themselves.[38] As a result, shareholder, board members, managers, creditors, employees, and other constituencies depend on each other to help realize goals at both the individual and collective levels. A corporate actor may depend on one or more other actors, and do so along a number of dimensions. It follows that a corporation's complexity will depend both on the number of participants and the nature of these dependencies, including their multidimensionality. Social dependence reveals an interest and willingness of corporate actors to engage in a cooperative enterprise; although they may each have different reasons for putting themselves in such a relation, these possibly divergent interests do intersect in an important way: the actors believe that others within the firm can help. A person who ceases to believe in the value of being part of the firm will eventually exit. Nonetheless, a willingness to cooperate is not a sufficient condition to bring it about[39]; cooperation also requires coordination,[40] at the physical, temporal, and epistemic levels.[41]

---

[38] I will refer to the various corporate constituencies as "corporate actors" or, where the context allows, merely as "participants"; and to board members and officers/managers collectively as "managers," unless the context requires drawing a distinction between the two.

[39] *See* Simon, *Administrative Behavior*, *supra* note __ at 72-73 (stating that "cooperation will usually be ineffective—will not reach its goal, whatever the intentions of the participants—in the absence of coordination"); Barnard, *Function of the Executive*, *supra* note __ at 6 (arguing that "the survival of an organization depends upon the maintenance of an equilibrium of complex character in continuously changing environment...which calls for adjustments of processes internal to the organization").

[40] *See* THOMAS C. SCHELLING, THE STRATEGY OF CONFLICT 54-57 (1960) (describing role of focal points in overcoming coordination problems); DAVID K. LEWIS, CONVENTION: A PHILOSOPHICAL STUDY (1969) (discussing coordination problem from philosophical perspective and developing concept of common knowledge); DAVID HUME, A TREATISE OF HUMAN NATURE 489-90 (L. A. Selby-Bigge ed. Oxford Univ. Press 1978) (classic treatment of coordination problem and contracting relationships); DREW FUNDENBERG & JEAN TIROLE, GAME THEORY 18-20 (1991) (providing formal treatment of coordination games).

[41] This general problem of epistemic coordination within organizations has received close attention in the transaction cost, agency, and property rights literatures. *See* KENNETH ARROW, THE LIMITS OF ORGANIZATION 53-59 (1974) (discussing the role of information channels and communication codes within organizations); OLIVER WILLIAMSON, MARKETS AND HIERARCHIES 31-33 (1975) (discussing "information impactness" and its relation to opportunistic behavior); Michael C. Jensen & William H. Meckling, *Specific and General Knowledge and Organizational Structure, in*

Achieving coordination along these three dimensions is not a straightforward exercise and one fraught with the potential for failure, which can be costly, even if that failure is temporary in nature.

D. Temporal Complexity

Corporations are embedded within a temporal frame. They are abstract entities, brought into existence by the filing of a certificate of incorporation and persisting until they are dissolved, merged, or terminated by the state. Temporal issues come into play whenever the consequences of decisions—in the form of costs and benefits—are experienced at different points in time, as well as in situations in which the order in which events occur affect the overall outcome. As a general matter, a rational person will take an action in the current period if it is intertemporally worthwhile: if given her belief of how she plans to act in the future, the action maximizes her current *and* future well-being.[42] In making the determination, she will try to predict two things that may change over time: (1) her preferences and those of others—e.g., other corporate actors; and (2) the environment in which her actions will unfold and payoffs materialize.

This means that corporate actors will be in a series of intertemporal dependent relations, not just with others, but also with their past and future selves.[43] In other words, even when parties do not need to coordinate their actions with others, they still may have to plan the behavior of their temporally extended selves.[44] For example, managers must determine how much general and firm-specific human capital to acquire, which in turn will be influenced by their age, the outside employment options they expect to have, and more generally by how long they expect to be employed by the firm.[45] In the same manner, a shareholder must determine how much effort to expend monitoring managers and when to do so, which in turn will depend on the size of its

CONTRACTS ECONOMICS 251 (Lars Werin & Hans Wijkander eds., 1992) (discussing agency costs associated with control of knowledge).

42 *See* Ted O'Donoghue & Matthew Rabin, *Choice and Procrastination*, 116 Q.J. ECON. 121, 128 (2001) (setting up a general model where people act with reasonable beliefs about future actions and choose current actions to maximize preferences in light of those beliefs).

43 Economists sometimes model an intertemporal decision-maker as: (1) a current self with current preferences, and (2) a series of separate "agents," one for each point in time between current choices and future consequences. The current agent will make choices to maximize her current preferences, but her future selves will control her behavior. *See* Ted O'Donoghue & Matthew Rabin, *Doing It Now or Later*, AM. ECON. REV., March 1999. *See also* Derek Parfit, *Personal Identity*, 80 PHIL. REV. 3, 26–27 (1971) (arguing that individuals discount future payoffs because of changes in identity over time—a diminution of the connection between our present and future selves); Roland Bénabou & Jean Tirole, *Self-Knowledge and Self-Regulation: An Economic Approach*, *in* 1 THE PSYCHOLOGY OF ECONOMIC DECISIONS 137, 138 (Isabelle Brocas & Juan D. Carrillo eds., 2003) (arguing that actors "who usually populate economic models have little doubt about 'who they are': they know their own abilities and basic preferences").

44 *See* MICHAEL E. BRATMAN, INTENTION, PLANS, AND PRACTICAL REASON 29–30 (1987) (defining "plans" as "mental states involving an appropriate . . . commitment to action" and discussing the contingent, reversible nature of plans).

45 *See* Bratman, *Intentions, Plans, supra* note __ at 33-34 (discussing how prior intentions and plans provide a background framework used to weigh various options regarding potential actions).

holdings, how long it expects to own the shares, tax considerations, and the level of diversification of its portfolio.[46]

E. Bounded Rationality

In making a decision, a fully rational actor will use all of the information in its possession that is relevant to that decision—this is true both for computers and individuals.[47] A computer may fall short of full rationality if given the speed of its central processing unit it does not have enough storage, memory, and time to carry out the requisite computations.[48] People too have limited time, memory, and computational power,[49] and thus will face the same type of "bounded rationality" constraints as computers.[50] The concept of bounded rationality was introduced into computer science by Herbert Simon in the 1950's and subsequently imported into economics[51] and law.[52] From a design perspective, complexity matters only to the extent that a decision-maker faces a bounded rationality constraint that is in fact binding.[53] As we will now see, one way to deal with the

---

[46] The rise of mutual funds, hedge funds, and securitization and derivatives markets over the last thirty years can all be seen, at least in part, as ways of helping individual shareholders, managers, employees, and debt-holders to resolve their own intertemporal coordination problems.

[47] *See* ROBERT NOZICK, THE NATURE OF RATIONALITY 64-75 (1993) (describing decision-making procedure of rational actors).

[48] *See* JOHN VON NEUMANN, THE COMPUTER AND THE BRAIN (1958) (describing computer architecture, whose only necessary components are immediately available storage—memory—and a processing unit to process instructions, and is generally known as von Neumann computer; other types of storage and peripherals to facilitate input and output are now common, but ultimately not necessary).

[49] *See* HERBERT A. SIMON, 1 MODELS OF THOUGHT 3 (1979) (arguing that "human thinking powers are very modest when compared with the complexities of the environments in which human beings live").

[50] *See* HERBERT A. SIMON, THE SCIENCE OF THE ARTIFICIAL 36 (2d ed. 1981) (describing the boundedly rational decision-maker as "a satisficer, a person who accepts 'good enough' alternatives, not because he prefers less to more, but because he has no choice"); ARIEL RUBINSTEIN, MODELING BOUNDED RATIONALITY 107-120 (1998) (discussing various approaches to modeling bounded rationality within groups).

[51] *See* Glenn Ellison, *Bounded Rationality*, *in* INDUSTRIAL ORGANIZATION IN ADVANCES IN ECONOMICS AND ECONOMETRICS: THEORY AND APPLICATIONS, NINTH WORLD CONGRESS, VOL. II 142, 150-52 (Richard Blundell, Whitney K. Newey, & Torsten Persson, eds., 2006) (summarizing theoretical and empirical literature on learning in complex environments, when parties interact repeatedly); OLIVER WILLIAMSON, THE ECONOMIC INSTITUTIONS OF CAPITALISM (1995) (setting forth options available to contracting parties generally, given bounded rationality, incomplete contracting, and transaction costs).

[52] *See* Christine Jolls, Cass R. Sunstein & Richard Thaler, *A Behavioral Approach to Law and Economics*, 50 STAN. L. REV. 1471, 1477-78 (1998) (discussing bounded rationality and heuristics issues within legal context).

[53] This means that one approach is to leave the level of complexity alone and instead reduce temporal constraints and/or supplement human computational power with that of a computer. This has become an increasingly attractive possibility given recent improvements in computer memory storage, and processor power, developments in peer-to-peer networks, and proliferation of highly sophisticated financial management systems. Interestingly, in a lecture entitled *Will the Corporation Be Managed By Machines?*, delivered in the early 1960s, Simon predicted "that we will have the technical capability, by 1985, to manage corporations by machines, although humans will continue to play an important role, given that machines will be able to engage in symbolic computation and problem solving, but will be constrained by their

design of very complex systems is through a divide-and-conquer technique in which different parts of the system are designed and tested independently and eventually glued together to create the complete system. However, in order to use such a recursive approach, the designer has to understand how the various components interact with each other. One way to reduce the complexity of making sense of these potential interactions is to create clear boundaries between components—for example, by specifying when they are allowed to interact, and when they are prohibited from doing so. This is in fact the very approach used to design concurrent systems.

II. A Theory of Concurrent Corporate Governance

Part I described three important sources of corporate complexity: the number of actors involved, their social dependence, and the intertemporal nature of their interactions. Complexity is not an absolute constraint, but one that can be managed by making adjustments along two dimensions: (1) reducing the number of system components; and (2) increasing the efficiency and reliability of the interactions between them by modifying the interface through which they communicate and engage in joint behavior. Of these two, the second one is the more important for the law, given that policymakers often want to add more rules to an already complex system of laws. For example, if one accepts that it would be valuable to simplify a set of rules, such as the tax code or a regulatory framework, it does not follow that one has to reduce the number of rules; instead one can make rules more self-contained, such as by limiting the way that they interact with or depend on other rules in the system. Engineers have given great attention to developing techniques to better describe, understand, and manage complexity so that they can continue to add additional components to already complex systems.[54] Since the bounded computational abilities of humans and machines are analogous, it makes sense to look at the way that engineers have handled the issue.[55] With this in mind, this Part will address the following two questions. If an engineer were hired to specify, design, and implement a corporate governance regime, how would she approach the task? What design methodologies would she use to address the problems raised by the inherent

relative inability to see and move." HERBERT A. SIMON, THE SHAPE OF AUTOMATION: FOR MEN AND MANAGEMENT 49 (1965).

[54] For example, computer scientists for example have been able to greatly increase the speed and efficiency of microprocessors and system memory, and developed algorithms whose execution take less time and space, computer languages that help produce source code that is easier to understand and change. *See* HANDBOOK OF ENGINEERING, *supra* note __.

[55] This is not to say that legal academics have not focused on identifying areas in which complexity, bounded rationality, and heuristics affect the behavior of actors; however, progress in the second part of the enterprise, that of developing tools and theories to directly and consciously address the complexity problem, has lagged behind.

complexity of corporations, discretion of corporate agents, and physical and strategic obstacles to observing their behavior?

A. Managing Complexity

The first step in designing any governance mechanism is to specify: (1) who will be using it—that is, the identity of the governing party and of the governed; (2) the types of actions available to each party, including when those actions are feasible, and whether they can be undertaken independently of each other or require the participation of both; (3) the information that each party has available at the time of acting; and (4) the consequences of those actions, including the payoffs received by each party.[56] However, given the complexity problems, the second task that the governance designer faces is that of identifying the sources of complexity, the tools available to it to make the actions of parties more transparent.

1. The Art of Abstraction

One of the principal ways in which engineers deal with complexity is through the use of abstractions. For example, if a system has 1,000 parts, each with their own independent identity, we may just choose to ignore the independence of some of them by embedding them in groups of like types.[57] We then attach a name or identity to each group and forget about their different, but conceptually equivalent members.[58] A user interacting with such a compound object will do so through a limited interface which, if all goes well, provides it with all of the information it needs to use the object. Information about the internal workings of the object is hidden from the user. There is often more than one way of abstracting from the underlying complexity of a system, and the one chosen will usually depend on the identity of the individuals using the system and the nature of their relationship with it. For example, a geneticist, neurologist, and painter will each have a

[56] This is partly the way that one would go about specifying a game, for a game theory model, although in the latter one would also specify other factors, such as the strategies available to each party, the equilibrium concept being used, and the extent to which the players have common knowledge about certain aspects of the game. *See* DREW FUNDENBERG & JEAN TIROLE, GAME THEORY 4-9 (1991).
[57] *See* Robert Cecil Martin, DESIGNING OBJECT-ORIENTED C++ APPLICATIONS: USING THE BOOCH METHOD 9 (1995) (stating that abstraction involves the "elimination of the irrelevant and the amplification of the essential").
[58] *See* Abelson & Sussman, *supra* note __, at 4 (describing abstraction technique by which "compound elements can be named and manipulated as units").

different take on the human body.[59] In other words, the interface between each of them and the bodies with whom they interact will differ: they will observe and communicate with them at different levels of abstraction.[60]

2. Choosing Corporate Abstractions

Thus, one way of reducing corporate complexity is to hide from corporate participants information that is superfluous to the type of governance decisions that they will have to make. But how should one do this? One way is to make certain behavioral assumptions about what motivates the various participants, and use these to categorize them; a second way is to adopt the ontology provided by corporate law, dividing participants into shareholders, managers, boards members, creditors, and so on. However, the resulting abstractions are not identical. For example, shareholders may have different goals, risk-tolerance, and time horizons, as may also board members and managers. There are other ways of categorizing corporate participants, but the key point in that the scheme chosen has positive and normative consequences; at the very least, it will carve out and privilege certain features of the real world for observation and manipulation by laws and contracts. Given that we are concerned with the way that social dependence affects the decision-making process of corporate participants, we will focus on abstractions that are well-suited for dealing with the complexity involved when parties are involved in repeated interactions, but are not in constant contact with each other. That is, contexts in which participants will come together intermittently to carry out particular corporate actions, and must predict the extent to which they will be able to coordinate their behavior when they are called to do so.

B. Designing Reliable Concurrent Systems

Concurrent systems are composed of socially dependent components or actors. In order to design reliable systems, the designer has to understand how the various components coordinate or synchronize their joint behavior over time. The inherent indeterminacy of concurrent systems makes it difficult to use standard abstraction techniques, which are best suited for contexts in which the nature of the interactions among components remains stable over time.[61] In order to deal with

---

[59] *See* Milner, *supra* note __, at 11 (stating that the level of decomposition used depends on the goal of the model: "we do not treat a person as a network of parts when we are interested in companies, though this treatment is essential for the anatomist").
[60] *See* Simon *supra* note __, at 84 (stating that fact "that many complex systems have a nearly decomposable, hierarchic structure is a major facilitating factor enabling us to understand, describe, and even 'see' such systems and their parts").
[61] The inherent indeterminacy of concurrent systems, means that it is not possible to test them in the usual manner—i.e., by executing them repeatedly with inputs chosen to identify deviations from the specification—since the same set of

this indeterminacy, an engineer will try to model or simulate the potential courses of action available to components and extent to which a component will be in a position to join in a joint action with other components when it is called to do so.[62].

1. The Concurrency Problem

The general concurrency problem can be stated as follows. Suppose that there are two socially dependent actors or components, each with a set of actions available to it. Moreover, each of these actions may be appropriate or available at particular points in an actor's *action-sequence*[63] but foreclosed or impossible at others.[64] More specifically, the actions available to an actor at any one point in time, will bc a function of the state in which it is then in; moreover, each time that an actor acts, it moves to a new state, which may have the same or some other actions available (or none).[65] Actors are expected to interact or participate in joint activities, at various points in time; however, given that the order in which actions occur matters, an actor will be able to participate in a joint activity only if it is at a juncture in its action-sequence in which the action called for in that joint activity is available to it—i.e., if it is in the appropriate state. When actors interact they are able to

---

inputs can trigger different interactions and thus lead to different results. In short, testing a system will provide only an incomplete assessment of reliability. *See* Hoare, *supra* note __ (discussing problems in testing concurrent systems).

[62] One important part of this exercise is to formally specify how two executions of system components can be compared to determine whether they are equivalent. Once a reliable solutions has been found, the designer can use it or substitute an equivalent one that has other properties, such as being more efficient. Efficiency by itself is not a sufficient condition for choosing between two potential approaches, given that neither may meet the specifications for the system. A similar approach can be used in designing legal institutions, where one would first create a specification, find a solution that meets that specification, compare it to other solutions that are equivalent along the dimensions in the specification, but which may differ along other ones, such as transaction costs or general operational efficiency. By separating the task of finding an actual solution from other normative goals, one can reduce the risk that normative constraints will reduce the space of institutional innovation.

[63] A sequence of n objects or components is an ordered set (or n-tuple) where the component are identified by their position in the set. More formally, if $a_1, a_2 \ldots, a_n$ are the components, then a sequence is an ordered n-tuple, $(a_1,a_2,\ldots,a_n)$, where n is the length of that sequence. For example, the following two sequences are not equivalent. A = (a, b, c, c) and B = (b, a, c, c). Moreover, unlike sets where we are only concerned about the identity of members, in a sequence we not only care about the identity and order of the components, but also how many times they occur. In other words, under set notation A and B would be the same set: {a, b, c}. *See, e.g.,* HARRY R. LEWIS & CHRISTOS H. PAPADIMITRIOU, ELEMENTS OF THE THEORY OF COMPUTATION 10 (2nd ed. 1998) (defining sequences).

[64] *See* Schneider, *supra* note __, at 85 (stating that an important property of an agent's behavior is the "occurrence of events in the right order, and that events do not occur at inappropriate times").

[65] Computer scientists model sequential behavior as automatons, each of which is defined by a set of states and transitions: (1) a start state; (2) an acceptance state; (3) a set of transition between states such that s1 → s2 means that there is an action that will cause a transition from s1 to s2. An automaton is finite if it has a finite set of states and deterministic if for each state s and transition there is only one state to which s can move. *See, e.g.,* HARRY R. LEWIS & CHRISTOS H. PAPADIMITRIOU, ELEMENTS OF THE THEORY OF COMPUTATION 55-57 (2nd ed. 1998) (defining finite automaton) *See* Abeson & Sussman, *supra* note __, at 80 (stating that state-variable can be used to capture the state of an actor at any one point).

observe the result of their joint behavior; or equivalently, they can ascertain the state to which each transitions. However, actors in concurrent systems are not in constant interaction; in fact, it is expected that, in between any two interactions, they will engage in independent or autonomous behavior, which may or may not be observable to others. If their independent behavior is always observable, then there is no concurrency issue but to the extent that it is not actors may be unable to participate in required or planned interactions.

To summarize. Actors in a concurrent system will each engage in a sequence of actions over time, where some will be independent and others will involve the participation of others. In order for these joint actions to occur (or to avoid mistakes or inefficient interactions), each actor has to be in a state in which that behavior is available to it. This means that the extent to which an actor can depend on another will be a function of its ability to predict whether that other actor will be able to engage in the required behavior at the appropriate time. That second actor will be completely "transparent" if all of its independent actions are observable, but will become increasingly opaque or indeterminate the more of those actions that are beyond observation.

2. Observation and Synchronization Events

Thus the designer of a concurrent system needs to find some way of dealing with the non-observable behavior of actors. The key breakthrough in the design of these systems came with the realization that in many cases one can simply ignore non-observable behavior; with the critical proviso, that they should be ignored in a principled, well-thought-out manner. The standard concurrency model has the following properties. First, an actor is completely defined by the set of *observable* actions that it can engage in,[66] the order in which these can occur, and the types of interactions with others that they are expected to undertake.[67] Moreover, an actor's behavior can be observable to one or more other actors, but may be unobservable to third parties. Second, two actors can observe each other if and only if they engage in a joint activity or interaction—which is

[66] More formally, an actor's complete action set is composed of the observable-action set and one or more internal actions available to it but which cannot be observed by others. It is nonetheless possible for other actors to infer the content of internal events by observing that actor's subsequent external behavior. *See* ROBIN MILNER, COMMUNICATING AND MOBILE SYSTEMS: THE PI-CALCULUS 38, 52-54 (1999) (describing action set of external and internal actions and proposing mechanism that allows one to disregard some occurrences of internal events).

[67] In other words, actors are modeled as independent "black boxes," whose behavior will include independent activity that cannot be observed by others, as well as joint actions or events involving two or more actors. *See* ROBIN MILNER, COMMUNICATING AND MOBILE SYSTEMS: THE PI-CALCULUS 13 (1999) (describing actors as "black boxes" which can be distinguished only by observing their external behavior).

usually referred to as a *synchronization* event.[68] This does not mean that two individuals in a joint event will observe the same thing, experience it the same way, or attach the same meaning to it.[69] However, it does mean that any time that one actor observes another they are by necessity involved in a joint activity, even if the second actor is oblivious that it is being observed.[70]

By requiring that whenever two actors need to share, disclose, signal, or in any way communicate or transfer information that they do so through a pre-defined interactions or synchronization, the concurrency model brings the observability/non-observability problem to the foreground, forcing system designers to make all design decisions with this general problem in mind. [71] Given that the only way to observe the occurrence of an event is to participate in it, whenever two actors interact, a third party who was not part of that interaction will not be able to observe what transpired between them: as far as third-parties are concerned, that interaction can be treated as a unit or black box.[72]

In order to get a better sense of the relationship between internal and external observable behavior and the constraints that may dynamically arise as agents engage in action-sequences, imagine that two chess players are playing a championship match. The game is a concurrent activity that will consist of each player undertaking a sequence of observable moves that will terminate when there is a checkmate, or they agree to a draw. Each move, beginning with the first one, will change the state of the game, as well as that of each of the players. The progress of a game can be characterized as a

---

[68] In other word, a necessary condition for person A to observes an action of person B is to interact with B in some specified manner; and by so interacting B in turn observes A. *See* Milner, PI-CALCULUS, *supra* note __, at 28 (stating that an agent observes the action of another agent by interacting with it).

[69] *See* ROSCOE, *supra* note __, at 8 (stating that communications should be thought of as a "transaction or synchronization between two or more processes rather than as necessarily the transmission of data one way"); P. Y. A. Ryan & Steve A. Schneider, *Process Algebra and Non-Interference* 18-24 (manuscript) (describing concurrent systems involving confidential information in which two actors may engage in the same joint-event, but each observes different things); Milner, supra note __, at 37.

[70] In fact, this approach has been used to model interactions in which messages are passed but the sender can remain anonymous, something that is sometimes important when securing networks. *See* Steve A. Schneider, *Anonymity and Security* (manuscript).

[71] *See* MILNER, *supra* note __, at 12 (stating that under this approach "the behavior of a system is exactly what is observable, and to observe a system is exactly to communicate with it"). Examples of synchronization events of this sort include "passing of a baton in a relay race; the delivery of a registered letter; the closure of a contract; becoming married," and more generally, any action involving two or more actors whose behavior intersect temporally in a meaningful way. *See* SCHNEIDER, *supra* note __, at 29. *See also* MILNER, *supra* note __, at 36 (describing handshake synchronizations as atomic or indivisible actions of two or more agents, where data may or may not be transferred and in which there is no necessary directionality in the "communication").

[72] For example, a computer has a clear interface, including a set of keys, communication ports, screen, and installed programs. When a person interacts with it, the only thing that she can observe is the behavior that is revealed via that interface. The rest of the computer is a black box that prevents her from observing the myriad operations occurring inside—the only way for her to interact with it is through the parts that have been externalized, or made available to her. This limited set of joint activities between a user and a system greatly reduce their complexity.

series of transitions from one state to the next, where each move is constrained by all of the moves up to that point and the rules of the games—e.g., the way that each piece may be moved. A player's observable state—their current position on the board—will not (if properly executed) betray her internal deliberations about sequences of moves that she expects to make. While some of these internal transitions may be inferable, given that players often adopt well known move-sequences from previous matches,[73] the great players are the ones who can make others believe that they are in fact engaged in such sequence, but eventually reveal that they were actually playing a new variation of a known sequence.[74]

3. Traces and Specifications

Since the only actions that are relevant for the model are observable ones, an actor can be described by setting forth the set of observable action sequences that are available to it. The *trace* of an action-sequence is a record of an agent's observable behavior,[75] in the order that they occur; a set of traces is a collection of all action-sequences that are possible.[76] In some cases, it is important to assure that an actor will abstain from certain types of behavior. One can create such a "safety" specification by setting forth a set of action-sequences that are prohibited and then checking to make sure that the observable actions of an actor, as captured by its trace set does not include one of those sequences. Such specifications do not require an actor to do anything, just to avoid certain bad outcomes. For example, an engineer designing a railway crossing would adopt safety specifications such as: "if a train is approaching crossing, do not allow cars from passing though, which can be met by having the gate lowered when a train is within a certain distance from the crossing." On the other hand, "liveness" specifications require that an actor engage in one or more observable actions; that is, refusing to take such an action at the required time would be deemed an error.[77] The engineer may, for example, want to require that the gate goes up after the train passes though so that cars can continue to use the crossing. The set of actions in an environment which an actor is able to refuse is

[73] The market for chess matches turns out to be highly informationally efficient: once a trap of variation of any importance has been introduced it is difficult to use it again in a professional match and expect to be able to engage an arbitrage opportunity.

[74] In fact sequences of those previously observed actions are given special names to identify their originators, they often also carry names of the variations that disrupted previous complacency—e.g., Ruy Lopez, Berlin Defense, including the Mortimer Trap.

[75] A trace is analogous to a history in a sequential game. *See* FUNDENBERG & TIROLE, supra note __, at 70-71 (describing sequential games and role of histories).

[76] *See* Schneider, *supra* note __, at 85-86 (describing traces as record of the events that may occur in connection with an agent's action-sequence, as if some observer were "recording all events in the order in which they occur").

[77] *See* Schneider, *supra* note __, at 193 (contrasting safety specifications, which require that "nothing bad will happen" with liveness ones, which require that "something good will happen").

that actors "refusal set." One way of defining a particular actor is by specifying the set of actions that it is able to take (the trace set) as well as the set of actions that it can refuse to take in all relevant contexts. Two actors can thus be considered equivalent if they have the same trace and refusal sets.[78]

4. The Designer's Task

This of course does not mean that we have eliminated the potential indeterminacy that can arise whenever actors engage in non-observable behavior. However, it does bring the transparency problem into clear focus: a designer who wants to make sure that two actors can coordinate their behavior at some point in time, will need to assure that: (1) the internal state transitions of each does not affect their ability to engage in that joint event; or (2) it will have to include one or more synchronization points along the way to assure that their knowledge of each other's state—i.e., future ability to engage in the joint event—do not diverge too much.

The designer's task is then to identify those contexts in which actors are socially dependent and the types of problems that can arise due to their potential inability to observe each other's behavior. Once that is determined, the designer has to ascertain the extent to which observation-events are needed, the nature of those observations, and their order or timing. The designer cannot simply assert that actors will come to know or should know a particular fact; it has to point to a specific observation event in which that communication can occur. If the designer is unsure that the actors have sufficiently synchronized their beliefs about a relevant fact, then it has to insert additional observation points, or explain why they are not needed.

Finally, let me summarize some of the benefits of the concurrency model. First, it provides a set of tools that greatly simplify the task of describing and reasoning about complex interactions within intertemporal contexts; for example, a lot of these systems are required to stay in constant operation for very long periods of time, and to provide real-time solutions when they interact with people.

[78] If at point *t*, actor A is placed in context C in which action *x* is available, there are three sets of behavior that may be observed by a third party. First, whenever A is faced with that choice in context C it does x. A designer who wants to guarantee this will have to make sure of two things. First, each time that A is in context C, it is in a position to do *x*—i.e., it is in a state in which *x* is a possible action. Second, the environment must also be in a position to offer action *x* to A. This is particularly important when the action in question is a joint-event with another. Third, the designer has to be able to guarantee that actor A will in fact take that action—i.e., that it cannot refuse to act. In any context, an actor who is in a stable state—i.e., one in which it is not able to engage in an infinite number of internal transitions—who is offered action *x* by the environment, will either have the ability to do it and will do it, or will have the ability to refuse to engage in that action. *See* Schneider, *supra* note __, at 171-76.

Second, the model makes it easier to specify, design, and implement systems, and formally determine places in which unreliable interactions may occur. Third, the key decision to model joint behavior as a single action or event helps reduce complexity of concurrent system by indicating the precise points at which the independent actions of two or more autonomous agents are required to intersect. Fourth, by treating all observable behavior in the same manner, it is much easier to compare the expected behavior of systems, given that what is important is not the number of components that are interacting within the system but the observable result that they produce as a group.

C. Concurrent Corporate Governance

How then can we test the reliability of governance structures and compare between different types—e.g., markets, contracts, mandatory or default legal rules? Can we identify design rules that will facilitate the process by which corporate governance goals—whatever they may be—can be translated into robust and reliable governance mechanisms? The approach introduced in this Paper provides a general framework that can be used by corporate actors, lawyers, and lawmakers to compare governance devices and identify potential problems that can arise when they are placed in real-world contexts, particularly given the social dependence and intertemporal complexity constraints described in Part I. However, the goal of this paper is relatively modest: to provide an overview of how the concurrency model would operate and to show how it can help with the first steps in the road towards governance transparency.

1. Governance Divergences

Shareholders delegate managerial tasks to board members and managers, knowing that they will generally be unable to observe their behavior. Agency problems are due precisely to this general inability of principal to observe the behavior of their agents. The concurrency approach allows one to model corporate governance events as a stream of snapshots across time, much in the same way that a balance sheet captures the financial state of a firm as of a certain date.[79] The reliability of a governance approach will depend, in part, on how often these observation events occur, the nature of the information that is transferred, and who is involved in those observation events. Some types of actions are what we can call *experience actions* in that their consequences are not fully apparent until

[79] See Abelson & Sussman, supra note __, at __ (describing lazy evaluation approach in functional languages in which functions are evaluated only when they are needed, giving impression of timeless execution).

after they occur.[80] We can generalize this notion of experience actions to take into account situations in which the aggregate effect of an actor's actions may not be completely obvious or cognizable until it has taken a sufficiently large number of them.[81] For example, managers make a series of management decisions over time, many of them of relatively small import by themselves. However, when taken together these decisions can have a material impact on the welfare of shareholders.

One principal obstacle to designing effective governance devices, is determining the types of contexts in which managers can undertake a sequence of non-observable actions harmful to shareholders—i.e., lead to an "unacceptable" divergence from the course of action most likely to maximize returns to shareholders. In order to identify and prevent these sorts of governance divergences, the designer of governance structures needs to be able to determine the number and types of observation or synchronization events that should be used.[82]

2. Concurrent Corporate Governance

The general rationale of the concurrent governance approach is straightforward: instead of trying to find transparency where there is none, policymakers and shareholders should take the opposite tack; they should assume that the actions of managers are completely *non-observable*, except where managers and shareholders have participated in a well-specified observation event. Under the concurrency approach, a governance mechanism includes one or more governance operations, with the following characteristics: (1) an operation involves two or more actors, who engage in a joint activity—an observation or synchronization event;[83] and (2) the only way to observe an occurrence of an event is to actually participate in it. While there may be limitations to the accuracy of an observation, a non-participant is by definition a non-observer, and thus is not involved in the governance exercise. At first glance, this approach may appear artificial or one difficult to implement. But drawing a sharp distinction between synchronizations/observation events based on

80 In economics, an "experience good" is a product whose value cannot be completely ascertained until after it is purchased and consumed.

81 *See* ARIEL RUBINSTEIN, MODELING BOUNDED RATIONALITY 63-84 (1998) (discussing problem of limited memory in the context of bounded rationality).

82 For example, concurrency models have been extended to describe markets and auction mechanisms. *See, e.g.*, Julian A. Padget & Russell J. Bradford, *A Pi-Calculus Model of A Spanish Fish Market: Preliminary Report*, *in* LECTURE NOTES IN COMPUTER SCIENCE 166 (Pablo Noriega & Carles Sierra eds., 1999).

83 Recall that we are assuming that a person can be modeled as a sequence of selves over time. *See supra* note __. Therefore, a person can engage in self-governance, involving her current and future selves.

participation and all other types of events acts as a commitment device to prevent designers of corporate governance regimes from adopting overly optimistic assumptions about non-observable behavior. Modeling systems solely based on observable events, forces designers to either say nothing about them—if the observations are not there—or revise their original design to allow for additional observations events. To the extent that complexity is making it difficult for policymakers to correctly determine how the behavior of socially dependent actors is affecting the overall behavior of corporations, the solution is not to try to impose axiomatic behavioral assumptions—e.g., that these actors are fully rational and do not face bounded rationality or informational asymmetry constraints—but to create additional observation points that take into account both the intertemporal nature of corporations and the intricate social dependence of participants.

3. Basic Governance Operations

One way to approach this general problem is to define a limited set of governance operations and way of combining them such that all that we need to know in order to reason about composite governance devices is how the primitive devices operate individually and extent to which their operation changers when they are combined. The first type of governance operation is what I have referred to as an observation event, which, as mentioned above, are, by definition, a joint activity of two or more actors. In the corporate context, observation events take a variety of forms, including securities disclosures and monitoring interactions between shareholders and managers, and between creditors and shareholders.[84] The second type of governance operation is a requirement that a corporate decision be made jointly—i.e., with the participation of two or more corporate actors. For example, if a manager wants to carry out a merger, she will have to engage in a joint event with the board of directors, in which the board will decide whether or not to proceed. If the board agrees, then control to make the decision will be handed to the shareholders. This type of externalized joint-decision needs to be contrasted with internalized independent decisions. Many of day-to-day corporate decisions are internal decisions of managers, in that those choices will not be directly observable by the board or shareholders, or require their participation. The board and shareholders may however engage in subsequent synchronization events with the managers in which they may be able to infer the content of one or more of those internal choices. The third general

[84] *See* Jensen & Meckling, *supra* note __.

governance operation is that of parallel composition.[85] This just allows us to combined two actors into a context in which they will interact. Under the concurrency model all corporate governance is parallel in nature. This is because by definition the only way to engage in a governance operation is to participate in a synchronization or joint event with one or more actors. An observation event involves the interaction of at least two actors and thus is a type of parallel composition.
For example, assume that the audit committee of a board of directors deliberates and makes a decision regarding the annual audit. The members of the committee participate in a joint event, where they engage in a set of reciprocal observations of each other, although some information will be internal to each committee member—i.e., not observable by the others. When the rest of the board reviews the minutes of the audit committee, the board becomes involved in a governance operation; however, it is an operation in which the board can only observe the joint output of the committee, as reported in the minutes and encapsulated in their decision to approve or reject the audit. Suppose that the managers also review the committee's minutes, by doing so they become part of a governance operation. Finally, the audit committee, board, and managers are involved in a symmetrical parallel governance operation involving each other.

4. Parallel Governance

When a person tells another "if you could only see yourself…" they are basically saying that if they were able to engage in a detached, objective observation of their behavior, they would, at the very least, begin to see the error of their ways. But encapsulated in that phrase is a second statement: that although her self-governance or self-observation is faulty, she is nonetheless being observed and, in this case, judged. In other words, the very fact of being involved in a joint event restricts the types

[85] One also needs to allow for an operation to capture the sequential observable behavior of actors. Suppose that an actor has the ability to choose an action from an action set. Then she will either make a choice or not; if she does not, then this is equivalent to saying that she is engaged in a sequence of non-observable behavior. After the actor makes an external choice, then she will transition to a state in which she may have additional choices and so on. The types of actions available to an actor and the set of states though which it can transition will be included as part of that actor's overall specification. Some economists have modeled contractual incompleteness due to complexity by positing that contracts are abstract computational machines, where the execution of a contract is equivalent to that of the machine. *See* Luca Anderlini & Leonardo Felli, *Incomplete Contracts and Complexity Costs*, 46 THEORY & DECISION 23 (1999) (modeling incomplete contracts as execution in abstract machine, where complexity is at level of contractual provisions being executed); Ariel Rubinstein, *Finite Automata Play the Prisoner's Dilemma Game*, 39 J. ECON. LIT. 83 (1986) (modeling repeated game as execution of abstract computational machine, where level of complexity is at level of structure). The difference between those approaches and the one here is that finite deterministic automata are not particularly useful in modeling concurrent systems, since they fail to distinguish with the type of non-deterministic behavior in these systems. *See* Milner, *supra* note __, at __ (discussing limitations of standard automaton approach when modeling concurrent systems).

of behavior that are available to each actor, whether it is because of the observation event or requirement that the decision be made jointly. More specifically, a necessary condition for a governance event is the participation of two or more actors, and it is through that interaction—joint observations, joint decisions, and so on—that governance will ultimately occur. The claim is not that a joint event will always be a sufficient condition for effective governance to occur. But existence of observation and the need to coordinate behavior limit the autonomy of each involved. A gatekeeper who is in collusion with a manager who is engaged in illegal behavior is both observing and being observed by the manager, and while this fact may not always be sufficient to constrain their joint misconduct, it can nonetheless be used in designing governance devices. The reason that the gatekeeper and manager can engage in the illegal activity is that the rest of the world cannot observe their internal behavior, their collusion. This suggests that adding an additional external actors to "participate" in the existing activity can further reduce their freedom to engage in misconduct. If the manager has to report to the board of directors, the ability of the board to observe the manager's behavior can constrain both the manager and gatekeeper, who now must account for the fact that the manager is involved in a joint event with the board that it cannot fully observe.[86]

5. Recursive Governance

If we take the general argument one step further, one can further argue that all governance is necessarily self-governance; or alternatively, all governance is recursive in nature. This follows from the manner in which I have defined the concept of governance: (1) it requires a joint observation event; (2) this is the same as saying that in order for a person to be involved in governance, they have to be in a parallel composition to one or more actors; (3) due to the first requirement a third party who is added to the governance scheme becomes part of that composite group—although it may not be at the same level as other members and thus may be unable to observe some of their behavior. Nonetheless, putting an additional actor in an parallel composition with an existing group will restrict that groups' autonomy, since it is exposed to some degree of observation by that new actor.

More specifically, whenever a corporation engages in misconduct it has to be because one or more individuals failed at self-governance; which may be either because the expected benefits of that

[86] This sort of recursive de-composition of conspiracies and collusive activity generally is well-known to prosecutors and antitrust enforcers.

misconduct exceeded the expected sanctions or because of self-control problems.[87] Suppose that a manager has not exercise proper self-governance and a shareholder has been harmed because of its inability to observe the manager's behavior. To protect itself, the shareholder may impose additional observation events, either involving its own interactions with managers or bringing in a gatekeeper. If it resorts to using a gatekeeper, the shareholder will face a similar agency problem, which may lead it to hire a second gatekeeper to monitor the first one. While this exercise is hierarchical in nature—we are building a governance scheme from the bottom up—it is not a hierarchy based on authority or fiat.[88] Instead it is one that is held together by mutual synchronizations involving individual members; moreover, it is one in which placing actors in a horizontal or parallel composition can serve as a valuable constraint. In other words, each time that a new actor is added to the composite governance group, the discretion of existing members to engage in non-observable, harmful behavior will be further reduced. This means that the oft-cited agent-watching-agents problem can be resolved by using parallel governance regimes. More generally, one can envision a parallel governance regime in which there are multiple gatekeepers, each of which knows of the existence of other gatekeepers, but not their identity. Such a regime would make it difficult for a gatekeeper to collude with managers, at least to the extent that they do not know whether all of the other gatekeepers have also agreed to collude with the managers, given that even one honest gatekeeper may discover and expose that gatekeeper's misconduct.

Someone might object that this approach is far too general to provide useful guidance in designing governance structures or that it avoid dealings with difficult issues, such as the general difficulty in observing the actions of managers and board members. It is thus helpful to explain what can and cannot be accomplished. First, the ability to observe the behavior of the governed party is a necessary condition for the operation of a any governance mechanism; therefore, drawing a sharp distinction between observable and non-observable behavior will help a designer identify contexts in which governance devices would not work unless one were to include an observation event. Second, corporate participants must coordinate their behavior over time; they thus need a way to

[87] *See* Utset, *Hyperbolic Criminals*, *supra* note __, at 642-45 (setting forth model of time-inconsistent misconduct, in which preference for immediate gratification lead actors to engage in misconduct that from long-term perspective had negative expected benefits).

[88] Using hierarchical structures for corporate governance comes at a cost. *See* Paul R. Milgrom, *Employment Contracts, Influence Activities, and Efficient Organization Design*, 96 J. POL. ECON. 42 (1988) (discussing influence costs and other types of rent-seeking within hierarchies); KENNETH J. ARROW, THE LIMITS OF ORGANIZATION 68-79 (1974) (discussing tradeoff between delegation and oversight within organizations).

predict whether the other parties with whom they need to coordinate will be in a position to do so at the appropriate time.

III. Legal and Corporate Governance Implications of Concurrency Model

A. The Modular Corporation

How can one use this modular design via abstraction to reduce corporate complexity? Corporate law has some built-in abstraction mechanisms. It requires that at least one person hold voting and residual rights,[89] and that that the corporation be managed by or under the control of a board of directors.[90] Additionally, boards can delegate some management tasks to committees[91] and officers.[92] These modularity-enhancing rules encourage a division of labor: officers engage in day-to-day management, the board in general managerial oversight, and shareholders in electing the board and approving extraordinary transactions. While there is general agreement that this governance scheme helps reduce corporate complexity, commentators have used this fact to make additional, albeit conflicting, normative claims as to who should be at the top of the corporate hierarchy—i.e., whose interest should trump all others—shareholders, the board, and other constituencies.[93]

The goal of modular design is to decrease complexity without at the same time introducing other costs into the system. Treating shareholders as a unit only works if they are in fact a unit, in that their preferences and other important characteristics are sufficiently similar, a fact recognized by courts dealing with conflicts between majority and minority shareholders.[94] The same is true with boards of directors: we cannot predict how a board will behave unless we have some sense about the identity of those within it—i.e., whether they are independent directors or officers. Moreover, even if they are all independent directors they may not be all equally able to engage in oversight of

[89] *See* Del. Code Ann. tit. 8, § 151(b) (1998) (at least one outstanding share must have residual and voting rights).
[90] *See* Del. Code Ann. tit. 8, § 141(a) (1998).
[91] *See* Del. Code Ann. tit. 8, § 141(c)(2) (1998)
[92] *See* Del. Code Ann. tit. 8, § 142 (1998)
[93] *See* Eugene F. Fama & Michael C. Jensen, *Separation of Ownership and Control*, 26 J.L. & ECON. 301 (1983) (stating that division of concerns is valuable and arguing for shareholder primacy); Stephen M. Bainbridge, *Director Primacy: The Means and Ends of Corporate Governance*, 97 NW. U. L. REV. 547, 550 (2003) (arguing that scheme shows that board of director should have final say—i.e., board primacy); Margaret M. Blair & Lynn A. Stout, *A Team Production Theory of Corporate Law*, 85 U. VA. L. REV. 247 (1999) (arguing that board acts as mediating hierarch to mediate interests of various constituencies).
[94] *See, e.g.,* Sinclair Oil Corp. v. Levien, 280 A.2d 717, 720 (Del. 1971) (drawing a distinction between actions in which all shareholders share same interest (payment of dividend) and those in which the majority shareholder received a benefit and the minority's expense, and applying duty of care to first and duty of loyalty to second).

certain matters, such as the audit process.[95] Moreover, a second characteristic of good modular design is that the different modules be de-coupled, such that they interact only through a pre-determined interface. In other words, the designer needs to specify the ways in which different modules can influence each other's behavior.[96] In corporations, the same person can be a shareholder, board member, and officer, something that is common in close corporations, and encouraged in public ones through the use of compensation schemes that give managers stock options.

There are of course important reasons for allowing such violations of modularity, but not surprisingly a large number of problems in corporate law revolve around how to make sense and judge the behavior of actors who operate in multiple domains.[97] But the problem is not that we allow someone to wear different hats, but that we create different roles, separate modules, and then allow someone to straddle them. It is the combination of these two that lead to problems with officers who are also board members, majority shareholders who, acting as a director, fire an employee, who also happens to be a minority shareholder, and corporate opportunity cases in which an officer or board member has to decide whether an opportunity is in the company's line of business. The same type of problems arise with gatekeepers such as auditors and lawyers who may be performing more than one task, something recognized in a number of provisions in the Sarbanes-Oxley Act.[98] Of course, this does not mean that it is necessary or prudent to adopt a blanket prohibition of such cross-domain behavior; however, it does suggest that a hidden cost of modular design is the false impression that it may give to an outside observer as to the thought and rigor that went into creating internal cohesion within a module and clear decoupling between them.

B. The Sarbanes-Oxley Act: Parallel Governance Par Excellence

Some provisions of the Sarbanes-Oxley Act that have been criticized for imposing significant financial burdens on corporations—in managerial time and effort and increased legal and accounting

[95] *See* Sarbanes-Oxley Act of 2002 § 301 (requiring wholly independent audit committee, thereby reducing ability of managers to increase immediate costs to board of directors of challenging financial statements prepared by managers).
[96] *See* Abelson & Sussman, *supra* note __, at 117 (arguing that this allows for the creation of library of modules that can be exported to other systems or modified without having to change all other modules with which they interact)
[97] *See* Tamar Frankel, *Fiduciary Law*, 71 CALIF. L. REV. 795, 811 (1983) (discussing role of fiduciary law in dealing with conflicts of interest).
[98] *See* Sarbanes-Oxley Act of 2002 § 303 (making it illegal for managers to increase immediate costs to auditors of refusing to go along with fraudulent financial statements).

fees[99]—can be explained in part as parallel governance schemes. The certification requirements and management's assessments of internal controls[100] were adopted to make it more difficult for senior managers to claim that they were unaware of problems with the company's financial statements, disclosures, and internal control mechanisms. However, the much criticized section 404 of the Sarbanes-Oxley Act adopts a series of cross-monitoring procedures that act as parallel governance devices. For example, these procedures require that managers make representations regarding the company's internal accounting controls and then requiring auditors "to attest to, and report on, the assessment made by the management."[101] This, in turn, leads accounting firms to hire lawyers to help prepare these attestations. It may well be that critics are correct that section 404 imposes potentially high compliance costs; however, the rule also increases the number of observation events involving these different actors, and thus impose the sort of parallel governance that we have been discussing. It is a gatekeeper scheme in which gatekeepers not only engage in their usual gatekeeping activities, but police each other.

C. Safety and Liveness Specifications in Corporate Law

A shareholder concerned with reducing the agency costs imposed by the board's un-observed behavior can make a list of all possible observable action sequences available to the board, as captured by their traces. It can then decide which of those action sequences it wants to allow the boar to undertake and which to exclude. The shareholder can create a specification of the board's legitimate behavior by setting forth a set of traces representing the *allowable* action-sequences. Such a *safety* specification only identifies the type of observable behavior that is prohibited. An example would be the prohibitions against self-dealing imposed by the duty of loyalty and the due care and informed decision-making requirements under the duty of care. Affirmative disclosure requirements under the securities laws can also be seen as safety specifications. In the fiduciary duty and disclosure cases, the law sets forth a set of triggering events that will exclude certain types of behavior, including doing nothing, but gives varying amounts of leeway on the set of action-sequences that will satisfy the legal requirements. However, in certain case we want to make sure

---

[99] *See, e.g.,* Andrew Countryman, *Sarbanes-Oxley Mandates Send Corporate Audit Expenses Soaring*, CHI. TRIB., June 4, 2005, at 1; *Sarbanes-Oxley Compliance Costs Exceed Estimates*, FIN. EXECS. INT'L, (Mar. 21, 2005), *at* http://www.fei.org/404_survey_3_21_05.cfm; Dan Roberts, *Sarbanes-Oxley Compliance Costs Average $5M*, FIN. TIMES, Nov. 12, 2004, at 1. For a discussion of the some of the problems associated with quantifying the true costs of Sarbanes-Oxley, *see* Carl Bialik, *How Much Is It Really Costing to Comply with Sarbanes-Oxley?* WALL ST. J., June 16, 2005, at **.

[100] *See* § 302 of the Sarbanes-Oxley Act of 2002 (general certification requirement); § 906 (certification for filings that include financial reports; criminal sanctions); and § 404 (management assessment of internal controls).

[101] Sarbanes-Oxley Act of 2002 § 404(b), 15 U.S.C. § 7262(b).

that an actor take one or more actions; this can be achieved with a liveness specification. Shareholders may require the board to consider any takeover offers presented to it or to monitor the behavior of managers on an ongoing basis. The recent Delaware decisions, *In re Caremark International* and *Ritter* can both be characterized as liveness specifications, since they impose an affirmative duty on the board to monitor managers on an ongoing basis and not just when they become aware of some act of misconduct.[102] The distinction between safety and liveness specifications may be sometimes blurred, particularly if one characterizes a required behavior as a way of avoiding some bad result. Nonetheless, the reason to draw distinguish between them is that there are certain types of bad behavior that designer of governance rules may want to clearly prohibit, while, in other cases, the goal is to reduce the discretion of a corporate actor from completely abdicating its duties. For example, the *Francis v. United Jersey Bank*[103] case stands for the proposition that a board member can violate its fiduciary duty of care and good faith by failing to acquire the rudimentary knowledge needed to discharge its duty as a board member.[104]

D. Hierarchies and Markets

Agency theory posits that markets are the source of synchronizations between shareholders and managers and that the non-observable behavior of managers between any two market-synchronizations is not important; what matters is the fact that the markets for corporate control, managers, and the company's products will provide managers with the correct governance incentives. These markets communicate certain things to managers,[105] such as "approval" or "disapproval" of the way they are running a company. But how does a manager figure out what it

[102] *See* In re Caremark International Inc. Derivative Litigation, 698 A2d 959 (Del. Ch. 1996) (stating that in order to discharge duty of acting in good faith, a director must attempt to assure that corporation has adequate information and reporting system so that information needed by directors to oversee corporate activities reaches board); Stone v. Ritter 2006 Del. LEXIS 597, *30-31 (Del. November 6, 2006) (in order to violate duty of loyalty based on lack of good faith directors must engage in a systematic failure to exercise oversight).

[103] 432 A.2d 814 (N.J. 1981)

[104] Id. (finding that a director has a continuing obligation to acquire the requisite information needed to discharge its duties).

[105] *See* HERBERT SIMON, ECONOMICS, BOUNDED RATIONALITY AND THE COGNITIVE REVOLUTION 27 (1992) (arguing that market help conserve information processing task, allowing participants "to behave rationally with relatively simple computations and on the basis of relatively little information"). Importantly, while Hayek underlined the importance of market prices in encapsulating economic information for market participants, he argued forcefully that economists at the time were not giving the requisite attention to the role played by time in markets. He stated that "since equilibrium is a relationship between actions, and since actions of one person must necessarily take place successively in time, it is obvious that the passage of time is essential to give the concept of equilibrium any meaning." *See* Friedrich A. Hayek, *Economics and Knowledge*, *in* INDIVIDUALISM, *supra* note __, at 33, 36-37 (in discussing neoclassical economists he also argued that "economists appear to have been unable to find a place for time in equilibrium analysis and consequently have suggested that equilibrium must be conceived as timeless").

should or should not do, in reaction to these coarse market signals? If managers sees that the market price of their company's stock has declined, they may conclude that the decline is due to some outside shock, and not a signal of disapproval. Even if a manager believes that the market is sending it signal, it still needs to decipher and react to it—is the market saying to take more or fewer risks, sell some of its assets or make more acquisitions, focus on long-term growth, short-term returns? One reason that markets sometimes fail to live up to expectations is because too much is asked of the price signal.[106] A price is a cost-effective, low-complexity signal because it hide all information regarding how that equilibrium price came about. At the same time, however, the information that gives rise to a market price is often be useful in other governance contexts, but once used to bring about a market price a lot of it gets discarded or forgotten—in fact, the weak form of the efficient capital market hypothesis tells us that once prices have incorporated all relevant information about a company, the historical information that is left behind is of no real value to future traders.

IV. Conclusion

This paper approached the problem of corporate governance from an engineering perspective. This paper argued that policymakers and shareholders should design and test corporate governance regimes using formal techniques such as the ones used by engineers to design, test, and update complex concurrent systems. Engineers have given close attention to the general problem of how to specify and design concurrent systems to identify potential catastrophic failures before they can materialize. The recent financial crisis showed that financial systems are susceptible to catastrophic failures and, as a result, that corporate governance is important not just at the level of individual corporations, but also at the system level in which shareholders and creditors and households interact via financial intermediaries and corporations. The concurrency approach to corporate governance is easily generalizable to the web of relationships between corporations and financial intermediaries, and thus helps provide a coherent approach for identifying and addressing governance failures at the micro and macro levels.

One possible objection to the concurrency approach is that it seems to introduce a new ways of talking about and characterizing behavior which can be described with our existing vocabulary. For example, economists have given a large amount of thought to the problem of information

106 *See* Manuel A. Utset, *Reciprocal Fairness, Strategic Behavior & Venture Survival: A Theory of Venture Capital-Financed Firms*, 2002 WIS. L. REV. 45, 100-04 (discussing over-optimism and self-serving bias in context of entrepreneur-venture capitalist relationships).

asymmetries within agency contexts. I have purposely taken a different approach to underline the complexity within corporations and how it is affected by the social dependence and intertemporal interactions of corporate actors. A second goal has been to introduce into the law the work of computer scientists in dealing with very similar issues in other types of concurrent systems. It is sometimes valuable to introduce languages that are specially tailored for capturing specific aspects of the world being described and studied. In fact, establishing new languages—domain specific languages—allows designers to represent a complex problem in different ways,[107] and thus is yet another technique used by engineers to deal with complexity.

While spontaneous emergence of legal rules and norms no doubt occur, spontaneity is always within institutional structures and thus constrain by them, and while institutions will sometimes emerge at the urging of invisible hands, those hands are only made invisible by the structures used to organize markets and market-like frameworks. In the end, there is not Archimedean point from which spontaneity can operate, there is no real way to do away with designers of legal rules, institutions, and markets. Legal commentators therefore need to pay much closer attention to the question of specifying, designing, and implementing legal rules and contracts. We should view complexity and indeterminacy as challenges that should spur, not hinder, innovation; not as fixed constraints or upper bound that limits the scope on our enterprise to that of describing behavior and the bookkeeping tasks associated with tallying what we have observed. At the very least, we should consider ways of improving the design and testing of legal rules. Adopting formal design and testing methods, such as the ones described in this paper, should make it easier to predict how legal rules will operate once implemented and lead to the creation of better metrics for measuring the reliability, fairness, and efficiency of legal interventions.

[107] See Abelson, supra note __, at 359 (making argument and using example of circuits, which engineers represent and model using the languages of networks and systems, each of which picks out different aspects of the problem).

Causes, Cure and Prevention of Future Financial Crises: An Ethical Analysis

Robert W. McGee

Abstract

The present financial crisis has been blamed on Wall Street greed, big banks, lack of government regulation, too much government regulation, bad accounting rules, failure of the capitalist system, market failure, government failure, several presidents and monetary policy, to name a few. In fact, there were several interrelated causes of the financial crisis, many of which were the result of not following basic ethical principles, as this article will show. This paper employs the tools of economic analysis as well as two ethical systems – utilitarianism and rights theory – to determine what went wrong, what must be done to alleviate the present situation and what can be done to prevent future financial crises.

INTRODUCTION

Blame for the financial crisis has been placed on a number of individuals and institutions. Some say market failure is to blame.[1] Others say deregulation, too much or too little regulation is the cause.[2] Wall Street greed[3] and/or capitalism have been blamed by some[4] while government has been

1 No triumphant return of the state. Financial Times, January 1, 2010 online edition; Robert Gordon, Did Liberals Cause the Sub-Prime Crisis? The American Prospect, online edition, April 7, 2008. Accessed 22 January 2010, Christopher A. Richardson, The Community Reinvestment Act and the Economics of Regulatory Policy, 29 Fordham Urban L.J. 1607-1632 (2002).

2 Jagadeesh Gokhale & Peter Van Doren, Would a Stricter Fed Policy and Financial Regulation Have Averted the Financial Crisis? Policy Analysis No. 648, October 8, 2009. Washington, DC: Cato Institute; Robert Gordon, Did Liberals Cause the Sub-Prime Crisis? The American Prospect, online edition, April 7, 2008. Accessed 22 January 2010; Johan Norberg, Financial Fiasco: How America's Infatuation with Homeownership and Easy Money Created the Economic Crisis (2009); Thomas E. Woods, Jr., Meltdown: A Free-Market Look at Why the Stock Market Collapsed, the Economy Tanked, and Government Bailouts Will Make Things Worse (2009).

3 Philip Augar, The Greed Merchants: How the Investment Banks Played the Free Market Game (2006); Barry Ritholtz, Bailout Nation: How Greed and Easy Money Corrupted Wall Street and Shook the World Economy (2009).

4 Loong Wong, The crisis: a return to political economy? 5(1/2) Critical Perspectives Int'l Bus. 56-77 (2009).

blamed by others.[5] This article examines the arguments that have been put forth and applies logic, ethical theory and economic analysis to determine the real causes of the crisis. Once the causes have been determined it is possible to recommend a cure and to determine what ethical policies can be adopted to prevent a recurrence.

The easiest allegation to dismiss is the charge that deregulation is to blame, since there were no major deregulation initiatives in the years leading up to the financial crisis. The last major piece of deregulatory legislation before the financial crisis was signed by President Clinton in 1999 -- the Financial Services Modernization Act of 1999, also known as the Gramm-Leach-Bliley Act,[6] which repealed the provisions of the Glass-Steagall Act[7] that prohibited banks from engaging in both commercial and investment banking at the same time.[8]

However, repealing those provisions merely put U.S. banks on an equal footing with the banks in most other countries,[9] which established a more level playing field and made it easier to compete internationally. Had those provisions not been repealed, it would not have been possible for JP Morgan to acquire Bear Stearns or the Bank of America to acquire Merrill Lynch, which would have made the crisis even worse.[10] Thus, that particular piece of deregulation actually

5 Bert Ely, Bad Rules Produce Bad Outcomes: Underlying Public-Policy Causes of the U.S. Financial Crisis. 29 Cato J. 93-114 (2009); Johan Norberg, Financial Fiasco: How America's Infatuation with Homeownership and Easy Money Created the Economic Crisis (2009); John B. Taylor, How Government Created the Financial Crisis, Wall Street J. February 9, 2009 at A19; John B. Taylor, Getting Off Track: How Government Actions and Interventions Caused, Prolonged, and Worsened the Financial Crisis (2009); Thomas E. Woods, Jr., Meltdown: A Free-Market Look at Why the Stock Market Collapsed, the Economy Tanked, and Government Bailouts Will Make Things Worse (2009).

6 Gramm-Leach-Bliley Act (a.k.a. Financial Services Modernization Act of 1999), Pub.L. No. 106-102, 113 Stat. 1338 (1999).

7 Glass-Steagall Act (a.k.a. the Banking Act of 1933). 12 U.S.C. 24; 48 Stat. 162 (1933).

8 Allan H. Meltzer, Reflections on the Financial Crisis. 29 Cato J. 25-30 (2009).

9 George Benston. The Separation of Investment and Commercial Banking (1990).

10 Lawrence H. White, How Did We Get into This Financial Mess? Cato Institute Briefing Papers No. 110, November 18, 2008. Washington, DC: Cato Institute.

strengthened the financial system. Subsequent research has shown that passage of that Act has had a beneficial effect on the banking, insurance and brokerage industries.[11] Thus, from the perspective of utilitarian ethics, the regulatory changes that did occur before the financial crisis were ethical because the result was a positive-sum game (more on this concept later).

The Gramm-Leach-Bliley Act[12] also made it possible for institutions and individuals to do things that they were prohibited from doing before the Act's passage, which strengthens property and contract rights. It must not be forgotten that government is force. Whenever government prohibits an activity it reduces the opportunity for individuals to exercise choice. Where there is no choice, there can be no morality, because morality involves choice. Thus, passage of the Gramm-Leach-Bliley Act expanded opportunities for making choices (to engage in both investment banking and commercial banking).

Wall Street greed can also be dismissed as a cause. The amount of greed in society is more or less constant. It does not change much from year to year. People who are greedy are going to continue to be greedy and people who are not greedy will not all of a sudden become greedy. There was no sudden surge in greed to cause the financial crisis.

Although greed might have been present, it was not the cause of the financial crisis. Even if greed did exist on Wall Street, that is not necessarily a bad thing, as Adam Smith pointed out in 1776.[13] Merely acting in one's self interest while playing within the rules has a beneficial effect on

11 Aigbe Akhigbe & Ann Marie Whyte, The Market's Assessment of the Financial Services Modernization Act of 1999, 36(2) Fin. Rev. 119-138 (2005).

12 Gramm-Leach-Bliley Act (a.k.a. Financial Services Modernization Act of 1999), Pub.L. No. 106-102, 113 Stat. 1338 (1999).

13 Adam Smith, An Inquiry into the Nature and Causes of the Wealth of Nations (1776/1937).

society.[14] Greed becomes a problem to other individuals or society only when the individual does not play within the rules.

People who act only in their own self interest often benefit society more than they intend by offering a higher quality product or service at a lower price than the competition. Offering higher quality and/or lower prices are the two main ways to gain profits and market share. The fact that the individuals who do so might act from the perspective of greed rather than altruism is irrelevant from the perspective of utilitarian ethics because the result is still a positive-sum game regardless of motive (Kant would disagree.[15] If the activity is voluntary it does not violate property or contract rights, and so is not unethical from the perspective of rights theory (more on this theory below).

It might be argued that the people who traded complex financial derivatives and bundled subprime mortgage securities were acting unethically because their activity constituted fraud. But while that might be true in some cases, it was not true in all cases. Merely trading in such instruments does not constitute fraud or unethical activity. Where there was no intent to defraud it cannot be said that engaging in such trading constituted unethical conduct unless some other element is involved.

The fraud argument would be strengthened if one points out that there was sometimes an element of negligence or deception on the part of those who bundled high and acceptable quality mortgage instruments with mortgage instruments of lower quality. The fact that some components of those bundled securities were poor investments, coupled with the fact that their low quality was

14 Adam Smith, An Inquiry into the Nature and Causes of the Wealth of Nations (1776/1937); Ayn Rand, The Virtue of Selfishness (1964).

15 See Immanuel Kant, Critique of Practical Reason (1997); Immanuel Kant, Groundwork for the Metaphysics of Morals (1998); Immanuel Kant, Lectures on Ethics (2001); Immanuel Kant, The Metaphysical Elements of Ethics (2009); Sally Sedgwick, Kant's Groundwork for the Metaphysics of Morals: An Introduction (2008); Roger J. Sullivan, Immanuel Kant's Moral Theory (1989); Roger J. Sullivan, An Introduction to Kant's Ethics (1994).

not disclosed, or was even hidden, might lead one to reasonably conclude that fraud was present in at least some cases. But in many other cases it was simply negligence (not making a sufficient attempt to determine the quality of the underlying financial instrument) or incompetence (not being able to place a value on the instruments due to lack of background or intelligence).

It might be pointed out that not all of that negligence and incompetence originated on Wall Street. Some of it emanated from the halls of Congress and the offices of Fannie Mae and Freddie Mac, two quasi-governmental agencies that pushed the sale of subprime mortgage backed securities.[16]

Was market failure to blame or was it government failure? Richard Rahn, chairman of the Institute for Global Economic Growth, answers that question with a question of his own:

> If government agencies pressure banks to give loans to people who are poor credit risks, do you view this as a failure of capitalism or a failure of government?[17]

The better view is that government policy caused the financial crisis. Several presidents have expounded on the desire to spread opportunities for home ownership, which they sometimes refer to as the American dream. While it might be a dream of many Americans to own their own homes, it does not follow that the federal, state or local government should help them to attain this dream, especially if it comes at the expense of someone else. In fact, it is questionable from the perspectives of ethics and political philosophy whether it is a legitimate function of government to use the force it has at its disposal to punish or reward private non-rights violating behavior of any kind. Yet the federal government of the United States has enacted a number of laws and regulations that subsidize

16 Anna J. Schwartz, Origins of the Financial Market Crisis of 2008, 29 Cato J. 19-23 (2009).

17 Richard W. Rahn, Lies or Ignorance? The Washington Times. October 1, 2008 online edition. Accessed 22 January 2010.

home ownership, often at the expense of landlords, renters and taxpayers. It rewards home owners at the expense of everyone else.

Ethical aspects of government intervention into the home ownership market have been almost totally ignored in both the literature and the public debate. Yet subsidizing home ownership requires someone to pay for part of the cost of owning a home that would otherwise be borne by the homeowners themselves, which seems inherently unfair. Using the force of government to encourage people to purchase homes also punishes landlords, since it reduces demand for rental properties. Worse yet, the landlords are forced to pay taxes to support this homeowner subsidy. Pressuring banks to grant below prime loans reduces their profits and increases defaults, which harms both the banks and their shareholders. It also harms other home owners, since mortgage loan defaults cause the market to become flooded with repos, which puts downward pressure on the price of homes that are not in default. It is a negative-sum game, which cannot be justified on utilitarian ethical grounds. It also violates the rights of those who are forced to subsidize the home purchases of others.

Renters are also forced, through their tax payments, to subsidize the purchase of homes by others. And since there is a tendency for homes to be purchased by those who have above-average incomes, some of the renters who are subsidizing those home purchases are actually subsidizing people who have higher incomes than they do, which results in the poorer classes subsidizing the richer classes.

The current financial situation cannot be blamed on market failure. Markets are not to blame for failing to regulate a market that is permeated with restrictive regulations and subsidies. Monetary policy, subsidies, misguided government regulations and financial safety nets have prevented the market mechanism from working.[18] It is a government failure, not a market failure.

METHODS OF ANALYSIS

This paper will employ two methods of analysis, utilitarian ethics and rights theory. The two methods overlap to a certain extent. However, they do not overlap 100 percent.[19] There are several reasons why both methods are employed. The utilitarian approach is used because the vast majority of economists take a utilitarian approach, either predominantly or exclusively. Portions of the U.S. and other legal systems are partially utilitarian based.[20] The *General Welfare Clause* of the United States Constitution is an example of how utilitarian philosophy is embedded into the legal system. The *General Welfare Clause* is the constitutional provision regulators use to justify their actions when they can find no other constitutional authority. Many other national constitutions contain their own version of the *General* **Welfare Clause**

The subfield of welfare economics is utilitarian based and many of the criticisms that have been made of welfare economics can also be made of utilitarian analysis.[21] Thus, utilitarian analysis

18 Bert Ely, Bad Rules Produce Bad Outcomes: Underlying Public-Policy Causes of the U.S. Financial Crisis. 29 Cato J. 93-114 (2009); Jagadeesh Gokhale & Peter Van Doren, Would a Stricter Fed Policy and Financial Regulation Have Averted the Financial Crisis? Policy Analysis No. 648, October 8, 2009. Washington, DC: Cato Institute; Robert L. Hetzel, Should Increased Regulation of Bank Risk-Taking Come from Regulators or from the Market? 95(2) Econ. Q. 161-200 (2009); Robert L. Hetzel, Monetary Policy in the 2008-2009 Recession. 95(1) Econ. Q. 201-233 (2009); Jeffrey M. Lacker, What Lessons Can We Learn from the Boom and Turmoil? 29 Cato J. 53-63 (2009); Allan H. Meltzer, Reflections on the Financial Crisis. 29 Cato J. 25-30 (2009); Johan Norberg, Financial Fiasco: How America's Infatuation with Homeownership and Easy Money Created the Economic Crisis (2009); Anna J. Schwartz, Origins of the Financial Market Crisis of 2008, 29 Cato J. 19-23 (2009); Lawrence H. White, How Did We Get into This Financial Mess? Cato Institute Briefing Papers No. 110, November 18, 2008. Washington, DC: Cato Institute; Thomas E. Woods, Jr., Meltdown: A Free-Market Look at Why the Stock Market Collapsed, the Economy Tanked, and Government Bailouts Will Make Things Worse (2009).

19 Robert W. McGee, Property Rights vs. Utilitarianism: Two Views of Ethics, 27 Reason Papers 87-115 (2004).

20 Richard A. Posner, Utilitarianism, Economics, and Legal Theory, 8 J. Legal Stud. 103-140 (1979).

21 Kenneth J. Arrow, Little's Critique of Welfare Economics, 41 Am. Econ. Rev. 923-934 (1951); A.E.C. Hare, The Theory of Effort and Welfare Economics, 18 Economica 69-82 (1951); Botond Köszegi & Matthew Rabin, Mistakes in Choice-Based Welfare Analysis, 97 Am. Econ. Rev. 477-481 (2007); I.M.D. Little, A Critique of Welfare Economics (1950/2002); Arthur C. Pigou, Some Aspects of Welfare Economics, 41 Am. Econ. Rev. 287-302 (1951);

suffers from some structural deficiencies. However, failure to consider utilitarian arguments would result in ignoring some of the main arguments that have been put forth on both sides of the financial crisis debate, so some utilitarian analysis is called for in spite of its structural deficiencies. Applying rights theory overcomes the structural deficiencies of utilitarian ethics. However, rights theory is also an imperfect tool of ethical analysis, as is discussed below.

Utilitarian Ethics

Utilitarian ethics may be summarized by the following flow chart.[22]

UTILITARIAN ETHICS

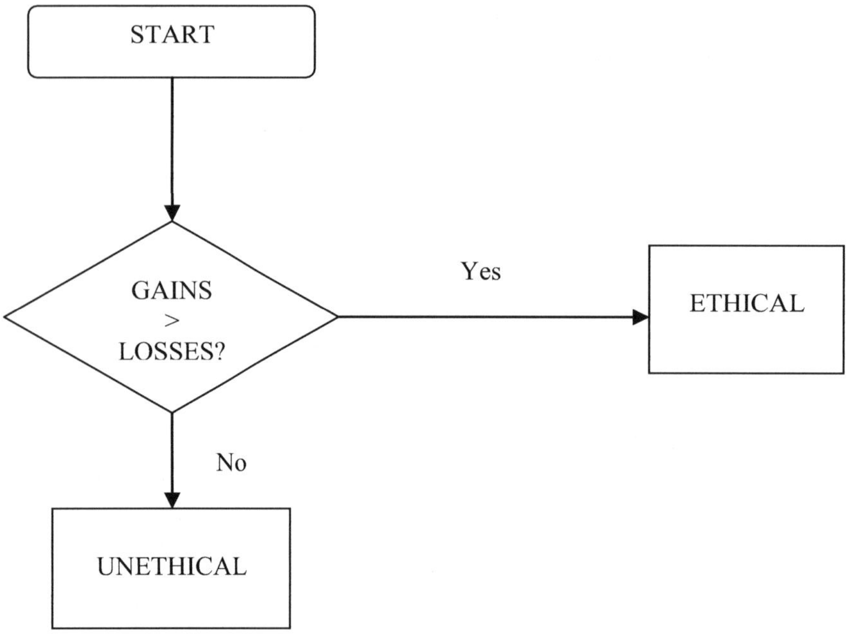

Arthur C. Pigou, The Economics of Welfare, 4th edition (1958); Charles K. Rowley & Alan T. Peacock, Welfare Economics: A Liberal Restatement (1975); Tibor Scitovski, The State of Welfare Economics, 41 Am. Econ. Rev. 303-315 (1951); Jacob Viner, The Utility Concept in Value Theory and Its Critics, 33 J. Pol. Econ. 638-659 (1925).

22 Robert W. McGee, Analyzing Insider Trading from the Perspectives of Utilitarian Ethics and Rights Theory, 91 J. Bus. Ethics 65-82 (2010).

Utilitarian ethics contains some structural defects that cannot be overcome by merely fine-tuning the theory.[23] For example, it is not always possible to measure gains and losses precisely,[24] which makes it difficult or impossible to determine with a high degree of reliability whether the gains exceed the losses or whether the result is a positive-sum or negative-sum game. One must make estimates and the accuracy of those estimates may leave something to be desired.[25] This measurement problem also occurs in cases where a small minority benefit greatly by a policy while the vast majority lose just a little,[26] which is the case with restrictive trade policies and most other special interest legislation. It also is not possible to measure interpersonal utilities,[27] which makes it impossible to determine in a one winner, one loser situation whether the result is a positive-sum game.

Early utilitarians such as Bentham[28] and Mill[29] believed that a policy is good if it results in the greatest good for the greatest number. Although this view appears sound on the surface, a mathematician would be quick to point out that it is mathematically impossible to maximize more than one variable at the same time.[30] One may adopt a policy that achieves the greatest good or one

23 Robert W. McGee, The Fatal Flaw in NAFTA, GATT and All Other Trade Agreements, 14 Nw. J. Int'l L. & Bus. 549-565 (1994); Robert W. McGee, The Fatal Flaw in the Methodology of Law & Economics, 1 Commentaries L. & Econ 209-223 (1997).

24 J.C.C. Smart & Bernard Williams, Utilitarianism – For and Against (1973).

25 Murray N. Rothbard, Man, Economy and State (1970).

26 William H. Shaw, Contemporary Ethics: Taking Account of Utilitarianism (1999).

27 Nicholas Kaldor, Welfare Propositions in Economics and Interpersonal Comparisons of Utility, 49 Econ. J. 549-552 (1939); Murray N. Rothbard, Man, Economy and State (1970);
Murray N. Rothbard, The Logic of Action One: Method, Money, and the Austrian School (1997).

28 Jeremy Bentham, The Principles of Morals and Legislation (1988).

29 John Stuart Mill, On Liberty and Utilitarianism (1993).

30 John von Neumann & Oskar Morgenstern, Theory of Games and Economic Behavior (1947), at 11; G. Hardin, The Tragedy of the Commons. 162 Science 1243-1248 (1968).

may choose a policy that benefits the greatest number but one may not have a policy that does both at the same time. One goal must yield to another goal.

Another inherent problem with utilitarian approaches is that it is not always possible to identify all the groups and individuals who may be affected. Some groups may be easy to identify while others may be difficult or impossible to identify. Frederic Bastiat (1801-1850) provides an excellent example of this problem in his essay, *What Is Seen and What Is Not Seen.*[31]

The essay begins with a parable, which has come to be known as *The Broken Window Fallacy.* The story is about a young hooligan who throws a rock through a window. A crowd gathers and begins to discuss what has happened. One spectator points out that some good has resulted from this destruction because it provides employment for glaziers. If no windows were ever broken, there would be no work for glaziers. What is seen is an expansion of employment in the glass making industry. Thus, some glazier wins. If one were to stop there, one might conclude that destruction is good because it benefits the economy. Those who have argued that war is good for the economy stop their analysis at this point.

If one continues to analyze the situation it is possible to identify a loser - the owner of the window. At this point an economist might conclude that the breaking of the window constitutes a zero-sum game because there is one winner and one loser.

But that analysis is also incomplete. There are really two losers. The owner of the window loses but so does the cobbler because the owner of the window would have used the six francs it cost to replace the window to purchase a pair of shoes. But instead of having a window and a new pair of shoes, the window owner now has only a window. He is not able to buy the shoes because he had to spend six francs to replace the window.

---

31 Frederic Bastiat, Selected Essays on Political Economy (1964), at 1-50. This essay was first published as a pamphlet and is reprinted in Oeuvres Complètes de Frédéric Bastiat, Vol. V, Paris: Guillaumin et Cie, 1862: 336-392.

The point of the parable is to show that some individuals and groups may be identified but others may not. No one except the owner of the window knows that the cobbler has lost as a result of the broken window, and even the owner of the broken window may not be able to identify the cobbler as a loser if he has not yet decided what he would have done with those six francs. But analysts must attempt to identify all winners and losers, or at least those who would be foreseeable. Failure to do so results in an incomplete utilitarian analysis.

Bastiat goes so far as to say that the failure to make this attempt is what separates a good economist from a bad economist.

> There is only one difference between a bad economist and a good one: the bad economist confines himself to the *visible* effect; the good economist takes into account both the effect that can be seen and those effects that must be *foreseen.*[32]

Thus, if we do not at least attempt to identify all affected individuals and groups and try to determine the effect a policy has on them we are being bad economists. As we shall see below, several of the policies that have been adopted over the years leading up to the financial crisis were the result of bad economics because those who advocated and adopted the policies failed to identify all affected individuals and groups and failed to take into consideration the effect the proposed policy would have on them.

Some philosophers, legal theorists and policy analysts believe that a policy is ethical if the result is an increase in efficiency. Richard Posner, a prolific American jurist and a co founder of the law and economics movement, is one such theorist.[33]

> The efficient society is wealthier than the inefficient – that is what efficiency means.[34]

32 Frederic Bastiat, Selected Essays on Political Economy (1964), at 1.

33 Robin F. Grant, Judge Richard Posner's Wealth Maximization Principle: Another Form of Utilitarianism? 10 Cardozo L. Rev. 815-845 (1989); Richard A. Posner, Utilitarianism, Economics, and Legal Theory, 8 J. Legal Stud. 103-140 (1979); Richard A. Posner, The Economics of Justice (1983), at 88-115; Richard A. Posner, Economic Analysis of Law, 5th edition (1998), at 284-287.

> ... the criterion for judging whether acts and institutions are just or good is whether they maximize the wealth of society. This approach allows a reconciliation among utility, liberty, and even equality as competing ethical principles.[35]

Some ethicists disagree with the ethics as efficiency argument.[36] For example, a government that finds a more efficient way to kill people or violate rights is not acting ethically. Hoppe[37] argues that efficiency can be maximized only with a strong property rights regime, and that economic efficiency can be justified, but on the basis of property rights rather than utilitarian ethics, a conclusion with which Norton[38] and Knight[39] would agree. .

Another structural flaw with any purely utilitarian analysis, perhaps the major flaw from the perspectives of ethics and political philosophy, is that it totally ignores all rights,[40] including property and contract rights and even the right to life in some cases. For example, if two wolves and one sheep vote to determine what is for dinner, a utilitarian would conclude that whatever outcome that benefits the majority is the correct outcome. Rights theorists would take the position that the rights of the one sheep are superior to the desires of a thousand wolves.

34 Richard A. Posner, The Economics of Justice (1983), at 205.

35 Id, at 115.

36 John B. Egger, Comment: Efficiency is not a Substitute for Ethics. In Uncertainty and Disequilibrium 117-125 (Mario J. Rizzo, ed., 1979).

37Hans-Hermann Hoppe, The Ethics and Economics of Private Property (1993).

38 Seth W. Norton, Poverty, Property Rights and Human Well-Being: A Cross-National Study, 18 Cato J. 233-245 (1998).

39 Frank H. Knight, Risk, Uncertainty and Profit (1971).

40 Utility and Rights (R.G. Frey, ed., 1984); Robert W. McGee, The Fatal Flaw in NAFTA, GATT and All Other Trade Agreements, 14 Nw. J. Int'l L. & Bus. 549-565 (1994); Robert W. McGee, The Fatal Flaw in the Methodology of Law & Economics, 1 Commentaries L. & Econ 209-223 (1997);

Robert W. McGee, Property Rights vs. Utilitarianism: Two Views of Ethics, 27 Reason Papers 87-115 (2004); Murray N. Rothbard, Man, Economy and State (1970).

The contrast between utilitarian ethics and rights based ethics has also permeated literature. For example, in *The Brothers Karamazov*, Dostoevsky[41] asks whether it would be permissible to torture one baby to death if the result would be happiness for every other member of the human race forever. A more recent variant of this contrast may be seen in the argument about whether it is permissible to torture alleged enemy combatants if doing so would result in extracting information that would save lives.

Rights-Based Ethics

The rights approach may be summarized by the following flow chart.[42]

41 Fyodor Dostoevsky, The Brothers Karamazov (1984).

42 Robert W. McGee, Analyzing Insider Trading from the Perspectives of Utilitarian Ethics and Rights Theory, 91 J. Bus. Ethics 65-82 (2010).

RIGHTS-BASED ETHICS

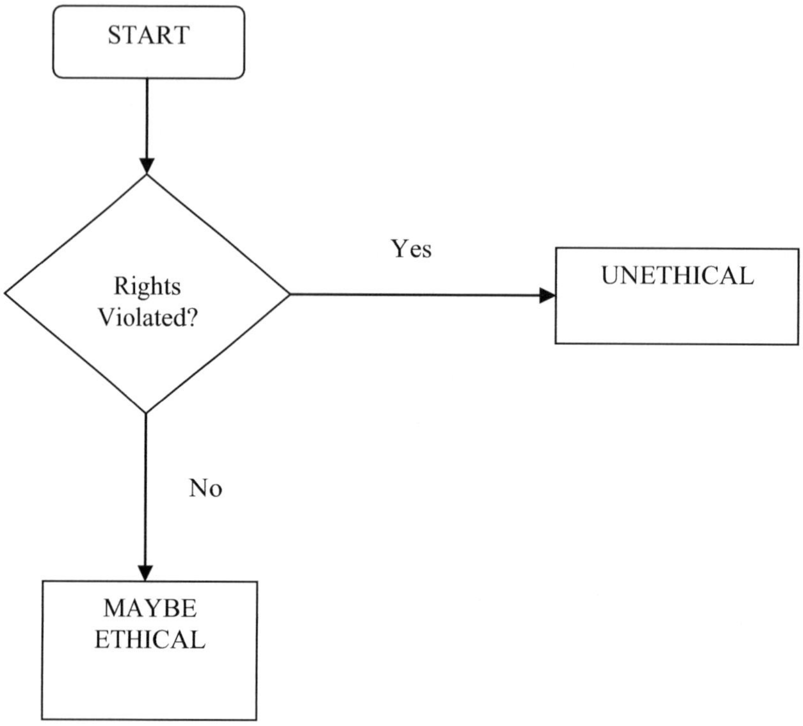

According to rights theory, all acts or policies that violate rights are automatically unethical, regardless of the utilitarian outcome.[43] One advantage of the rights approach is that it negates the need to make estimates about relative gains and losses. It is not necessary to identify all affected groups. All that need be determined is whether anyone's rights have been violated.

The rights approach is also embedded in the U.S. Constitution and the constitutions of many other countries. Portions of the Bill of Rights contained in the first ten amendments to the U.S. Constitution are some examples that might be given. The right to free speech, free press, assembly,

43 Robert W. McGee, Property Rights vs. Utilitarianism: Two Views of Ethics, 27 Reason Papers 87-115 (2004).

religion, and so forth do not include any utilitarian escape clause. The rights of one individual are superior to the wishes of the whole world.

Although the rights approach overcomes the structural flaws of utilitarianism, the rights approach is not perfect. It merely makes it possible to identify acts and policies that are unethical. It does not help us to decide whether non-rights violating activities are ethical or unethical. Prostitution, gambling, taking certain drugs, working on the Sabbath and so forth may or may not constitute unethical or immoral conduct but we cannot apply rights theory to arrive at any conclusions. All we can conclude is that no rights are violated by these practices. We must apply some other criteria to determine whether the acts are ethical.

The rights approach has been criticized by utilitarians. Bentham, for example, takes the position that there is no such thing as inherent rights; all rights come from government.[44] He even goes so far as to state that rights are "nonsense on stilts."[45] One wonders whether Bentham would continue to hold this position if he were a sheep confronted by two hungry wolves.

Although Bastiat often applied a full and complete version of utilitarian ethics to analyze public policy issues, he did not limit himself to utilitarian analyses. He also employed rights theory at times.[46] He also identified rent seeking activity wherever he found it.

The most complete exposition of his rights position was laid out in *The Law*.[47] In it, Bastiat points out that the law can be perverted to be a tool of legal plunder.

> Under the pretense of organization, regulation, protection, or encouragement, the law takes property from one person and gives it to another; the law takes the wealth

44Jeremy Bentham, The Principles of Morals and Legislation (1988).

45 Jeremy Bentham, The Principles of Morals and Legislation (1988); Nonsense upon Stilts: Bentham, Burke and Marx on the Rights of Man (Jeremy Waldron, ed., 1987).

46 Frederic Bastiat, The Law (1968). Originally published in 1850 as a pamphlet, La Loi. Reprinted in Sophismes Économiques, Ouevres Complètes de Frédéric Bastiat, Vol. I, 4th edition. Paris: Guillaumin et Cie, 1878: 343-394.

47 Id.

> of all and gives it to a few – whether farmers, manufacturers, shipowners, artists, or comedians.[48]

Economists would call this practice rent-seeking, or using the law to feather the nests of the few (special interests) at the expense of the many.[49]

> But how is this legal plunder to be identified? Quite simply. See if the law takes from some persons what belongs to them, and gives it to other persons to whom it does not belong. See if the law benefits one citizen at the expense of another by doing what the citizen himself cannot do without committing a crime.
>
> Then abolish this law without delay, for it is not only an evil itself, but also it is a fertile source for further evils because it invites reprisals. If such a law – which may be an isolated case – is not abolished immediately, it will spread, multiply, and develop into a system.[50]

In summary, this paper employs two approaches – utilitarian ethics and rights based ethics – in order to have a fuller and more complete analysis. Omitting either of the approaches results in an incomplete analysis. The next few sections will examine some of the alleged causes of the financial crisis. The examination will take place through the lens of utilitarian ethics and rights theory.

THE COMMUNITY REINVESTMENT ACT

The Community Reinvestment Act[51] was passed during the Carter administration to encourage (pressure?) banks to provide credit to the communities where they are located. While such a

48 Id., at 17.

49 Towards a Theory of a Rent-Seeking Society (James M. Buchanan, Robert Tollison & Gordon Tullock, eds., 1980); 40 Years of Research on Rent Seeking 2: Applications: Rent Seeking in Practice (R.D. Congleton, A.L. Hillman & A. Konrad, eds., 2008); Efficient Rent-Seeking: Chronicles of an Intellectual Quagmire (A. Lockhard & Gordon Tullock, eds. 2001); The Political Economy of Rent-Seeking (Charles K. Rowley, Robert Tollison & Gordon Tullock, eds., 1988); Gordon Tullock, Private Wants, Public Means: An Economic Analysis of the Desirable Scope of Government (1970); Gordon Tullock, The Economics of Special Privilege and Rent Seeking (1989); Gordon Tullock, Rent Seeking (1993).

50 Frederic Bastiat, The Law (1968), at 21.

51 Community Reinvestment Act. 1977. 12 U.S.C. §§2901-2907 (1977); Pub.L. No. 95-128; 91 Stat. 1147 (1977), effective October 12, 1977. Also see www.fdic.gov/regulations/laws/rules/6500-2515.html.

requirement might seem harmless, such is not always the case. For example, what if a bank establishes a branch in a community where a large proportion of residents are unemployed, underemployed and/or otherwise poor? Such people generally have a difficult time paying their rent on time. Presumably they would also have difficulty paying a mortgage, especially if the mortgage payment is higher than their rent payment. Yet the Community Reinvestment Act (CRA) pressures banks to make loans to such uncreditworthy customers as a condition of doing business.

The main provisions of the law are summarized in Sec. 802 of the Act:

> SEC. 802. (a) The Congress finds that--
>
> (1) regulated financial institutions are required by law to demonstrate that their deposit facilities serve the convenience and needs of the communities in which they are chartered to do business;
>
> (2) the convenience and needs of communities include the need for credit services as well as deposit services; and
>
> (3) regulated financial institutions have continuing and affirmative obligation to help meet the credit needs of the local communities in which they are chartered.
>
> (b) It is the purpose of this title to require each appropriate Federal financial supervisory agency to use its authority when examining financial institutions, to encourage such institutions to help meet the credit needs of the local communities in which they are chartered consistent with the safe and sound operation of such institutions.

One might criticize the very premises of the Act on philosophical and ethical grounds. Companies are generally in business to make a profit, which includes servicing the communities in which they do business. If they do a good job they are rewarded with profits and if they do a bad job they are punished with losses and perhaps bankruptcy. The market already does an excellent job of regulating performance by rewarding those who service consumers well and punishing those who do not.[52] There is no need to pass a law requiring companies to serve their communities. However,

52 Ludwig von Mises, Human Action: A Treatise on Economics (2008).

there is a danger of making such a law, and the Community Reinvestment Act (CRA) serves as an excellent example of what can happen when politics is injected into the market process.

The CRA was passed in response to evidence that some banks were "redlining," or drawing red lines on a map around low-income neighborhoods deemed not to be credit worthy.[53] The original 1977 act was more concerned with reporting data than with enforcement. However, amendments enacted during the Clinton administration put some teeth into the law and pressured banks into making a certain percentage of their total loans to customers who would not otherwise have qualified because of low income and/or poor credit ratings.

One impetus for the CRA was the perception that banks were discriminating along racial lines. However, one of the main studies that reached that conclusion did so using flawed data.[54] Other studies have found that discrimination in lending practices tended to be based on credit worthiness rather than race.[55]

One alleged reason for the passage of the CRA was to increase the availability of credit to poor and minority communities. However, there was seldom a lack of competition for lending in these communities. Thus, from the perspective of enhancing credit opportunities, the argument for passage of the Act does not hold up to analysis. Various scholars[56] have pointed out this fact.

---

53 J.I. Brannon, Renovating the CRA, 23(2) Regulation 8-9; Michelle Minton, The Community Reinvestment Act's Harmful Legacy: How It Hampers Access to Credit. CEI On Point No. 132 (March 20, 2008). Washington, DC: Competitive Enterprise Institute.

54 Michelle Minton, The Community Reinvestment Act's Harmful Legacy: How It Hampers Access to Credit. CEI On Point No. 132 (March 20, 2008). Washington, DC: Competitive Enterprise Institute; Fred J. Phillips-Patrick & Clifford V. Rossi, Statistical Evidence of Mortgage Redlining? A Cautionary Tale, 11 J. Real Estate Res. 13-23 (1996).

55 George J. Benston, The Community Reinvestment Act: Looking for Discrimination That Isn't There. Policy Analysis No. 354, October 6, 1999. Washington, DC: Cato Institute; Andrew Holmes & Paul Horvitz, Mortgage Redlining: Race, Risk and Demand, 49 J. Fin. 81-99 (1994); Andrew Holmes & Joe F. James, Discrimination, Lending Practice and Housing Values: Preliminary Evidence from the Houston Market, 11 J. Real Estate Res. 25-37 (1996).

56 Jeffery W. Gunther, Should CRA Stand for "Community Redundancy Act"? 23(3) Regulation 56-60 (2000); Vern McKinley, Community Reinvestment Act: Ensuring Credit Adequacy or Enforcing Credit Allocation? 17(4) Regulation 25-37 (1994); Lawrence J. White, The Community Reinvestment Act: Good Intentions Headed in the Wrong Direction. 20 Fordham Urban L.J. 281-292 (1993).

White[57] goes so far as to say that the CRA is ill advised, redundant, and shackles the banking system while providing opportunities for various groups to extract tribute.

Complying with the provisions of the CRA is not a costless venture. Both the direct and indirect costs can be substantial. Some direct costs include preparing the various government reports, hiring compliance officers, dealing with CRA examiners and meeting with various community groups that threaten to complain to the government if the bank does not grant a certain number of loans to local members of the community who have poor credit scores.[58]

One study found that the CRA cost relatively small banks an average of 4.5 percent of their pretax income and 0.25 percent of their total assets.[59] There is evidence to suggest that the financial soundness of banks decreases as they better conform to CRA rules. Studies comparing bank CRA ratings to their CAMELS rating (a formula bank regulators use to assign safety and soundness of lending institutions) found that the better a lender was rated according to CRA standards, the worse its CAMELS rating was.[60] These studies provide strong evidence that the Community Reinvestment Act weakened the banking system.

Benston[61] identified three important adverse effects that the CRA has had on borrowers and distressed neighborhoods.

---

57 Lawrence J. White, The Community Reinvestment Act: Good Intentions Headed in the Wrong Direction. 20 Fordham Urban L.J. 281-292 (1993).

George J. Benston, The Community Reinvestment Act: Looking for Discrimination That Isn't There. Policy Analysis No. 354, October 6, 1999. Washington, DC: Cato Institute.

58 George J. Benston, The Community Reinvestment Act: Looking for Discrimination That Isn't There. Policy Analysis No. 354, October 6, 1999. Washington, DC: Cato Institute.

59 George J. Benston, The Community Reinvestment Act: Looking for Discrimination That Isn't There. Policy Analysis No. 354, October 6, 1999. Washington, DC: Cato Institute, at 10; Anjan V. Thakor & Jess C. Beltz, An Empirical Analysis of the Costs of Regulatory Compliance, in Proceedings of the 29th Annual Conference on Bank Structure and Competition, May 1993, Chicago: Federal Reserve Bank of Chicago, 549-568. Cited by George J. Benston, The Community Reinvestment Act: Looking for Discrimination That Isn't There. Policy Analysis No. 354, October 6, 1999. Washington, DC: Cato Institute at p. 10.

60 Jeffery W. Gunther, Should CRA Stand for "Community Redundancy Act"? 23(3) Regulation 56-60 (2000); Michelle Minton, The Community Reinvestment Act's Harmful Legacy: How It Hampers Access to Credit. CEI On Point No. 132 (March 20, 2008). Washington, DC: Competitive Enterprise Institute.

61 George J. Benston, The Community Reinvestment Act: Looking for Discrimination That Isn't There. Policy Analysis No. 354, October 6, 1999. Washington, DC: Cato Institute.

- Banks that try to fulfill their CRA obligations tend to siphon off customers from other banks, sometimes on less beneficial terms to the borrowers. Minority owned banks have complained that they have to compete against banks that subsidize their loans through CRA pressure in order to obtain regulatory approval for mergers or acquisitions.
- The CRA makes it very difficult for banks to close branches that are in distressed neighborhoods. Because that is the case, it serves as a negative incentive for other banks to enter those neighborhoods and offering their services to minorities.
- Some borrowers may be harmed because of the CRA policy that requires banks to lend to members of certain specified groups. For example, banks that have experience lending to members of other groups, such as Polish-Americans or Chinese-Americans or to other groups that the CRA does not consider to be disadvantaged, might have to reduce their services to those groups in order to shift their resources to the CRA preferred groups.

Allowing politics to enter the realm of bank lending also provides opportunities for special interest groups to engage in rent seeking activities. Community organizers and groups like ACORN (Association of Community Organizations for Reform Now) can threaten to oppose proposed bank expansions or mergers by filing complaints with various federal government agencies. Sometimes banks find it easier to donate hundreds of thousands of dollars to such groups to buy their silence.[62] Time is of the essence in mergers. Delays can cost money even if the delay is for a short time. ACORN and other groups realize this fact and use it to their advantage. One ACORN representative has stated: "When you're talking a billion-dollar merger, every day of delay costs lots

62 Michelle Minton, The Community Reinvestment Act's Harmful Legacy: How It Hampers Access to Credit. CEI On Point No. 132 (March 20, 2008). Washington, DC: Competitive Enterprise Institute.

of money. It's cheaper to negotiate than fight."[63] The CRA has been used as a form of legalized extortion by these groups to coerce contributions out of banks and to force them to make subprime loans to uncreditworthy people.

Pressuring and intimidating banks into making below market loans may be criticized on several counts. From the perspectives of ethics and political philosophy, using the force of government to coerce law abiding business people into channeling their assets and the assets of their shareholders into relatively unproductive, inefficient and risky uses is not a legitimate function of government in any conceivable liberal democracy.

Since there is a limited amount of credit to go around, funds that are lent to less credit worthy customers cannot be lent to more credit worthy customers. Such practices discriminate against the prudent and reward the less prudent. Forcing banks to lend to some groups at the expense of other groups violates the bank's property rights and also the contract rights of both banks and their more credit worthy customers. It also violates utilitarian ethics, since it forces banks to operate less efficiently and results in negative-sum games, since there are more losers than winners. Banks and their shareholders lose, as do their more credit worthy clients who are no longer able to borrow the funds they need, and taxpayers lose because they are ultimately called upon to pay for the defaults. As foreclosures increase, housing prices in the entire community decline as the supply of housing that is for sale increases. The only winners are the less credit worthy customers and the politicians who have purchased their votes with promises of low interest mortgages.

Another unethical aspect of this practice of subsidizing mortgage loans is that it is off the books. If the government adopts a policy of subsidizing mortgage loans, it should at least make it a budget item rather than hiding it.[64] Making it part of the federal budget would at least force

63 Vern McKinley, Community Reinvestment Act: Ensuring Credit Adequacy or Enforcing Credit Allocation? 17(4) Regulation 25-37 (1994), at 34-35.
64 Allan H. Meltzer, Reflections on the Financial Crisis. 29 Cato J. 25-30 (2009).

Congress to acknowledge that the policy is not cost-free and would force the government to at least disclose what the true cost is.

Macey and Miller[65] conducted a major economic study of the CRA and concluded that it does more harm than good. They found that it allocates credit inefficiently, encourages banks to make risky and unprofitable investment and product-line decisions, penalizes banks that try to reduce costs by consolidating services or closing or relocating branches, deters transactions that would improve efficiency and solvency, impairs the safety and soundness of the banking system, selectively taxes certain depository institutions, imposes significant compliance costs, and harms the very groups the Act was intended to help. In other words, the Act violates utilitarian ethics. One might also point out that it violates property rights because it uses coercion, threats and intimidation to force bankers to invest shareholder assets in places that would not otherwise receive them in the absence of coercion.

Bierman, Fraser and Zardkoohi[66] examined the Macey and Miller study[67] and were in major agreement with it. They point out that, ironically, banks that have high CRA ratings may actually harm the communities they are supposed to help because some of their policy choices may result in having less funds available to lend in the community.

Economists are divided about what should be done. Some economists call for mere reform,[68] perhaps because they believe that outright repeal is not feasible.[69] Overby[70] advocates

65Jonathan R. Macey & Geoffrey P. Miller, The Community Reinvestment Act: An Economic Analysis, 79 Va. L. Rev. 291-348 (1993).

66 Leonard Bierman, Donald R. Fraser & Asghar Zardkoohi, The Community Reinvestment Act: A Preliminary Empirical Analysis, 45 Hastings L.J. 383-412 (1994).

67 Jonathan R. Macey & Geoffrey P. Miller, The Community Reinvestment Act: An Economic Analysis, 79 Va. L. Rev. 291-348 (1993).

68 Christopher A. Richardson, The Community Reinvestment Act and the Economics of Regulatory Policy, 29 Fordham Urban L.J. 1607-1632 (2002).

69 J.I. Brannon, Renovating the CRA, 23(2) Regulation (2001) 8-9.

70 A. Brooke Overby, The Community Reinvestment Act Reconsidered, 143 U. Pa. L. Rev. 1431-1531 (1995).

extending the CRA to finance companies and mortgage companies. Klausner[71] advocates a system of tradable obligations.

Others have called for repeal. In fact, calls for repeal have been made since the mid-1990s,[72] before the most damaging provisions of the CRA became generally known.

White[73] suggests several alternatives to the CRA. If discrimination is the problem, the solution is vigorous enforcement of antidiscrimination laws. If lack of credit availability is the problem, the rules that restrict interstate and branch banking should be loosened to increase competition. If it is determined that low income neighborhoods still are not being adequately served, direct subsidies by the federal government should be used rather than regulation, the reason being that direct subsidies would be more open and transparent and a better, cleaner form of government.

Repeal seems to be the best solution to the problem of subprime loans and misallocation of resources. Anything less than repeal would allow credit to continue to be misallocated and would allow special interest groups such as ACORN to legally extort millions of dollars from banks and their shareholders. The present situation violates utilitarian ethics because it misallocates resources, causing the economy to work less efficiently. The present result is a negative-sum game because there are more losers than winners. The present regime also violates the property and contract rights of bankers, shareholders and potential customers who are unable to obtain bank credit because credit is being channeled to others through coercion.

FREDDIE MAC AND FANNIE MAE

71 Michael Klausner, Market Failure and Community Investment: A Market-Oriented Alternative to the Community Reinvestment Act, 143 U. Pa. L. Rev. 1561-1593 (1995).

72 Vern McKinley, Community Reinvestment Act: Ensuring Credit Adequacy or Enforcing Credit Allocation? 17(4) Regulation 25-37 (1994); William A. Niskanen, Repeal the Community Reinvestment Act. Testimony before the Subcommittee on Financial Institutions and Consumer Credit Committee on Banking and Financial Services, United States Senate, March 8, 1995. Published in Cato Congressional Testimony, www.cato.org/testimony/ct-ni3-8.html. Accessed 22 January 2010.

73 Lawrence J. White, The Community Reinvestment Act: Good Intentions Headed in the Wrong Direction. 20 Fordham Urban L.J. 281-292 (1993).

Freddie Mac and Fannie Mae were government creations. They were founded in order to increase the number of mortgage loans to people with low income. The Department of Housing and Urban Development (HUD) gave Freddie and Fannie explicit targets to achieve. In 1996, the target was that 42 percent of their mortgage loans had to go to borrowers whose income was below the median income in their area. This target increased to 50 percent in 2000 and to 52 percent in 2005.[74]

HUD also required Fannie and Freddie to purchase a certain percentage of mortgages from borrowers whose incomes were less than 60 percent of the median income in the areas where they live. That percentage was 12 percent of all mortgage purchases in 1996, and rose to 20 percent in 2000 and 22 percent in 2005. That goal was to increase to 28 percent in 2008. As a result, they funded hundreds of billions of dollars of loans, many of them at subprime rates. Many of the borrowers purchased homes with less than 10 percent down payments. Fannie and Freddie fueled much of the demand for subprime securities.[75] These subsidies were all off budget. If private banks have tried to omit this volume of loans from their balance sheets, the bank officers would have gone to jail for fraud. Yet when the government resorts to the practice of off balance sheet financing it is business as usual. This is exactly the kind of practice Frederic Bastiat warned against in the 1840s ["See if the law benefits one citizen at the expense of another by doing what the citizen himself cannot do without committing a crime."[76]

Freddie and Fannie have squandered hundreds of billions of dollars by channeling funds into relatively unproductive uses. They have helped fund the housing bubble and misallocated resources. It is time for the federal government to get out of the mortgage business.

74 Anna J. Schwartz, Origins of the Financial Market Crisis of 2008, 29 Cato J. 19-23 (2009).
75 Anna J. Schwartz, Origins of the Financial Market Crisis of 2008, 29 Cato J. 19-23 (2009).
76 Frederic Bastiat, The Law (1968), at 21.

Economists and policy analysts are split on what to do about Freddie Mac and Fannie Mae. Some advocate reform while others advocate abolition[77] or privatization.[78] One thing that is clear is that doing nothing – the status quo – is not acceptable. Pouring more money into those institutions would also be an improper policy, since they have proven they are not capable of investing capital efficiently.

From an ethical perspective the choice is quite clear. Any form of government subsidy violates someone's property rights because it forces one group of individuals to pay for the benefits of other individuals. Furthermore, forcing credit to flow into areas where it would not otherwise flow causes credit to be misallocated, which decreases efficiency, thus violating utilitarian ethics. The only ethical choice is abolition. There are a few ways to accomplish this goal. One way would be to just shut them down. Another option would be to privatize them by selling them to the highest bidder.

OTHER FEDERAL LENDING PROGRAMS

Although this paper cites the Community Reinvestment Act, Freddie Mac and Fannie Mae as part of the problem, other federal lending programs could also be mentioned and analyzed if space permitted. The Small Business Administration lending program, Ginnie Mae and the CDFI (Community Development Financial Institutions) program also distort credit markets. The Federal Housing Administration continues to use its power to loosen downpayment standards. The Department of Housing and Urban Development continues to abuse its power by pressuring lenders to grant mortgage loans to uncreditworthy customers.[79] There is no need for these agencies

77 Allan H. Meltzer, Reflections on the Financial Crisis. 29 Cato J. 25-30 (2009).

78 Lawrence J. White, Fannie Mae, Freddie Mac, and Housing Finance: Why True Privatization Is Good Public Policy. Policy Analysis No. 528, October 7, 2004. Washington, DC: Cato Institute.

79 Tad DeHaven, Three Decades of Politics and Failed Policies at HUD. Policy Analysis No. 655. November 23, 2009. Washington, DC: Cato Institute.

to exist. Their only reason for existence is to subsidize some groups at the expense of the general public. They should also be abolished.

THE FEDERAL RESERVE BOARD

A number of economists have blamed expansive monetary policy for being one of the primary causes of the financial crisis.[80] Alan Greenspan, the former chairman of the U.S. Federal Reserve Board, established a policy of keeping interest rates below the market level. The purpose was worthy. Low interest rates make it easier for businesses to borrow and expand, thus creating jobs. Low rates make it easier for individuals to purchase homes. It seemed like a win-win situation.

However, regulating interest rates so they are below the rates that would be present in a free market has its downside. Low interest rates lead to overexpansion of credit. Businesses that would find it unprofitable to invest in certain projects if interest rates were at the market level find it profitable to invest in some marginal projects if interest rates are below the market level. Individuals who would not otherwise be able to purchase a home on credit now find it possible to purchase a home. Those who already have a home now find it possible to purchase a larger home. The housing market expands beyond what would be the case in a market where interest rates are not kept artificially low. Housing prices are artificially increased because of the excess demand, causing a market bubble. The housing bubble would not have been possible without the Fed's expansive monetary policy.

This overexpansion of credit leads to market distortion, which eventually leads to a reversal, causing either a recession or a depression, depending on the severity of the reversal. F.A. Hayek won

80 Anna J. Schwartz, Origins of the Financial Market Crisis of 2008, 29 Cato J. 19-23 (2009); Lawrence H. White, How Did We Get into This Financial Mess? Cato Institute Briefing Papers No. 110, November 18, 2008. Washington, DC: Cato Institute; Lawrence H. White, Federal Reserve Policy and the Housing Bubble, 29 Cato J. 115-125 (2009).

the Nobel Prize in economics in 1974 for his work in this area,[81] but his work was basically just an extension of the work done by Ludwig von Mises before World War I.[82]

There is a common belief among economic historians that the Federal Reserve Board's mistakes in the area of monetary policy of the 1920s led to the Great Depression of the 1930s.[83] Some economists believe that it was the primary or only cause[84] while others argue that it merely deepened the depression.[85] The evidence is clear that the Fed played a role.

One of the arguments put forth to keep the Fed is because of the stabilizing role it plays in the economy. It supposedly regulates interest rates in the public interest, keeps the money supply growing at the appropriate rate and reduces the severity of economic fluctuations. However, the massive study by Milton Friedman and Anna J. Schwartz of U.S. monetary history[86] dispels that notion. In fact, they found that since the creation of the Federal Reserve Board in 1913 there have been more frequent and more severe economic fluctuations than before the creation of the Fed.

81 F.A. Hayek, Geldtheorie und Konjunkturtheorie (Beitrage zur Konjunkturforschung, herausgegeben vom Österreichisches Institut für Konjunkturforschung, No. 1). Vienna, 1929;
F.A. Hayek, Monetary Theory and the Trade Cycle (1933). Available online at http://mises.org/books/monetarytheory.pdf; F. A. Hayek, Money, Capital & Fluctuations: Early Essays (1984); F. A. Hayek, Prices, Production and Other Works on Money, the Business Cycle and the Gold Standard (2008).

82 Ludwig von Mises, The Theory of Money and Credit (1971). First published in German in 1912 under the title Theorie des Geldes und der Unlaufsmittel.

83 Milton Friedman & Anna J. Schwartz, A Monetary History of the United States, 1867-1960 (1963); Jeffrey M. Lacker, What Lessons Can We Learn from the Boom and Turmoil? 29 Cato J. 53-63 (2009); Allan H. Meltzer, Reflections on the Financial Crisis. 29 Cato J. 25-30 (2009); Murray N. Rothbard, America's Great Depression, 5th edition (2000).

84 Alan Brinkley, American History: A Survey, 12th ed. (2010). Available online at http://highered.mcgrawhill.com/sites/0073124923/student_view0/chapter25/bibliographies.html; Milton Friedman & Anna J. Schwartz, A Monetary History of the United States, 1867-1960 (1963);
Milton Friedman & Anna J. Schwartz, The Great Contraction, 1929-1933 (2008); Ludwig von Mises, On the Manipulation of Money and Credit (1978).

85 Alan Brinkley, American History: A Survey, 12th ed. (2010). Available online at http://highered.mcgrawhill.com/sites/0073124923/student_view0/chapter25/bibliographies.html; Peter Temin, Did Monetary Forces Cause the Great Depression? (1976).

86 Milton Friedman & Anna J. Schwartz, A Monetary History of the United States, 1867-1960 (1963).

If the Fed is to blame, what is the solution? The Fed is nominally independent of the federal government. However, its chairman is appointed by the president and confirmed by the Senate. One proposed solution by Milton Friedman is to end this independence and make it part of the U.S. Treasury.[87] However, that is Friedman's second best solution. His first choice would be to end the Fed.[88]

After President Andrew Jackson failed to renew the charter for the first central bank in the 1830s the United States did quite well without a central bank.[89] The nineteenth century was an almost continuous period of economic growth. The present Federal Reserve Bank was not established until 1913, so it cannot be said that a central bank is essential to a country's economic growth because it is not.

Abolishing the Federal Reserve Board might sound like a radical idea, but actually there is a lot of high-powered intellectual support for it. Milton Friedman and F.A. Hayek, both Nobel Prize winning economists, have called for its abolition.[90] A number of economists have explained how the functions of the Fed could be performed by the market.[91] The clearing function could be taken over easily by the twelve regional banks.

87Milton Friedman & Rose Friedman, Free to Choose (1980), at 308; Milton Friedman, Monetary Policy: Tactics versus Strategy. In The Search for Stable Money 361-382 (James E. Dorn & Anna J. Schwartz, eds., 1987).

88 Brian Doherty, Best of Both Worlds (an interview with Milton Friedman. Reason, June, 1995, online edition, http://reason.com/archives/1995/06/01/best-of-both-worlds.

89 Murray N. Rothbard, The Mystery of Banking (1983).

90Brian Doherty, Best of Both Worlds (an interview with Milton Friedman. Reason, June, 1995, online edition, http://reason.com/archives/1995/06/01/best-of-both-worlds; F. A. Hayek, Choice in Currency. Occasional Paper 48. London: Institute of Economic Affairs, 1976; F. A. Hayek, Toward a Free-Market Monetary System, in The Search for Stable Money 383-390 (James E. Dorn & Anna J. Schwartz, 1987); F. A. Hayek, Denationalisation of Money – The Argument Refined, 3rd edition (1990).

91 F. A. Hayek, Choice in Currency. Occasional Paper 48. London: Institute of Economic Affairs, 1976; F. A. Hayek, Toward a Free-Market Monetary System, in The Search for Stable Money 383-390 (James E. Dorn & Anna J.

The main thing the Fed would no longer be able to do would be to make mistakes in monetary policy, since this function would be assumed by the market. Lawrence H. White (not to be confused with Lawrence J. White) has written two books that outline how free banking has worked in the past[92] and how competing currencies would function.[93] F.A. Hayek[94] outlined a plan for competing currencies that would be created in the private sector and that would be based on some defined basket of goods and services.

The theory of competing currencies has its foundation in monopoly theory. Two inherent characteristics of monopoly are that the cost is higher and the quality is lower than what would be the case under competition. If the Fed is the only legal creator of money, it is a monopolist. If a number of private issuers, such as Citibank, Bank of America, Barclays, and so forth each issue their own money, the monopoly is broken and the doors of competition are open, leading to higher quality money at reduced cost. One might raise the Gresham's Law argument, that bad money drives good money out of circulation. However, Gresham's Law only applies when exchange rates are fixed. Since the collapse of the Bretton Woods Agreement and the reintroduction of flexible exchange rates, there is no longer any need to worry about the Gresham's Law effect. Superior money would be traded at a premium and inferior money would trade at a discount

Space does not permit a full exposition of the theory. Hayek[95] gave us a basic outline in 140 pages and White[96] expanded on the idea with 260 pages of additional analysis. George Selgin[97] has

Schwartz, 1987); F. A. Hayek, Denationalisation of Money – The Argument Refined, 3rd edition (1990); Murray N. Rothbard, The Mystery of Banking (1983); George A. Selgin, The Theory of Free Banking: Money Supply under Competitive Note Issue (1988); Lawrence H. White, Competition and Currency: Essays on Free Banking and Money (1989).

92 Lawrence H. White, Free Banking in Britain: Theory, Experience and Debate, 1800-1845 (1984).

93 Lawrence H. White, Competition and Currency: Essays on Free Banking and Money (1989).

94F. A. Hayek, Choice in Currency. Occasional Paper 48. London: Institute of Economic Affairs, 1976.

95 F. A. Hayek, Choice in Currency. Occasional Paper 48. London: Institute of Economic Affairs, 1976.

also written a book on the subject and White and Selgin co-authored an article available on the internet that provides the basic outline, with links to additional publications.[98]

Suffice it to say that it is an idea worth exploring. If the Fed played a decisive role in the present financial crisis by its cheap money policy, and if the abolition of the Fed's monetary policy function could prevent such mistakes from happening again, the concept of competing currencies and the denationalization of the money supply appear to be a good alternative to the status quo.

The idea of competing currencies meets both the utilitarian ethics test and the rights test. Competing currencies would improve quality and reduce cost, thus increasing efficiency. The fact that the government monopoly would be broken strengthens property and contract rights, since the present government monopoly punishes private money issuers and prevents them from entering into contracts and trading the property they have for the property they want. Hülsmann,[99] writing from the perspective of Christian ethics, holds that the present government monopoly monetary system creates unjust incomes, destroys wealth, subverts the moral foundations of society and ultimately paves the way for hyperinflation and totalitarianism.

---

96 Lawrence H. White, Competition and Currency: Essays on Free Banking and Money (1989).

97 George A. Selgin, The Theory of Free Banking: Money Supply under Competitive Note Issue (1988).

98 Lawrence H. White & George Selgin, Why Private Banks and Not Central Banks Should Issue Currency, Especially in Less Developed Countries. Library of Economics and Liberty. April 19, 2000. http://www.econlib.org/library/Features/feature3.html. Accessed 25 January 2010.

99 Jörg G. Hülsmann, The Ethics of Money Production (2008).

FEDERAL TAX LAW

Several provisions of the federal tax code[100] subsidize home purchases. Perhaps the largest and most visible subsidy is the provision that allows taxpayers to deduct mortgage interest and real estate taxes on their primary homes and, in some cases, on secondary homes as well. For people in the 25 percent tax bracket, monthly interest and tax payments of $2000 reduce their tax liability by $500.

Many people in the lower income brackets do not pay any federal income taxes, or if they do pay taxes, they take the standard deduction rather than itemize their deductions, which means that many people with low incomes are not able to take advantage of this subsidy. The federal mortgage interest and real estate tax deduction are beneficial mostly to middle and upper income individuals. At least one study[101] has found that eliminating the mortgage interest deduction would increase horizontal equity.[102]

This subsidy distorts both the housing market and the credit market. Making homes artificially cheaper on an after-tax basis causes home price inflation. Diverting capital into the mortgage market also results in less capital being available for other types of loans, including business loans, thus increasing the cost of capital to businesses and making it more difficult to stay in business and to compete internationally.

What is not seen is the depressing effect the subsidy has on rental property. If the demand for homes increases, the demand for rental units must decrease, leading to reduced profits in the real estate rental market and increased bankruptcies, as marginal providers are unable to generate sufficient revenue to stay in business. Landlords who do survive will have fewer funds available to maintain and improve their properties, to both their detriment and the detriment of their tenants.

---

100 Title 26 U.S.C.

101Susan Rhame & Robert Walsh, Measuring Increases in Horizontal Equity In The Absence Of Certain Itemized Deductions And Phase Outs, 7(10) J. Bus. & Econ. Res. 39-45 (2009).

102 Horizontal equity means that people earning about the same income pay about the same amount of taxes.

There are several ways to eliminate this subsidy. One solution would be to repeal the provision that allows homeowners to deduct their mortgage interest and property taxes. However, doing so would result in a tax increase for those affected by the repeal, which is not a good idea, given the fact that taxes are already taking too much money out of the private economy. If this solution were tried, it would be necessary to reduce tax rates so that the change would not result in a heavier tax burden.

Another solution would be to allow renters to deduct the cost of their rent. Doing so would level the playing field between those who rent and those who own. It would also increase the desirability of rental housing, which would remove the present bias against landlords. The problem with this solution, from an ethical and philosophical perspective, is that it is a form of subsidy, which is a step in exactly the wrong direction. Subsidies result in market distortion and housing subsidies of any kind artificially inflate housing prices, leading to bubbles in the housing market. The best policy would be to abolish all subsidies and adjust taxes downward to offset what would otherwise be tax increases.

Another, lesser known effect of interest deductibility is the effect it has on income shifting from mortgage holders to banks. A study by Harris and Kilic[103] found that mortgage rates vary positively with both banks' tax costs and mortgage holders' interest tax deductions, with the effect that banks are able to pass on their tax costs to consumers and also capture a portion of their borrowers' tax benefits. The annual magnitude of this tax shift was estimated to be $23 billion.

The federal government has enacted a number of tax credits to encourage potential home buyers to purchase a home. The rules in this area are changing rapidly and the rules about to be discussed may be replaced or supplemented by other rules by the time this article appears in print, so

103 David G. Harris & Emre Kilic, Bilateral Implicit Taxes and Anti-Competitive Banking Regulation, 31(2) J. Am. Tax. Assn. 45-73 (2009).

this discussion should be considered as an example of how the Internal Revenue Code is used to subsidize home purchases rather than an up-to-date tax treatise that can be relied on for investment purposes.

The Housing and Economic Recovery Act of 2008[104] established a $7500 tax credit for first-time home buyers. The American Recovery and Reinvestment Act of 2009[105] increased that amount to $8,000 and changed the repayment and qualification rules.[106] The Worker, Homeownership and Business Assistance Act of 2009[107] extended the tax credit into 2010 and expanded the rules by allowing existing homeowners to get the credit as well.[108] IRS Form 5405 can be used to claim the credit. The effect of the credit is to increase demand for homes, which leads to an artificially induced boom in housing prices. It also makes it easier for uncreditworthy individuals to purchase homes that they otherwise would not be able to afford.

Some governments at the sub-federal level also subsidize mortgage interest payments. Some states issue Mortgage Credit Certificates, which allow homeowners to take a tax credit rather than a tax deduction for home mortgage interest.[109]

Another federal tax provision that encourages debt is the business interest deduction. Businesses are allowed to deduct interest but not dividend payments, leading to an after-tax reduction in the cost of debt capital relative to equity capital. As a result, businesses are encouraged to use debt rather than equity to finance their operations. Increasing the ratio of debt also results in

104 PL 110-289 (2008).
105 PL 111-5 (2009).
106 Nell Adkins & B. Charlene Henderson, Help for Homebuyers: A Guide to the First-Time Home Buyer Credit. 27(5) J. Accountancy 34-37 (2009).

107 H.R. 3548.
108 Anonymous. Worker, Homeownership, and Business Assistance Act of 2009, 23 Tax Mgmt Tax Practice Series Bull. 14-15 (2009).

109 Erica Greulich & John M. Quigley, Housing subsidies and tax expenditures: The case of mortgage credit certificates. 39 Regional Science & Urban Econ. 647-657 (2009).

increasing the return on equity capital, since there is less of it. However, it also increases the after-tax cost of equity capital.

This bias in favor of debt financing is especially relevant for banks, since the debt bias encourages them to become less solvent. It is obvious that less solvent banks pose a threat to the financial system, yet federal tax policy encourages banks to become less solvent.

The federal government also gives special tax breaks to certain lenders, such as credit unions, Fannie Mae, Freddie Mac and the Federal Home Loan Banks, a practice that is inherently unfair to other lenders. These tax breaks are little more than subsidies. In the case of Fannie Mae and Freddie Mac they are subsidies that reward poor performance. They should be eliminated in the interests of fairness and efficiency.

MARK-TO-MARKET ACCOUNTING

Mark-to-market accounting, the financial reporting rule that requires companies to list certain assets on their balance sheets at current market value instead of historical cost, has been cited as one of the contributing causes of the financial crisis.[110] In a sense, the allegation has some merit. If the market value of investments falls far below historical cost, and if the companies holding those investments are forced to disclose that fact to the public in their annual and quarterly reports, investors and analysts who read those reports could decide to sell their shares in those companies, thus causing a decline in stock price. If a sufficient number of investors decide to sell it could lead to insolvency.[111]

---

110 Gary Wolfram, Accounting Rules at Heart of Bank Crisis. March 13, 2009. HumanEvents.com. Accessed 24 January 2010.

111 Franklin Allen & Elena Carletti, Mark-to-Market Accounting and Liquidity Pricing, 45 J. Acct. & Econ. 358-378 (2008).

But that is only part of the story. One reason why some securities declined so much in value is because of the rise and increased popularity of some derivatives and securitized mortgage instruments. Combining thousands of subprime mortgages that are thought to be federally secured into a single instrument causes valuation problems that are not easy to unwrap. Many of those complex financial instruments were issued before the market became aware of their flaws. Neither the designer of those instruments nor their purchasers understood the risks.[112] As those risks started to become known, the prices of those instruments declined and the mark-to-market accounting rule required corporate holders of those securities to report them at current market value rather than historical cost. Mark-to-market accounting merely exposed these bad investment decisions to the light of day. It is a case of the messenger being blamed for reporting the collapse of market values.[113]

That is not to say that the mark-to-market rule could not be amended to take temporary declines into account, provided one can be reasonably sure that the decline is only temporary. One might even make the case that debt securities, which have a clearly defined maturity date, should not be included in the list of securities that should be listed at current market value, since their market value and maturity value will be identical at the maturity date. But arguing that merely reporting the facts about market values "caused" the financial crisis is a losing argument. What is the alternative? To not report the facts in order to avert or delay the crisis, which would only allow the situation to fester and get worse over time? If one is to look for causes and cures, requiring companies to report their investments at historical costs when their value has declined is not a good policy option. It also is not honest because it results in deliberately reporting inaccurate numbers.

112 Anna J. Schwartz, Origins of the Financial Market Crisis of 2008, 29 Cato J. 19-23 (2009).

113 Sharon S. Seay & Mimi Ford, The Ethical Implications of Fair Value Accounting Pursuant to the December 28, 2008 SEC Study on Mark-to-Market Accounting. Proceedings of the Allied Academies International Conference, 2009, New Orleans, at 49.

THE ETHICS OF BAILOUTS

> The state is the great fictitious entity by which everyone seeks to live at the expense of everyone else.[114]

> The illegitimate use of a state by economic interests for their own ends is based upon a preexisting illegitimate power of the state to enrich some persons at the expense of others.[115]

> Through the years, some men have discovered how to satisfy their wants at the expense of others without being accused of theft: they ask their government to do the stealing for them.[116]

Corporate bailouts are always and everywhere a violation of both utilitarian ethics and rights. They necessarily violate utilitarian ethics because they cause assets to be taken from the more productive sectors of the economy and transferred to the less productive sectors. They violate property rights because taxpayers are forced to part with their property (money) to pay for it.

Bailouts are inherently unfair because they force the productive and successful members of the community to subsidize (reward) the inefficient and the incompetent. Bailouts are nothing more than special interest legislation that benefits some favored minority interest at the expense of the general public. Bailouts serve to socialize risks and privatize gains. They also create moral hazards. Bankers feel they can make riskier loans if they know they will be bailed out. Insurance executives are less restrained in insuring risky ventures if government regulators tell them they are too big to fail.

114Frederic Bastiat, Selected Essays on Political Economy (1964) at 144. This essay was first published as a pamphlet and is reprinted in Oeuvres Complètes de Frédéric Bastiat, Vol. V, Paris: Guillaumin et Cie, 1862: 336-392.

115 Robert Nozick, Anarchy, State and Utopia (1974), at 272.

116 William M. Curtiss, The Tariff Idea (1953), at 19.

One might argue that some bailouts are justified on economic grounds because they prevent worse things from happening. The auto bailout saved jobs. The banking and insurance industry bailouts prevented a collapse of the financial system.

Such arguments sound plausible on the surface. However, if one digs below the surface one soon realizes that such arguments are incomplete and that those who advocate them are acting as what Bastiat referred to as bad economists[117] because they fail to take into account the effect the policy would have on all groups, both in the short-run and in the long-run.

One must remember that government has no resources of its own. Whatever resources it has it must first take from someone. If some government program pumps $500 billion into a particular failing industry, it must take the money out of some other sectors of the economy. The sector that receives the funds expands and prospers while the sectors that have the capital sucked out of them must necessarily shrink.

However, the shift from the productive sector to the relatively unproductive sector is not a zero-sum game. It is a negative-sum game because resources are being shifted from sectors that are relatively productive to a sector that is relatively unproductive. This shift can be illustrated mathematically as follows:[118]

If:
a = the rate of return in the average industry,
b = the rate of return in the bailed out industry,
c = cash injection,
m = multiplier, and
$b < a$, then
$bcm - acm < 0$

If we set:
a = 5%,

117 Frederic Bastiat, Selected Essays on Political Economy (1964) at 1.
118 Robert W. McGee, Obama, Bastiat and Economic Stimulus Packages. Proceedings of the International Academy of Business and Public Administration Disciplines Winter 2010 Conference, 3-6 January 2010, Orlando, USA: 858-864, at 862.

$b = 1\%$,
$c = \$1$ trillion, and
$m = 5$, then
$bcm - acm = 0.01(\$1 \text{ trillion})(5) - 0.05(\$1 \text{ trillion})(5) < 0$

All bailouts thus fail the Pareto, Posnerian[119] and Primeaux and Stieber[120] efficiency tests. They also violate property rights, since the property transfers are not voluntary.

THE CURE

The financial crisis could have been prevented by applying utilitarian ethical principles and rights theory – Don't do anything that results in negative-sum games and don't violate property or contract rights. The cure starts by undoing all the things that got us into this mess. End all subsidies. Abolish any federal agency that produces negative-sum games or that violates property or contract rights.

Those who call for more regulation almost unanimously assume that it is the government that must be the regulator. However, such is not necessarily the case. The market can also act as a regulator. In fact, the market can be a very good regulator. The market did an excellent job of punishing the accounting firm of Arthur Andersen for its failed audits of Enron. The market acted much more swiftly and efficiently than did the government. Once the word got out that Arthur Andersen conducted a bad audit, its audit clients left in droves, well before the government lawsuits got to court, a process that took years. So it cannot be assumed that the government is the only regulator of corporate behavior. The market has a track record of being a very efficient regulator.[121]

119 Richard A. Posner, Utilitarianism, Economics, and Legal Theory, 8 J. Legal Stud. 103-140 (1979); Richard A. Posner, The Economics of Justice (1983); Richard A. Posner, Economic Analysis of Law, 5th edition (1998).

120 Patrick Primeaux & John Stieber, Managing Business Ethics and Opportunity Costs, 16 J. Bus. Ethics 835-842 (1997).

121 Ludwig von Mises, Human Action: A Treatise on Economics (2008).

If the goal is to make it more difficult and costly for banks and other financial institutions to engage in risky and speculative schemes, why not take away the government created safety nets that subsidize this behavior and make those institutions subject to market discipline? If financial institutions knew that the government would not insure them or bail them out if they failed, they would be far less likely to engage in risky ventures. The moral hazard problem would be greatly reduced.

THE HIDDEN LAW: UNCOVERING THE SPIRITUAL FOUNDATIONS FOR TRANSFORMATIVE LEGAL REFORM

MAURICE R. DYSON[†]

The Hidden Law patiently teaches
It quietly guides the soul but never preaches
If we only listen and humbly abide
It will bring harmony in good stride
Disobey and all it will say
Bid as your ego wills on this day
For you are the Judge of your own transgression
And the Cause of your own perdition
But the Hidden Law reminds
It is for our own benefit that it binds
I to Thou and Thou to I
Star to star and galaxy to sky
Lovingly it accepts our mortal flaw,
Yet alas elevates us in its Law —M. R. Dyson[1]

The world is confronting profound change and challenge like never before. Revolutionary changes swelling in Iran, the manmade engineered disasters of the Great Global Recession, the conquest of natural resources in the face of profound climatic global change, massive demoralization and restructurings of America's public schools, civil strife over religion, sexual identity, ethnicity and race since the election of a first Black president has pointed society to both profound change in the air and significant challenges on the ground, perhaps of our own doing. Has society itself manifested

† Maurice R. Dyson, J.D., Columbia University School of Law; A.B., Columbia College, Columbia University; Associate Professor of Law, Thomas Jefferson School of Law; Professor Dyson practiced law with the firm of Simpson Thacher & Bartlett where he participated in the landmark Department of Education finance litigation, and in federal civil rights enforcement as the Special Projects team attorney for the U.S. Office for Civil Rights (OCR), where he was recognized for his work in inter district funding equity analysis. A member of the Bar of the U.S. Supreme Court, Professor Dyson has also served as the national chairperson of the Association of American Law Schools (AALS) Section on Education Law, a national executive board member of the AALS Section of Minority Groups, a member of the board of directors of the Mildred Quinn Foundation, and as the N.Y. program coordinator of the Merrill Lynch Philanthropic Foundation. In addition, he has served as educational policy adviser to the Texas State Legislature Joint Select Committee on Public School Finance, and various elected officials, and has taught law on the faculties of Columbia University, the City University of New York, and the Southern Methodist University Dedman School of Law. He is the recipient of numerous awards including the prestigious King's Crown Award, the Kluge Award, the Albert Roothbert Endowment, the Lester A. and Stella Porter Russell Endowment, the Society of the Order of the Barristers and the Taft Samuel Carpenter Award for Teaching Excellence. This work is dedicated to the late MaryAnne L. Lee, a devoted mother, friend and spiritual teacher.

1 See Maurice R. Dyson, Voices of the Apocrypha: Collected Poems (2009); For another poetic verse of the hidden law, see also W.H. Auden, The Hidden Law ("The Hidden Law does not deny our laws of probability, but takes the atom and the star And human beings as they are, and answers nothing when we lie. It is the only reason why No government can codify, And verbal definitions mar.").

these challenges into the reality of existence under the influence of some hidden law at work not previously perceptible in our legal framework? Perhaps most of these profound events around the globe today may be attributed to an ego-centered conscience inculcated in our law, policy and societal ethos. New revelations about humankind's ability to adapt to profound changes and successfully overcome these challenges with a new spiritual consciousness has begun to emerge with greater conspicuousness in the popular conscience. This article seeks to illustrate and explore how our legal systems foster an ego conscience approach to domestic and global concerns and the ways in which this approach has not only been a disservice to society by fomenting greater conflict but in fact how the law functions to subverts itself in the quest to promote meaningful solutions. The manifested realities of an ego conscience jurisprudential approach in the face of increasingly globalization today, which comes at the expense of what is termed a soul centered conscience, may be evidentially clear and worse, significantly dire. This article proposes incorporating a novel soul conscience approach to sociolegal reform and reveals some new ways in which it can and has yielded effective transformative legal change in an era of post-enlightenment globalization. However, revealing the spiritual foundations for transformative sociolegal reform grounded in a soul centered conscience approach will require profound but an important reexamination in three primary arenas that have fostered an ego centered conscience approach. First, is to explore the ways in which the law generally obscures the spiritual interrelatedness of societal, political and economic relations and its practical implications within which it arises. Second, is to explore the ways in which the law is practiced and taught, so that the primary individuals of interest are those who practice and teach law that reveals the discouragement of discourse about spiritual well being, values and legal morality. A third major task of the article to explore the ways in which the law spiritually affects the individual well being of those who may be specifically touched by its intrinsic ego centered assumptions as well as its outcomes, in terms of practicing lawyers as well as those individual clients, claimants, victims and alleged perpetrators who are caught up in the legal system.

INTRODUCTION

Much of the nation's attention has been captured by the law of attraction and the laws of the universe with the publication of recent works *The Secret*[2] *The Power of Intention*[3] and the books of Esther and Jerry Hicks' *Ask and It Shall Be Given* and other such works. [4] The works of Abraham-Hicks has captured both our attention and popular imagination raises the question about whether

2 Rhonda Byrne, The Secret (2006); see also Michael J. Losier, Law of Attraction, The Science of Attracting More of What You Want and Less of What You Don't (2006).

3 Wayne W. Dyer, The Power of Intention 3 (2004) ("In the universe there is an immeasurable force which shamans call intent and absolutely everything that exists in the entire cosmos is attached to intent by a connecting link." (quoting Carlos Castaneda)).

4 Ester and Jerry Hicks, A New Beginning I: Handbook for Joyous Survival, by Jerry and Esther Hicks (1988); A New Beginning II: A Personal Handbook to Enhance Your Life, Liberty and Pursuit of Happiness (1991); Sara and the Foreverness of Friends of a Feather (1995); Ask and It Is Given: Learning to Manifest Your Desires by Esther and Jerry Hicks (2005); The Amazing Power of Deliberate Intent: Living the Art of Allowing (2005); The Law of Attraction: The Basics of the Teachings of Abraham Esther and Jerry Hicks (2006); Sara, Book 1: Sara Learns the Secret about the Law of Attraction (2007); Sara, Book 2: Solomon's Fine Featherless Friends (2007); Sara, Book 3: A Talking Owl Is Worth a Thousand Words!, by Esther and Jerry Hicks (2008); Money and the Law of Attraction: Learning to Attract Health, Wealth & Happiness by Esther and Jerry Hicks (2008). The Vortex: Where the Law of Attraction Assembles All Cooperative Relationships (2009).

there exist a hidden law of the universe known as the law of attraction[5] that bases a life approach upon the notion that each of us is a deliberate creator of our reality.[6] It has been suggested that this unseen law of attraction regulates the universe of seemingly appearing physical matter that in actuality comprises pure energy. This pure energy permeates the environs of our being which has long confounded humanity's wisdom to understand it under outdated conceptions of Newtonian physics.[7] Subscribers to the belief suggest we are beginning to witness since the revelation of Einstein's theory of relativity and Niels Bohr's refinement of that theory an emerging consensus in both scientific and spiritual literature that everything and every living being existing in the universe, including what appears as solid mass itself, is at its subatomic core, merely a vibrating frequency of energy. This energy which binds together with other energies of the same harmonious frequency to constitute what we perceive to be reality determines all of what we experience in the physical world.[8] Further, as each of us are vibrating masses of pure energy that is intricately interconnected to everything else, we begin to see our interconnectedness and the ability of energy to attract similar energy to create harmonious frequencies. Much of the body of scholarship in modern humanistic psychology, holistic medicine and wellness, religion and economics, both positive thinking and unconditional love has been viewed as the most potent pure invisible energy vibrational frequency in which the energy in the universe responds to through intention and thought to manifesting correlative outcomes in our physical reality.[9]

---

5 See See Abraham Hicks, Law of Attraction Quotes ("Every thought that you think is vibrating at a very personal frequency . . . and by the powerful Law of Attraction (the essence of that which is like unto itself, is drawn), that thought is now attracting another thought that is its Vibrational Match. And now, those combined thoughts are vibrating at a frequency that is higher than the thought that came before; and they will now, by the Law of Attraction, attract another and another and another, until eventually the thoughts will be powerful enough to attract a "real life" situation or manifestation. Excerpted from Money and the Law of Attraction — 3/31/09"), available at http://www.abraham-hicks.com/lawofattractionsource/index.php (last visited Feb. 22, 2010).

6 See generally Abraham Hicks, The Teachings of Abraham-Hicks (Abraham is said to be a spiritual entity that speaks through Ester Hicks provide as follows: "You are a physical extension of that which is non-physical; You are here in this body because you chose to be here; The basis of your life is freedom; the purpose of your life is joy; You are a creator; you create with your every thought; Anything that you can imagine is yours to be or do or have; You are choosing your creations as you are choosing your thoughts; The Universe adores you, for it knows your broadest intentions; Relax into your natural well-being. All is well; You are a creator of thoughtways on your unique path of joy; Actions to be taken and money to be exchanged are by-products of your focus on joy; You may appropriately depart your body without illness or pain; You can not die; you are everlasting life.") available at http://www.abraham-hicks.com (last visited Feb. 22, 2010)); The Vortex: Where the Law of Attraction Assembles All Cooperative Relationships (2009).

7 See generally Karen Kingston, Creating Sacred Space with Feng Shui: Learn the Art of Space Clearing and Bring New Energy into Your Life (1997).

8 See generally Brian Greene, The Elegant Universe: Superstrings, Hidden Dimensions, and the Quest for the Ultimate Theory (1999) Cf. John Polkinghorne, Quantum Physics and Theology: An Unexpected Kinship (2007); U.S. Department of Energy, Office of Science, What is Physics?, available at http://www.science.doe.gov/Sub/Newsroom/News_Releases/DOE-SC/2005/What_is_ Physics.htm (last visited Sept. 12, 2008); E. WIGNER, SYMMETRIES AND REFLECTIONS 192 (1967); see F. CAPRA, THE TAO OF PHYSICS (1975); D. POSTLE, FABRIC OF THE UNIVERSE (1976); B. TOBEN, SPACE-TIME AND BEYOND (1975).

9 These findings were purportedly confirmed by a cohort of quantum physicists and other scientists in an experiment later known as The Copenhagen Interpretation which reached the conclusion that energy acted and responded in exact proportion to the thoughts and beliefs that the scientist who was studying them had at that moment and that as these particles form they attract additional particles that harmonize with their vibrational match which transmutes from the quantum field and become the physical form of visible matter. See generally Brian Greene, The Elegant Universe: Superstrings, Hidden Dimensions, and the Quest for the Ultimate Theory (1999); John Polkinghorne, Quantum Physics and Theology: An Unexpected Kinship (2007).

These notions that thoughts are creative vibrational energy and may result in physical appearing particles of energy based on one's belief however are not new. This law of attraction find its roots in both modern and centuries of theological teachings including those of Jesus Christ, St. Thomas Aquinas and Dr. Martin Luther King, Jr. who embraced an eternal, universal law predicated upon unconditional love and intentionality of faith "that could move mountains with faith the size of a mustard seed."[10] Nonetheless, the purported emerging consensus between quantum physics, medicine and theology raise important questions about the ability and role of law in manifesting societal outcomes based upon the intentions and expectations of law and policymakers and those who the law impacts. However, the law of attraction thesis has come under sharp attack in recent times, raising profound questions about the power of harnessing positive energy through positive thinking to order one's lives and by extension to positively manifest positive order in the world. Conversely, some have begun to wonder what role has negative energy of global human conflict, competition for natural resources and the unethical pursuit of wealth has played in the manifestation of the realities concerning our current economic crisis, ponzi investment schemes as well as religious and social conflict.

Perhaps America has much cause for optimism in positive thinking as part of its spiritual awakening. But the once optimistic America that embraced optimistic hope and change to catapult its first African-American into the presidency has given way to a growing cynicism and doubt as of late as we grow mired in partisanship and discord. In this article, I attempt to unpack the assumptions in the beliefs of positive thinking as a means to understand our ability to effectuate meaningful educational and socio-legal transformational reform. However, I nonetheless suggest one should not misapprehend law of attraction principles in ways that unwittingly undermine our spiritual growth as a society by fostering denial, complacency, lack of empathy or concern for our human condition including the least of these among us, to wit—those victims of discrimination, poverty and illness. As I argue and attempt to show, the spiritual pitfalls that accompany the misapprehension of the popular positive thinking law of attraction movement has, and will only continue to lead to the embrace of a narrow ego-centered construction of a post-racial, acontextual, anti-Islamic, anti-gay, anti-education society. I also suggest this misapprehension and dogged adherence to a myopic notion of the law of attraction may justify a passive complacency in our jurisprudence on issues of equity, fairness and restorative justice with regard to a whole host of domestic and international matters. To this end, we explore the unraveling of spiritual values or soul conscience in the law that has only contributed to the promotion of societal conflict rather than the resolution of it. Accordingly, a return to the principles of fairness which have now fallen to the wayside of the American common law system is needed to move to an inclusive system of educational and legal reform predicated upon positive reinforcement, conciliatory system of legal dispute resolution that enhances the spiritual well being and equality of all stakeholders involved and which embraces what some refer to as the universal law of divine oneness. I suggest that it is when we defy this law of oneness, and thus deny our interconnectedness, that humanity begins to witness

10 See Holy Bible, New Testament, Matthew 17:20. ("And Jesus said unto them, Because of your unbelief: for verily I say unto you, If ye have faith as a grain of mustard seed, ye shall say unto this mountain, Remove hence to yonder place; and it shall remove; and nothing shall be impossible unto you."); Holy Bible, New Testament, Luke 17:6 ("And the Lord said, "If you had faith like a mustard seed, you would say to this mulberry tree, 'Be uprooted and be planted in the sea'; and it would obey you."); Holy Bible, New Testament, Mark 11:23 ("Truly I say to you, whoever says to this mountain, 'Be taken up and cast into the sea,' and does not doubt in his heart, but believes that what he says is going to happen, it will be granted him.").

some of its greatest suffering including the recent global economic and climatic crisis. Conversely, it is ultimately by embracing our oneness that America and the world will resolve its karmatic challenges of globalization including those related to race, economic growth and climatic change. These challenges can be met by a full embrace of the role of spiritual values of inclusiveness, positive visualization, reconciliation, forgiveness and restoration of the individual and community relationship in the administration of educational policies and justice.[11] Therefore, if we are to transform the spiritual ethos of educational and legal reform, a change in the ethos of educational and legal culture in society itself is needed. Yet in the search for that culture we must be vigilant that notions of purported laws of the universe that harness the enormous potential of the human mind to create our realities are not delinked from the spiritual values of inclusiveness, well-being, acceptance, love, justice and oneness that permeate, hold and bind us all together.

THE LAW OF DIVINE ONENESS / INTERRELATEDNESS

The Law of Divine Oneness "helps us to understand that we live in a world where everything is connected to everything else. Everything we do, say, think and believe affects others and the universe around us."[12] As further explained, this law of divine oneness exist for a reason:

> "Every Soul, living and discarnate, is connected at the level of the collective unconscious, deep within the Higher-Self. We are all part of a great energy gestalt called God, and because we are part of God, we are God. It is the goal of the gestalt to move the energy forward, creating more energy. So, in living harmoniously, we each increase

11 This article suggests a return to the principles in the system of equity that promoted fairness which have now fallen to the wayside of the American common law system. In so doing, it is advised that we embrace the metaphysical nature of positive law professed by Aquinas, Kant and King to ensure the relationship between law and justice do not remain unraveled but rather reflect the best traditions of spiritual post-enlightenment values to move the collective gestalt karma of the nation and world forward in the face of increased globalization. I suggest the nation must move to a conciliatory system of dispute resolution that enhances the well being of all stakeholders involved: the client, attorney, and community groups alike if it is to reunite law and justice and uplift the standing of the legal profession as a whole. To this end, the comprehensive law movement and critical jurisprudential theories should not be viewed separately from, but as a manifest realization of the law and spirituality movement wherein spiritual consciousness in the practice, teaching and conception of laws become manifest. Experience suggests society is better off when it embraces the universal law of oneness implicit in the teachings and examples of Kant, King and the Dalai Lama. It is when we defy this law of oneness, and thus deny our interconnectedness, that humanity begins to see its greatest suffering. As we have seen, when we defy the law of oneness, we also deny the Kantian categorical imperative. To put it another way, when we begin to treat each other as a means to an end rather than as an end in itself in violation of the Kantian conception of the categorical imperative, we deny each other's inherent intrinsic value, and thus our interrelated oneness as humanity. Defying this metaphysical law of oneness will continue to see genocide, global environmental destruction, wall street corruption, more Great Recessions and racial subjugation. Further, it is ultimately by embracing our oneness that America and the world will resolve its karmatic challenges of globalization. These challenges are not merely related to race, but economic growth and climatic change. However, to the extent each are an outgrowth of our collective failure to see beyond ourselves to our interrelatedness, and thus see our destinies as interconnected, race serves as a good metaphor for the challenges we confront today which at its core, is to understand the effect of one's action upon another and to accordingly respect one another's humanity. Only by embracing our collective interrelatedness, are we able to overcome the interest-convergence dilemma and fully take accountability for cause and effect, a universal law of metaphysics at the heart of America and the world's karmatic lesson. For in order to spiritually grow as individuals and as a collective gestalt, it is our responsibility to acknowledge the cause and effect of our own actions on another and to ultimately take accountability for it.

12 Deepak Chopra, The Seven Spiritual Laws of Success (2007), available at http://www.ofspirit.com/deepakchopra1.htm (last visited Feb. 4. 2010).

> our vibrational rate and intensify the vibration of the entire gestalt. When we are disharmonious, we decrease the vibration of the entire gestalt, because we are one, everything you think, say and do, affects every other Soul."[13]

The law of oneness, also bears some relation to the law of potentiality, the notion that all of us are not only at our subatomic core as Einstein discovered, energy, but in possessing the ability to manipulate malleable energy by our thought and expectations that we are are pure potentiality which cannot be fully realized in an individual without acknowledging our collective oneness.[14] The soul conscience level of awareness accepts our commonality as a collective composed of the same common energy. Among many others, it was Dr. Martin Luther King Jr. who appeared to be keenly aware of the universal law of divine oneness as evidenced in his writings. He fully acknowledged the interconnectedness of each of us and as a result the effect of one's behavior upon another. In other words, our interrelatedness is really also a reflection of our interdependence. He was able to understand that "[w]hatever affects one directly, affects all indirectly."[15] He boldly proclaimed "I can never be what I ought to be until you are what you ought to be. This is the interrelated structure of reality." Consequently, we do not have the luxury of passive indifference to the injustice of others."[16]

INTERRELATEDNESS (SOUL CONSCIENCE) V. FALSE INHERENT EXISTENCE (EGO CONSCIENCE)

As social psychologist Edward Deci observed, whether an individual internalizes external norms corresponds to the level in which they feel autonomous yet related to others because these are the "innate psychological nutriments that are essential for on-going psychological growth, integrity, and well-being."[17] Moreover, self esteem that rest upon the external need for approval is the very

---

13 Id.

14 Id. Pure potentiality can only be realized through an acknowledgement of our divine oneness. ("This law is based on the fact that we are, in our essential state, pure consciousness. Pure consciousness is pure potentiality; it is the field of all possibilities and infinite creativity. When you discover your essential nature and know who you really are, in that knowing itself is the ability to fulfill any dream you have, because you are the eternal possibility, the immeasurable potential of all that was, is and will be. This law could also be called the Law of Unity, because underlying the infinite diversity of life is the unity of one all-pervasive spirit. There is no separation between you and this field of energy. One way to access the field is through the daily practice of silence, meditation and non-judgment. Spending time in nature will also give you access to the qualities inherent in the field: infinite creativity, freedom and bliss.").

15 James M. Washington ed., A TESTAMENT OF HOPE: THE ESSENTIAL WRITINGS AND SPEECHES OF MARTIN LUTHER KING, JR. 626 (1986)("All men are interdependent. Every nation is an heir of a vast treasury of ideas and labor to which both the living and the dead of all nations have contributed. Whether we realize it or not, each of us lives eternally 'in the red.' We are everlasting debtors to known and unknown men and women. When we arise in the morning, w go into the bathroom where we reach for a sponge which is provided for us by a Pacific Islander. We reach for soap that is created for us by a European. Then at the table we drink coffee which is provided for us by a South American, or tea by a Chinese or cocoa by a West African. Before we leave for our jobs we are already beholden to more than half the world.").

16 See id. ("I am cognizant of the interrelatedness of all communities and states. I cannot sit idly by in Atlanta and not be concerned about what happens in Birmingham. Injustice anywhere is a threat to justice everywhere. We are caught in an inescapable network of mutuality, tied in a single garment of destiny. Whatever affects one directly, affects all indirectly. Never again can we afford to live with the narrow, provincial "outside agitator" idea. Anyone who lives inside the United States can never be considered an outsider anywhere within its bounds.").

17 Deci & Ryan, The "What" and "Why" of Goal Pursuits, at 227, 229 (2000) cited in Katharine T. Bartlett, Making Good on Good Intentions, 95 Va. L. Rev. 1893, 1932 (2009).

embodiment of insecurity that becomes the defining characteristic ego conscience. The more insecure their self-esteem, the more approval from others is required to maintain it, and the further one moves away from their own alignment with their inner healing energy of soul conscience. The unhealthy ego mind is often the result of low self esteem that is solely concerned with its own unquenchable gratification in materiality, maintaining its separate identity, its continued survival over death at all costs, and the false illusion that which exists outside of oneself will bring lasting satisfaction as each of these provide the needed "feel" for security.[18] As a result, insecure self-esteem "does not support the internalization of legal and social norms, such as nondiscrimination; it works against them.[19] Ego conscience has as its own agenda its continued survival predicated on creating false distinctions between people and groups as separate and apart from oneself. Since death is the only occurrence that the ego believes is absolutely sure exists in the world, it continually "lives in fear of everything" for there is "no way to know which part of the "separate" Universe will attempt to claim its life" preferring to seek security for its survival in grandiose houses, cars, false distinctions between people and groups that give it a false sense of security from death.[20] The result of this false distinction and illusion of independent, separate existence often obscures the cause and effect relationship between people and their actions. The next sections below will demonstrate what happens when the ego conscience illusion of independent and inherent existences is embodied in legal systems and human actions. As we will see, much of the current global economic and social crisis confronted today bear witness to this truth and the consequences of this illusion. In Buddhist thought it is quite interesting to see the truth of interrelatedness operate with prominence in its explanation of the dependent arising nature of the world. Because every cause is viewed in itself as an effect of its own preceding cause, it is dependent upon its own respective causes. Since a cause is labeled so in relations to its future designated effect, it is not truly an independent cause but interrelated to its effect in a way that shows the dependent arising nature of matter and all human beings. Buddhist thought explains that there is no inherent existence that is independent as the ego conscience driven individual believes. As the Dalai Lama explains, "if you understand that, no matter what appears, whether to your senses or to your thinking mind, those objects are established in dependence upon thought, you will get over the idea that phenomena exist in their own right."[21] Further, it is this false notion that things, events and persons have an inherent existence of their own beyond and apart from their counterparts that extreme action, ignorance, self interest motive and afflictive emotions are engendered in error.[22] Therefore to overcome the dilemma of the interest-convergence,[23] one must see their own action, their own survival and well being as dependent upon

18 James F. Twyman, The Moses Code: The Most Powerful Manifestation Tool In The History of the World (2008) at 84-86 ("The ego believes that everything is separate from everything itself is separate from everything that it perceives. In other words, you're split apart from the person sitting next to you, the house in which you live, the world that supports your existence, and the Universe that contains all life…Because you're isolated and alone, you must find a way to defend you life from all other things that may and probably will attack you. If you don't then something, at one point or another, is going to come along and claim you. This is what the ego calls death.")

19 See Katharine T. Bartlett, Making Good on Good Intentions, 95 Va. L. Rev. 1893, 1932 (2009).

20 Id. at 85.

21 Dalai Lama, How To See Yourself As You Really Are (2006) at 194.

22 Under a model of self interest, one labors under the false assumption that this is their school, their car, their home, their money, their "stuff," thereby exaggerating its disadvantages, faults, and attractiveness in ways that will undermine their standing and security that is interdependent on others they may despise.

23 See Derrick A. Bell, Jr., Racial Remediation: An Historical Perspective on Current Conditions, 52 Notre Dame L. Rev. 5, 12 (1976). As Bell notes, "[r]eform is seldom forthcoming until white policymakers perceive some self-interest-based benefit for themselves or, occasionally, for other whites. When the reform is adopted, justice for blacks is given as the sole motivation. . . ." Dudziak also emphasizes the significance of the impact of race discrimination on foreign relations, a "cold war imperative" for civil rights reform, as one of the factors motivating

another through closer, meditative contemplation to remove ignorance in order to perceive the full benefits and costs of their bounded mutuality that they will come to see nonetheless exists.

AWAKENED COMPASSION (SOUL CONSCIENCE) V. CONCEALED CONDITIONING (EGO CONSCIENCE)

Today we exist in a world dominated primarily by the ego conscience and there has yet to be a more comprehensive spiritual awakening of one's self from the explicit and concealed conditioning inherited from our ego driven socialization, upbringing and other external pressures. Yet the conscious decision to be free from the ego mind also liberates the world from the unhealthy ego of the self.[24] When the collective ego mind is also free from its unhealthy conditioning and fixation with its gratification and moves toward humanitarian well being, the world will begin to see sustained, meaningful evolution of consciousness and constructive resolution of societal legal conflict. To do so requires a conscious engagement and clarity of pure intentions on an individual and collective level that can forge the evolution of consciousness from sincere, awakened compassion. "Awakened compassion is to figure out a way to show someone that they are much more than just the conditioned fears and desires of the culturally-created self."[25] Awakened, sincere compassion that is the byproduct of the awakened self sustains philanthropic and humanitarian compassion well after the camera lights disappear, and news headlines fade to indifference. At its best, awakened compassion leads to unconditional love. This is what we will refer to as soul conscience level of awareness, an awareness and memory of which humanity has been robbed of, leaving us to believe all that exist before our eyes in our incarnate state of flesh is all that there is. The ego that does not know death is a fiction (for life eternally persists after physical death), it seeks to "get" what it feels will ensure its survival yet the soul conscience individual who knows his own eternal invulnerable nature, fears neither the illusion of death that it knows is but a fiction nor that anything can harm it under a divine loving protection that makes a demonic hell also a fiction of the same ego-driven illusion of reality created by the physical world's desire for control, contest and conquest of religious converts. Secure it in its own right, it "never seeks to get anything because it knows it already possesses everything of value, preferring instead to "give." It does not fear losing what it gives or seek to "get" because the soul knows that "everything flows easily and naturally in its direction when its aligned with its Divine Source."[26] This is the basis of the law of attraction theme taken up later in this article. For now, it is important to see that the self-esteem of the soul conscience is grounded in an internal sense of autonomy, competence, and connectedness does not require continuous external reinforcement on superficial benchmarks of approval or false inherent existence that ego conscience requires. The soul conscience draws on internal norms that are *self-reinforcing*. It is significant to see that the soul conscience level of awareness will seek its expression not through external approval, but through unconditional love that in turn will eventually result in harmony if society seeks to free itself of its own ego mind. But "[u]nconditional love is not

Eisenhower's handling of the Little Rock crisis. She notes that the protection of the nation's image abroad would not require massive social change but was susceptible to cheap talk as "the token desegregation upheld in Little Rock made clear that the "equality" ultimately achieved in that case was more formal than substantive." Mary L. Dudziak, The Little Rock Crisis and Foreign Affairs: Race, Resistance and the Image of American Democracy, 70 S. Cal. L. Rev. 1641 (1997).

24 Mick Quinn, The Uncommon Path of Awakening Authentic Joy: An Integral Guide To Uncovering Concealed Conditioning 248 (2009).

25 Id.

26 Id.

romantic love. It is the acceptance of others as they are without judgment or expectations…The law of unconditional love says, 'If you go out of your way to express unconditional love, you automatically rise above fear, and, as you transcend your fears, you automatically open to the expression of unconditional love.'"[27] It should thus come as no surprise that recent experimental studies demonstrate that individuals with high levels of internal motivation characterized by the high self esteem of soul conscience and low levels of external motivation characterized by the low self esteem of the ego conscience were more autonomous, and more effective in regulating race bias.[28] It is not a coincidence then that this law of unconditional love was the highest calling for Dr. Martin Luther King Jr. in the quest to overcome societal racial biases. He knew when realized, this unconditional love of the soul conscience would lead humankind to transcend its racial differences to find an expression in the ultimate love.[29] As he proclaimed elsewhere, "I believe that unarmed truth and unconditional love will have the final word in reality. This is why right, temporarily defeated, is stronger than evil triumphant." He stressed the need for loving, non-violent unconditional love for his fellow brethren, even for those enemies that demonstrated the most vitriolic hatred to peaceful demonstrators.[30] One must take into account the specific theological basis upon which King's understanding of justice rests; namely, that the spiritual law of love is dependent on and flows
from the love of God, a dependency which requires a very specific understanding of God as all loving, all forgiving and transformative. Thus, for King, the power of unconditional love was formidable: "Love is the only force capable of transforming an enemy into friend." It was the spiritual task of humankind to "evolve for all human conflict a method which rejects revenge, aggression and retaliation..[and for King and humankind's sake] [t]he foundation of such a method is love." But the reasons for this were not merely just moral or altruistic, but practical and logical. As he explained: "Darkness cannot drive out darkness; only light can do that. Hate cannot drive out

27 Dick Sutphen, The Lighting the Light Within (1987), available at http://www.radioastrology.com/TFG/20PrUniL.htm (last visited feb. 22, 2010).

28 See Patricia G. Devine et al., The Regulation of Explicit and Implicit Race Bias: The Role of Motivations to Respond Without Prejudice, 82 J. Personality & Soc. Psychol. 835, 845 (2002).

29 See Holy Bible, New Testament, Luke 6:27-37 (NRS)("But I say to you that listen, Love your enemies, do good to those who hate you, bless those who curse you, pray for those who abuse you... Do to others as you would have them do to you. If you love those who love you, what credit is that to you? For even sinners love those who love them. If you do good to those who do good to you, what credit is that to you? For even sinners do the same... But love your enemies, do good... and your reward will be great, and you will be children of the Most High; for he is kind to the ungrateful and the wicked. Be merciful, just as your Father is merciful... Forgive, and you will be forgiven "); See Holy Bible, New Testament, Eph 4:31-32 (Phi)("Let there be no more bitter resentment or anger, no more shouting or slander, and let there be no bad feeling of any kind among you. Be kind to each other, be compassionate. Be as ready to forgive others as God for Christ's sake has forgiven you."); See Holy Bible, Old Testament, Heb 12:15 (Jer)("Be careful that no one is deprived of the grace of God and that no root of bitterness should begin to grow and make trouble; this can poison a whole community."); See Holy Bible, New Testament, Rom 12:17-21 (Phi)("Don't pay back a bad turn by a bad turn, to anyone. See that your public behavior is above criticism. As far as your responsibility goes, live at peace with everyone. Never take vengeance into your own hands, my dear friends: stand back and let God punish if he will. For it is written: "It is mine to avenge, I will repay," says the Lord. And it is also written: "If your enemy is hungry, feed him; if he is thirsty, give him something to drink. In doing this, you will heap burning coals on his head." Don't allow yourself to be overpowered by evil. Take the offensive--overpower evil with good!").

30 Taylor Branch, Parting the Waters: America in the King Years, 1954–1963 (1988); David Garrow, Bearing the Cross: Martin Luther King, Jr., and the Southern Christian Leadership Conference (1986); Martin Luther King, Jr.: Civil Rights Leader, Theologian, Orator (D. Garrow ed.1989) (3 vols.) [hereinafter Martin Luther King, Jr.]; D. Lewis, King, A Biography (2d ed.1978); S. Oates, Let the Trumpet Sound: The Life of Martin Luther King, Jr. (1982).

hate; only love can do that."[31] Thus, if love is a force so powerful that it can transform our nature for the betterment of humankind, then it comes as no surprise that some have called for love to be the governing, organizing principle behind the law's quest to achieve equality because it will inevitably lead to acts of compassion.[32]

As horrific as the natural disasters of Hurricane Katrina was, it demonstrates perhaps a far more tragic nature of the ego-mind and a turning away from the law of unconditional love that is characteristic of the soul conscience driven individual and society. In the aftermath of the hurricane hitting New Orleans and devastating the lower 9th Ward, and the Bush Administration's lackluster emergency response to the cries of desperate residents on stranded rooftops without food and drinkable water for five days, pledges of reinvestment and renewal abounded. New Orleans was to re-emerge better than ever. Politicians, celebrities, and public figures gave the clarion call for renewal and restoration of New Orleans. But that result did not materialize. Much of the lower 9th ward remains today exactly as it did after the hurricane. One may well speculate that after the national spotlight left the plight of suffering New Orleans residents in the dark, the lower 9th ward appears to stand just as devastated today as it did before. Perhaps the calculated decision to feign humanitarian interest for the well being of fellow human beings was calibrated to the degree necessary to save face, and to appear altruistic just enough to restore the status quo of the ego mind or to yield to the concealed conditioning of society to gratify self image, self guilt or self interests. For the ego mind, a cold calculation likely took root. The French Quarter and Bourbon Street were the only areas of New Orleans standing above sea level and thus unaffected by Hurricane Katrina. But it was and is a source of revenue for the city and state that remained untouched and unharmed, but for the lower 9th ward occupants where no revenue is to be found; these devastated and displaced residents were left bereft. Some did heed the call for true compassion to those displaced by providing shelter and long term solutions for their living conditions in other states and cities, but these were by far the exception. An awakened, sincere compassion of the soul conscience level of awareness the other hand would resemble public office holders and celebrities to sustain their philanthropy and generosity well after the attention of the media outlets fade. Telethons, donation hotlines, celebrity commercial spotlights for charities and aid organizations would continue as long term, sustained commitment to the flight of our misfortunate fellow human beings. A truly empathetic, concerned president and public over the recent Haiti earthquake disaster would see that humanitarian resources reach their intended recipients as soon as possible, not merely motivated to prevent a public relations disaster that a late FEMA emergency response. A true altruistic concern for those devastated would be the impetus for the soul conscience level of awareness based upon

31 Dick Sutphen, The Lighting the Light Within (1987), excerpted text available at http://www.radioastrology.com /TFG/20PrUniL.htm (last visited Feb. 22. 2010).

32 Barbara Attwell, The Jurisprudence of Love, 85 U. Det. Mercy L. Rev. 495, 501-502 (2008)(" Given that the universe is energetic in nature and that we are all energetically interconnected, the special energy of Love needs to be explored, for it is because of the special power of Love that [it should be used] as the driving force behind our laws. There is a large body of spiritual literature in the marketplace that discusses the nature of Love. Although this broad-based and somewhat diverse body of literature may originate from different vantage points, one area of general agreement relates to the unique power of Love. ... One of the reasons why Love is uniquely powerful is that of all the different frequencies of energy, Love is the highest or most all encompassing kind: 'Love is the ultimate answer. Love is not an abstraction but an actual energy, or spectrum of energies . . . . Since everything is energy and love encompasses all energies, all is love.' Thus, it is Love rather than some other underlying premise that should be the fundamental driving force behind the law.").

our common humanity, our interrelated oneness.[33] Only for the ego conscience level of awareness would an us v. them set the stage for limited if any engagement of humanitarian effort for fellow human beings.

THE GOLDEN RULE AND THE CATEGORICAL IMPERATIVE

Of course, it seems that when we defy this soul conscience level of awareness of our interrelatedness and the law of oneness, and so deny our interdependence, is when humanity begins to see its greatest suffering which we are doomed to repeat unless this vital law is observed. Thus, the genocide in Rwanda yesterday becomes today's genocide in Darfur, someone else's suffering and death becomes a mirror of our own. In the biblical reciprocity of the Golden Rule, in adhering to the dictates of a kingdom of ends where the categorical imperative governs, can we rekindle our common humanity and the need for change. Thus, whether it is a genocide of a people, hurricane Katrina victims, the uninsured dying of a preexisting condition on a hospital bed, as Tibetan philosophy would encourage, one must place themselves in the shoes of their fellow man and woman?[34] In fully answering in the reciprocity of the Golden Rule to do unto others as we would have them to unto us where it would also be morally just. Under Kant's moral categorical imperative to encourage a certain action, we can also determine and provide for needs but an action is moral, Kant argues, only to the extent that it is performed purely out of duty. Love and compassion, for Kant, are
secondary concerns in ways that are fundamentally at odds with the compassionate character of Tibetan philosophy or even Dr. King's theology, yet the end result of taking a specific moral action appears to be the same, although the underlying reasons and justifications for it may differ. A reciprocal consideration nonetheless appears as their common denominator from differing sources of justification that becomes the basis of a hidden governing law, whether based on duty rationality or compassionate experience. Thus, without such a common denominator construct built into in our law; one that might emanate from theological or even non-theological sources of justification, we are left bereft in a society where yesterday's slave trade becomes today's sex traffic trade, yesterday's Great Depression becomes today's Great Recession, all because we principally continue to uphold greed rooted in the false notion of inherent existence separate and apart from considerations of reciprocity, whether grounded in duty, compassion, or our inter-connected, interrelated reality of oneness. The Kantian principle that every rational being is an end in itself is universal and applies to all rational beings comes from reason, not from experience.[35] Now, if

33 The earthquake disaster in Port-Au-Prince, Haiti may resemble a similar fate as Hurricane Katrina victims. After celebrity telefons, the limited self interest of Bell's interest–convergence dilemma between politicians, celebrities and native will unravel, will the children of Haiti be forgotten? How will the nation of Haiti recover and will it do so with the sustained support and generosity of those who profess philanthropic generosity today? Will society turn a blind eye not merely to the suffering of earthquake victims, but to the rampant desperation of poverty, or the police violence against those accused of stealing rice amidst a crisis?

34 See generally Sogyal Rinpoche, The Tibetan Book of Living and Dying (Patrick Gaffney and Andrew Harvy eds., 1994)("First, look at the dying person in front of you and think of that person as just like you, with the same needs, the same fundamental desire to be happy and avoid suffering, the same loneliness, the same fear of the unknown, the same secret areas of sadness, the same half-acknowledged feelings of helplessness. You will find that if you really do this, your heart will open toward the person and love will be present between you. . . . [S]econd . . . is to put yourself directly and unflinchingly in the dying person's place. . . . What would you most need.").

35 See generally Immanuel Kant, The Critique of Pure Reason (1781). Kant believed in an afterlife where the potential to achieve the summum bonum could be realized and that God must exist to advance eschatological justice. There are three categorical imperatives according to Kant which guides us in determining which actions are morally obligatory and those which are forbidden. The first imperative is to ask oneself if the action about to be engaged

rational beings are ends in themselves (in what he termed a kingdom of ends), and not means to some other end (as in the kingdom of means), then the will of a rational being must be thought of as the maker of universal law and where the Golden Rule abides as part of the eternal law that comprises a larger societal context than the individual which can govern legal systems.[36] As with St. Thomas Aquinas, Dr. King believed there is an eternal law, rooted in the existence of God and the very universe this divine entity has created.[37]

In this way, it is easier to see that moral duty and spirituality is that unseen characteristic of our rational mind, personality and spirit which unites us to this universal eternal law despite our separate bodies, races, colors, national origins or sex. It is also then feasible to see that humankind's law is that unseen force which orders relationships between our separate fleshly bodies and mediates conflicts between them in social, political and economic terms of societal construction. Spirituality and law are thus inextricably intertwined. Where one finds harmony in society, is it because one finds peace and happiness flourishing where spirituality is supported by humankind's law animated by principles of reciprocity within the eternal universal law? Concomitantly, one must likewise speculate that where conflict, inequality, discrimination and warfare exists, is it where the law has lost its spiritual bearing with the Aquinas/King universal law of justice, or where spirituality that uplifts the human personality and spirit has lost its safeguards and pedestal of legal protection? Perhaps. As Dr. King admonished us to remember, "everything Adolf Hitler did in Germany was "legal" and everything the Hungarian freedom fighters did in Hungary was "illegal." It was "illegal" to aid and comfort a Jew in Hitler's Germany."[38] This discord, inequality, discrimination and warfare reflected a disharmony between the unjust laws of man and the eternal just laws of the

should be applied universally. If so, it should apply to everyone under all circumstances with no exception." Although Kant would take issue with Dr. King's theology, presumably Dr. King would also be clearly dismayed at the hypocrisy of laws that some are required to follow or which subjugate minorities while those who pass such laws are not subject to its subjugation. Take the following proposition: "It is good to discriminate against African-Americans in education, voting rights and in housing." One would have to decide if it would be a good thing for this rule to apply to everyone to determine its morality. The question must be asked, would it be a good thing for everyone to be discriminated against in education, voting rights and in housing? If the answer is no, then this action cannot be universal in its application and thus is immoral. The second categorical imperative requires one to regard humans as ends in themselves and never as a means to some end. Only in this way does humanity promote equality and outlaw societal evils such as slavery, or racial exploitation. Finally, the third categorical imperative required one to act as is one lived in a kingdom of ends without regard to the utilitarian concept of punishment which could justify sanctions against the innocent if the majority benefit.

36 This would include reference to the universal law of the Golden Rule embodied in biblical teaching as well as arguably in the first categorical imperative, albeit for different reasons. The Golden Rule that is, do unto others as you would have them do unto you as Christ asserted, see Holy Bible, New Testament, at Luke 6:31.

37 See James M. Washington, A Testament of Hope: The Essential Writings of Martin Luther King, Jr. 217, 219 (1986). Under this view, because this eternal, universal sense of justice is rooted in this eternal law of the universe, then humankind's conception of justice best finds its expression in laws that are harmonized with this higher spiritual sense of justice. Aquinas, like Dr. King, held the belief that humans could also know God's law by the exercise of intellect (through natural revelation) as well as by divine insight (supernatural revelation), particularly with regard to matters of faith. Like Kant, Aquinas contended that all truth was available to all through correct human reasoning which would include rational proofs for God's existence. Kant's theory is not without its critics. Some philosophers have argued that in practice our moral beliefs are based more so on intuitions, rather than reason. Hegel argued that moral beliefs are often societal or culturally bound and can never be unconditional because moral questions must be resolved in the context of the society in which we live. Nietzsche argued that reason is not the source of moral freedom, but is rather an impediment to free choice.

38 Id.

universe rooted myopic self interests where each is seen as only a means and not an end in itself. That is not only the danger we saw most recently in our national and international economic crisis.

HOW THE LAW PROMOTES EGO CONSCIENCE OVER SOUL CONSCIENCE: THE GREAT RECESSION AND THE KINGDOM OF MEANS

To see this, the destabilization of the global economy in today's reality of a Great Recession is evidence of the impact of the ego conscience level that views self interest rooted in an extreme adherence to individualistic gain and ego mind rather than as the soul conscience level that accepts and is able to see our collective interrelatedness. It is a testament to the suffering that happens under the ego conscience level when treating each other as a means to an end in violation of the categorical imperative. No where else is the ego conscience level more dominant over soul conscience level than in the banking world in what Thomas Friedman terms as IBG/YBG—"Ill be gone or you'll be gone" syndrome. As he aptly explains, this practice was responsible for bringing down the world economy:

> "The mortgage broker who first sold a family a mortgage and then passed it off to a bigger institution, like Fannie Mae or Citibank, knew that he would be "gone" if and when the family holding the mortgage defaulted: He would no longer own the mortgage—Fannie or Freddie or some investment bank would. So there was no risk for him personally in the high risk deal. And he told the family that the same was true for them. There would be no problem if it turned out that they couldn't make the payments because "you'll be gone"—because housing prices would always go up, they could just flip the house for more than they paid for it, or just walk away. The rating agencies, whose fees and revenues depended on how many of these bonds of subprime mortgages they got to rate, ad a great incentive to give them high ratings so they would sell more easily and therefore more investment houses and banks would want to use their rating services. And if those bonds blew up, well, said the raters, IBG—"I'll be gone." The investment banks had a great incentive to bundle more and more mortgages into bonds as long as they didn't hold too many on their own balance sheets, if they blew up, who cared? IBG—"I'll be gone."[39]

There are many ways in which the reciprocal law of oneness embodied in the categorical imperative is violated. The above example demonstrates just one. The above demonstrates we are far from a Kantian kingdom of ends, failing to view one another not as beings with intrinsic worth, or as an end in themselves, but as a means to an end. If the categorical imperative requires you to treat all your fellows as "ends in themselves" or as objects of intrinsic value--and not as mere instruments for the attainment of your personal goals, then we have not only violated the categorical imperative, but the metaphysical law of oneness which not only affirms our interrelatedness, but our universal intrinsic value. In actuality, it is easy to see that it is not possible to violate the categorical

39 Thomas L. Friedman, Hot, Flat and Crowded: Why We Need a Green Revolution—And How It Can Renew America 17 (2009).

imperative, and live up to our divine oneness. Therefore, elevating unjust means to justify a legitimate end in the law, even during times of national hysteria and fear only promotes further injustice as the epitome of the kingdom of means. Many times through history, law has treated people as means to an end.[40]

In treating each other as a means to an end, we construct an artifice of separation that reflects the illusion of separation, a false impression that is fostered at the ego-conscience level that most of society still mistakenly labors under. This ego-conscience level artifice of separation is a concept that fosters the us v. other dynamic and thus promotes a disconnect between ourselves and our actions. As the above excerpt demonstrates, we see how greed and fear can function as a self imposed barrier to ignore and disregard this law of unitary interrelatedness and the soul-level conscience of the inherent intrinsic value as human beings. It does so for purposes of self gain to the detriment of others as a gratification of the ego-level of conscience. The impact of de-linking one's intrinsic self from another is to disregard the consequences of one's actions that creates negative karma and the universal law of cause and effect is invoked. But greed alone is not the only barrier. Indeed, there are many to chose from that operate to serve the same purpose.

THE EGO CENTERED PITFALLS OF THE POSITIVE THINKING MOVEMENT & THE LAW OF ATTRACTION

What assumptions are laden in the critique of positive thinking as an instrument for organizing societal change and manifesting individual harmony? Does a distorted and myopic focus in the positive thinking movement, if left unchecked, lead to perverse stunting of spiritual growth through self denial, complacency or lack of social empathy? By over promoting the individual self over the community at the expense of a global conception of our interconnectedness, proponents may unwittingly conceal conditioned intentions in actions and laws that lead to undesired karmatic consequences.[41] These karmatic consequences ultimately undermine the utility of positive thinking and stunt the evolutionary progress of spiritual consciousness of the collective gestalt.

---

40 See Paul Savoy, The Spiritual Nature of Equality: Natural Principles of Constitutional Law, 28 How. L.J. 809, 864-865 (1985)("A law may have a legitimate, or even 'compelling,' purpose such as preventing espionage during wartime, but the means used to accomplish that purpose may classify people in such an unreliable manner that a substantial number of persons whose situations bear no reasonable relation to the purpose of the law are subjected to its restraints. The term used to describe this vice of legislative line-drawing is over-inclusiveness of which the wartime internment of Japanese-Americans was a striking example. More than 100,000 Americans of Japanese ancestry were forcibly evicted from their homes during World War II and confined in detention camps 'because of the presence of an unascertained number of disloyal members of this group.' By using such a broad racial classification to identify persons who endangered the national security, the government subjected an indeterminate but substantial number of innocent persons to severe deprivations of liberty despite the fact that their detention served no purpose other than administrative convenience.").

41 In one sense, the notion of karma (that which you sow you reap) can be said to be just another way of describing the law of attraction, that is, what you offer is what you receive. See Abraham Hicks, Law of Attraction Quotes ("Appreciation and love, and alignment to that which is Source, is the ultimate "giving back," so to speak, for in your pain or struggle, you have nothing to give back. What you are living is always an exact replication of your vibrational patterns of thought. Nothing could be more fair than life as you are living it, for as you are thinking, you are vibrating, and as you are vibrating, you are attracting—for by the Law of Attraction, you are always getting back the essence of what you are giving. Excerpted from Money and the Law of Attraction — 3/31/09") available at http://www.abraham-hicks.com/lawofattractionsource/index.php (last visited Feb. 22 2010).

In her recent work, entitled: *Bright-Sided: How the Relentless Promotion of Positive Thinking Has Undermined America*,[42] Barbara Ehrenreich advances the proposition that the universal Law of Attraction (that which you think you attract)[43] has the deleterious effect of making the unemployed, ill and misfortunate condition of the less serendipitous the product of their own doing. For instance, she points to assertions such as those by Rhonda Byrne of *The Secret* who opined that tsunami victims had attracted their own misfortune condition.[44] Ehrenreich also posits how this positivist philosophy has advanced wall street greed by justifying lopsided material gain with a brand of passive self acceptance by society not to question, complain or place fault on the global economic downturn on oneself.

She further discusses how Emerson and the Transcendentalists sought to liberate themselves from the rigidity and pre-determinism of Calvanism only to note that such attempts were later thwarted by the likes of Phineas Quimby, Mary Baker Eddy and others.[45] It was in the 1860s when Mary Baker Eddy, the founder of Christian Science, met Phineas Parker Quimby, a metaphysician and inventor who launched the cultural movement of positive thinking. From William James' pragmatism movement[46] to Napolean Hill's 1930's classic *Think and Grow Rich!*,[47] and finally to Norman Vincent Peale's work, *The Power of Positive Thinking*,[48] Ehrenreich traces the intellectual lineage of the positive

---

42 Barbara Ehrenreich, Bright-Sided: How the Relentless Promotion of Positive Thinking Has Undermined America (2009).

43 Deepak Chopra, The Seven Spiritual Laws of Success (2007) available at http://www.ofspirit.com/deepakchopra1.htm (last visited Feb. 4, 2010)("This Universal Law demonstrates how we create the things, events, and people that come into our lives. Our thoughts, feelings, words, and actions produce energies which, in turn, attract like energies. Negative energies attract negative energies and positive energies attract positive energies." It is worth spending some time unpacking the ramifications of this law since it has been the subject of much discussion in popular print and media. Does it result in a demoralization of self, a descent into self pity or self blame? Is this belief that the world's suffering is brought on by ourselves the price some pay for dispelling all notions in an all knowing and all loving God that is capable of allowing such suffering? Perhaps we have taken our own cross so to speak as a way to explain and cope with a world that is replete with suffering, tragedy or disaster in the human condition? In other words, does the fault dear Brutus lie not in the stars but in ourselves? Positive visualization may sharpen our focus so we are in a better position to perceive when the promising opportunities arise, but action as we have seen, is nonetheless is required. Recent literature on the law of attraction such as The Secret discount inspired action as a means to manifesting the desired positive visualized event. It also discounts the other laws of the universe. Deepak Chopra explains that this law of attraction, which he terms the law of intention and desire, is not to be followed in isolation. He states: "This law is based on the fact that energy and information exist everywhere in nature. A flower, a rainbow, a tree, a human body, when broken down to their essential components are energy and information. The whole universe, in its essential nature, is the movement of energy and information. The only difference between you and a tree is the informational and energy content of your respective bodies. You can consciously change the energy and informational content of your own quantum mechanical body, and therefore influence the energy and informational content of your extended body--your environment, your world--and cause things to manifest in it. The quality of intention on the object of attention will orchestrate an infinity of space-time events to bring about the outcome intended, provided one follows the other spiritual laws of success. Intention lays the groundwork for the effortless, spontaneous, frictionless flow of pure potentiality. The only caution is that you use your intent for the benefit of mankind.").

44 Rhonda Byrne, The Secret 21, 88, 116 (2006).

45 Gillian Gill, Mary Baker Eddy (1998) at 43; Donald Meyer, The Positive Thinkers: Popular Religious Psychology From Mary Baker Eddy to Norman Vincent Peale to Ronald Reagan (1998).

46 William James, The Varieties of Religious Experience: A Study in Human Nature (2002).

47 Napoleon Hill, Think and Grow Rich! 52, 29, 71, 28, 30, 74 (2004).

48 Norman Vincent Peale, The Power of Positive Thinking (1994)(Propounding that if positive thoughts bring positive events than negative thoughts bring negative events. ("If we are our own chief problem, the basic reason must be found in the type of thoughts which habitually occupy and direct our minds.")); see also Norman Vincent Peale, The Positive Principle Today (1994).

thinking movement and criticizes it for its increasingly sharp focus on "prosperity" and get-rich-quick schemes. The popularity of this positive thinking movement, Ehrenreich explains, can be partially explained by the workplace where much more emphasis on livelihood requires one to be "likeable to employers, clients, coworkers, and potential customers..."[49]

But the results are even more profound for Ehrenreich who posits much of today's crises can be traced to the positive thinking movement that has characterized the law of attraction. In the present day, she unpacks how many recently seen phenomenon at its core has its roots in this cult of positive thinking as she sees it: evangelical mega-churches have espoused the "God wants you to be rich!" gospel evangelism, the pseudo scientific investigation into happiness became popular and most recently, the downturn in the global economic crisis. Three of the four nation's largest mega-churches, she notes, subscribe to the "prosperity gospel."[50] It was positive thinking that led confused and even deluded many people from their limited economic reality, including borrowers who were proactively seduced by this positive thinking mentality to buy more house than one could afford.[51] Likewise, lenders took advantage of such positive thinking by offering predatory leveraging instruments like the subprime mortgage.[52] During the credit bubble, lenders became not only motivated out of sense of greed, but perhaps were equally susceptible to the notion and focused on the short-term positives rather than the long-term risks of subprime mortgage loans.[53]

If the foregoing is not a sufficient attack on the positive thinking, where Ehreneich's critique is most salient, although not always explicit, centers around the notion of self interest. As someone confronting breast cancer herself, Ehrenreich was confounded to see that positive thinking rather than more concrete advice became a way of addressing cancer victims. Further, those having a less optimistic disposition and label of "cancer victim" were quickly dismissed as negative rather than seeing oneself as a cancer "survivor."[54] "The effect of all this positive thinking is to transform breast cancer into a rite of passage," she writes, "not an injustice or a tragedy to rail against but a normal marker in the life cycle, like menopause or grandmotherhood."[55]

In some sense, positive thinking then can have several nefarious and more demoralizing effects according to Ehrenreich: First, it can cause one to blame themselves when misfortunate events based upon natural disasters, mother nature, economic crises, or other environmental phenomena do occur as noted earlier. This leads to a self blame for things truly out of one's control thereby negating the very purpose and purported effect of positive thinking if one accepts the proposition that what you think as your mental focus is what you will attract without exception, chance, or circumstance.[56] The teachings of the law of attraction according to some if its ardent adherents

49 Ehrenreich, Bright Sided, at 96.

50 The prosperity gospel can be summed as a divine desire for man to be rich. The reason for this is made manifest in the contention that "[i]t is in the use of material things that a man finds full life for his body, develops his mind, and unfolds his soul. It is therefore of supreme importance to him that he should be rich." See Wallace D. Wattles, The Science of Getting Rich 108 (2007).

51 Ehrenreich, Bright Sided, at 177-195.

52 Id.

53 Id.

54 Id. at 15-44

55 Id.

56 See Abraham Hicks, Law of Attraction Quotes ("When you begin to understand Law of Attraction, and you understand that which is like unto itself is drawn, then it is easier and easier to understand that you are offering a

embrace this notion that indeed nothing happens in one's life that is not the product of their own present, active belief. This notion raises the thorny question of whether every tragedy, natural disaster, or terrorist calamity that befalls humankind is the product of one's own thinking. According to this view of the law of attraction, the answer must undoubtedly be yes. No wonder Ehrenreich suggest that the positive thinking movement might lead one to self blame for all cancers, family deaths, hurricanes, earthquakes one suffers is their own doing. Secondly, a narrow adherence to the law of attraction, she suggests, creates a tendency to accept the status quo as a result, even if that status quo operates to one's own detriment in the hope that something later will positively develop. That is, rather than challenging or questioning the propriety of wall street greed in the subprime loan, or motivating society's to find and find a cure for cancer rather than promoting an acceptance of cancer as a right of passage, positive thinking as practiced by some, it is said, has done us a great misservice.

WHERE THE LAW OF ATTRACTION MEETS SOCIAL REFORM

Other than the law of attraction, Ehrenreich does not specifically take into account law into her analysis. Yet it is conceivable to see the ramifications of her thesis on one's ability to bring inspired change in the form of legal reform through positive thinking alone.[57] After all, as commentator Ruthann Robinson notes,

> "[i]f Homer Plessy had only been more of a positive thinker about that Louisiana statute mandating separation of the races! ... But in the power of positive thinking world that Ehrenreich describes, low self-esteem - - - what would be named "negativity" now - - - is in the control of the individual and is not attributable to legal or social conditions. Instead of suing to end segregated schools, should the plaintiffs (and attorneys) in *Brown* have looked "within" and tried to be more "positive" about the "situation"? ...Why advocate for better jobs and schools, safer neighborhoods, universal health insurance, or any other liberal desideratum if these measures will do little to make people happy? Social reformers, political activists, and change-oriented individuals can all take a much-needed rest. . . . the baton has been passed to the practitioners of "optimism training" . . . . ."[58]

signal, and the entire Universe responds. And when you finally get that, and you begin to exercise some deliberate control about the signal that you offer, then it really begins to be fun, because then you recognize that nothing happens outside of your creative control. There are no things that happen by chance or by circumstance. There is nothing that is happening because of something you vibrated a long time ago or in a past life. It is not about what you were born into. It is only about what you are, right now, in this red hot fresh moment emitting. --- Abraham, Excerpted from the workshop in Seattle, WA on Saturday, June 20th, 1998") available at http://www.abraham-hicks.com/lawofattractionsource/index.php (last visited Feb. 2, 2010).

57 This proposition is dubious when legal reform is entrenched in racial discriminatory thought as seen in the context of both Plessy v. Ferguson, 163 US 537 (1896), where Justice Henry Billings Brown famously wrote: "We consider the underlying fallacy of the plaintiff's argument to consist in the assumption that the enforced separation of the two races stamps the colored race with a badge of inferiority. If this be so, it is not by reason of anything found in the act, but solely because the colored race chooses to put that construction upon it."

58 Ehrenreich, Bright Sided, at 172.

The above passage is telling for several reasons if only to demonstrate Ehrenreich misapprehends the notion of the law of attraction as exercised by those "practitioners of optimistic training." As those adherents to the law of attraction would undoubtedly argue, an observational concentrated focus of thought energy on what is lacking in their social, political or economic condition rather that on what is desired is the basis of one's unhappiness that often manifests in accordance with the unhappy thoughts of lack based upon the perceiver.[59] Therefore, according to this approach, their focus on the emotions, thoughts, energy and all conscious and unconscious associations attributed to inequality would only result in the perpetuating on the desired realities associated with equality, fulfillment and happiness.[60]

Ehrenreich's positive thinking is less transformative than its allure might seem if viewed in this particular way as it suggest a defeatist approach with overtones of "why bother?" Under this view of the law of attraction, she suggest it discourages taking action when adherents contend that thought alone is sufficient. To be fair to Ehrenreich, the teachings of the authors of the Secret and the Abraham Hicks teachings, thought alone is indeed said to be sufficient standing alone independent of action.[61] Yet not all are in agreement on this point. However, this is a misapprehension of the positive law of attraction as embraced by many of its practitioners who nonetheless call upon embracing a positive belief as well as taking inspired action based upon that belief as if it were already a reality in their life existence.[62] Thought, when coupled with harmonious

59 See Abraham Hicks, Law of Attraction Quotes ("When you focus upon lack in an attitude of complaining, you establish a vibrational point of attraction that then gives you access only to more thoughts of complaint. Your deliberate effort to tell a new story will establish a new pattern of thought, providing you with a new point of attraction from your present, about your past, and into your future. The simple effort of looking for positive aspects will set a new vibrational tone and the Law of Attraction will begin the immediate attraction of thoughts, people, circumstances, and things that are pleasing to you, Excerpted from Money and the Law of Attraction — 3/31/09.") available at http://www.abraham-hicks.com/lawofattractionsource/index.php (last visited Feb. 22, 2010).

60 Id. ("The realization that something is not as you want it to be is an important first step, but once you have identified that, the faster you are able to turn your attention in the direction of a solution, the better, because a continuing exploration of the problem will prevent you from finding the solution. The problem is a different vibrational frequency than the solution—and all thoughts (or vibrations) are affected by (or managed by) the Law of Attraction. Excerpted from Money and the Law of Attraction — 3/31/09").

61 Id. ("That which is like unto itself is drawn." Vibrations are always matched. So, as you experience the contrast which inspires the new desire, this new desire, whether it is a strong one or a soft one, is summoning unto itself proportionately. And as it summons, it is always answered. It is the basis of our Universe: When it is asked, it is always given. Humans think they are asking with their words, or even with their action, and sometimes you are, but the Universe is not responding to your words or your action. The Universe is responding to your vibrational calling. --- Abraham, Excerpted from the workshop in Cincinnati, OH on Saturday, July 15th, 2000").

62 According to some new age spiritual belief, the law of attraction is to be complemented with the law of Action which "must be applied in order for you to manifest things on earth. Therefore, we must engage in actions that support our thoughts, dreams, emotions and words." Dr. King, a prime spiritual leader and activator of social change appeared to fundamentally understand this law when confronted by his critics and fellow clergymen who admonished him to be patient and wait in advocating social change or to be passive in accepting the human social condition as it was in 1964. Although he had been told many times that "the teachings of Christ take time to come to earth," he knew that action, rather than passive belief or the passive passage of time itself would bring about the kind of manifested change on earth he sought. As he was able to understand, without action, little can be accomplished. James M. Washington, A TESTAMENT OF HOPE: THE ESSENTIAL WRITINGS AND SPEECHES OF MARTIN LUTHER KING, JR. 49 (1986)("Human progress never rolls in on wheels of inevitability; it comes through the tireless efforts of men willing to be co workers with God, and without this hard work, time itself becomes an ally of the forces of social stagnation."). King's prophetic words and philosophy embraced this concept of the forward march of collective progress as advanced by one's own actions. ("Actually, time itself is neutral; it can be used either

action consistent with it leads to an amplification of creative ability to manifest what is desired. Thus, it does not follow under the law of attraction that social reformers, political activists, and change-oriented individuals can now all take a much-needed rest. Rather, it suggests that social reformers focus their thoughts, emotions, beliefs as well as their collective synergistic actions on the desired outcomes and solutions as if actualized based upon their empowerment derived from their own self-efficacy to effectuate change. Rather than offering of a vibrational match of energy that aligns with further inequality being observed, positive visualizations, beliefs, emotions and self empowerment based actions are more likely to find constructive approaches to achieving equality. One might well ask how does such social reformers, political activists and change-oriented individuals focus on desired outcomes and solutions in a practical and meaningful way? Psychology appears to have already given us the answer to this question in the form of what has been referred to as Appreciative Inquiry. Appreciative Inquiry is the brainchild of Dr. David Cooperrider,[63] who posited that in shifting from our usual, problem-centered approach to a solutions-possibilities approach, leaders can effectuate positive change by capitalizing on what works.[64] It is with this approach in mind, that re-thinking educational law and indeed all sociolegal reform can lead to transformative model of interpersonal relationships that by enhancing individual well being can achieve the underlying policy goals of reform geared toward a love of learning, self actualization and personal achievement. We need only look at our current approach to educational law and policy to see its system of punitive accountability and non-individual assessment neither promotes or enhances individual student well being nor takes a positive appreciative inquiry approach.

THE EGO-CENTERED USE OF THE LAW OF ATTRACTION & THE DESPERATE NEED FOR SOUL CONSCIENCE VALUES

destructively or constructively. More and more I feel that the people of ill will have used time much more effectively than have the people of good will….We must use time creatively, in the knowledge that the time is always ripe to do right. Now is the time to make real the promise of democracy and transform our pending national elegy into a creative psalm of brotherhood. Now is the time to lift our national policy from the quicksand of racial injustice to the solid rock of human dignity."). In response to critics of his advocacy of direct action, he was even more bold and clear about the need to observe this universal law of action ("We know through painful experience that freedom is never voluntarily given by the oppressor; it must be demanded by the oppressed. Frankly, I have yet to engage in a direct action campaign that was "well timed" in the view of those who have not suffered unduly from the disease of segregation. For years now I have heard the word "Wait!" It rings in the ear of every Negro with piercing familiarity. This "Wait" has almost always meant "Never." We must come to see, with one of our distinguished jurists, that "justice too long delayed is justice denied.").

63 David Cooperrider is Professor of Organizational Behavior at Case Western Reserve University's Weatherhead School of Management and cofounder of Appreciative Inquiry Consulting.

64 See Kathy Clark, Appreciative Inquiry: It's Not Easy, But It Is Simple (Sept. 2004) (stating that Appreciative Inquiry, (AI) is "inquiry based on positive questions. In Appreciative Inquiry, a clear, concise topic is chosen, positive questions are developed, and the consultant (or whoever is asking the questions) sits down with the client and asks the questions. Stories start to develop; patterns begin to emerge. Individuals recall and tap into positive achievements and stories that strengthen and inspire. The process, which is more fully described below, doesn't ignore problems—it just approaches them from the other side. The other side being what IS working rather than what is NOT working. It can be used informally, such as in a conversation or in a formal context, such as at a strategic planning conference or retreat. It can be used with two people or two thousand. AI builds on several assumptions, including: 1. In every society, organization, or group, something works. 2. What we focus on becomes our reality.3. The act of asking questions of an organization or group influences the group in some way.4. What we want already exists in ourselves, our firms, our organizations, and our communities.") available at http://www.abanet.org/lpm/lpt/articles/mgt09041.html (last visited Feb. 22, 2010).

But it may be said that Ehrenreich's thesis is less about positive mentality and more about the self denial. What she is really identifying is the denial, self blame and dissonance experienced with the reality when positive desire is not manifested. For now it telling to note that under this view, labeling anything negative is a cause to brush aside its relevance, to dismiss its significance and to relegate it to oblivion in an active resistance that may nonetheless attract or to become that which one persistently resists (law of resistance).[65] We have already seen the deleterious effects of ignoring collective co-created reality particularly when it brings the global economy to the brink of destruction, but there are other important implications to consider as well. Arguably, in all that Ehrenreich identifies as dangerous and undesirable about positive thinking, denying anything and anyone that is remotely perceived as negative can have significant impact on societal acceptance of those less fortunate, those needy, those sick, those poor and those marginalized. This leads us to perhaps the most profound adverse impact that this denial which accompanies positive thinking has on the spiritual consciousness and evolution of spiritual values.

Thirdly, and perhaps the most troubling in terms of human interpersonal relations is that an extreme approach to the law of attraction is that it causes one to dismiss all too easily those disheartened, distressed or simply in doubt as merely having negative thinking rather than actively engaging them in a dialogue that is characteristic of compassion, commiseration or empathy. Taken to its most extreme in the cult phenomenon it has become, positive thinking persons tend to socially castrate or write off those who struggle with and grapple with the demons of fear, depression and anxiety. In a world that seems less secure in economic, political and military terms, we have come to dismiss and blame our downtrodden brethren rather than display empathy and understanding as if demonstrating a modicum of either might somehow being validating negativity. Perhaps then, in following this line of belief, it is not surprising then when Pat Robertson, the tele-evangelical Christian who once suggested God was punishing Americans with Hurricane Katrina, also proclaims that a "pact to the devil" brought on the devastating earthquake in Haiti.[66]

In Wallace D. Wattles' classic 1910 book recently updated in translation in The Science of Getting Rich, we are told that positive thinking requires us not to look upon the poor and to turn our mind and focus away from the least fortunate of these. The better way to advance the poor is not through donations, or pity but the visualization of seeing them succeed. As he asserts, the poor don't need charity or pity, but rather need inspiration.[67] Undoubtedly, inspiration is key, but visualization without inspired action accompanying it is less effective practically and spiritually. In this sense, advocates of positive thinking often downplay the role of action and its significance in manifesting desires. Similarly, we are told in medicine not to study disease for that focus only leads to the prolonging of it, but to instead place our focus upon wellness.[68] The focus on wellness is surely

65 See infra, fn. 92-94 and accompanying text. The law of resistance states that which one attempts to resist, one becomes or is compelled to confront it. Here again, one might rightfully speculate that the law of resistance is yet another nomenclature and iteration that describes the law of attraction. Since what one attempts to resist often is accompanied with thought attention to the displeasing thing, event of person to be resisted, according to the law of attraction, they are attracting what they resist by virtue of their focus upon it.

66 Pat Robinson: Haiti Cursed By Pact to The Devil, The Huffington Post, available at http://www.huffingtonpost.com/2010/01/13/pat-robertson-haiti-curse_n_422099.html (last visited Feb. 22, 2010). Quixotically, no similar proclamations came from Rev. Robinson in connection with the 8.8 earthquake that rocked Chile only a few weeks later in late February, 2010.

67 See generally Wallace D. Wattles, The Science of Getting Rich (2007)

68 Id.

valuable and laudable as means of focusing more on a solution than a problem. Yet ignoring a medical diagnosis as negative thought is questionable. Perhaps being mindful of a diagnosis only to sharpen a contrasting desire for wellness may be the best way to straddle the healing benefits of positive mind thought and energy while taking concrete steps to overcome illness without unduly focusing upon it. Finally, we are told that "nature is an inexhaustible storehouse of riches; the supply will never run out" and that if "individuals are poor, it is because they do not follow the Certain Way of doing things which makes the individual man rich."[69] The idea here to project abundance may as the proponents suggest attract abundance, but for mother earth, such thought and action has plundered environmental resources that has exacerbated man's imbalance with his environment. In the competition of resources, and the conflict to usurp power and dominate through capturing another's energy at the expense of the other through competitive means has remained at the heart of all human conflict including the conflict of nations over natural resources. A limited notion of nature will surely enhance a competition for resources, yet a view of nature as an inexhaustible storehouse of riches as this positive thinking movement suggest may encourage overplundering the earth's resources for profit rather than need and without creating a giving, reciprocating, sustainable give and take relationship with the earth that is in balance. Left to stand alone, these assertions may promote dangerous detachment and self interest over the human condition.[70] Such thinking may leverage the power of deliberate creation of the law of attraction to create abundance and on a global scale of such vibrational thought were sustained, the world might indeed see abundance but it does not reconcile a notion of deliberate creation with existing realities or with spiritual values.[71] Proponents of Abraham-Hicks law of attraction seem to reject the notion that surrounding global conditions may be the product not of just one individual but of countless

---

69 Id. at 116.

70 Chopra's law of detachment must also fail on its own terms for similar reasons that his law of least effort must if universally applied. This law provides that:

"... in order to acquire anything in the physical universe, you have to relinquish your attachment to it. This doesn't mean you give up the intention to create your desire. You give up your attachment to the result. This is a very powerful thing to do. The moment you relinquish your attachment to the result, combining one-pointed intention with detachment at the same time, you will have that which you desire. Anything you want can be acquired through detachment, because detachment is based on the unquestioning belief in the power of your true Self. Attachment comes from poverty consciousness, because attachment is always to symbols. Detachment is synonymous with wealth consciousness, because with detachment there is freedom to create. True wealth consciousness is the ability to have anything you want, anytime you want, and with least effort. To be grounded in this experience you have to be grounded in the wisdom of uncertainty. In this uncertainty you will find the freedom to create anything you want." Deepak Chopra, The Seven Spiritual Laws of Success (2007), available at http://www.ofspirit.com/deepakchopra1.htm (last visited Feb. 4. 2010).

Here again, there will certainly be times that a call for detachment may enhance spiritual growth and soul perfection but it should be noted that detachment is not usually the natural result of spirituality. Spirituality at its best does not encourage one to become detached from the world but to become more deeply connected to it in interpersonal relationships in order to fully embrace the karmatic lessons of love, fear, loss, disappointment, hate, evil and courage. Having detachment for a particular outcome or thing may at times promote objectivity or freedom to overcome affliction. However, as we have also seen, detachment has lead to lack of empathy, discrimination, subjugation and the artifice of social construction that perpetuates paradigms of dominance and subdominance as a racialized "other".

71 See Abraham Hicks, Law of Attraction Quotes ("Everything is valid and everything is truthful, because Law of Attraction lets everything be. The question is not whether it's right or wrong, whether their approach is right or wrong, or whether my approach is right or wrong. The question is: Does their approach feel good to me? And if it doesn't, then I choose a different approach. --- Abraham, Excerpted from the workshop in Los Angeles, CA on Sunday, August 2nd, 1998.") available at http://www.abraham-hicks.com/lawofattractionsource/index.php (last visited Feb. 22, 2010).

millions of co-creators manifesting contrasting realities that nonetheless impact an individual by virtue of being in the same plane of reality. Those proponents of the Abraham-Hicks teachings of the law of attraction do not accept this, holding firm to the belief that "[i]f man understood that 'what I create has nothing to do with what anybody else is creating…"[72] However, it is here where adherents to the law of attraction misapprehend the quantum physics and spiritual teachings upon which they base their belief for it fails to acknowledge the interconnected of all energy as being one. This would mean that realities are based upon the thought-emotion-action creations of the individual as well as that of the collective gestalt of society which may require collective societal synergistic creation in order to manifest its global reality. Her thesis and those of law of attraction adherents also ignores the important role of subconscious thoughts and concealed conditioning of karmatic intentions and actions of the ego mind that can unwittingly undermine ones' efficacy to manifest what is desired. The impact of karmatic concealed conditioning and the influence of the collective gestalt is taken up later in this article. But this does not mean that there is no place for positive thinking nor is it, as the cynicists suggests, that positive thinking does not have profound implications on one's destiny. For Barbara Ehrenreich and others who remain skeptical of the role of positive thinking on health, medical treatments, psychology, behavioral sciences, educational promise or career success would do well to re-think the critical role positive thinking can still nonetheless play in shaping one's destiny in each and all of these varied arenas of concern. As Ghandi once admonished:

> Keep your thoughts positive because your thoughts become your words. Keep your words positive because your words become your behaviors. Keep your behaviors positive because your behaviors become your habits. Keep your habits positive because your habits become your values. Keep your values positive because your values become your destiny.[73]

POSITIVE THINKING & POST RACIAL SOCIETAL CLAIMS

What the foregoing discussion all reveals on a deeper level has less to do with positive thinking, self blame, accepting the status quo or even denial for that matter. It is the more fundamental question of what society identifies as negative. If simply labeling or associating something with negative energy or mentality, one is given license to dismiss it. This might not only include illness or poverty if you accept the foregoing propositions, it would also conceivably include anything perceived as different, marginalized, undesirable or connected with inequality, discrimination, etc. Could this popular notion as of late with the election of the nation's first African-American president of post-racial America suggest that we have moved beyond race suggest that society has attached negative connotations to it? Does a post-racial society take into account when race can be used to for benign purposes to track or identify racial profiling or is it more likely a post-racial society simply delude itself into the notion that racial profiling or discrimination no longer exists? Although it might be reasonable to take into account race in order to track and therefore make more accountable those would engage in discriminatory treatment as a way of redressing wrongs committed against those of a particular race, this reality would simply be dismissed as negative.

72 See id. ("Excerpted from the workshop in El Paso, TX on Saturday, November 14th, 1998.") available at http://www.abraham-hicks.com/lawofattractionsource/index.php (last visited Feb. 22, 2010).
73 Mahatma Ghandi, An Autobiography The Story of My Experiments With Truth (1954).

Taken to its radical and extreme, a populace enamored with this positive thinking cultural phenomenon may lead to a perception of a post-racial society that not only fosters the status quo with blatantly accepted self denial of the fact that race matters or that racial discrimination still exists would also justify blaming the victims of racial discrimination themselves as somehow having attracted their own misfortunate lot in ways that are certain to strain inter-racial and interpersonal relations. As a society we have yet to reach King's status in what Cornel West has termed the "race-transcending prophet"–"someone who never forgets the significance of race but refuses to be confined by race."[74] As philosopher Robert Birt observed: "various forms of social oppression and domination obstruct the actualization of that freedom which constitutes the being of human reality, thereby blocking the ultimate source of energy for the creative formation of identity. Thus, oppression may be seen as an existential violation, an ontological crime. Is this not what is meant when we describe oppression and exploitation as dehumanizing?"[75] Where subjugation leads one to internalize the inferiority they feel whether it is racial, ethnic or national origin discrimination of for that matter discrimination on any basis, it is that internalization that misalign one's self from their own inner source of love and well being that is their natural state of being.

Not surprisingly then, psychology professor Richard Eibach reportedly found that in evaluating the relative racial progress in America, Caucasians and African-Americans often use different criteria of measurement. For instance, it was recently reported that "whites use the yardstick of how far we have come from the nation we used to be" while "Blacks use the yardstick of how far we have yet to go to be the nation we ought to be."[76] What accounts for this difference? Does the self denial that often accompanies extreme positive thinking shed some light on this issue? Is it perhaps the negative connotations one attaches to race relations really a reflection of the shortcomings in ones' self?[77] The answer really lies in what one is apt to perceive as negative and all too often that negative perception is rarely connected with anything about oneself, whether it is their own behavior or their own flaws. As Dr. King astutely observed: "Everything that we see is a shadow cast by that which we do not see."[78] Sadly, that statement might be true for a vast majority of us and for those adhering to an extreme law of positive thinking, we miss a valuable opportunity for spiritual growth. If so, then one who subscribes to this extreme notion of positive thinking is more inclined not to look at oneself as being part of any societal problem. After all the alternative clearly seems better or

---

74 Cornel West and bell hooks, Breaking Bread: Insurgent Black Intellectual Life 49 (1991).

75 Robert Birt, Existence, Identity, and Liberation, in Lewis R. Gordon, Introduction to Existence in Black: An Anthology of Black Existential Philosophy 3, 206 (1997).

76 See Leonard Pitts Jr., Post-Racial America Isn't here Yet, available at http://www.cnn.com/2009/POLITICS/03/28/pitts.black.america/index.html (last visited Nov. 21, 2009).

77 Many of us hold conscious and subconscious negative associations and unchallenged connotations reflecting racial bias, prejudices, stereotypes on the basis of race, sex and disability status, see Anthony G. Greenwald & Linda Hamilton Krieger, Implicit Bias: Scientific Foundations, 94 Cal. L. Rev. 945 (2006); Alexander M. Czopp & Margo J. Monteith, Confronting Prejudice (Liter-ally): Reactions to Confrontations of Racial and Gender Bias, 29 Personality & Soc. Psychol. Bull. 532, 541–42 (2003); Jerry Kang & Mahzarin R. Banaji, Fair Measures: A Behavioral Realist Revision of "Affirmative Action," 94 Cal. L. Rev. 1063, 1072 (2006); Samuel L. Gaertner & John F. Dovidio, Understanding and Ad-dressing Contemporary Racism: From Aversive Racism to the Common Ingroup Identity Model, 61 J. Soc. Issues 615, 625 (2005); Brian A. Nosek et al., Harvesting Implicit Group Attitudes and Beliefs From a Demonstration Web Site, 6 Group Dynamics: Theory, Res., & Prac. 101, 112 (2002); Russell H. Fazio & Michael A. Olson, Implicit Measures in Social Cognition Research: Their Meaning and Use, 54 Ann. Rev. Psychol. 297, 299–300 (2003).

78 James M. Washington, A TESTAMENT OF HOPE: THE ESSENTIAL WRITINGS AND SPEECHES OF MARTIN LUTHER KING, JR. 49 (1986).

easier by comparison—Point the finger at perceived negativity that lies elsewhere rather than at ourselves. As one commentator observes:

> "who can be surprised that blacks and whites each tend to gravitate toward the measure [of racial progress] that is most forgiving of their individual groups, that shoves the onus for change off on the other? The black yardstick, after all, leaves black people no obligation other than to demand justice and equality from white people. The white yardstick requires of white people only that they exhort black people to become more self-reliant and take more responsibility for their own problems."[79]

The problem with both notions fails to see the power of one's self efficacy one has to effectuate change under the law of attraction and the ability of the collective consciousness of all races to join together to play an active part. Surely, the costs of positive thinking should not have to come at the costs of placing the onus of critical reflection on the "other." The above quote suggest the vast majority of us become more self justificatory, more condemning, more procrastinating or worse yet more jaded, paternalistic or passive to those injustices of which we each have played a modest or subconscious part or where we fail to invoke our own power to manifest change. By that yardstick, the focus of Caucasians to look only at the past to see what has been achieved, focuses an energy of thought and positive visualization, but only on the past whereas the yardstick of African-Americans to see only what is lacking in their present circumstance only emanates a vibration to bring more of the same undesired circumstance into their present vibrational reality. Whether by our own judging conduct, ambivalence, or indifference to injustice when our voices could make a difference, we may each silently acquiesce in the proposition that injustice is only morally blameworthy to those who suffer at the hands of it when such a notion defies our very interconnectedness as collective energy and our each of our abilities to change it. Perhaps "[t]he ultimate tragedy is not the oppression and cruelty by the bad people but the silence over that by the good people."[80] In his narrow jail cell, Dr. King acknowledged this in his writing of his famous Letter in a Birmingham Jail.[81] So what the foregoing discussion reveals is a perversion in our understanding of the laws of the universe for it is not merely the law of attraction that we abide by in the universe.[82] Nor is it perhaps the case that the law of attraction was ever meant to supplant the need for the agency of human action or for that matter that we accept the status quo in all cases uncritically where change is indeed feasible or even necessary. Further, a narrow conception of positive thinking or law of attraction should not be an invitation to dismiss empathy, compassion, humanitarian engagement with our fellow human beings and the global challenges that confront our economy, our environment and our inter-personal relations. It should not serve to oblige the conscience to deny our interrelatedness. But what it does teach minority and non-minority alike is that if we align our yardstick of measurement to

79 See Leonard Pitts Jr., Post-Racial America Isn't here Yet, available at http://www.cnn.com/2009/POLITICS/03/28/pitts.black.america/index.html (last visited Nov. 21, 2009).

80 James M. Washington, A TESTAMENT OF HOPE: THE ESSENTIAL WRITINGS AND SPEECHES OF MARTIN LUTHER KING, JR. 49 (1986).

81 Id. ("We will have to repent in this generation not merely for the hateful words and actions of the bad people but for the appalling silence of the good people….Shallow understanding from people of good will is more frustrating than absolute misunderstanding from people of ill will. Lukewarm acceptance is much more bewildering than outright rejection.").

82 Perhaps it is the case that we also abide by the law of cause and effect, and the law of unconditional love.

affirmatively reflect that love, acceptance, respect and equality which is desired, we cultivate powerful synergy of vibrational energy to create that reality in our present time. Through fostering respect, mutual understanding rather than punitive sanctions in law for the subconscious biases, we better reflect these spiritual and psychological insights that may lead individuals to constructively confront rather than resist their own biases, flaws and shortcoming. Coercive threats of the law may indeed further entrench biases that promote the false illusion of separate inherent existence that engenders discrimination against "others." As some scholars are just now coming to realize, most recently in employment workplace law, "[p]ositive strategies that affirm people's good intentions, in contrast, engage people constructively in defining their better, nondiscriminatory selves and aligning their conduct accordingly. While coercion and threat make people defensive, opportunity and engagement leverage people's good intentions into a deeper commitment to a more inclusive, nondiscriminatory workplace. It is this type of commitment—not legal coercion—that will best address the implicit bias that is most characteristic of today's workplace."[83] Such an approach affirms our interrelatedness and promotes the individual positive intention in ways that encourage us to constructively address the cause and effect of our behavior upon another.

INTERRELATEDNESS AND THE LAW OF CAUSE AND EFFECT

The universal law of cause and effect holds that "nothing happens by chance or outside the Universal Laws. Every action has a reaction or consequence and we "reap what we have sown." In actuality, the law of cause and effect is intertwined with the law of oneness. Indeed, to better understand the law of cause and effect is to understand the relationship between two or more interrelated actors and events. The applications of this interdependent approach of oneness are manifold when examining cause and effect.

Climate Change

Today, we need not look far to see this universal law animating events all around us. Indeed, it is the increased globalization of intertwining economic, climatic and political realities that as a body politic we must awaken to the spiritual reality of oneness that underscores, informs and reinforces our physical reality. To begin with, we can easily see how this interconnected manifested in the nexus between nations in the economic meltdown beginning prominently in 2008 and beyond. We saw how the reckless greedy actions of a few bad market actors in the U.S. wall street market have perilously brought whole world economies to its knees on the brink of collapse. In our global environmental climate, we can see how the increased demands for natural resources and energy needs of newly developing regions like India, China and South America can have profound economic and devastatingly climatic impacts on the rest of the world. By demonstrating true mutual benefit and cooperation has a practical and spiritual synergy that compounds positive and desirable outcomes with the least imposition for all, great strides could be made on the need to conserve global energy. Otherwise, how can sustainable development be achieved for all while addressing global climate change? [84] How can everyone have sufficient clean water without conflict?[85] How

83 See Katharine T. Bartlett, Making Good on Good Intentions, 95 Va. L. Rev. 1893, 1901 (2009).

84 See Global Changes Facing Humanity, The Millennium Project ("The December 2009 Climate Change Conference in Copenhagen has focused analysis on the practical details of how to manage cap and trade, pay for adaptation, stimulate technology transfer to reduce emissions, estimate when peak GHG emissions will be reached, and set goals to address climate change. Without a global strategy to address climate change, the environmental movement may turn on the fossil fuel industries. The legal foundations are being laid to sue for damages caused by greenhouse gases.

can population growth and resources be brought into balance?[86] How can growing energy demands be met safely and efficiently?[87] As Thomas Friedman notes in his work, *Hot, Flat and Crowded*, the challenge can still be met by calling upon small, incremental sacrifices that do not cramp individual lifestyles.[88]

Large reinsurance companies estimate the annual economic loss due to climate change could reach $300 billion per year within a decade. Coastal urbanization is increasing the numbers of people vulnerable to coastal flooding. Environmental damage to developing nations caused by richer countries is more than the entire Third World debt of $1.8 trillion. To help developing countries leapfrog unsustainable practices to more sustainable ones, the Global Environment Facility provided $7.4 billion in grants and $28 billion in cofinancing since 1991 and an addition $3 billion to 2010; more funds are being established by the World Bank ($5.5 billion), Japan ($10 billion for five years), and the Asian Development Bank ($1.2 billion). The UN estimates that developing countries will need $100 billion annually to finance climate change mitigation and $28–67 billion for adaptation by 2030.Other suggestions include retrofitting coal plants to burn leaner and to capture and reuse carbon emissions…") available at http://www.millennium-project.org/millennium/Global_Challenges/chall-01.html (last visited Feb. 20, 2010).

85 Id. ("About 700 million people face water scarcity today (defined as fewer than 1,000 cubic meters per person per year), which could grow to 3 billion by 2025 due to climate change, population growth, and increasing demand for water per capita. Water stress (1,000–1,700 cubic meters per person per year) could affect half the countries by 2025 and 75% of the world's population by 2050. …China and Saudi Arabia have started buying land in other countries to grow crops. Cooling systems for energy production require large amounts of water. Energy demand may increase 50% in 20 years, coupled with increased food demands, dramatic changes in water management will be required. Global demand for meat may increase by 50% by 2025 and double by 2050, further accelerating the demand for water per capita. Nature also needs sufficient water to be viable to support all life. Development planning should integrate the lessons learned from producing more food with less water via drip irrigation and precision agriculture, rainwater collection and irrigation, watershed management, selective introduction of water pricing, and replication of successful community-scale projects around the world.").

86 Id. ("The world's population is 6.8 billion. It is expected to grow to 9.2 billion by 2050 and could reach 11 billion if fertility rates do not continue to fall. If the rates do continue to fall, then world population could actually shrink by 2100, creating an elderly world difficult to support. Nearly all the population increases will be in developing countries. Today, 18 countries have falling populations, which could increase to 44 countries by 2050, with the vast majority of them in Europe. Scientific and medical breakthroughs over the next 50 years are likely to change these forecasts, giving people longer and more productive lives than most would believe possible today. Some forecast that life expectancy by 2030 could increase one year per year. In either case, global population is changing from high mortality and high fertility to low mortality and low fertility. A quarter of the world (excluding Africa) will be over 60 years old in 2050. There will be more people over 60 than under 15 by 2045, according to the UN medium forecast. To reduce the economic burden on younger generations and to keep up living standards, people will work longer and create many forms of tele-work, part-time work, and job rotation.").

87 Id. ("World energy demand could nearly double by 2030, with China and India accounting for over half of the increase. Without major policy and technological changes, fossil fuels will meet 80% of primary energy demand by 2030. If so, then large-scale carbon capture, storage, and/or reuse should become a top priority to reduce global climate change…Some 73 countries have national renewable energy goals. Meanwhile, over a quarter of humanity has no access to electricity and a third still relies on traditional biomass for cooking and heating, while billions of gallons of petroleum are wasted in traffic jams around the world…The global market for liquid biofuels was worth $30.3 billion in 2008 and should increase to $42.8 billion in 2013. Japan plans to have a working space solar power system in orbit by 2030; such systems could meet the world's electricity requirements indefinitely without nuclear waste or GHG emissions. A global collective intelligence could provide the overviews and details necessary to create more coherent energy policy and better informed consumer choices.").

88 Thomas L. Friedman, Hot, Flat and Crowded: Why We Need a Green Revolution—And How It Can Renew America 238 (2009) ("Telling every individual on the planet who wants or can afford a car that they cannot have one would be changing our lifestyle. But banning cars over a certain weight or engine size, or bringing maximum speed limits back down to 55 miles per hours, or banning taxis that are not hybrids—such efforts do not strike me as fundamentally cramping anyone's lifestyle. Telling people that henceforth we are going to ration electricity would certainly involve changing one's lifestyle. But making it illegal for office building…to leave their lights on after hours, as tens of thousands of companies mindlessly seem to do…does not strike me as fundamentally cramping

When the bottom line of increased productivity, less energy consumption and more economic growth becomes manifest in a critical mass of nation's adopting such conservation incremental approaches that do not unduly impinge upon lifestyle, many more not initially inclined to cooperation except by their narrow self interest may eventually fall in line. When greater than expected, or mutual benefit becomes clearer to all stakeholders, the more inclined will a critical mass gain momentum to serve as a catalyst for change. These may all still be justified by the ego conscience level of awareness. Yet the soul conscience level of awareness of the universal law of oneness, there remains the capacity to bring about significant and profound practical change. A soul level conscience recognizing the interdependent nature of our interrelatedness and its attendant cause and effect will see that mutuality of humanity and the need for cooperation where an ego conscience will persist with the destructive self gratification of resources that will hasten climatic change and perhaps disaster. Further, for where the ego seeks to get, the soul seeks to give what is desired and in return receives what is desired threefold. Give the efficient environment technology to developing nations that is desired for a clean global environment, and a clean global environment is what is yielded.

International Politics & Terrorism

In international politics, an ego conscience President might see a problem of Somali sea piracy of American ships as the work of a handful of bad apples, who then become an easy target force of assassination. But in actuality the existence of bad apples crops up again because their actions may be dependent upon finding economic opportunities. These economic opportunities in turn may be dependent upon establishing a stable, functional government in Somali and a lasting peace with Eritrea. A soul conscience level awareness of interdependent nature of humanity and its cause and effect would extend and give that which is desired, for giving peace and stability to Somali will be a peace and stability given to all American and seagoing ships and ferries around the horn of Africa. Likewise, knowing how many troops to station or deciding upon a strategy of intervention in Afghanistan might require an understanding of the dynamics in conflict between the elite and the rural Taliban, the development of a civil society, the elimination of governmental corruption, the reinforcement of a legitimate electoral structure and our past historic and current role as an intervenor. Simply responding with a military solution would be too simplistic in ways that deny the complexity of issues that we noted myopic ego driven positive thinking tended to engender. We see our interdependence under a soul conscience level of awareness and give the very thing that is desired—a Marshall Plan that promotes a civilly educated, economical prosperity affirming of highest human potential. So the same would also hold true for an earthquake stricken Haiti, a country in dire need of its own Marshall plan.

Medicine

Likewise, in medicine, it may be too simplistic under an ego conscience approach to examine just the liver where circulatory issues, the heart, lymphatic system and the whole body needs to be considered. This is the dependent arising nature of our existence. The mind-body connection

one's lifestyle. Telling people that they cannot have an iPod or laptop would certainly involve changing our lifestyle. But requiring all iPods and laptops to be made with easily recyclable materials doesn't strike me as fundamentally cramping anyone's lifestyle.").

cannot be ignored where depression lends itself to lesser physical activity, or mental stress manifest itself in ulcer, hypertension and high cholesterol compromise the body's overall health. Where the mind remains focused, so our thought will effect behavior which in turn impacts our health condition. In other words, the health of the soul conscience impacts the body overall. For these reasons, doctors have only recently acknowledged the role that prayer and positive thought plays the convalescence and healing of individual patients. With regard to the possible role of the law of attraction and its cause and effect at work in medicine, it is telling that doctors who prescribe placebos while telling the patient of its purported effects, show biological responses that demonstrate the power of the mind to effect individual biochemistry.[89] In some instances, "patients were told they were undergoing internal mammary artery ligation to bring new blood to their hearts, but, in fact, when their chests were opened, the artery was not tied off. The success rate of sham surgery in alleviating the symptoms of angina was equal to that of the real procedure, proving that this widely endorsed operation acted as a placebo treatment."[90] Likewise, as noted earlier, if, as the law of attraction provides, the focus of thought, belief and intention effects energy to manifest the particular belief in reality, then the study of medicine should not primarily focus on disease. Such an emphasis on disease alone without attention to the soul need for growth places intensive and nearly exclusive focus on the problem that will only lead to the prolonging of the condition of disease. Rather than focus medicine on the study of disease, treat disease with what is desired, a greater focus upon wellness and health.[91] This is similar to the notion discussed earlier with regard to the concept of Appreciative Inquiry, that focuses on solutions rather than a problem-based approach, or he soul conscience level of awareness to focus and give that which is desired rather than a focus on that which is not. At the end of the day, our very cognitive-biochemical nexus is a testament to not only an internal micro-biological level of interrelatedness and inter-dependency, but the macro-level nature of our interrelatedness, and its very relationship to cause and effect.

Business and Economics

In business and economics, the ego conscience of our society saw yesterday's savings and loans scandals, Worldcom, Enron and Arthur Andersen debacles become today's Fannie Mae and Freddie Macs whenever the soul conscience level awareness of the core principle of interrelatedness is transgressed. We see it currently with Greece's economic debt crisis resulting in instability that had threatened to spread to Portugal and Spain and which places a heavy burden on the European Union's powerful member state, Germany, to support its bailout.[92] The ramifications are as far reaching beyond the single currency of sixteen eurozone nations as even the United States as part of the International Monetary Fund are also significantly impacted.[93] These developments once again

89 See generally Daniel E. Moerman, Meaning, Medicine and the Placebo Effect, Cambridge Studies in Medical Anthropology (2002).

90 See The Placebo Effect of Surgery, available at http://fanaticcook.blogspot.com/2009/12/ placebo-effect-of-surgery.html (last visited Feb. 22, 2010).

91 Id.

92 Ian Traynor, Crisis in Greece Leaves EU Future in Balance,Warns Angela Merkel, Guardian (May 5, 2010), available at http://www.guardian.co.uk/world/2010/may/05/greece-crisis-threatens-eu-future-merkel-germany (last visited May 24, 2010).

93 Greek Crisis Stirs Debate, Forbes (May 20, 2010), available at http://www.forbes.com/2010/05/19/greece-economy-europe-currency-oxford-analytica.html (last visited May 24, 2010)("The fundamental connections between Greece's crisis and membership in a currency union are contained in the optimum currency area (OCA) theory put forward by Robert Mundell in 1961. The main point of the theory is the need for adjustment mechanisms to replace

affirm our interrelatedness and should caution us all against ego conscience approaches, whether it is fiscal miscreants that break euro rules or Wall Street firms that take irresponsible risks at public taxpayer expense which contributed to the Great Recession in 2008.[94] The ego conscience disregarded our interrelatedness which created a domino cause and effect of near cataclysmic events during the subprime mortgage economic meltdown when self takes precedence over the collective good:

> "[T]he whole system depended upon people who originated the risk profiting from that origination, then transferring that risk to someone else and never having to be responsible for it afterward. So people who never should have been taking out mortgages took them out, people who never should have granted them granted them, people who never should have bundled them [in mortgage back securities] bundled them, people who never should have rated them AAA rated them AAA, people who never should have sold them to pension funds and other financial institutions worldwide sold them. And companies that never should have been insuring them, like AIG, insured them, without setting aside sufficient assets to cover a massive default. Everyone just assumed they could profit personally in the short term and never have to worry what happened in the long term after they passed the bond along."[95]

Education

To see our soul conscience awareness of our interrelatedness is to acknowledge our interdependence. Yet the limited ego conscience level of awareness proffers forth educational policies that deny or exclude individuals with differences that in effect deny our very interdependence and common humanity. Indeed, one can see that a societal ethos of ego conscience and its falls illusion of separate inherent existence is pervasively promoted in our educational legal system, whether it was the racial segregation laws of Jim Crow at issue in Brown v. Board of Education,[96] or today's racially segregated classroom practices enforced by tracking and ability grouping,[97] linguistically segregative policies that partition students into unequal resource tracks,[98] racially exclusionary admissions practices of magnet schools,[99] discriminatory community

---

the exchange-rate adjustment mechanism....When a shock leaves domestic prices and wages at levels that are uncompetitive internationally, they must fall to restore competitiveness. (In the case of Greece, the shock was the credit boom.) However, coordinating this reduction is difficult, as various sectors will only accept wage cuts if they see other sectors doing likewise. In the meantime, although wages and incomes are falling, the amount owed to creditors is not. Indeed, it is rising in real terms. This situation rarely ends without a default and devaluation. In a currency union, the latter is possible only by exiting the union.")

94 The description of the economic crisis as the "Great Recession" comes from the work of Thomas Friedman, see Friedman, Hot, Flat and Crowded, at 18.

95 Id.

96 347 U.S. 483 (1954).

97 See Charles T. Clotfelter, After Brown 137-46 (2004). This factor captures race indirectly based upon the prevalent racially identifiable character of schools. See generally Jeannie Oakes, Keeping Track: How Schools Structure Inequality (Yale Press 1985); Thomas Good, Two Decades of Research on Teacher Expectations: Findings and Future Directions, J. of Teacher Ed., 32, 38-47 (1987).

98 Plyler v. Doe, 457 U.S. 202 (1982); Lau v. Nichols, 414 U.S. 563 (1974); Castenada v. Pickard, 648 F.2d 989, 1009-10 (5th Cir. 1981) (establishing a three-part test for determining whether a school district has taken "appropriate action

district zoning laws of neighborhood schools, discriminative zero tolerance policies,[100] discriminatory educational finance systems,[101] sexually segregative schools and admissions policies,[102] the harassment and separation of LGBT students,[103] or the systemic exclusions of individuals with disability from the mainstream classroom and curriculum,[104] individual difference becomes the ego conscience cornerstone for justifying segregation and exclusionary practices. Law at its worse, endorses and promotes this ego conscience approach by creating the necessary conditions for its thriving. But, at its best, law can seek to promote a soul conscience interrelatedness of humankind. In fact, one can view the educational, constitutional and civil rights reform of the past three decades as a grand social saga to strike at the heart of the ego centered denial of our interrelatedness. As one commentator notes:

> "[Dr.] King understood, and the experiences of individuals with disabilities confirm, that exclusion spills directly from the denial of our interdependence. Prejudice would have us see no connection between ourselves and others, and therefore no reason to

---

to overcome language barriers," requiring that the school district's program (1) be based on sound educational theories, (2) effectively implement the education theories, and (3) produce results showing that language barriers are being overcome); Keyes v. Sch. Dist. No. 1, 576 F. Supp. 1503 (D. Colo. 1983). See also The Civil Rights Project, Report, What Works for the Children? What We Know and Don't Know About Bilingual Education (2002); Kevin R. Johnson & George Martinez, Discrimination By Proxy: The Case of Proposition 227 and the Ban on Bilingual Education, 33 U.C. Davis L. Rev. 1227, 1227 (2000); Lynn Olson, Mixed Needs of Immigrants Pose Challenges for Schools, Educ. Wk., Sept. 27, 2000; Susan Baker & Kenji Hakuta, Bilingual Education and Latino Civil Rights (Stanford University working paper, available at http://www.civilrightsproject.ucla.edu/research/latino97/Hakuta.pdf);

99 See e.g., Parents Involved in Community Schs., 127 S. Ct. at 2738; see also Grutter, 539 U. S. at 306.

100 See generally Anne J. Atkinson, Zero Tolerance Policies: An Issue Brief, available at http:// ednews.org/articles/1609/1/ZERO-TOLERANCE-POLICIES-AN-ISSUE-BRIEF/Page1.html (last visited Jan. 5, 2008).

101 Jonathon Kozol, Savage Inequalities: Children in America's Schools 99-101 (1992); Council of the Great City Schools, Adequate State Financing of Urban Schools: An Analysis of State Funding of the New York City Public Schools 40-43 (2000), available at http:// www.cgcs.org/pdfs/NYCAdequateFinanceReport.pdf; Council of the Great City Schools, Adequate State Financing of Urban Schools: An Analysis of State Funding of the Philadelphia Public Schools 30-33 (1998), available at http:// www.cgcs.org/pdfs/PhiladelphiaAdequateReport.pdf.

102 Verna L. Williams, Reform or Retrenchment? Single-Sex Education and the Construction of Race and Gender , 2004 Wis. L. Rev . 15, 21 (2004).

103 Nat'l Mental Health Ass'n, Bullying in Schools: Harassment Puts Gay Youth at Risk, available at http:// www.nmha.org/pbedu/backtoschool/ bullyingGayYouth.pdf First Public Gay H.S. Opens in NYC, MSNBC.com, Sept. 8, 2003, http:// www.msnbc.com/news/963392.asp.

104 See e.g., Florence County Sch. Dist. Four v. Carter, 510 U.S. 7 (1993); Zobrest v. Catalina Foothills Sch. Dist., 509 U.S. 1 (1993); Honig v. Doe, 484 U.S. 305 (1988); Irving Indep. Sch. Dist. v. Tatro, 468 U.S. 883 (1984); Bd. of Educ. v. Rowley, 458 U.S. 176 (1982); Hobson v. Hansen, 269 F. Supp. 401 (D.D.C. 1967), aff'd sub. nom. Smuck v. Hobson, 408 F.2d 175 (D.C. Cir. 1969) (en banc); Oscar Cohen, Inclusion Should Not Include Deaf Students, Educ. Wk., Apr. 20, 1994, at 35; Lisa Fine, More Disabled Students Graduating, Ed. Dept. Report Says, Educ. Wk., Dec. 6, 2000, at 26; Daniel J. Losen & Kevin G. Welner, Disabling Discrimination in our Public Schools: Comprehensive Legal Challenges to Inappropriate and Inadequate Special Education Services for Minority Children, 36 Harv. C.R.-C.L.L. Rev. 407, 434 (2001); John O'Neil, Q & A, A Better IDEA, N.Y. Times, Apr. 14, 2002, at A17; U.S. Dept. of Education, "IDEA Final Regulations: Major Issues" (1999); U.S. Dept. of Education, "IDEA Topic Brief 10: Parentally Placed Children in Private Schools" (1999); U.S. Dept. of Education, "IDEA Final Regulations: Discipline for Children with Disabilities" (1999); U.S. Dept. of Education, "Questions and Answers About Provisions in the Individuals with Disabilities Act Amendments of 1997 Related to Students with Disabilities and State and District-wide Assessments" (Aug. 24, 2000); David Krantz, Separate Is Not Equal, Educ. Wk., June 21, 1993, at 38, 40.

> acknowledge or respect our common humanity. Systematic and pervasive impediments to human interaction in the significant arenas of human life are corrosive of individual dignity and the maintenance of community, and thus isolation should be seen to be at a heart of the evil to be combated through our constitutional protections. Indeed, the purpose of all civil rights statutes, implementing those protections, is to enhance and ensure human interaction for the sake of human rights, the health of our democracy, and our common humanity. James Somerset, upon his arrival in England, breathed in the pure air of rights, air that carried to him the holy symbols of his humanity. As all of us take in from the same air, slavery cannot be allowed to exist because it poisons the atmosphere of rights upon which our humanity depends. Each relies upon the other to protect the air, and each is necessary to the effectuation of rights that have no meaning or consequence except within a web of relationship. Rights respiration can only occur within our social context, and thus isolation constitutes social asphyxiation and the death of self."[105]

Yet our failing to achieve these laudable sociolegal goals comes not from a misguided soul conscience legal approach. Rather our failing to achieve the full promise and potential of a soul conscience approach is predicated upon the ego-centered attempts to subvert enforcement of those very same laws, sometimes with the tacit and explicit accomplice of the law subverting itself in order to do so. Of course, one need only read the psychological impact of racial segregation or the emotional effects commonly detailed in student bullying and harassment opinions to see the acceptance of their legal legitimacy may be all too common in our education system.[106] We may also come to see where the ego conscience denial of interrelatedness (soul conscience) occurs that produces inequality, and nonetheless results in a denial of interdependence that overall adversely affects all stakeholders involved: (1) Native speakers are deprived of meaningful opportunities to learn language dynamically side by side in dual immersion language programs with other non-native speakers that may have beneficial cognitive benefits for the mastery of math, music and science skills of all involved;[107] (2) Opponents of diversity and affirmative action are deprived of interpersonal human skills of understanding, communication, tolerance and acceptance to function in a multiracial society;[108] (3) Opponents of restorative school finance and inclusive housing policies may end up

105 See Allan H. Macurdy, Rights Respiration. Disability, Isolation and a Constitutional Right of Interaction, The Boston University School of Law Working Paper Series Index, available at http://www.bu.edu/law/faculty/scholarship/workingpapers/2006.html).

106 Theno, 377 F. Supp. 2d at 968. ("[The plaintiff] began suffering from stomach problems that required prescription medication and depression so severe that his physician prescribed medication and he sought counseling. He was diagnosed with post-traumatic stress disorder, anxiety disorder, and avoidant personality disorder that likely stemmed from the harassment. The harassment was so humiliating that he eventually left school.... The school district's argument that the harassment is not actionable because it involved only name-calling and crude gestures, not physical harassment, [is] without merit.").

107 Joetta L. Sack, Riley Endorses Dual Immersion Programs, Educ. Wk., Mar. 22, 2000, at 34, available at http://www.edweek.org/ew/articles/2000/03/22/28hisp.h19.html;

108 See generally William G. Bowen & Derek Bok, The Shape of the River: Long-Term Consequences of Considering Race in College and University Admissions (1998); Jack Greenberg, Diversity, the University, and the World Outside, 103 Colum. L. Rev. 1610 (2003). Peter Schmidt, New Research Complicates Discussions of Campus Diversity-in a Good Way ("The book, No Longer Separate, Not Yet Equal: Race and Class in Elite College Admission and Campus Life (Princeton University Press), also says that whether students report benefiting from crossracial

bearing the costs of educational inequity in higher crime rates in their neighborhoods;[109] (4) Opponents of racial inclusiveness and acceptance in university ROTC educational programs may result in lack of legitimacy and racial tolerance that threatens to undermine the collective national security of America both domestically in army unit dissension and homogenous composition that abroad adversely impacts its ability to function effectively to win the hearts and minds of diverse global environments;[110] (5) Opponents of affirmative action compromise the ability of corporate America do engage in international business;[111] (6) Proponents of sexually segregated schools may often reinforce sexual stereotypes, intolerance to the opposite sex and encourages sexist conduct in the workplace and in interpersonal relationships;[112] (7) Opponents of educational tuition benefits for undocumented immigrants may result less economic growth for a nation in need of greater skilled labor to transition to a green economy.[113]

Race Relations

Whether it is greed, fear, anger, jealousy, ego superiority, ignorance, racial prejudice or discrimination, each contrived barrier created by the ego-conscience level of awareness serves as the pre-text for individual separation from the soul conscience level of awareness of our interdependent interrelatedness and its ability to take accountability for cause and effect of one's actions. Rather than the law demanding greater accountability, it invokes the coercive force of the state to escape it. These barriers, like racism, justify action without regard to consequence, establishing cause without regard to accountability for its effect or acting in narrow self interest by treating others as a means to an end rather than as ends themselves. Similarly, overcoming racial subjugation, disability

interactions depends heavily on what those interactions are. Students with freshman-year roommates from different racial backgrounds, for example, are much more likely than others to have crossracial interactions later during college. Casual contact and superficial exchanges appear to have little impact on students' thinking. "Diversity work does not begin or end with the admission office," says Mr. Espenshade, who based his analysis on data on 9,000 students at 10 selective colleges collected through the National Survey of College Experience. At most colleges, he says, "there is not enough attention paid to relevant issues of mixing or mingling." Of course, diversity initiatives operating with social stigmas and racial exclusivity may nonetheless have adverse effects. "The book, The Diversity Challenge: Social Identity and Intergroup Relations on the College Campus, written by Mr. Sidanius and three other scholars, also says the UCLA study found not only that some black students' grades had suffered from their belief that they were admitted through race-conscious admissions policies, but also that involvement in racially or ethnically oriented campus groups appeared to hurt students' ability to relate to peers from other racial and ethnic backgrounds. Among some studies currently under way is one by a collaborative of colleges based at the University of Michigan at Ann Arbor to measure the educational impact of "intergroup dialogue," <http://chronicle.com/article/Intergroup-Dialogue-Promo/985/> a teaching approach that brings students from different backgrounds together and encourages them to grapple with points of conflict. On another front, the Higher Education Research Institute at UCLA is developing a national survey of colleges to measure students' experiences with diversity and how they are affected.").

109 Susan H. Bitensky, Theoretical Foundations for a Right to Education Under the U.S. Constitution: A Beginning to the End of the National Crisis, 86 Nw. U. L. Rev. 550, 551 (1992); Shilesh Muralidhara, Deficiencies of the Low-Income Housing Tax Credit in Targeting the Lowerst-Income Households and In Promoting Concentrated Poverty and Segregation, 24 Law & Ineq. 353 b (2006).

110 See generally Consolidated Brief of Amici Curiae Lt Gen Julius W. Becton, Jr, et al, in Support of Respondents, Grutter v Bollinger, No 02-241 (US filed Feb 19, 2003).

111 Brief for Amici Curiae 65 Leading American Businesses at 7, Grutter v. Bollinger, 123 S. Ct. 2325 (2003) (No. 02-241).

112 Verna L. Williams, Reform or Retrenchment? Single-Sex Education and the Construction of Race and Gender , 2004 Wis. L. Rev . 15, 21 (2004).

113 Plyler v. Doe, 457 U.S. 202, 102 S. Ct. 2382, 72 L. Ed. 2d 786, 4 Ed. Law Rep. 953 (1982).

discrimination, gender bias and distinctions on the basis of sexuality compels extraordinary efforts at transcendence. Therefore, race can serve as a metaphor to offer humanity a tool to see how divine oneness and its resulting cause and effect of actions must be properly in balance to advance the consciousness of the subjugator and the subjugated alike if there is to be true transcendence.[114]

When Caucasians fled in white flight from the city schools to avoid desegregation orders in the inner city, when entire white colleges, professional programs, and universities were shut down rather than submit to desegregation mandates, or football teams dismantled to prevent desegregation of its team members, Caucasians fundamentally denied the dependent arising nature of their co-reality with blacks. What resulted in effect was a palpable, practical harm to white revenue, educational opportunity and recreational enrichment if not more so given their vested interests than what existed for Blacks at the time. The injuries of race and racialization not only affect the racially subjugated, but they do harm to the collective constitutive humanity of the subjugators themselves. Artificial contrivances in the legal doctrine of segregation fostered a legal and societal fiction of separation that would need to be challenged. What was needed then as is now is a shift in thinking where a talented nexus of organic, spiritually based leaders cultivated among their own peers that would need to make plain in moral authority and in practicality how these true hidden costs fundamentally and adversely impact the oppressor, perhaps even more so than the oppressed.

In race relations, we see the law of cause and effect based upon our interdependent nature. This interrelated nature of the races can be gleaned from the thesis of the Miner's Canary.[115] Has Lani Guinier and Gerrald Torres noted: "Race is like the miner's canary. Miners often carried a canary into the mine alongside them. The canary's more fragile respiratory system would cause it to collapse from noxious gases long before humans were affected, thus alerting the miners to danger. The canary's distress signaled that it was time to get out of the mine because the air was becoming too poisonous to breathe. Those who are racially marginalized are like the miner's canary—Their distress is the first sign of a danger that threatens us all. We watch the canary, seeking to improve the air quality in the mines, and to reconnect individual experiences to democratic faith, to social critique, and to meaningful action that improves the lives of everyone in the mine."[116] Although the races are equally situated and those most vulnerable in society are the first to feel the effects of efforts to sever humanity's interrelatedness, it does lend support to the notion that what effects one, will

114 Dr. King also understood this concept of divine interrelated oneness and its relationship to cause and effect with regard to viewing race as a barometer for the progress of society. When advocating a bus boycott as part of the Montgomery Improvement Association (MIA), Dr. King confronted the exaggeration from whites who held as their attitude that it was their city, their buses, their right to ride that was theirs alone as if it and they were inherently existing independently of Blacks. Accordingly, whites exaggerated, and thus in their ignorance underestimated or ignored the interdependent nature of things, i.e., the bus transportation system and the city's reliance on the revenue of African-Americans to support its economic life. Whites had no choice but to ultimately relent and yield to the interrelated and interdependent nature of reality.

115 See generally, Lani Guinier & Gerald Torres, The Miner's Canary: Enlisting Race, Resisting Power, Transforming Democracy (2002). See also http://www.minerscanary.org/ about.shtml ("Ignoring racial differences – color blindness – has failed, they argue. Race and power intertwine at every level of social interaction, from classrooms to courtrooms to congressional districts. Only cross-racial coalitions can expose these embedded hierarchies of privilege and – through innovative power sharing and democratic engagement – demolish them. Guinier and Torres call this concept of enlisting race to resist power political race. The methodology of political race has policy implications for affirmative action, racial profiling, criminal justice, access to educational opportunity, voting and democracy. It is a methodology for diagnosing systemic injustice and then organizing to resist it.").

116 See generally, Lani Guinier & Gerald Torres, The Miner's Canary: Enlisting Race, Resisting Power, Transforming Democracy (2002).

ultimately impact all of humanity if left unchecked and we must cease to isolate one another or the relationship of one's actions upon another.

As noted essayist Jean-Paul Sartre acknowledged, the temptation to view effect as separate from its cause allows us to justify things being simply as they are rather than as the outcome of a particular cause:

> "[i]f I observe that a balloon rises, I say it rises because it is light. If I observe, as a child, that Blacks do not behave as we do, I say that is because they are Black. A changed point of view is required to be able to comprehend that the air carries the balloon up and that we require Blacks to act as they do, because in both cases, the determining factor is hidden."[117]

Yet a wholesale ignorance or willful ego conscience blindness in our society to see how the oppressed affects the oppressed is blatant rejection of the soul conscience level awareness of our interrelatedness and its attendant cause and effect principle. As Paulo Freire observed, "the behavior of the oppressed is a prescribed behavior, following as it does the guidelines of the oppressor."[118] Similarly, it is also a patent rejection of the cause and effect principle to turn a blind eye to see or our past actions impact our present reality. This causal relationship was at the heart of King's exposition about the causes of the mass protest and demonstrations. He chided those who criticized this form of direct action without comprehending the root causes that spurned so many to action. He urged the reader to remember that for the consequence of mass protest being witnessed in the streets, there was a cause of injustice that prompted such discontent and civil disobedience. He reminded us that to castigate the demonstrators without fully castigating the racist behavior that led to it amounted to a fundamental misunderstanding of the cause and effect of past and present human behavior.[119] Dealing with the root causes of discriminatory attitudes in the workplace, in the classroom, or the insensitivity and false assumptions that excuse inappropriate behavior must be addressed through legal, educational and spiritual means for there to be a just justice; one not predicated merely on money judgment but on transformative individual and institutional practices that compel us as individuals to lovingly confront one another as a family of human beings and to resolve our conflicts within the context of interdependence.

Societal Evasiveness In Addressing Root Causes

---

117 Jean-Paul Sartre, Revolutionary Violence, in Notebooks for An Ethics 561-74 (1992) (David Pellauer, trans., University of Chicago Press 1992).

118 Paulo Freire, Pedagogy of the Oppressed 34 (Myra Bergman Ramos trans., Continuum Publishing Company 1970).

119 Martin Luther King, Jr., Letter From A Birmingham Jail, reprinted in A TESTAMENT OF HOPE: THE ESSENTIAL WRITINGS AND SPEECHES OF MARTIN LUTHER KING, JR. 49 (James M. Washington ed., 1986)(" "If one recognizes this vital urge that has engulfed the Negro community, one should readily understand why public demonstrations are taking place. The Negro has many pent up resentments and latent frustrations, and he must release them. So let him march; let him make prayer pilgrimages to the city hall; let him go on freedom rides - and try to understand why he must do so. If his repressed emotions are not released in nonviolent ways, they will seek expression through violence; this is not a threat but a fact of history. So I have not said to my people: "Get rid of your discontent." Rather, I have tried to say that this normal and healthy discontent can be channeled into the creative outlet of nonviolent direct action.").

It is thus ironic to see that those conservatives who would profess personal responsibility as a banner call for reform are the first to curtail concrete efforts to promote personal responsibility through greater accountability for cause and effect, whether it be banking, regulatory reform, environmental reform or educational reform. What accounts for this evasive approach to address the root causes inequity? Perhaps to acknowledge root cause is to acknowledge that we, ourselves, have contributed to it.[120] But more often than not it is a realization that we are unwilling to muster the desire to, or unable to understand its full complexity or find it simply too costly to do so. [121] Yet this inaction, futility are often borne out of the same thing—that is, the failure to see the inherent interrelatedness of all human condition and its attendant cause and effect for if we did, we would see the need to act as fates inextricably intertwined. Taking a spiritual approach, we may overcome the defeatist attitudes of futility that prompt inaction to addressing root causes of inequity by reaffirming, as King did, our ability move progress and time forward. We may come to see, as the Dalai Lama and Deepak Chopra suggest, that our root causes can be examined as interlinked with its effect. Further, sloppy analysis is almost always certain to be the byproduct of approaches that fail to take a hard look at the adverse impact our actions and behaviors sanctioned by our laws upon others without any compassionate regard to their realities. Addressing the superficial symptoms of a problem is not tantamount to addressing the effects of a problem. The former fails to take into account the realities of all stakeholders except in cosmetic, formalistic fashion, whereas the latter does not; it concerns itself not only with its own actions but its adverse impact upon all stakeholders and invites them to participate in real, meaningful change.

This would lead to more lasting settlements, greater productivity, sound employee or student well being in the work and learning environment respectively. But often such efforts fail to establish anything meaningfully beyond political correctness our mutuality, our connectedness or a divine oneness. True transformative lawyering and counseling of clients must begin with ourselves as practitioners and as consensus shapers in seeing clients interests intertwined and fostering beneficial interest for the collective good. Whether this is for families in family law, for employees and employers alike in the workplace discrimination law, or for businesses, government and customers alike in administrative regulatory law, the collective good should remain at the heart of the matter. It is our final embrace of our oneness and positive change for the collective good that we can begin to fully utilize the law of cause and effect in ways that harmonize and maximize opportunities that will promote individual growth, economic growth and global growth in truly responsible, sustainable ways that protect and rejuvenate our earth and our inter-personal relationships. The post enlightenment spiritual values of community, and restoring people's relationships to each other and to their communities are to be embraced in our legal system as much as possible to achieve justice through individual and collective well being.

KARMA AS CAUSE AND EFFECT

---

120 Peter H. Schuck, Affirmative Action: Past, Present, and Future, 20 Yale L. & Pol'y Rev. 1, 83 (2002).

121 Id. ("Root causes usually remain root causes for one of three reasons: we do not know how to eliminate them, or we (think we) know how but consider it too costly to do so in terms of resources or competing values, or we believe it is worth doing but simply cannot muster the necessary political will. When these impediments to attacking root causes exist…our best course may be to focus on managing symptoms until we can figure out how to remove the more fundamental causes. In such cases, insisting on a root cause strategy may in effect be a prescription for inaction, futility, rhetorical excess, and (because root causes are hard to understand) sloppy analysis.").

Deepak Chopra explains that this cause and effect, or what he refers to as karma, is rooted in actions of the past. Thus, to understand the present, one must understand their past actions and its impact upon their reality.

> “"Karma" is both action and the consequence of that action; it is cause and effect simultaneously, because every action generates a force of energy that returns to us in kind. There is nothing unfamiliar about the Law of Karma. Everyone had heard the expression, "What you sow is what you reap." Obviously, if we want to create happiness in our lives, we must learn to sow the seeds of happiness. Therefore, karma implies the action of conscious choice-making.”[122]

Our nation’s status, prosperity and growth has experienced the negative karma that comes from the actions of the past five years of decreased regulation, rewarding of corporatized greed, the devolution of the collective good ideal and the morally bankrupt notion of personal responsibility of leaders and whole business sectors.

But what are the implications of karmatic spiritual development on race relations? To fully explore the ramifications of karma on race, it is first necessary to understand the laws of soul evolution, reincarnation and karma which are often intertwined concepts in a universal scheme to achieve a collective justice and harmonious balance. According to this universal law, it is the responsibility and role of all seven billion people on the face of the earth to achieve their own individual and collective soul evolution whether they realize this is the case or not.

THE LAW OF KARMA AND RESTORATIVE JUSTICE

In Hinduism and Buddhism, karma is a concept that refers to the effects of a person's actions that will ultimately determine one’s destiny. Under this conception, karma is not retribution, but merely the balancing of experiences to refine the process of soul evolvement.[123] Karma also may or may not involve religious conceptions of reincarnation to some believers.[124] For these believers, one’s

122 Deepak Chopra, The Seven Spiritual Laws of Success (2007)[hereinafter Spiritual Laws] available at http://www.ofspirit.com/deepakchopra1.htm (stating that “[w]hether you like it or not, everything that is happening at this moment is a result of the choices you've made in the past. Unfortunately, a lot of us make choices unconsciously, and therefore we don't think they are choices--and yet, they are. If you step back for a moment and witness the choices you are making as you make those choices, then in just this act of witnessing, you take the whole process from the unconscious realm into the conscious realm. This procedure of conscious choice-making and witnessing is very empowering. You can use the Law of Karma to create money and affluence, and the flow of all good things to you, any time you want. But first, you must become consciously aware that your future is generated by the choices you are making in every moment of your life. If you do this on a regular basis, then you are making full use of this law. The more you bring your choices into the level of your conscious awareness, the more you will make those choices which are spontaneously correct--both for you and those around you.”).

123 Dick Sutphen, The Lighting the Light Within (1987), excerpted text available at http://www.radioastrology.com/TFG/ 20PrUniL.htm

124 Id. (“what you most need to learn and in your earthly sojourns, and for each life experience you seek out other souls, often with shared histories, and always with Karmic configurations matching your needs. Whenever you act with intention you create Karma. Actions are considered to be thoughts, emotions, words and deeds, and the motive, desire and intent behind each. Disharmonious acts must be balanced in the future in this life or in a future lifetime, to have Soul growth.”)

lessons are determined according to the individual during the afterlife, when one is presumably free of the self-justificatory rationalizations and the imperfections of the personality that dominated the flesh to honestly evaluate one's life just lived to assess their spiritual progress. Previously unconscious or subconscious resistance or hostility to race can be clearly viewed now through the prism of self reflection.[125] Wisdom may be the byproduct of suffering and the reflection of love, but it is wisdom that in turn erases karma so that lessons once learned through love can mitigate suffering.[126]

In a manner of speaking one reaps what one sows not as a punishment, but as learning experience to embrace lessons that lead to a change of heart, and thus a change in behavior. This is the thrust of the role of forgiveness as seen in the South Africa's Truth and Reconciliation Commission[127] following the end of apartheid and in the corrective justice movement that has informed reforms to the criminal justice system.[128] Under this view, our law misplaces its focus on punishment and incarceration rather than adequately restoring the "destruction of trust between people that crime tends to produce."[129] Viewed in this way, we come to see that "what is annulled in the act of

125 Perhaps the role of suffering destroys and burns up ego which is an impediment to obtaining wisdom. In this sense of an interdependent tautology that confounds our limited understanding, is it man's ego that creates suffering in the world while it is also suffering that burns up the ego, thereby allowing one to freely remove barriers to achieving wisdom?

126 It is also sometimes through suffering and pain that lessons are learned most effectively and efficiently which are further red in the incarnate life. Therefore, if you "you greedily take from others, and instead of learning through wisdom and love that this is wrong, you have to experience from others someone greedily taking from you, whether later in this life or in a future lifetime." Id.

127 See Peter Gabel, Imagine Law, available at http://www.spiritlawpolitics.org/gabel_ imaginelaw.html ("The power of this re-imagining of the healing power of law has been nowhere better revealed than in the work of South Africa's Truth and Reconciliation Commission (TRC) under the leadership of Bishop Desmond Tutu. That commission has sought to avoid the vengeance that almost inevitably accompanies revolutions against a legacy of oppression by seeking, on behalf of the black majority, to forgive the white minority for the crimes of apartheid so long as the offenders acknowledged the truth of what they had done. With all its limitations, including the immense political complications accompanying the TRC's work (hearing and televising a review of some 22,000 cases often involving extreme violence), the TRC is one of the greatest experiments in human history in a spiritual approach to healing social conflict. Imagine if we began now to take the next millennium to build our entire legal culture on the TRC's premise announced in the title of Bishop Tutu's recent book: No Future Without Forgiveness.").

128 See David M. Lerman, Forgiveness in the Criminal Justice System: If It Belongs Then Why Is It So Hard To Find? available at http://www.spiritlawpolitics.org/lerman_forgiveness. html#5; see also Restorative Justice: Principles, Practices, and Implementation. U.S. Department of Justice, National Institute of Corrections "(One abbreviated definition of Restorative Justice focuses on the basic inquiries pursued by the traditional justice system as opposed to a restorative approach. If the traditional system seeks answers to:1.Who did the act, 2. What rule/law was violated, and 3. How should that person be punished; then the restorative approach seeks answers to: 1. What is the harm done by an act, 2. What needs to be done to correct the harm, and 3. Who is responsible for that? Restorative Justice is predicated upon a set of core principles. These include: 1. Crime is an offense against human relationships. 2. Victims and the community are central to justice processes. 3. The first priority of justice processes is to assist victims. 4.The second priority is to restore the community to the degree possible. 5. The offender has personal responsibility to victims and to the community for crimes committed. 6. Stakeholders share responsibilities for restorative justice through partnerships for action. 7. The offender should develop improved competency and understanding as a result of the restorative justice experience.").

129 See David M. Lerman, Forgiveness in the Criminal Justice System: If It Belongs Then Why Is It So Hard To Find? available at http://www.spiritlawpolitics.org/lerman_forgiveness. html#5

forgiveness is not the crime itself but the distorting effect that this wrong has upon one's relations with the wrongdoer and perhaps with others."[130] The benefits of the spiritual role of forgiveness is twofold, a benefit for the victim and for the perpetrator.[131]

The role of forgiveness in the law also has a benefit for the perpetrator and the community as well.[132] Yet lawyers, judges, and legal scholars have not fully understood the spiritual role of seeking and granting forgiveness outside the limited corrective justice model in the criminal law context. Indeed, all of law requires a restoration of relationships as part and parcel of providing legal redress. Whether it is restoring trust and relations in a bitter fought divorce or custody battle in family law, or restoring trust between a lax Securities and Exchange Commission, Congress and defrauded Madoff Ponzi scheme investors who lost their college and retirement savings, or seeking and granting forgiveness for the committed wrongs of slavery, for ambivalence in the face of genocide, or acquiescence in human trafficking, Dr. King understood this principle as did the lawyers Nelson Mandela and Mahatma Ghandi.

Nor does the law fully recognize the spiritual roots of forgiveness that has taken prominence in various faiths. For instance, in the Gospel of Matthew, Jesus commands His followers to forgive those who have wronged them.[133] In Matthew, Apostle Peter came to Jesus and asked, "Lord, how many times shall I forgive my brother when he sins against me? Up to seven times?" Jesus answered, "I tell you, not seven times, but seventy-seven times."[134] In the Gospel of Luke, it proclaims "Do not judge, and you will not be judged. Do not condemn, and you will not be condemned. Forgive, and you will be forgiven." [135] The same is true under Judaic law.[136]

---

130 Id. citing J. North, J. Wrongdoing and Forgiveness. Philosophy 62: 409-508, at 500 (1987).

131 See David M. Lerman, Forgiveness in the Criminal Justice System: If It Belongs Then Why Is It So Hard To Find? available at http://www.spiritlawpolitics.org/lerman_forgiveness. html#5 Example 1 clearly shows the benefit to the victim? (Example 1: "in rural Wisconsin two young men sought to steal a car from a home they thought was empty. When the middle-aged woman of the house came outside to investigate they brutally attacked her and left her for dead. She survived, but faces severe physical limitations because of the attack. The young men were caught, convicted, and sentenced to long prison terms. Two and one-half years later the victim began a series of conferences with one of the young men. The first face-to-face meeting with her offender was important for her. Meeting her attacker, speaking with him, hearing his fears allowed her forgive him so that she could move on with her life. She also clearly stated that she hoped he never left prison, because he needed to be there for the safety of the community.")

132 Id. (Example 2: "At the other end of the spectrum is the case of K.T., an eighteen-year-old cashier awaiting entry to college. Her older brother is in prison, her mother has a cocaine habit, and her younger siblings at home sometimes suffer because their mother disappears for days. During one of these disappearances, K.T. was fed up, and tempted by the cash at her fingertips, manipulated the "no sale" key in a way she thought would hide her thievery. But she was caught, and confessed to prior incidents totaling just over $1,000. Prior to conviction, a conference was held with two representatives of the store. K.T. was tearful while listening to the human resources manager who had hired her describe the loss of trust. This manager, however, spoke of forgiveness after hearing the details of K.T.'s life, and her expressions of remorse during the conference. Eventually, the store representatives suggested that K. T. return to the store to speak at new employee orientations sessions. She in fact spoke at six sessions for her former employer, thus doing more to "earn" the forgiveness than simply saying "I'm sorry." She also developed greater competencies through this forward-looking approach to justice, which took into account the needs of the victim. Her case was ultimately dismissed.").

133 See Holy Bible, New Testament, at Matthew 5:44.

134 See Holy Bible, New Testament, at Matthew 18:21-22.

135 See Holy Bible, New Testament, at Luke 6:37; Mat 18:21-27 (NIV)(" Then Peter came to Jesus and asked, "Lord, how many times shall I forgive my brother when he sins against me? Up to seven times?" Jesus answered, "I tell you,

Like the many faiths of the world that the call for forgiveness, the role of restoring individuals and human relationships must be at the heart of law itself beyond criminal justice and to all avenues of domestic and international civil and human rights law. These faiths appear to subscribe to the same view demonstrated above, that forgiveness and the restoration of relationships is beneficial to the individual and their spiritual ability to heal and move beyond a crime. The converse then must also be true, that is, that the failure to forgive leaves human relationships in disrepair, and the victim and perpetrator worse off. Viewed in this way, law can advance one's karma. In a similar vein, karma is not intended to be a wrathful judgment of God (who is loving) but rather intended merely as experiential learning to understand fully the impact of our intentions and actions upon another when we defy our interrelatedness and the cause and effect relationship of our oneness. Karma is learning by experience wisdom in an earthly plane of negativity since it is only in a realm of negativity that we can understand what goodness is in its juxtaposition with negative reality.[137] Like Kant himself believed, the reincarnation schematic is necessary to reach that *sonnum bonnum* as that individual soul has chosen for its own level of perfection over several lifetimes. This does not mean, however, that one should succumb to negativity and evils of the earthly plane. Nor should one indulge or remain complacent to it for each advances their soul's growth and God's core of love when attempting to overcome it. [138]

---

not seven times, but seventy-seven times. "Therefore, the kingdom of heaven is like a king who wanted to settle accounts with his servants. As he began the settlement, a man who owed him ten thousand talents was brought to him. Since he was not able to pay, the master ordered that he and his wife and his children and all that he had be sold to repay the debt. "The servant fell on his knees before him. 'Be patient with me,' he begged, 'and I will pay back everything.' The servant's master took pity on him, canceled the debt and let him go."); see also Mat 18:28-35 (NIV) "But when that servant went out, he found one of his fellow-servants who owed him a hundred denarii. He grabbed him and began to choke him. 'Pay back what you owe me!' he demanded. His fellow-servant fell to his knees and begged him, 'Be patient with me, and I will pay you back.' But he refused. Instead, he went off and had the man thrown into prison until he could pay the debt. When the other servants saw what had happened, they were greatly distressed and went and told their master everything that had happened. Then the master called the servant in. 'You wicked servant,' he said, 'I canceled all that debt of yours because you begged me to. Shouldn't you have had mercy on your fellow-servant just as I had on you?' In anger his master turned him over to the jailers to be tortured, until he should pay back all he owed. This is how my heavenly Father will treat each of you unless you forgive your brother from your heart.").

136 Maimonides, Laws of Teshuva, 2:9 Generally, see also Lerman, D. "Restorative Justice and Jewish Law," Full Circle, 2:2, April 1998. ("[r]epentance and prayer on Yom Kippur (the Day of Atonement) only atone for sins between people and the Almighty. Wrongs between people, for example when someone injures, curses, or steals from someone else, will never be forgiven until the wrongdoer makes the injured party whole. The injured party must also be appeased. Appeasement means asking for forgiveness and assuaging the emotional discomfort caused by the original act. Jewish tradition actually urges a victim to be receptive to a wrongdoer's overtures.").

137 This will mean that the earth as a school for the soul will remain an existence filled with negativity since overcoming negativity is not possible on the Other Side where only pure positive vibration exist in the presence of the Creator. In this sense, there is a balance and harmony that is restored that might not always be present to the eye or in the limited view of an individual lifetime that a broader schematic provides.

138 Dick Sutphen, The Lighting the Light Within (1987), excerpted text available at http://www.radioastrology.com/TFG/20PrUniL.htm:

"Example 1: In your last life you were married to a Soul who is your mate today, and whom you cruelly left far another in that previous lifetime. Before you were born into your current life, you agreed to be left by your mate, under similar circumstances—this will allow you to balance your Karma—and directly experience the pain of abandonment. If through the wisdom of Master-Life-Awareness it is easier to detach consciously from the relationship with love, you will ease the pain of parting while also passing your own test, and thus absolving Karma and evolving from within.

RACE & THE LAW OF RESISTANCE

In accordance with the law of resistance, "that which you resist you draw to you, and you will perpetuate its influence upon your life. Resistance is fear, so it is something you need to karmically resolve. The Law of Resistance assures that you let go of the fear by encountering it until you are forced to deal with it..."[139] To be sure, evil in the world is something to resist, and the notion that resisting evil makes one bound to become evil is a false assertion in so as we recognize evil does not promote justice, well being or positive manifestations of behavior. The law of resistance tells us that where the individual racist, unrepenting and unrelenting in his or her vitriol of a minority fails to acknowledge and rectify their behavior may be subject to continual confrontation.[140]

Example 2: Assume that you have Astrologically destined a severe relationship test for May of your 35th year. If you have learned through past life awareness, as well as present life learning, to be positive, non-judgmental and without expectations in your relationship you may only experience an argument with your mate on that fateful day in May, but if you haven't learned your past lessons, and have intensified your disharmony during your relationship you might experience a divorce in may of your 35th year."

As noted above, in the afterlife, or the interlife (in between incarnate lives), one is able to honestly assess without false justification their own life how well lessons were learned and what additional ones may need to still be addressed in a future incarnation. It is here where what some psychics, Gnostics and spiritualists refer to as the "Hall of Orientation" they view during astral visits to "the other side" that a soul reflects on one's life and makes the determination to reincarnate or not. It is here that an individual soul with the assistance of spirit guides and Orientator facilitators acclimate a soul that has just crossed over to the other side of spiritual dimension (what is referred to heaven) and to help the individual understand where strengths and weaknesses were and to assess whether a new life incarnate is indeed needed. Learned behaviors, previously unknown or subconscious patterns of racial discrimination or hostility can be seen in the "screening machine" a device where one can view their full life from the moment of conception until the moment of death. Psychologically buried resentments, unfair, harsh behavior and outright resistance to those belonging to a different faith, race or gender would be clearly and undeniably seen in the light of the day.

139 A slight variation of this law is the law of reflection: "The Law of Reflection. This Law says that the traits you respond to in others, you recognize in yourself, both positive and negative. It has four primary manifestations: "The Law of Reflection. This Law says that the traits you respond to in others, you recognize in yourself, both positive and negative. It has four primary manifestations: 1. That which you admire in others, you recognize as existing within yourself; 2. That which you resist and react to strongly in others is sure to be found within yourself; 3. That which you resist and react to in others is something which you are afraid exists within you; and, 4. That which you resist in yourself, you will dislike in others. In other words, you have chosen to incarnate upon the manifest plane to learn to rise above the effect of fear. Those fears will always be reflected in your reactions to others, Thus your goals are very obvious once you recognize how to perceive them. As you let go of the fear, you automatically open to expressing more unconditional love."

140 Dick Sutphen, The Lighting the Light Within (1987), excerpted text available at http://www.radioastrology.com/TFG/20PrUniL.htm (""Example: You may have a strong resistance toward people of the Asian race; Black race, Jewish faith...Your resistance is fear. The quickest way to overcome that which you fear is through direct experience, thus you will reincarnate as an Asian, Black, Jew...in a future lifetime. When you attain Master of Life awareness and stop resisting [your fear] by consciously detaching from the negativity, the problem will be resolved. Most disharmonious situations are solved through a change in your viewpoint. By changing your perspective, you can usually eliminate the effects of a problem, and if you are no longer affected by a problem, you no longer have a problem, although nothing about the problem situation may have changed. Another aspect of the Law of resistance states, that which you resists, you become....").

Consider a possibility that is beyond these worries that has a larger schematic in mind. One that is focused on a soul that has a more long term view of its own development, its own evolution of understanding. What if challenges are pre-selected in the non-physical dimension of our reality as a way to refine our character, our soul's growth and perfection within the cauldron of a tumultuous earthly life's existence complete with hardship that transforms challenges into opportunities, heartbreaks into triumphs and sorrows into joys for the ultimate self-actualization.

If we take the law of dharma (responsibility undertaken in life by an individual soul)[141] seriously, then it follows that those incarnate in a particular race or ethnicity have chosen to do so to help fulfill their life's purpose.[142] This does not mean, however, as the above suggests, that in all cases a racial minority is one that has previously led a life of resistance to other racial minorities.[143] As suggested earlier, we could conceive of a soul like Dr. Martin Luther King, Jr. who may have decided to accept a life dharma to help bring racial reconciliation to the world by assuming a particular racial identity to help perfect souls around him and in the process advance his own spirituality as well as that of the nation. But this spiritual law contains both promise and pitfalls in its ramifications. If we take the view that by changing one's perspective, we can eliminate the effects of a problem, then conceivably where that perspective involves fear, prejudice or hate to any one demographic group, then it might be quite feasible to eliminate the effects of racism as a societal problem. But this

---

141 Dharma is a Sanskrit word that means "purpose in life." This law provides that:
"we have taken manifestation in physical form to fulfill a purpose. You have a unique talent and a unique way of expressing it. There is something that you can do better than anyone else in the whole world--and for every unique talent and unique expression of that talent, there are also unique needs. When these needs are matched with the creative expression of your talent, that is the spark that creates affluence. Expressing your talents to fulfill needs creates unlimited wealth and abundance. There are three components to the Law of Dharma. The first says that each of us is here to discover our true Self. The second component is to express our unique talents; the expression of that talent takes you into timeless awareness. The third component is service to humanity. When you combine the ability to express your unique talent with service to humanity, then you make full use of the Law of Dharma."

142 Indeed, perhaps there is another way to view the metaphysics of our world and our purpose in it. Consider as we start out at the outset of this inquiry that there is a world seen and unseen, a physical world and an non-physical world, where the course of human events in the individual and on the world stage are shaped by both these physical and non-physical worlds. And yet, despite this assumption, the end conclusion is that we are ourselves the captains of our ship, the cause of our own destiny whether it be sublime or in calamity. What if the cancer that is brought about exist because it a manifestation of our own doing on both in a physical and non-physical plane that exist only in the energy of thought? What if there is a physical world we are all born into and yet a non-physical world where we have pre-selected our challenges, our triumphs, our family or friends in a blueprint of life that is minutely planned. Does this smack of predetermined Calvanism? Not quite. Calvanism would have us believe that everything no matter what our actions have all been predetermined. But what if there is a blueprint that serves as the primer for all our life lessons that we ourselves for reasons that become clear only when we return to the non-physical dimensions of our reality as pure spiritual beings do we understand the choices we made both before assuming life in the flesh and the choices we made once incarnated into a life of flesh. In this paradigm, challenges are presented, but they themselves are not pre-determinative as in Calvanism. But for what reason would one have to pre-select such challenges? Or to endure such painful hardships? What rational mind would voluntarily assume such woeful burdens? It is said that by astrologically selecting one's time and place of your birth, a decision is consciously made in the interlife to determine the nature or the effects you will experience in life as well as all the relevant details including your parents, other souls to interact with you, challenges and yes, even some illness and it is the astrological configurations existing at the time of birth which determine character, personality, abilities, restrictions, and timing for strengths and weaknesses all for the soul's evolution of its life purpose.

143 Such a limited understanding might also lead to the same kind of justificatory blame and ambivalence to the plight of racial minorities we saw with the positive thinking movement. Instead, we can also conceive of those who incarnate in a particular racial identity as those who have courageously undertaken as their purpose to help perfect the lives of others around that soul.

presupposes that the material effect of long term discrimination would no longer be a problem when in actuality its effects could be felt for generations to come if the systematic racial impediments to equality embodied in law and institutions is not removed once one's perspective has been transformed. It is worth bearing in mind the Ghandian approach of devising remedies for past wrongs where no individual or individual race would have to suffer the crushing burden of redressing a collective wrong, but rather in the spirit of equity would award public compensation to those who suffer the effects of remedial measures to correct past wrongs (such as affirmative action) as a form of 'inverse condemnation' to the cause of the overall social good.[144]

Here again, however, the need to understand and embrace one's interconnectedness under the law of divine oneness is manifest for once one's perspective is changed, what would compel a person to move beyond their own perspective to change the underlying discriminatory conditions one no longer subscribes to as their own personal perspective, particular if it is no longer perceived as a problem? A change of heart without a change of material impact or effect may in fact perpetuate in concrete and subtle ways the underlying racial inequality produced from one's racially biased behavior. It is here where we might consider the role of Kantian principles in our conception of the law of karma. Thus one's motives will lack universal validity unless it respects the fact that all rational beings have intrinsic worth. Since the categorical imperative requires one to treat all their fellow beings as "ends in themselves"--that is, as objects of intrinsic value--and not as mere instruments for the attainment of one' personal karma goals, one can move beyond narrow self interest and address the underlying discriminatory conditions that impact others which no longer affect the individual self. Another particular salient consideration remains: that just as an individual has their own path of karma, so do nations in a collective gestalt of groups and nation-states based upon their thoughts, feelings, and actions.[145]

KARMA OF THE U.S. & THE COLLECTIVE GESTALT: THE FEAR OF A BROWNING AMERICA

Obama, Anti-Immigrant Law & Ethnic Studies Ban

Given the above discussion, it comes with additional urgency that spiritual principles will uplift not merely "the personality" as King suggests, but in fact the heart of a nation to address its shortcomings. Only one U.S. President, Bill Clinton, and a congressional resolution have formally

144 Paul Savoy, The Spiritual Nature of Equality: Natural Principles of Constitutional Law, 28 How. L.J. 809, 818-819 (1985).

145 Dick Sutphen, The Lighting the Light Within (1987), excerpted text available at http://www.radioastrology.com/TFG/20PrUniL.htm Drs. Milanovich and McCune in, The Light Shall Set You Free, explain the concept of a collective gestalt in terms of a collective energy: ("The Universal Laws are all inter-related and are founded on the understanding that everything in the universe is energy, including us, and that energy moves in a circular fashion. At the microscopic level, we are a whirling mass of electrons and energy atoms spinning rapidly. In fact, everything in the world is comprised of energy and we are intimately connected with this sea of energy, this sea of whirling electrons. Our thoughts, feelings, words, and actions are all forms of energy. What we think, feel, say, and do in each moment comes back to us to create our realities. Energy moves in a circle, so what goes around comes around. The combined thoughts, feelings, words and actions of everyone on the planet creates our collective consciousness, it creates the world we see before us. The exciting news is, because our thoughts, feelings, words and actions create the world around us, we have the power to create a world of peace, harmony and abundance. In order to do this, it is essential that we learn to control our thoughts and emotions. Understanding the Universals Laws help us to do this.").

apologized for slavery and Jim Crow era injustice,[146] but its impacts can still be felt today. Until the U.S. confronts its past and overcomes its racially biased perspective, one might correctly speculate if this spiritual principle truly operates as articulate above, that nation may experience the impact of a its collective gestalt karma. Indeed, if that which we resist is that which we become, then query perhaps that process has already began. We have in the first time in our history, its first African-American president elected in part by large minority demographics; an event never before believed to be possible given the history of racism, slavery, Jim Crow, racial profiling and hate crimes. With hate crimes now on the rise since the election of Barack Hussein Obama, the nation is again called upon to address and confront head on its karmic lessons and challenges. How our nation rises or falls in relation to this challenge remains up to the collective gestalt. A positive visualization and belief held by millions that of a person of color could be president may have been the possible creative force assembling all cooperative relationships among voter citizens, political action groups, superdelegates and electoral college electors to manifest that reality before us. It is now for us to ask why and to shape that reality.

If that which we resist we are bound to become, then for a nation that has long resisted racial mixing, integration and its intertwining mutual destiny, it should come as no surprise to anyone to witness the national phenomenon that has been characterizes as the "browning of America" with increased immigration and intermixing of the races that will compel America to confront its own racial fears and resistance. Yes, one can say that the expanded opportunity America provides immigrants are the cause of increased legal and illegal immigration that has "browned" America. But even as spiritualists contend, patterns are often the result of the natural creative forces at work in and through the regular channels of action that direct all cooperative relationships to a particular end. Thus for karma to be realized, there need not be always a reincarnation of being as karma may be realized in ones' lifetime. The recent enacted legislation in Arizona banning certain ethnic studies programs for fear of encouraging solidarity among Chicanos or other minority groups[147] and the legislation criminalizing illegal immigration status and which targets individuals for detention, questioning and arrest under the "reasonable suspicion" of being of illegal immigrant status[148] may all represent current manifestations of a nation that continues to exemplify fear or resistance in more profound ways to the nation's changing demographics.

146 Krissah Thompson, Senate Backs Apology for Slavery: Resolution Specifies It Cannot Be Used In Reparation Cases, The Washington Post, Jun. 19, 2009 (last visited Dec. 8, 2009) available at http://www.washingtonpost.com/wp-dyn/content/article/2009/06/18/AR2009061803877.html.

147 Frank James, Arizona Gov. Signs Ethnic Studies Ban, National Public Radio, available at http://www.npr.org/blogs/thetwo-way/2010/05/arizona_gov_signs_ethnicstudie.html (last visited May 24, 2010). This law presumably is designed to prohibit programs that encourage resentment but may go too far in discouraging solidarity among students of color. Solidarity need not mean the same as resentment and solidarity in keeping with a first amendment freedom of association could mean promoting pride among a particular ethnic group. However, for a Caucasian majority quickly seeing itself become a minority, "solidarity" can signify a growing fear or resistance to race and ethnicity in a browning America.

148 Randal C. Archibold, Arizona Enacts Stringent Law on Immigration, N. Y. Times (April 23, 2010) available at http://www.nytimes.com/2010/04/24/us/politics/24immig.html (last visited May 24, 2010). While illegal immigration has always been illegal, criminalizing immigrant status is a new development. Rather than targeting resources against criminal actions of illegal immigrants on the border where limited resources are most needed, criminalizing immigrant status may place an undue burden among police forces and may invite an unwarranted harassment of American citizens of color or illegal immigrants not engaged in otherwise criminal behavior. Where the electoral power of immigrants through an amnesty or other naturalization program threatens to forever change electoral politics and perhaps national demographics of eligible voters, the criminalization of such status assuages fears of a racial non-minority majority.

But if the lessons of karma are to be learned, the end result will not merely mean the browning of America, but rather the ability of a nation to transcend its own fear or resistance to those racial or ethnic differences in order to reach a higher state of spiritual consciousness. This would mean that for a nation that has not only merely (a) separated the minority races, but (b) subjugated them psychologically, socially and legally to unjust inequity will mean that in order to karmically resolve its lessons, America will not only become racially intermixed, but become a nation of racial equality that fully embraces such equality psychologically, socially and legally. We must move to, as one colleague artfully stated, a humanity consciousness in our jurisprudence. A more humane interpretation of our law, and the Fourteenth Amendment law could conceivably achieve four important objectives. It would:

> "(1) facilitate the acknowledgement of harm done, (regardless how much time has passed); (2) facilitate the uplifting or restoration of the community to a state of humanity consciousness; (3) seek gently to disrupt the re-creation of, and orientation of human Being around, false communities; and (4) embody, to the extent possible, the community's objective of recognizing and validating our inner impulse toward a "genuine We" or, perhaps more appropriate in light of the particular rhetoric of our Constitutional democracy, a genuine "We, The People." Each of these would assist us in grappling with the presently under-remedied substantive and material existential violations described above presently purportedly addressed by antidiscrimination law, as well as the spiritual violations not presently addressed, or even recognized, by the law."[149]

Has America resolved its karmatic lessons of race? Here it is worth revisiting our earlier discussion on measuring standards of racial progress to demonstrate that America has and yet still remains in the process of doing just that. If "whites use the yardstick of how far we have come from the nation we used to be" while "Blacks use the yardstick of how far we have yet to go to be the nation we ought to be" what we quickly come to see is a reality of an America that has and remains in the throes of its karmatic challenges of race. The challenges of globalization, whether economic, political, or climatic, present similar concerns about our ability to reinvent ourselves and spiritually rise to the challenge of interrelated oneness.

THE KARMATIC IMPACT OF LAW: RELIGIOUS STRIFE & ANTI-HOMOSEXUALITY LAWS

What karma will come of those who engage in racial discrimination or abandon those left behind in the rubble of the Haitian earthquake? For those who intention is predicated on concealed conditioning by society might very well find themselves confronted with scenarios where they or the larger society are in dire need of the same need for compassion that was so fleeting or sparingly offered. Not yet realizing their life is entangled in a cycle of events designed to prompt one to

149 Rhonda V. Magee Andrews, Racial Suffering As Human Suffering: An Existentially-Grounded Humanity Consciousness As A Guide To A Fourteenth Amendment Reborn, 13 Temp. Pol. & Civ. Rts. L. Rev. 891, 920 (2004).

spiritually awaken to its own concealed intentionality, this fate might repeat until one evolves in their own consciousness.[150]

Intentionality thus informs the consequences of any given action.[151] Likewise, law must not obfuscate positive with negative intention or make it unduly burdensome to prove the nefarious intentions of wrongdoers as we currently do in constitutional and civil rights law.[152] For instance, we have difficulty in our civil rights jurisprudence to allow victims of racial discrimination to establish a prima facie case of discriminatory intent unless there is a clear, definitive smoking gun and often asserted pretext justifying such discrimination is often overlooked. As a society, perhaps looking beyond pretext and even at times beyond actions, to the core of our intentions as individuals or in a given law to understand its karmatic impact. The karmatic impact of law is often animated by the intention behind the law's purpose and that purpose is often gleaned by examining closely its unmitigated effect upon stakeholders if our interconnectedness is to be accepted. "We will have to repent in this generation not merely for the hateful words and actions of the bad people but for the appalling silence of the good people….Shallow understanding from people of good will is more frustrating than absolute misunderstanding from people of ill will. Lukewarm acceptance is much more bewildering than outright rejection." As we have noted above, this intention should not be merely confined to the text of a statute or the words uttered or withheld by a legislator on the legislative record, but instead gleaned from its effect on individuals of different races, religions or sexual orientations when that affect is known to the lawmaker that nonetheless refuses to mitigate and/or eliminate its harmful discriminatory effect. Where the intention behind the law is to stifle, repress or oppress those of different backgrounds and beliefs, the karma of such legal regimes will eventually call upon the society that enforces it to confront and reflect on its own negative intentionality in order to reach a higher evolution of spiritual consciousness and the reality of our interrelatedness despite outwardly perceived differences.

Anti-Burqa Laws

Beyond race, one might examine all the differences that separate us as a challenge to embracing our oneness. In today's age, we are not only seeing racial, ethnic or cultural strife, but religious strife. These are exacerbated by beliefs enshrined in law and policy that further inflame tensions. Rather than embracing our own truth while allowing another theirs, law has sought to impose the force of the state on its citizens of varying beliefs. In the Sudan, an Islamic government imposes its beliefs upon in a devastating fashion upon its Christian citizens, in Iran, questioning the religious legitimacy of a Supreme leader may lead to harsh punishment, imprisonment or death. France legal system of laïcité which bans individuals from wearing Muslim burqas in the classroom suggests an anti

150 Id.

151 Viewed in this way, we may come to see that karma is not just predicated upon one's actions as we have already discussed, but that it is also predicated upon one's intentions. As in law, intention becomes the cornerstone of karma rather than just the action. The action of killing another remains the same, but it is the intention to commit murder, self defense, or accidental involuntary manslaughter that determines and seals the sentencing fate of the individual. Similarly, intentions behind one's actions today may in turn shape tomorrow's karma. If the collective karma of society is predicated upon intentions, then society must come to terms with its conscious and unconsciously conditioned concealed intentional actions. This remains at odds, however, with an Abraham-Hicks interpretation of the law of attraction that bases all manifestations on present vibrational offering of thought, not upon past actions or supposed past lifetimes.

152 City of Richmond v. J.A. Croson Co., 488 U.S. 469 (1989); Metro Broadcasting, Inc. v. FCC, 497 U.S. 547 (1990); Adarand, 515 U.S. 200. Croson, 488 U.S. at 477-78.

clericalism which prevents the believer from observing his or her religion.[153] In Italy, wearing burkahs, hijabs, abayas may result in a $700 legal fine if worn at swimming pools or along riversides in the northern Piedmont town of Varallo Sesia.[154] In the United States, a Muslim student is subject to racial profiling for wearing burqas or garb. Denying one's self, one's expression of their religious belief may do spiritual harm and stifle the well being of the individual. In this way the law further mandates this unhealthy practice which in turn may bring a collective karmatic impact upon the society that enforces the law.

The law of resistance may well mean that a society that continues to resist the acceptance of religious pluralism out of fear may result in a nation being forced to confront it repeatedly until it is resolved and no longer seen as a problem. This resistance brought on by fear may be the animating reason behind such restrictive laws enforced heavily since the September 11, 2001 terrorist attack much like the racial strife the U.S has seen since its election of its first African-American president. The law of resistance and the accompanying law of karma may be invoked. If that which we resist we become, perhaps karma becomes the operating means in which experience balances out and evolves the soul's understanding of itself by encountering, experiencing and even becoming part of the experience of those we fear, subjugate and resist. A reckoning of religious beliefs with the spiritual values of love, tolerance and compassion religious society professes remains at the heart of a recent global appeal of religious and political leaders in Geneva to encourage acceptance and tolerance without regard to religion.[155] It is likely that such a need will persist until religion ceases to be used as the blunt instrument to foment global violence and intolerance.

Anti-Homosexuality Laws

Although the U.S. Supreme Court has only recently overturned its influential decision in *Bowers v. Hardwick*[156] criminalizing sodomy as applied to homosexual couples which it held did not violate

---

153 Stefanie Walterick, The Prohibition of Muslim Headscarves from French Public Schools and Controversies Surrounding the Hijab in the Western World, 20 Temp. Int'l & Comp. L.J. 251, 252 (2006); Mukul Saxena, The French Headscarf Law and the Right to Manifest Religious Belief, 84 U. Det. Mercy L. Rev. 765, 767 (2007).

154 Italian City To Fine Mulsim Women in Burqinas, Pattay News, Aug. 29, 2009, available at http://www.pattayadailynews.com/shownews.php?IDNEWS=0000010102 (last visited Dec. 18, 2009); Burqini Banned in Italian Town, Asian News International, Aug. 20, 2009, available at 2009 WLNR 16226930. City Outlaws Burqini, Geelong Advertiser, Aug. 21, 2009, available at 2009 WLNR 16323773; Italian City Bars Muslim "Burqini" Swimsuit, Daily News Egypt, Aug 21, 2009, available at 2009 WLNR 16348935; see Italy: Curbs the Growth of Islam with Mosque Law, US Federal News, Sept. 19, 2008, available at 2008 WLNR 23939213).

155 The Geneva Spiritual Appeal." Available at http://www.religioustolerance.org/ rel_prom.htm Is a global effort that ask political and religious leaders and organizations to ensure that "religious faiths are not used to justify future violence." Because our personal convictions or the religions to which we owe allegiance have common a respect for the integrity of humankind. Because our personal convictions or the religious to which we owe allegiance have common a rejection of hatred and violence. Because our personal convictions or the religions to which we owe allegiance have common the hope for a better and more just world. Representing religious communities and civil society we appeal to the leaders of the world, whatever their field of influence, to strictly adhere to the following three principles: 1) A refusal to invoke a religious or spiritual power to justify violence of any kind, 2) A refusal to invoke a religious or spiritual source to justify discrimination and exclusion; 3) A refusal to exploit or dominate others by means of strength, intellectual capacity or spiritual persuasion, wealth or social status; Grounded in the Genevan tradition of welcome, refuge and compassion, our appeal is open to all whose convictions are in accordance with these three demands.").

156 478 U.S. 186 (1986); see also Marcum v. McWhorter, 308 F. 3d 635, 640-642 (CA6 2002) (relying on Bowers in rejecting a claimed fundamental right to commit adultery); Mullins v. Oregon, 57 F. 3d 789, 793-794 (CA9 1995)

substantive due process, since its new decision in *Lawrence v. Texas*,[157] we see referendums invoking the power of law to deny gay citizens the same equal protection rights in weddings denied heterosexual citizens primarily on religious grounds.[158] Law has not only entered the bedroom and marriages of heterosexuals but also homosexuals in some of the most intimate ways possible. The "Don't Ask and Don't Tell" military law towards gays[159] not only further hampers the spiritual well being of homosexuals, but justifies their dismissal and segregation that undermines cohesive oneness in purpose.[160] Currently, Uganda has proposed its own anti-homosexual law inspired by the U.S. religiously conservative anti-gay movement.[161] Originally envisioned, it would have imposed a death penalty for being gay and for sexually active HIV-positive patients who could be found guilty of practicing the capital crime of "aggravated homosexuality.[162]

Are there karmatic implications arising from the national and global resistance to homosexuality? In a nation that has resisted homosexuality forthrightly and violently before and since Matthew Shepard, a Wyoming student murdered in 1998 because of his sexuality which made national headlines,[163] we are seeing a nation that in the throes of confronting its own resistance. The more resistance, the more we may come to see a nation confronting its own hostility, prejudice, and inner turmoil. Karma may play its role as educator, imbibing the consciousness of a nation and a world to embrace the common humanity, our collective one both in quantum physics terms and in spiritual terms despite our own individual sexual orientation preferences. We may come to see the role of

(relying on Bowers in rejecting a grandparent's claimed "fundamental liberty interes[t]" in the adoption of her grandchildren); Doe v. Wigginton, 21 F. 3d 733, 739-740 (CA6 1994) (relying on Bowers in rejecting a prisoner's claimed "fundamental right" to on-demand HIV testing); Schowengerdt v. United States, 944 F. 2d 483, 490 (CA9 1991) (relying on Bowers in upholding a bisexual's discharge from the armed services); Charles v. Baesler, 910 F. 2d 1349, 1353 (CA6 1990) (relying on Bowers in rejecting fire department captain's claimed "fundamental" interest in a promotion); Henne v. Wright, 904 F. 2d 1208, 1214-1215 (CA8 1990) (relying on Bowers in rejecting a claim that state law restricting surnames that could be given to children at birth implicates a "fundamental right"); Walls v. Petersburg, 895 F. 2d 188, 193 (CA4 1990) (relying on Bowers in rejecting substantive-due-process challenge to a police department questionnaire that asked prospective employees about homosexual activity).

157 539 U.S. 558 (2003).

158 Ian Ayres & Jennifer Gerarda Brown, Straightforward: How to Mobilize Heterosexual Support for Gay Rights (2005).

159 Pub.L. 103-160 (10 U.S.C. § 654) prohibits anyone who "demonstrate(s) a propensity or intent to engage in homosexual acts" from serving in the armed forces of the United States, because "it would create an unacceptable risk to the high standards of morale, good order and discipline, and unit cohesion that are the essence of military capability."

160 See 10 U. S. C. §654(b)(1) ("A member of the armed forces shall be separated from the armed forces ... if ... the member has engaged in ... a homosexual act or acts").

161 Zoe Alsop, Uganda Anti-Gay Bill Inspired By The U.S., Time (Dec. 19, 2009) available at http://www.time.com/time/world/article/0,8599,1946645,00.html ("The bill has an American genesis of sorts, inspired to a large extent by the visits of U.S. evangelicals who are involved with a movement that promotes Christianity's role in getting homosexuals to become "ex-gays" through prayer and faith. Ugandan supporters of the bill appear to be particularly impressed by the ideas of Scott Lively, a California conservative preacher who has written a book, The Pink Swastika, about what he calls the links between Nazism and a gay agenda for world domination, which, by itself, would have raised the anti-colonial sensitivities of Ugandan society. Says the Rev. Kapya Kaoma, an Episcopalian priest from Zambia who authored a recent report on anti-gay politics in Uganda, Nigeria and Kenya: "The U.S. culture wars have been exported to Africa.").

162 For more information on the proposed anti-homosexuality bill as first envisioned, see http://www.time.com/time/world/article/0,8599,1946645,00.html#ixzz0a5jizXWA

163 See, e.g., James Brooke, Gay Murder Trial Ends With Guilty Plea, N.Y. Times, Apr. 6, 1999, at A20. His death culminated in legislation, see GovTrack.us S. 1105 — 110th Congress (2007): Matthew Shepard Local Law Enforcement Hate Crimes Prevention Act of 2007, available at GovTrack.us (database of federal legislation) http://www.govtrack.us/congress/bill.xpd?bill=s110-1105

law as less invasive on individual rights or a protectorate of individual expression, even religious expression with reasonable accommodations for religious beliefs.[164] In so doing, the law furthers a therapeutic, spiritual well being of an individual human spirit by allowing the person to be free in authenticity and self-expression. By hampering individual rights by denying the basic rights of dignity, safety and marriage, the law sanctions violence and ignorance that demeans the intrinsic human worth of the individual and so works at cross purposes with spiritual evolvement of both the oppressed and the oppressor.[165] In realizing this, perhaps where one is compelled to confront issues related to gender in a similar way society's resistance to race compels it to confront it, we are in the process of collective evolution. In realizing the law of resistance where one is compelled to confront issues related to gender in a similar way we discussed race and the law of resistance. For those skeptical of reincarnation as a belief, we may see that by the law of cause and effect, and interrelatedness that spiritually, psychologically and personally, will we be compelled to confront that part of our own psychological resistance to others in society that becomes the artificial bulwark and justification of discriminatory separation? Viewed in this light, where does harsh societal judgment, discrimination and the legal denial of civil rights protections to the LGBT community fit in? What role does it play? Ultimately, the goal is not to indulge in intolerance, incivility, inequity, but to confront and overcome it if our spirituality is to advance. Where our mind, heart and soul evolve, so will our law and legal systems. In this way, the law is a reflection of our human nature, and by extension, the evolvement of our spiritual growth as individuals and a society. Therefore, we would do well to remember that in the machinery of law, we must embrace well being and spiritual growth at the heart of justice:

> A spiritualized society would treat . . . the individual, from the saint to the criminal, not as units of a social problem to be passed through some skillfully devised machinery and either flattened into the social mold or crushed out of it, but as souls suffering and entangled in the net and to be rescued, souls growing and to be encouraged to grow, souls grown and from whom help and power can be drawn by the lesser spirits who are not yet adult.[166]

SPIRITUAL DISINVESTMENT UNDER THE NO CHILD LEFT BEHIND (NCLB) ACT

---

164 When at its best, law affords reasonable accommodations for religious beliefs, see "Making Room For Religious Differences," The Rights Stuff (Minn. Dept. of Human Rights, St. Paul, Minn.), May-July 2004, at 5, available at http://www.humanrights.state.mn.us/acrofiles/ Feb01RS.pdf; EEOC Compliance Manual, Directives Transmittal No. 915.003, Section 12, Religious Discrimination (July 22, 2008) available at http://www.eeoc.gov/policy/docs/religion.html.

165 For those who embrace the notion of reincarnation, the notion of gay identity as the rounding out of experience and the perfection of the soul becomes even more nuanced, whether it is for the benefit of the oppressed, the oppressor or both. For example, the soul created as a man, or who has reincarnated many lifetimes as a man that might chose in the next to live as a woman, there may be many reasons: (a) to round out an individual experience to know what it is like to live as a woman, (b) to balance out past behavior subjugating women in order to gain experiential knowledge of the effect of his own demeaning behavior on women or (c) to live as an inspiring exemplar for other women and men to follow and lead. Might it be feasible, as some have suggested, under this view, that where there is past cell memory or morphic resonance in one's subconscious memory as having lived many past lifetimes as a man, that a woman will identify their sexual orientation as a lesbian?

166 SRI AUROBINDO (A. GHOSE), THE HUMAN CYCLE 197 (1971).

Yet we are far from that spiritualized society. We see under the No Child Left Behind (NCLB) Act, that indeed children are treated as units of a social problem to be passed through a less than skillfully devised accountability and assessment machinery that are either flattened into the social mold or crushed out of it under the weight of its punitive sanctions. It is a law that fails to see children as souls nor is it a law that encourages the individual soul of a child to grow. To say no child is left behind presupposes the child is being evaluated when it is in fact a system of assessment based upon randomized and fluctuating enrollment from grade to grade. Assessments, student placements and accountability are not based upon the child's creative expression of their intellect in writings, projects and portfolios, or on their individual interests in music, literature, math, sports, art in any meaningful curricular depth. Nor is their assessment dynamically tailored to the relevant life, personality, talents and interests of the child.[167] In fact, NCLB assessment is not tied to the individual child at all as he or she progresses from year to year, grade to grade. Rather, assessment is tied to mechanistic, warehouse-factory conveyor belt-style group performance. A group performance consisting of any subset of students passing through certain arbitrary grade level markers becomes the relevant assessment benchmark for student achievement. One is left to wonder just what is being measured by this approach and what focus does this place on the individual child? Rather than a growth model of assessment that measures how ***that*** individual child is progressing in subjects throughout the K-12 system, we fail to invest in the necessary attention and time to the child's academic success and spiritual well being.

The NCLB, which is an act that in and of itself is named in terms of a negative (no child left behind) than in terms of a desired positive (achievement), attaches a whole host of negative, punitive educational and unintended spiritual consequences to unsatisfactory student performance based upon its accountability machinery. "In this system of academic performance, the federal purse is the carrot; the pressure, using sanctions of measurable student performance through high-stakes testing, is the stick."[168] Besides the threat to students under high stakes testing schemes to be retained in grade or denied a diploma, sanctions for underperforming schools and school districts also become increasingly punitive in nature.[169] Sanctions without rewards however are a paltry substitute for creating the necessary conditions to inspire academic success. It is said that "the argument on the

---

167 Linda McSpadden McNeil, Faking Equity: High-stakes Testing and the Education of Latino Youth, in leaving children behind: how "texas-style" accountability fails latino youth 57, 91 (Angela Valenzuela ed., State U. of N.Y. 2005).

168 Philip T.K. Daniel and Maurice R. Dyson, Bringing Every Child Forward: Lessons Learned Under No Child Left Behind & A Roadmap for Obama's Educational Reform, ___Temple. Pol. & Civ. Rts. L. Rev. __ (2010)(forthcoming); Sharon L. Nichols, Gene V. Glass, & David C. Berliner, Education Policy Studies Laboratory, Arizona State University, High-stakes Testing and Student Achievement: Problems for the NCLB Act 1-2 (Sept. 2005).

169 20 U.S.C. § 6311(g)(2); The NCLB Act requires each state to provide a formula for measuring success defined by adequate yearly progress (AYP), Id. § 6311(b)(2)(B), which must include test scores and at least a ninety-five percent participation rate of all students, including those in sub-groups. Id. § 6311(b)(2)(I)(ii). AYP is achieved each year only if students attain the state prescribed incremental improvement which must eventually reach one hundred percent. Id. § 6311(b)(2)(F). If schools or school districts have not made AYP for two years they are designated as "in need of improvement." Id. § 6316(b)(1)(A). Schools so designated may be compelled to develop two-year academic improvement plans. 20 U.S.C. § 6316(b)(3)(A). Parents may also be offered the option of transferring their children to a school that has reached AYP. Id. § 6316(b)(1)(E)(i). Schools or school districts must achieve AYP for two consecutive years. Id. § 6311(b)(2)(H)(i). If the status continues beyond the second year, schools face other sanctions, including loss of federal funds, options for parents to send their children to other schools including charter schools and private schools, and possibly, school restructuring. Id. § 6311(b)(1)(E). Mandated restructuring actions include turning over the school's operation to the state educational agency; id. § 6316(b)(8)(B)(iv); contracting with an education management organization (EMO) to run the school; id. § 6316(b)(8)(B)(iii); "replacing all or most of the school staff who are relevant to the failure to make adequate yearly progress"; id. § 6316(b)(8)(B)(ii); "[a]ny other major restructuring of the school's governance arrangement that makes fundamental reforms ... to improve student academic achievement in the school." Id. § 6316(b)(8)(B)(v).

part of supporters of high-stakes testing is that when faced with federal fiscal incentives and sanctions for poor performance, educators will spend more time and energy exhorting students to work harder and become smarter."[170] But if we take the insights of spiritual based approach, then it is the positive impact of creative thoughtful inspiration, and the genuine demonstrated regard for the success and well-being of students and teachers that are the impetus behind constructive energy creation. It is not then the fear of sanctions or even the loss of federal funds that "inspire" success. In this way, the NCLB fails to adopt positive spiritual-based incentives for favorable student performance like positive reinforcement, self expression, cooperative interactive learning, and discovery-focused skills acquisition. Moreover, under the NCLB, students are isolated in dead end, segregated, academic tracks based upon standardized tests rather than student placements in academic tracks that would encourage interaction with motivated students of varying skills, interests, linguistic abilities or cultural backgrounds.[171] The Act, through its Title III provisions, has the effect of discouraging bilingual education or dual immersion languages in the classroom.[172] It has the effect

170 Sharon L. Nichols, Gene V. Glass, & David C. Berliner, Education Policy Studies Laboratory, Arizona State University, High-stakes Testing and Student Achievement: Problems for the NCLB Act 1-2 (Sept. 2005).

171 See Barbara J. Brunner, Bilingual Education Under the No Child Left Behind Act of 2001, 169 Ed. Law. Rep. 505, 510-514 (2002) (observing bilingual education programs were replaced with intensive English immersion instruction under Arizona's Proposition 203 notwithstanding the presence of a significant bilingual student population within the state); William Ryan, Note, The Unz Initiatives and the Abolition of Bilingual Education, 43 B.C.L. Rev. 487, 487 (2002) (noting the end of bilingual education under Ron Unz's initiative and in the passage of Proposition 227 in California). See Kirsten Gullixson, Note, California Proposition 227: An Examination of the Legal, Educational, and Practical Issues Surrounding the New Law, 17 Law & Ineq. 505, 505-06 (1999) (observing limited English immersion classrooms under California's Proposition 227).

172 What is significant to note is that Title III funds do not mandate a specific bilingual educational model and provides for the usage of alternative bilingual education programs such as dual immersion and ESL. For purposes of Title III, a language instruction educational program is defined as a program of instruction: . . . that may make instructional use of both English and the native language to enable the child to develop and attain English proficiency, and may include the participation of English proficient children if such course is designed to enable all participating children to become proficient in English and a second language. Schools offering bilingual education programs must, of course, adhere to state law regarding the placement of students in these programs. See section 3301, Title III of the No Child Left Behind Act of 2001, Pub. L. No. 107-110, § 3102(1), 115 Stat. 1425, 1689 (2002). However, notwithstanding this apparent flexible approach, there are a few observations that can be gleaned from the new Title III that suggest a contradictory posture. First, it appears after the Bilingual Education Act and the Equal Educational Opportunity Act, Title III of NCLB was designed to disturb the status quo viewed by many to be wholly unsatisfactory. Such a drastic measure presupposes that the current system of educating limited English proficiency students ("LEP")—i.e. bilingual education—is in itself fundamentally flawed and ineffective. Second, the drafters' disfavor towards bilingual education is evident in the Purpose section of Title III of NCLB. The Purpose section states that one goal of NCLB is for "students [to] develop high levels of academic attainment in English." Id. at 115 Stat. 1425, 1689 (2002). This goal runs counter to the typical goal of bilingual education—attainment of English proficiency, while achieving academic success by educating LEP students primarily in their native language. Thus, while bilingual education focuses on academic success in the LEP student's native language, NCLB demands that academic success be in English. Third, Title III's stated purpose seems to reflect attitudes similar to those who drafted Proposition 227. Much of the enacting language of NCLB is comparable, if not the same, to that of Proposition 227. NCLB is closely tied to anti-bilingual and pro-English immersion movement in that it "reflects the spirit of state initiatives such as California's Proposition 227 to the extent that it contends that bilingual education has largely failed to accomplish its goals and that English proficiency is the key to success in American society," see Barbara J. Brunner, Bilingual Education Under the No Child Left Behind Act of 2001, 169 Ed. Law. Rep. 505, 510-514 (2002). Lastly, post-NCLB funding shifts seem to indicate disfavor towards bilingual education. Title III nonetheless requires that states hold LEAs accountable for meeting two annual measurable achievement objectives (AMAOs) for English learners. Under Title III, States must develop and meet two related annual measurable achievement objectives ("AMAOs") regarding English language proficiency. First, States must define a progress goal that requires States to demonstrate "annual increase[s] in the number or percentage of children making progress in English." Second, States must establish a proficiency objective that requires "annual increase[s] in the number or

through its school choice transfer policies after consecutive school failure,[173] student bullying,[174] or if designated as a persistently dangerous school,[175] to remove the brightest talent rather than those in greater need or those bullied rather the bully from the learning environment.[176] In so doing, it emphasis is to remove the few positive elements from a school than to transform the negative learning environment itself for the many more students left to languish in spiritually demoralized schools because basic bread and butter issues prevent them. Under our current accountability approach, students retained are more likely to be retained in grade. Thus, they see their friends and classmates leave them behind for the next grade making the chance of drop out seventy percent more likely to occur. Consequently, genuine student self-esteem and self-efficacy that appears to be a core spiritual component of academic achievement fails to be nurtured. It fails to be nurtured through realistic and increasingly challenging benchmarks but rather based upon academic standards that have been lowered to avoid federal sanctions and a watered down curricula that only furthers the cultural, intellectual and social alienation a child experiences. This alienation from his or herself occurs by not allowing the child to align with their own spiritual source of well being through the discovery of their own talents and passions. It also alienates the child from the free association and expression of intermingling with peers of different linguistic, academic, cultural and racial backgrounds. In this way, we as a society of parents, teachers, administrators and lawmakers commit the same "spiritual harm" in creating a stifling, repressive, control-centered, racially segregative system of Jim Crow. This was a system that engendered low self-esteem, low well-being and by extension low student achievement.[177] Where is the opportunity for children to reach beyond their comfort zone to meet successful and motivated peers from around the town, state, country? Where is the exposure to different cultures and people that offer an inspiring new outlook on life and a curiosity to explore the world around them? Where is the cultivation of self esteem or respect for non-native speaker's language or culture in enriching the classroom learning environment? In choosing between positive and negative attention, our educational law and policy has in many instances focused on the latter to the near exclusion of the former. In this way, education law and policy only furthers the neglect of cognitive and affective needs of the child and the negative social stigma of failure without a meaningful positive investment in success through positive attention, focus, and incentives for learning, succeeding and improving.

---

percentage of children attaining English proficiency by the end of each school year." Pub. L. No. 107-110, § 3102(1), 115 Stat. 1425, 1689 (2002).

173 No Child Left Behind § 6316(E); 34 C.F.R. § 200.44. These provisions are also difficult because it disregards its financial impact on the schools identified as needing improvement, see generally 20 U.S.C. § 1116.

174 Douglas E. Abrams, A Coordinated Public Response to School Bullying, in Maurice R. Dyson & Daniel B. Weddle, Our Promise: Achieving Educational Equality for America's Children (2009) at 399.

175 20 U.S.C. § 6316; 20 U.S.C. § 7912. (providing that a student may be given the opportunity to transfer to one or more designated schools if he or she attends a school designated by the state as persistently dangerous or if he or she is subject to a violent criminal offense while on school grounds. A transfer offered from a school identified as persistently dangerous will be in effect until the original school is no longer identified as persistently dangerous. A transfer offered to a victim of violent crime will be in effect for the remainder of the school year, placing a stigma and onus on the victim rather than the victimizer).

176 Daniel B. Weddle, Brutality and Blindness: Bullying in Schools and Negligent Supervision by School Officials, in Maurice R. Dyson & Daniel B. Weddle, Our Promise: Achieving Educational Equality for America's Children (2009) at 425.

177 See e.g., http://www.loc.gov/exhibits/brown/brown-brown.html ("In the "doll test," psychologists Kenneth and Mamie Clark used four plastic, diaper-clad dolls, identical except for color. They showed the dolls to black children between the ages of three and seven and asked them questions to determine racial perception and preference. Almost all of the children readily identified the race of the dolls. However, when asked which they preferred, the majority selected the white doll and attributed positive characteristics to it. The Clarks also gave the children outline drawings of a boy and girl and asked them to color the figures the same color as themselves. Many of the children with dark complexions colored the figures with a white or yellow crayon. The Clarks concluded that "prejudice, discrimination, and segregation" caused black children to develop a sense of inferiority and self-hatred.").

The situation remains the same for teachers who only face negative consequences for failure, but no positive consequences or incentives for success. Any critical mass of good quality teachers would be loathed to teach in such despair concentrated schools where they face the potential for job loss so that those most in need of the best teachers are the most likely to be the ones first deprived of them. Rather than encouraging or affirming the creative expression of the teacher and being a shared partner in developing dynamic teacher lesson plans that speak to children's interests, the NCLB discourages the teachers contribution, input, ideas or creative expression that fall outside the confines of a narrow exam format. "Under a high-stakes scheme, all aspects of education including teaching, classroom facilities, subjects taught, teacher training, and even library collections become secondary to standardized test taking instruction, because school teachers and school administrators are held accountable only for producing passing scores on the state-based exams.[178] While teachers are made full aware of the negative performance for job loss, school restructuring and the threat of federal funds, but where is the promise and benefits of their success? Where is the encouragement to develop long lasting relationships with their students? Where is the incentive to provide a dynamic environment for learning? What perverse effects can one expect to incentivize teacher merit pay when no effort is similarly made to incentivize students or to see such incentives for both aligned to maximize their well-being and by extension their enthusiasm for engaging in any learning environment? It is not success, but rather failure that truly triggers and makes relevant the NCLB statute in the lives of students, teachers and administrators through the failure to meet adequate yearly progress benchmarks that threatens sanctions. But where is there room for inspiration for students and teachers alike? A prolonged attention in the negativity of failure with the force of law behind it is a recipe for only more failure and spiritual disinvestment of our students and children.

A POSITIVE SPIRITUAL BASED APPROACH TO THE NCLB

Now imagine a NCLB Act that promotes a dynamic learning environment that draws upon the best teacher expectations of their students that they already are a success and that the only task of a teacher is to help the child realize it for herself by eliciting the best attitude, work habits and problem solving skills of that student. Imagine now a teacher is given the free expression and liberation from an overly managed state mandated syllabus to draw up lesson plans based upon positive music, clothes, movies, sports, interests and abilities that motivate and dynamically engage the individual child. Imagine a child that is actively learning by hands on experience, in cooperative learning environments with people of different races, cultures, languages of the world via class trips to experiment-based science and math camps, interactive museum exhibits, diverse schools, neighborhoods, countries. Imagine if you would a curriculum that brings Shakespeare, Jazz, Lauryn Hill and the Fugees into an English class lesson on lyrical writing or where a 3-D in class movie on the pyramids of Egypt are used to teach Pythagoras' theorem in math. Imagine the massive recruitment and retention of a highly motivated, highly paid, high quality teachers certified by a master teaching apprenticeship, that are positive energy channels, rather than just receptacles of the passive accumulation of graduate school credits. Where the two largest impact factors affecting student success is the competency and quality of the teacher standing in front of the classroom and the well being, confidence and self esteem impacted by external family home life, teachers. Or imagine a safe space where teacher, social worker, psychologist, linguist, fellow high school and

178 Philip T.K. Daniel and Maurice R. Dyson, Bringing Every Child Forward, supra note 36.

college educated mentors from the same neighborhood who look like the child regularly meet with the student and her family to design a learning program or to check in on what unmet emotional, psychological, economic, cultural needs of child and family can be better addressed that positively empowers and magnifies the positive energy and self-actualization of all involved. Where is the exposure to different cultures and people that offer an inspiring new outlook on life and a curiosity to explore the world around them? Imagine both teachers incentivized with merit pay that is actually correctly aligned not only with student performance but in depth, scope and vision of incentives for the student as well. The best of human potential is not borne from fear of failure except perhaps the formulation of desire for a contrasting new reality to pursue success or what is truly desired, the dreams and goals that are predicated upon an individual's emotional, psychological and spiritual well being. If we apply lessons learned from the therapeutic jurisprudence explored later in this article, a focus on re-thinking the role of education law, people and learning environments to promoting the overall wellbeing of the individual student is and has always been the most effective basis to rest successful educational reform. Empower and educate teachers and students alike that they can be the deliberate creators of their realities, and a K-12 education system can be transformed where well-being and individual self worth catapult an individual personal sense of fulfillment.

THE LAW OF ATTRACTION & EDUCATION: POSITIVE BEHAVIOR SUPPORTS

Schools have a definitive role in promoting social and emotional well-being for all students, faculty, and staff. In comprehending the needs that affirm the whole child, we are better positioned in society to leverage the insights of positive thinking, positive modeling and the benefits derived therefrom for educationally dynamic learning experiences that focus on individual positive potential. Rather than acting on the often stigmatic perception of students as unruly problem children unconcerned with learning, as educators, mentors, educational lawyers and policymakers, we model the positive attitude, behavior and love of learning we wish to instill in our students. By remaining well informed about "children's mental health through preservice teacher education programs that build into their curricula an awareness of children's mental health and its impact on student social emotional development and academic achievement, we begin to provide an education that treats students and teachers as the individuals that they are. Schools should employ Positive Behavior Supports (PBS), which is a scientifically based approach that promotes building a safe and secure "host" environment for all students and school personnel to reinforce the learning environment."[179] In wing upon the insights gleaned from positive thinking law of attraction movement and the Appreciative Inquiry solutions based approach to transformative, PBS provides wrap around interventions resulting from social, behavioral, and biomedical sciences that can be applied at the individual, classroom, and school level to achieve reductions in problem student behavior and

179 See Deann Lechtenberger and Frank Mullins, Achieving the Promise: The Significant Role of Highly Qualified Teachers in Transforming Children's Mental Health in America, in America's Promise: Achieving Educational Equality For America's Children,505-507 (Carolina Academic Press, Maurice R. Dyson, Daniel B. Weddle, eds.); See generally George Sugai & Robert H. Horner, The Evolution of Discipline Practices: School-Wide Positive Behavior Supports, 24 Child & Family Behavior Therapy 23, 23–50 (2002); George Sugai & Robert H. Horner, Features of Effective Behavior Support at the District Level, 11(1) Beyond Behavior 16, 16–19 (2001); Robert H. Horner & George Sugai, School-Wide Behavior Support: An Emerging Initiative, 2 Journal of Positive Behavioral Interventions 231, 231–33 (2000); George Sugai & Robert H. Horner, Discipline and Behavioral Support: Preferred Processes and Practices, 17(4) Effective School Practices 10, 10–22 (1999).

improved quality of life.[180] "PBS works to change both adult and student behaviors to support a positive learning environment where students can connect, contribute, and be successful. Such a positive learning environment provides the foundation for more instructional time for teachers to teach and students to learn, and supports good mental health outcomes aligned with the report from the President's New Freedom Commission on Mental Health.[181] As more educators are trained and become implementers of this evidence-based practice, schools can take the lead in meeting the needs of students with emotional behavior disorder (EBD) and their families."[182] But the goal of PBS should not be to push against certain behavior that do not conform to an external standard of expectation as it is the goal to help the individual student align with their own source as to be more authentically as they really are. In all of education, the goal to optimal learning is to allow the child to discover their own truth free from pain and into the joy of life that is love.

PROMOTING SOUL CONSCIENCE IN THE LAW: POST-ENLIGHTENMENT LEGAL SPIRITUALITY

It is significant to see that law and legal systems today embody and promote an ego-level conscience. While the American legal system has placed high on the pedestal the Enlightenment values such as personal freedom, independence, autonomy, will, and individual liberty for years, in a Post-Enlightenment period, this self interest conception of separation gives way to an "emerging culture of connectedness" where individuals have to work collaboratively in an on-going legal arrangement or relationship.[183] But this culture of connectedness is neither easy nor always desirable and it is the challenge of the law to mediate between separationist functions when necessary while preserving core relationships.[184]

So it is possible that the ignorance, limited self interest and the false paradigm of the ego conscience level of separate, inherent existence implicit in the interest-convergence dilemma can be overcome. Perhaps by feeling the adverse impact of ignoring this soul conscience level of interrelatedness or oneness that is the foundation of cause and effect can ego centered ignorance be overcome thereby behooving greater accountability by the collective body and putting forth positive incentives for

180 Tim Knoster et al., Emerging Challenges and Opportunities: Introducing the Association for Positive Behavior Support, 5(3) Journal of Positive Behavior Interventions 183, 183–86 (2003).

181 New Freedom Commission on Mental Health, Achieving the Promise: Transforming Mental Health Care in America, Final Report (2003).

182 See Deann Lechtenberger and Frank Mullins, Achieving the Promise: The Significant Role of Highly Qualified Teachers in Transforming Children's Mental Health in America, in America's Promise: Achieving Educational Equality For America's Children, (Carolina Academic Press, Maurice R. Dyson, Daniel B. Weddle, eds); Terrance M. Scott, Positive Behavioral Support: A School-Wide Example, 3(2) Journal of Positive Behavioral Interventions 88, 88–94 (2001).

183 Thomas D. Barton, Troublesome Connections: The Law and Post-Enlightenment Culture, 47 EMORY L. J. 163, 163-64 (1998).

184 Id. ("In a given case the law may oscillate between either separationist functions or connectedness values. This is because the desired outcomes often involve both protection and the building of a stronger relationship. In many instances of domestic violence, for example, the victim certainly wants and needs protection. The victim, however, may not want or may not be able to afford for the underlying relationship to be terminated. Instead, the victim desires the underlying relationship to be made more healthy and respectful. Yet this is precisely the sort of solution for which the Enlightenment legal process is poorly equipped.... Cases involving communities which are hostile to racial, ethnic, or sexual orientation minorities, cases involving unruly children, and even cases involving noisy neighbors may present the same challenges—to build stronger relationships among the parties while simultaneously stopping whatever immediately threatening behaviors escalated the problem to the legal domain. The fundamental need is for an integrative solution that works with, rather than ignores, the given social context.").

collective action for the overall good. Further, by seeing the tangible, synergistic, positive impact of inspired mutual cooperative action is there an incentive to overcome such ignorance and its results.[185]

We are also better positioned to see what the focus of our body of law, as a normative matter, should be.—to bring people together, to promote interaction, and to begin constructive dialogue around the soul conscience level that is able to perceive humankind as it may truly exist in its interrelatedness and interdependence. New methods of lawyering are rising to meet this shifting paradigm of post-Enlightenment values of the soul-level of conscience through collaborative approaches to divorce and child custody, creative problem solving, transformative mediation, victim-offender mediation in criminal law, and community-based criminal sentencing of criminals.[186] These same holistic approaches can inform and enrich our substantive jurisprudence to constitutional anti-discrimination law only when we"…come to recognize that our quest for the elusive ideal of equality is ultimately a moral and spiritual aspiration." [187] No where is this more apparent in constitutional law. [188]

Thus, in our laws and in our lawyering, we come to see a viable role for law and education in bringing clients together exists to effectively advise them from a holistic standpoint which become essential to see that perceived differences (of the ego level conscience) can give way to observed commonalities (soul level conoscience).[189] Here, the law can promote dialogue amongst diverse or diametrically opposed groups where "some kind of legal force is necessary to bring members of the two groups into a close enough relationship for the discriminators to learn from experience how inadequate their stereotypes have really been."[190] Only then can we come to see that our

185 By understanding that whatever arises dependent upon causes and conditions is not operating exclusively under its own power, we are also better able to take more effective action to curb the abuse of that power, whether it be a Montgomery bus boycott, better regulating markets, conditioning socialized recovery and bailouts when they do become necessary on empowering the collective body of all citizens.

186 Id.

187 Paul Savoy, The Spiritual Nature of Equality: Natural Principles of Constitutional Law,, 28 How. L.J. 809, 812 (1985).

188 Id.("Constitutional law is laced with an unconscious spirituality which our legal education compels us to consciously deny while seeking to cultivate within us values such as the inherent dignity and worth of the individual, equality, fairness and justice, all of which are, in reality, substitute objects for our lost belief in the human soul.").

189 MORTON DEUTSCH & MARY EVANS COLLINS, INTERRACIAL HOUSING: A PSYCHOLOGICAL EVALUATION OF A SOCIAL EXPERIMENT 78–88 (1951); NATIONAL COMMITTEE ON SEGREGATION IN THE NATION'S CAPITAL, SEGREGATION IN WASHINGTON 37–38 (1948); PRESIDENT'S COMMITTEE ON CIVIL RIGHTS,, TO SECURE THESE RIGHTS 103 (1947) at 85–87; Charles Abrams, Our Chance for Democratic Housing, NATION, Aug. 16, 1947, at 160–62;Charles Abrams, Race Bias in Housing, NATION, July 19, 1947, at 67–69; Charles Abrams, Will Interracial Housing Work?, NATION, Aug. 2, 1947, at 122–24; Marie Jahoda & Patricia Salter West, Race Relations in Public Housing, 7 J. SOC. ISSUES 132, 133–36 (1951); Daniel M. Wilner, Rosabelle Price Walkley, & Stuart W. Cook, Residential Proximity and Intergroup Relations in Public Housing Projects, 8 J. SOC. ISSUES 45, 45 (1952).

190 Gene Weltfish, Some Problems on Which We Need More Facts–and Some Implications for Action, 1 J. SOC. ISSUES 47, 52 (1945); ARTHUR M. SCHLESINGER, JR., THE VITAL CENTER: THE POLITICS OF FREEDOM 190 (1949) ("While we may not be able to repeal prejudice by law, yet law is an essential part of the enterprise of education which alone can end prejudice."); LILLIAN SMITH, NOW IS THE TIME 19 (1955) ("[T]his process of bringing about change in laws, or deciding on the validity of old laws, is also an important means of educating the people whom these laws affect . . . .").See also PRESIDENT'S COMMITTEE ON CIVIL RIGHTS, TO SECURE THESE RIGHTS 103 (1947) ("The argument is sometimes made that because prejudice and intolerance cannot be eliminated through legislation and government control we should abandon that action in favor of the long, slow, evolutionary effects of education and voluntary private efforts. We believe that this argument

differences in health, wealth, skin color, language, sex, sexual orientation or disability do not outweigh our common humanity and our interconnectedness.

LAW, SPIRITUALITY AND JUSTICE

It should be remembered that no one religion, nor any one set of precepts or principles of adherence to any one God is the focus of the law of divine oneness. Each comes with their own truth and belief systems and all are welcome. Rather, it is merely the recognition that as a collective gestalt, we are each inextricably intertwined to one another. Each action of one impacts the reality of another. But query whether our legal system promotes this principle of divine oneness, or whether it promotes dissention, discord and disharmony that ultimately lowers the energy of the entire gestalt. But has our system of law, rules and regulations become a secular form of religion that is bent on a notion of justice that promotes divisiveness rather than oneness, vengeance rather than understanding, empathy or compromise.[191]

How far have we really come from the lawyers, tax collectors, Pharisees and Saducees of Jesus day when the letter of the law took priority over the spirit of the law? Cloaked in robbers of self righteousness, the lawyers of the day observed the technical doctrine of Moses Ten Commandments but it took Jesus to bring the message of love that was the animating spirit behind Moses law. Where conflict exists, has it been the role of lawyers to seek reconciliation or to further fan the flames of contention, self aggrandizement and greed? Do we seek to promote understanding of the other litigant's circumstances and predicament or do we encourage in our legal practice the placement of narrow horse blinders that foster tunnel vision of self interest.

As Professor Joseph Allegretti wrote: "Let me be clear: At its core the legal profession faces not so much a crisis of ethics, or commercialization, or public relations, but a spiritual crisis. Lawyers and the profession have lost their way."[192] Anthony Kronman recognizes the implications of this crisis not only in the result of the law produced but on the practitioners themselves: "This crisis is, in essence…the product of growing doubts about the capacity of a lawyer's life to offer fulfillment to the person who takes it up. Disguised by the material well-being of lawyers, it is a spiritual crisis that strikes at the heart of their professional pride."[193] Yet we have become pessimistic in our view of

---

misses the point and that the choice it poses between legislation and education as to the means of improving civil rights is an unnecessary one. In our opinion, both approaches to the goal are valid, and are, moreover, essential to each other.").

191 James P. Kimmel, Suing for Peace: A Guide For Resolving Life's Conflicts (2004) excerpt, available at http://www.hamptonroadspub.com/bookstore/product_info.php? cPath=71_97&products_id=401 ("Not only has the broken relationship between law and spirituality led to violence, but it has had the unforeseen and quite paradoxical effect of elevating the pursuit of this new form of justice (vengeance) to the status of a secular religion. Having successfully separated government from organized religion, the vacuum has been filled by the justice system. But look closely. In our modern justice system, lawyers have become the high priests of our society and judges the popes and prophets, delivering justice to the masses. We erect great temples in which to practice and worship justice (courthouses); we create sacred vestments (judicial robes) and devise sacred liturgies to be carried out in these temples (oaths, legal creeds, complex rules of evidence and procedure); we even empower our lawyers and judges with the authority once held by the clergy to withhold and bestow property, freedom, and life itself. Viewed up close, our justice system looks and behaves increasingly like the Roman Catholic Church in the days before the Protestant Reformation.").

192 Joseph G. Allegretti, The Lawyer's Calling: Christian Faith and Legal Practice 3 (1996).

193 Anthony Kronman, The Lost Lawyer 2 (1993).

the law as this imbalance between the legal rules and justice has conceptually unraveled under increased skepticism.[194] What is justice and how do we define its relationship to law? Plato contemplated a theory that justice that involved a numerical as well as a proportional equality. This theory was advanced further by his pupil Aristotle in his *Nicomachaean Ethics*. He regarded the essence of justice was equality. "Equal is the middle between too much and too little..., since equal is a middle, also fair is a middle... Fair exists in a certain proportion ..., for proportional is in the middle, and fair is what is proportional."[195] In his *On Law of War and Peace,* Hugo Grotius, the father of rationalistic natural law, embraced fairness as the defining core characteristic of justice.[196] He regarded natural law as premised upon the man's social nature and his ability to act rationally. In his opinion, the principles of natural law are based on the corresponding supreme divine guidance. Thus, while common conceptions as natural law staked out the claim that the law reflected preexisting, divine laws independent of humankind as St Thomas Aquinas, Immanuel Kant and Dr. Martin Luther King Jr. also suggested, the movement of legal positivism that would later predominate took the perspective that laws were simply objective rules governed by rules of logic and precedent that were the embodiment of legal principles which afforded predictability to the law.[197] However, a subsequent and much more pessimistic school of thought known as legal realism proffered the notion that the law reflected the biases and predilections of judges and juries without regard to case precedent or rules and without regard to notions of inherent justice under natural law.[198] Instead of affording greater harmony with the universal law of justice, could it be that the legal systems of our society have exacerbated its disharmony by resorting to a distorted notion of justice based upon bias, predilection or a taste for vengeance justice? Or perhaps in our zeal to root out religion indoctrination from the state in our first amendment establishment clause jurisprudence, our classrooms and our government, we have unwittingly promulgated a misguided conception of justice that reflects a morally bankrupt, spiritually devoid disharmony with the just eternal law of the universe?[199] As one commentator put it: "Today in the United States, we have become so successful at separating law from organized religion that we have undermined the relationship between law and spirituality. This is manifest in our national obsession with using law to obtain justice against those who wrong us. Instead of using the law to unite us with each other (to achieve oneness), we use law to conquer and divide. The word "justice" itself, which once meant fundamental fairness and equity for all (the state of tangible oneness), is now debased by our society as the politically-correct synonym for revenge, retribution, payback, and vengeance-the very opposite of equity and oneness."[200] A hollow desire to pursue justice in contemporary jurisprudence

194 Dan Edwards, Reflections on Three Stories: "Practicing" Law and Christianity At The Same Time, 27 Tex. Tech L. Rev. 1105, 1111 (1996)("If one practices law without working very hard to keep one's blinders in place, one encounters the sharp edges of reality that prompt consciousness. Suffering, evil, injustice and the whole axle-grinding not-rightness of the world are laid bare in the practice of law. And so we are pricked into consciousness; but consciousness can endure only ephemerally without faith, without a sustaining trust in a narrative or world view sufficiently comprehensive to preserve consciousness from falling into despair in the face of the absurd and wrong.").

195 Roger Crisp, Aristotle: Nicomachean Ethics (2000).

196 See Hugo Grotius, On the Law of War and Peace (1814).

197 David M. Hunsaker, Law, Humanism and Communication: Suggestions for Limited Curricular Reform, 30 J. LEGAL EDUC. 417, 419 (1979-80).

198 Susan Daicoff, Law as Healing Profession: The Comprehensive Law Movement, available at http://ssrn.com/abstract= 875449 at 37-38.

199 James P. Kimmel, Suing for Peace: A Guide For Resolving Life's Conflicts (2004) excerpt, available at http://www.hamptonroadspub.com/bookstore/product_info.php? cPath=71_97&products_id=401 (last visited Feb. 22, 2010).

200 Id.

is often a desire to seek vengeance rather than resolution.[201] The result is a broken society where law sows discord and conflict that destroys communities and leaves individuals with a vein victory.[202]

Yet there remains hope that the pendulum has swung back and the role of spirituality in law will continue to grow as it already has with regard to a plethora of concerns including: "human rights, jurisprudence, privacy rights, family law, criminal liability for parental religious convictions, judicial resolution of intra-church disputes, the legal structure of specific religious faiths, legal education, regulation of spiritual advisors, the First Amendment religion clauses, legal history and environmental justice" just to name a few.[203] While not perfect, we recognize as human beings there is a place for righteous anger to true injustice and that it should be the aim of our legal system and attorney practitioners to promote practical solutions to realistic concerns while respecting spiritual principles such as the law of divine oneness where we see each other as interconnected. Furthermore, in viewing each other as interconnected, we will see more of our challenges and promises as citizens, attorney practitioners and spiritual beings in ways that reflect more of the reality we confront. As Mahatma Gandhi insightfully observed:

> "I had learnt the true practice of law. I had learnt to find out the better side of human nature and to enter men's hearts. I realized that the true function of a lawyer was to unite parties riven asunder. The lesson was so indelibly burnt into me that a large part of my time during the twenty years of my practice as a lawyer was occupied in

201 Id.

202 Id. ("In other words, the relationship between law and spirituality in our society has been broken. As a consequence, we experience increasing levels of conflict-in our homes, schools, businesses, communities, and within the world around us. Why? Because when we are wronged, our instinct to seek revenge is encouraged and rewarded by our justice system, rather than being discouraged and redirected toward the restoration of peace, happiness, and oneness. We excuse and rationalize our retaliatory lawsuits, violence, and warfare under the guise that we are only seeking "justice."").

203 Robert F. Blomquist, Law and Spirituality: Some First Thoughts on An Emerging Relation, 71 UMKC L. Rev. 583, 595-6 (2003); Maurice F. Reidy, Edmund Burke and the Natural Law, 72 Harv. L. Rev. 1395 (1959) (book review); Charles Fairman, Foreward: The Attack on the Segregation Cases, 70 Harv. L. Rev. 83 (1956); Michael Moore, Moral Reality, 1982 Wis. L. Rev. 1061 (1982); Richard Weisberg, How Judges Speak: Some Lessons on Adjudication on Billy Budd, Sailor With an Application to Justice Rehnquist, 57 N.Y.U. L. Rev. 1 (1982); Ingrid Michelsen Hillinger, The Article 2 Merchant Rules: Karl Llewellyn's Attempt to Achieve the Good, the True, and the Beautiful in Commercial Law, 73 Geo. L. J. 1141 (1985); Robin West, Jurisprudence as Narrative: An Aesthetic Analysis of Modern Legal Theory, 60 N.Y.U. L. Rev. 145 (1985); James Boyd White, Law as Rhetoric, Rhetoric as Law: The Arts of Cultural and Communal Life, 52 U. Chi. L. Rev. 684 (1985); Helen Silving, Testing of the Unconscious in Criminal Cases, 69 Harv. L. Rev. 683 (1956); Survey on the Law, Survey on the Constitutional Right to Privacy in the Context of Homosexual Activity, 40 U. Miami L. Rev. 521 (1986); Chad D. Naylor, Note, The Role of the Family in Cadaveric Organ Procurement, 65 Ind. L.J. 167 (1989);Notes, Litigation Between Husband and Wife, 79 Harv. L. Rev. 1650 (1966); Anthony B. Ullman, Note, The Domestic Relations Exception to Diversity Jurisdiction, 83 Colum. L. Rev. 1824 (1983); Note, The Establishment Clause and Religion in Child Custody Disputes: Factoring Religion into the Best Interest Equation, 82 Mich. L. Rev. 1702 (1984); Charles Wolfson, Midwives and Home Birth: Social, Medical, and Legal Perspectives, 37 Hastings L.J. 909 (1986);Thomas N. O'Neill, Jr. & Robert L. Trescher, Comment, Medical Care for Dependent Children: Manslaughter Liability of the Christian Scientist, 109 U. Pa. L. Rev. 203 (1960).

> bringing about private compromises of hundreds of cases. I lost nothing thereby—not even money, certainly not my soul."[204]

MEDIATING JUSTICE IN THE LAWYERING PROCESS

Much has been said about our adversarial gladiator system of justice that exacerbates retaliatory conflict, litigation costs and the promotion of gaming behavior through procedural mechanisms designed to suppress truth through the form of evidence, confessions and witness testimony. Even more, it would appear this adversarial approach to justice is finding further global reach.[205] Still, there has also been an admirable push toward mediation as alternative dispute resolution (ADR) mechanisms.[206] Much of this trend can be traced back to Roscoe Pound's speech to the American Bar Association in 1906, entitled "The Causes of Popular Dissatisfaction with the Administration of Justice,"[207] which threw down the gauntlet before the legal profession to confront these ills of the existing legal regime.[208] ADR seeks to resolve putative litigants claims outside the context of a formal courtroom case and to the extent it seeks resolution of substantive issues without the collateral gamesmanship and vindictive incentives that often cloud the justice system's pursuit of justice, it is to be encouraged.

More relational spiritually focused justice achieved through mediation is needed and many would agree with Lon Fuller characterization of mediation as having the unique "capacity to reorient the parties towards each other, not by imposing rules on them, but by helping them to achieve a new and shared perception of their relationship, a perception that will redirect their attitudes and dispositions toward one another."[209] In this way, mediation bears some commonality with a system of equity that allows more flexibility to concerns of fairness over strict common law rules. Indeed, "[m]ediation, like equity, was conceived of as justice without law. Mediation also offers the possibility of individualized justice, which may be in tension with strict legal justice and [j]ust as equity moderated the rigidity of the common law by integrating fairness and moral values into the judicial process, mediation offers fair alternatives to legal values and judicial decision-making."[210]

However, regrettably, some predict ADR will fall to the same fate as the system of equity in our stubborn adherence to a legal regime that elevates formalism over fairness and justice. ADR, like equity, it is feared will be reduced and subsumed into a common law adjudicatory system that has ultimately marginalized fairness principles.[211] As Dean Roscoe Pound and Professor Nolan-Haley observed, "legal rules were superseding equitable rules in some cases, and that equitable rules were

---

204 Mahatma Ghandi, An Autobiography The Story of My Experiments With Truth (1954).

205 Daniel Keleman, Suing for Europe: Adversarial Legalism and European Governance, 39 Comp. Pol. Stud. 101 (2006); Robert A. Kagan, Globalization and Legal Change: The "Americanization" of European Law?, 1 Reg. & Governance 99 (2007); David Levi-Faur, The Political Economy of Legal Globalization: Juridification, Adversarial Legalism, and Responsive Regulation, 59 Int'l Org. 451 (2005).

206 See, e.g., Jonathan M. Hyman and Lela P. Love, If Portia Were a Mediator: An Inquiry into Justice in Mediation, 9 Clinical L. Rev. 157, 177 (2002).

207 Roscoe Pound, The Causes of Popular Dissatisfaction with the Administration of Justice, Address Before the American Bar Association Convention (Aug. 26, 1906), 35 F.R.D. 273 (1964).

208 Id. at 273, 277-78.

209 Lon Fuller, Mediation: Its Forms and Functions, 44 S. Cal. L. Rev. 305, 325 (1971).

210 Jacqueline Nolan-Haley, The Merger of Law and Mediation: Lessons from Equity Jurisprudence and Roscoe Pound, 6 Cardozo Journal of Dispute Resolution 57, 65 (2004).

211 Id.

either disappearing, becoming rigid in their application, or being adopted in ways that confused rather than supplemented legal rules."[212] Where our contemporary legal system creates incentives for conflict by seeking "leverage" in a suit, whether that leverage is children in a custody suit, a spouse's illness, or a party's perceived weakness, a great missed opportunity to promote reconciliation and resolution where the rules reward just the opposite is deleterious to our social fabric and moral fiber. It is perfectly legal to bury an ailing party in a hospital with litigation maneuvers designed to financially cripple that party rather than promote compassionate justice; technical violations of procedure become a pretext to extract concessions from a vulnerable or resource limited litigant, and attorneys promising their clients big judgments appear all too willing to compromise moral integrity to deliver on their promises. These concerns have not dissipated with the increased merging of mediation into the common law. The increased "[r]eports of coercion, threats, strong-arming, and other abusive behaviors by mediators and attorneys suggest that the privacy of mediation has created space for behaviors that would hardly be tolerated in public courtrooms."[213]

The need for greater accountability to justice principles within mediation and ADR is thus needed. Additionally, a full restoration of our fairness principles embodied in equity is needed within the common law system. These two approaches point to two significant areas as a practical place to begin meaningful reform of our legal system so that the unraveled nexus between law, spiritual values and justice can be restored. Some of the more prominent answers to this call for action now include humanistic movements such as holistic lawyering,[214] comprehensive law,[215] therapeutic jurisprudence,[216] preventive law,[217] restorative justice,[218] collaborative lawyering,[219] as well as

212 Id.

213 See Jacqueline Nolan-Haley, The Merger of Law and Mediation: Lessons from Equity Jurisprudence and Roscoe Pound, at 68; James Alfini, Trashing, Bashing, and Hashing It Out: Is This the End of "Good Mediation"?, 19 Fla. St. U. L. Rev. 47 (1991); Vitakis-Valchine v. Valchine, 793 So.2d 1094 (2001); Allen v. Leal, 27 F. Supp.2d 945 (1998). See also cases discussed in Jacqueline Nolan-Haley, Lawyers, Clients and Mediation, 73 Notre Dame L. Rev. 1369 (1998).

214 Steven Keeva, Once More, With Healing: Ex-Law Dean Heads Center Dedicated to Alternative Approaches to Practice, 90 A.B.A.J. 74 (2004); Ellen Ostrow, The Lawyer's Life: Clear The Obstacles to a Balanced Life, 39 TRIAL 27 (2003); Carole L. Mostow, Holistic Lawyers Hope to Transform Conflict Resolution, 12 NO. 4 PROF. LAW 24 (2000).

215 Jean Hellwege, 'Comprehensive Law' Makes the Case for a Kinder, Gentler Law Practice, 39 TRIAL 12 (2003).

216 Tom R. Tyler, The Psychological Consequences of Judicial Procedures:Implications for Civil Commitment Hearings, in DAVID B. WEXLER & BRUCE J. WINICK, LAW IN A THERAPEUTIC KEY: DEVELOPMENTS IN THERAPEUTIC JURISPRUDENCE 3 (1996); Carwina Weng, Multicultural Lawyering: Teaching Psychology to Develop Cultural Self-Awareness, 11 CLINICAL L. REV. 369 (2005); David B. Wexler, Therapeutic Jurisprudence, 20 TOURO L. REV. 353 (2004); David B. Wexler, Lowering the Volume Through Legal Doctrine: A Promising Path for Therapeutic Jurisprudence Scholarship, 3 FLA. COASTAL L. J. 123 (2002); David B. Wexler, Therapeutic Jurisprudence and Legal Education: Where Do We Go From Here? 71 REV. JUR. U.P.R. 177 (2002); see also database of resources by David Wexler and Bruce Winick at http://www.therapeuticjurisprudence.org.

217 James L. Nolan, Jr., Redefining Criminal Courts: Problem-Solving and the Meaning of Justice, 40 AM. CRIM. L. REV. 1541 (2003); Marjorie A. Silver, Lawyering and Its Discontents: Reclaiming Meaning in the Practice of Law, 19 TOURO L. REV. 773 (2004); Ann E. Freedman, Fact-Finding in Civil Domestic Violence Cases: Secondary Traumatic Stress and the Need for Compassionate Witnesses, 11 AM. U. J. GENDER SOC. POL'Y & L. 567 (2003).

218 James Coben & Penelope Harley, Intentional Conversations About Restorative Justice, Mediation and the Practice of Law, 25 HAMLINE J. PUB. L. & POL'Y 235 (2003-04); Center for Restorative Justice at the University of Minnesota, Mark Umbreit at http://2ssw.che.umn.edu/rjp/People/ Umbreit.htm).

transformative and narrative mediation.[220] New models of lawyering as problem solving have transformed not only substantive assumptions of the law, but their very processes of achieving justice itself.

A COMPARISON OF TRANSFORMED AND TRADITIONAL COURT PROCESSES[221]

Traditional Process	Transformed Process
• Dispute resolution	
Problem-solving dispute avoidance	
• Legal outcome	Therapeutic outcome
• Adversarial process	Collaborative process
• Claim- or case-oriented	People-oriented
• Rights-based	Interest- or needs-
based	
• Emphasis placed on	Emphasis placed on
• adjudication	
Post-adjudication and	
	alternative dispute resolution
• Interpretation & application of law	Interpretation and application of social
science	
• Judge as arbiter	Judge as coach
• Backward looking	Forward looking
• Precedent-based	Planning-based
• Few participants and stakeholders	Wide range of participants
• Individualistic	Interdependent
• Legalistic	Common-sensical
• Formal	Informal
• Efficient	Effective

In this way, the law can enjoy more legitimacy by all stakeholders but also a greater sense of fairness and justice in the Aquinas, Kantian, and King worldview. Indeed, a spiritual, compassionate wisdom to resolve societal conflict has perhaps never been greater and a vibrant system of mediation, ADR and system of equity should be vehicles to that can promote such a development.

219 Pauline H. Tesler, Collaborative Family Law, 4 PEPP. DISP. RESOL. L.J. 317 (2004); Carolyn Copps Hartley & Carrie J. Petrucci, Practicing Culturally Competent Therapeutic Jurisprudence: A Collaboration Between Social Work and Law, 14 WASH. U.J.L. & POL'Y 133 (2004).

220 See, e.g., Leonard L. Riskin, Mindfulness: Foundational Training for Dispute Resolution, 54 J. LEGAL EDUC. 79 (2004); Leonard L. Riskin, The Contemplative Lawyer: On the Potential Contributions of Mindfulness Meditation to Law Students, Lawyers, and Their Clients, 7 HARV. NEGOT. L. REV. 1 (2002): ROBERT M. HARDAWAY, PREVENTIVE LAW: MATERIALS ON A NONADVERSARIAL LEGAL PROCESS (1997); Douglas A. Codiga, Reflections on the Potential Growth of Mindfulness Meditation in the Law, 7 HARV. NEGOT. L. REV. 109 (2002); J. Kim Wright & Dolly M. Garlo , Law As a Healing Profession, 63 OR. ST. B. BULL. 9 (2003).

221 Roger K. Warren, Reengineering the Court Process, Madison, WI, Presentation to Great Lakes Court Summit, September 24-25, 1998; see also Susan Daicoff, Law as Healing Profession: The Comprehensive Law Movement, available at http://ssrn.com/abstract= 875449 at 37-38.

LAWYER AS SPIRITUAL PEACEMAKER

We need, as Chief Justice Warren Burger called for, a new generation of lawyers as peacemakers.[222] Instead of hired guns, we need, in the words of Professor Mary C. Szto, a "hired dove who engages in empathetic dialogue with her clients. She urges others to radically question their views of their legitimate rights, natural needs and inclinations. If a lawsuit is filed, the "hired dove" urges her clients to do good to their adversaries, not to inflict pain on them. If there is a principle of justice involved, she may litigate, but she should avoid being a tool of malice and bitterness. She is to be an active and deliberate peacemaker who seeks restraint, reconciliation, and healing." [223] A hired dove goes beyond the call of duty, remains generous with her gifts, skills and still lobbies on behalf of her client.[224] Thus, it simply need not be the case that the pessimism of legal realism and its critical legal studies progeny that attacked the certainty of legal realism's predecessors, natural law and legal positivism mean that we have to lose faith in the ability of our legal system to achieve justice. The model of lawyers as problem solvers, as hired doves, gives us cause for optimism and suggest a more comprehensive manner to practice law. In the practice of remedial law, spiritual principles may also inform the types of solutions that parties might reach. As Paul Savoy suggests with regard to remedial affirmative action law, a Ghandian approach to law "would permit the preferential treatment of racial minorities but provide for a more equitable means of allocating the costs of affirmative action by implementing worksharing plans, for example, so that no individual employee would have to suffer the crushing burden of unemployment."[225] Beyond affirmative action, this Ghandian approach could be applied to "all those public works that benefit some at the expense of

222 Warren E. Burger, The Decline of Professionalism, 61 TENN. L. REV. 1, 5 (1993) citing Warren E. Burger, TheRole of the Law School in the Teaching of Legal Ethics and Professional Responsibility, 29 CLEV. ST. L. REV. 377, 378 (1980)(" [Lawyers] must be legal architects, engineers, builders, and from time to time, inventors as well. We have served, and must continue to see our role, as problem-solvers, harmonizers, and peacemakers, the healers – not the promoters – of conflict.").

223 Mary C. Szto, Lawyers as Hired Doves: Lessons From the Sermon on the Mount, 31 Cumb. L. Rev. 27, 28-30 (2000).

224 Id. ("If there is a governmental regulation or law to be complied with, the hired dove remembers the "second mile" analogy and urges her client to comply wholeheartedly. However, this does not preclude lobbying for legislative change. As long as a law exists, lawyers should counsel their clients to cheerfully comply with the spirit of the law. Finally, the hired dove is concerned with charity to the poor. She remembers Christ's command to give generously. This generosity includes not only her own pro bono service but also counsel to clients. The "hired dove" may encourage her clients to give generously to others; giving is part of the spirit of the law.").

225 Paul Savoy, The Spiritual Nature of Equality: Natural Principles of Constitutional Law, 28 How. L.J. 809, 818-819 (1985)("The Ghandian way, which we know in the West as the way of equity, assumes that in any dispute there is a measure of truth on each side and proposes a process of decision-making that seeks a higher order of resolution, one that will embrace the essential truth in each point of view and accord each party the respect owed to every person. Applied to the problem of affirmative action, this would require courts to abandon the old alternatives of either validating or invalidating the governmental action, and move toward a more creative and inclusive position that would transcend the traditional adversary model and enable both sides to emerge as winners. One such approach would permit the preferential treatment of racial minorities but provide for a more equitable means of allocating the costs of affirmative action by implementing worksharing plans, for example, so that no individual employee would have to suffer the crushing burden of unemployment. Another alternative in the spirit of equity would award public compensation to those who suffer the effects of affirmative action, a model of judicial review that would treat all forms of discrimination that serve a legitimate public purpose—not only affirmative action programs but all those public works that benefit some at the expense of others—as a form of 'inverse condemnation' requiring public compensation for those who lose their jobs or other economic benefits to the cause of the overall social good.").

others—as a form of 'inverse condemnation' requiring public compensation for those who lose their jobs or other economic benefits to the cause of the overall social good.".[226]

LEGAL EDUCATORS AS STEWARDS OF LEGAL DISCOURSE ON MORALITY

If attorneys are to effectively serve as problem solvers, hired doves and practice law in a comprehensive manner, there remains no doubt that legal education is in need of a major overhaul. First, problem solving requires a greater emphasis on practice in legal education.[227] This includes a focus on client interaction, problem solving law office management and legal ethics in particular.[228] The Carnegie Foundation recently observed: "Professional schools are not only where expert knowledge and judgment are communicated from advanced practitioner to beginner; they are also the place where the profession puts its defining values and exemplars on display, where future practitioners can begin both to assume and critically examine their future identities."[229] In its recent report, *Educating Lawyers: Preparation for the Profession of Law,* the Carnegie Foundation recommended a stronger emphasis on doctrine and practice, finding that the latter received inadequate attention in national law school curriculums.[230] Secondly, it requires a focus on educator should serve a steward of responsible discourse on legal morality and spirituality in the classroom and clinical education which has already begun to receive resounding calls.[231] As medical schools that have moved beyond

226 Id.

227 See Jerome Frank, A Plea for Lawyer-Schools, 56 Yale L.J. 1303 (1947); Jerome Frank, Why Not a Clinical Lawyer-School?, 81 U. Pa. L. Rev. 907 (1933); See The MacCrate Report (Joan S. Howland & William H. Lindberg eds., 1994); Task Force on Law Sch. & the Profession, Am. Bar Ass'n, Legal Education and Professional Development (1992). More recently, see Roy Stuckey et al., Best Practices for Legal Education (2007); See Lani Guinier et al., Becoming Gentlemen: Women, Law School, and Institutional Change (1997); Milton C. Regan, Jr., Eat What You Kill: The Fall of a Wall Street Lawyer (2004); Susan Sturm & Lani Guinier, The Law School Matrix: Reforming Legal Education in a Culture of Competition and Conformity, 60 Vand. L. Rev. 515 (2007); Elliott S. Milstein, Clinical Legal Education in the United States: In-House Clinics, Externships, and Simulations, 51 J. Legal Educ. 375, 375-76 (2001); Jill Schachner Chanen, Re-Engineering the JD: Schools Across the Country Are Teaching Less About the Law and More About Lawyering, A.B.A. J., Jan. 2007, at 42; Jonathan D. Glater, Training Law Students for Real-Life Careers, N.Y. Times, Oct. 31, 2007, at B9; see Bruce A. Kimball, Young Christopher Langdell, 1826-1854: The Formation of an Educational Reformer, 52 J. Legal Educ. 189 (2002).

228 See James E. Moliterno, An Analysis of Ethics Teaching in Law Schools: Replacing Lost Benefits of the Apprentice System in the Academic Atmosphere, 60 U. Cin. L. Rev. 83 (1991); see also Harry T. Edwards, The Growing Disjunction Between Legal Education and the Legal Profession, 91 Mich. L. Rev. 34 (1992); See John S. Elson, Why and How the Practicing Bar Must Rescue American Legal Education from the Misguided Priorities of American Legal Academia, 64 Tenn. L. Rev. 1135, 1135-36, 1138-39 (1997); Philip C. Kissam, Lurching Towards the Millennium: The Law School, the Research University and the Professional Reforms of Legal Education, 60 Ohio St. L.J. 1965, 1968-78 (1999); See generally Elizabeth Mertz, The Language of Law School: Learning to "Think Like a Lawyer" (2007); See Debra Moss Curtis, Teaching Law Office Management: Why Law Students Need to Know the Business of Being a Lawyer, 71 Alb. L. Rev. 201 (2008); see also Thomas C. Grey, Langdell's Orthodoxy, 45 U. Pitt. L. Rev. 1 (1983); Edward Rubin, What's Wrong with Langdell's Method, and What to Do About it, 60 Vand. L. Rev. 609 (2007); See Elizabeth Mertz, Inside the Law School Classroom: Toward a New Legal Realist Pedagogy, 60 Vand. L. Rev. 483, 494-508 (2007).

229 Alfred v. Alferi, Against Practice, 107 Mich. L. Rev. 1073 (2009) at fn. 10.

230 Carnegie Report, Educating Lawyers: Preparation for the Profession of Law, available at http://www.carnegiefoundation.org/ publications/educating-lawyers-preparation-profession-law

231 See Jane Harris Aiken, Striving to Teach "Justice, Fairness, and Morality," 4 Clinical L. Rev. 1 (1997); Thomas Shaffer, Legal Essay, The Profession as a Moral Teacher, 18 St. Mary's L.J. 195 (1986); Russell G. Pearce, Foreword: The Religious Lawyering Movement: An Emerging Force in Legal Ethics and Professionalism, 66 Fordham L. Rev. 1075, 1075-77 (1998); Symposium, The Relevance of Religion to a Lawyer's Work: An Interfaith Conference, 66 Fordham L. Rev. 1075 (1998); See Symposium, Faith and the Law Symposium, 27 Tex. Tech L. Rev. 911 (1996); Symposium on Religiously Affiliated Schools, 78 Marq. L. Rev. 247 (1995); Symposium, Religion and the Judicial

the question of if medical education should incorporate spirituality, the central issue they have embraced is how.[232] As the Carnegie Foundation observes: "Professional schools are not only where expert knowledge and judgment are communicated from advanced practitioner to beginner; they are also the place where the profession puts its defining values and exemplars on display, where future practitioners can begin both to assume and critically examine their future identities."[233] In fact, this past fall, I was confronted with a scenario in my Torts course where a student posed the following question: "How is it that the law does not punish people who stand idly by while witnessing another being violently attacked, harmed or killed? I was reminded of the Kitty Genovese case where it was widely thought, though perhaps inaccurately, that fully aware neighbors looked on silently as Ms. Genovese was being murdered right before their eyes, without intervening or calling the police.[234] Fueling the debate that reflected the low state of humanity and the law's moral failing was a New York Times article written by Martin Gansberg and published just two weeks after the murder which bore the headline "Thirty-Eight Who Saw Murder Didn't Call the Police."[235] Despite some of the perceived inaccuracies of the tragedy,[236] it provoked a slew of social psychology debates into the human psyche finding that most are reluctant to act when others are watching.[237] However, this incident was not what prompted the student's perplexed curiosity. This student raised the tragedy that took place in California where a number of students stood idly by while watching a fellow female student raped without so much as lifting a finger to help, call for assistance or try to

---

Process: Legal, Ethical, and Empirical Dimensions, 81 Marq. L. Rev. 177 (1998); See Roger Cramton, Beyond the Ordinary Religion, 37 J. Legal Educ. 509 (1987); See Melissa Harrison, Searching for Context: A Critique of Legal Education by Comparison to Theological Education, 11 Tex. J. Women & L. 245 (2002); See also Calvin G.C. Pang, Eyeing the Circle: Finding a Place for Spirituality in a Law School Clinic, 35 Willamette L. Rev. 241 (1999); Lucia Ann Silecchia, Integrating Spiritual Perspectives with the Law School Experience: An Essay and an Invitation, 37 San Diego L. Rev. 167 (2000);See Margaret E. Montoya, Introduction, Religious Rituals and LatCrit Theorizing, 19 Chicano-Latino L. Rev. 417 (1998); Russell G. Pearce, Forward, The Religious Lawyering Movement: An Emerging Force in Legal Ethics and Professionalism, 66 Fordham L. Rev. 1705 (1998); see also Amelia J. Uelmen, An Explicit Connection Between Faith and Justice in Catholic Legal Education: Why Rock the Boat?, 81 U. Det. Mercy L. Rev. 921 (2004); See Milner S. Ball, The Promise of American Law: A Theological, Humanistic View of Legal Process (1981); Thomas L. Shaffer, Faith and the Professions 1-38 (1987); See Steven K. Berenson, Institutional Professionalism for Lawyers: Realizing the Virtues of Civic Professionalism, 109 W. Va. L. Rev. 67 (2006); See generally Mary Ann Dantuono, A Citizen Lawyer's Moral, Religious, and Professional Responsibility for the Administration of Justice for the Poor, 66 Fordham L. Rev. 1383 (1998).

232 See Christine Kilgore, Some Medical Schools Push for Spirituality Training, Internal Med. News, June 15, 1997, at 1, 5.

233 Alfred v. Alferi, Against Practice, 107 Mich. L. Rev. 1073 (2009) at fn. 10.

234 Maureen Dowd (1984-03-12). "20 years after the murder of Kitty Genovese, The question remains: Why?". N.Y. Times at B1.

235 Martin Gansberg, "Thirty-Eight Who Saw Murder Didn't Call the Police," N.Y. Times, (March 24 1964).

236 Other reported accounts by the witnesses showed that no one saw the entire attack and it was not the case that many ignored the screams of a dying woman. "The Witnesses That Didn't". On The Media. 2009-03-27 at http://www.onthemedia.org/transcripts/2009/03/27/05 (last visited April 7, 2009)(The following exchange was reported following the incident. "BROOKE GLADSTONE: Wasn't she screaming during the second attack? JOSEPH DE MAY: The wounds that she apparently suffered during the first attack, the two to four stabs in the back, caused her lungs to be punctured, and the testimony given at trial is that she died not from bleeding to death but from asphyxiation. The air from her lungs leaked into her thoracic cavity, compressing the lungs, making it impossible for her to breathe. I am not a doctor, but as a layman my question is, if someone suffers that type of lung damage, are they even physically capable of screaming for a solid half hour?").

237 R. Manning et al.,"The Kitty Genovese murder and the social psychology of helping: The parable of the 38 witnesses". American Psychologist 62 (6): 555–562 (Sept. 2007).

intervene.[238] The student was naturally disturbed by the doctrine of nonfeasance which holds that in the absence of a special relationship or other exception, there is no legal duty to act and a failure to act will not result in legal liability. The rule always presents a moral dilemma for students who agonize with the soundness of this rule, showing that students do not, at least not immediately, check their soul or conscience at the door. How could I advise this student?[239] Sure, I mentioned that those who recorded and distributed the video of the assault on their cell phones could be prosecuted under some state pornography law, but what about those who did not do that? How does the law reach them? Moreover, how does one deal with the larger moral failing of the law? I ultimately decided the best way to counsel the student was to advise her that where the law's admittedly imperfect reach ends, one's moral conscience begins and that we have to work to promote such consciousness in young and old alike. That the fault really lies in our selves as an imperfectly flawed human race really suggest the law is but a reflection of our imperfect selves. That prompted the follow up question of whether the law should reflect our human flaws or prompt us to appeal to our better angels. I had to conclude that both were true. Although I contended that law could be a source of moral good at times,[240] that the human flaws of passion that informed the "heat of passion" defenses, "insanity" defenses or "battered woman's syndrome" arguments were a reflection of our flawed humanity just as the nonfeasance rule reflected our flawed moral judgments as a human race. But I advised her that imperfect as the law is, it should at the very least, not punish people of good moral conscience who do act upon their better angels and decide to intervene. For these individuals, we allow the good samaritan law to protect and sanction such actions in the hope of encouraging us to follow our higher conscience. I also explain that moral freedom has its benefits and its necessary evils, but that the law takes this most minimally moral approach to regulating morality because the course of human history has shown that law and government have abused its power in imposing morality in ways that undermine democratic value and human rights.[241] Christians and non-Christians may have good reason to embrace moral freedom in the law.[242] This does not,

238 Stephanie Chen, Gang Rape Raises Questions About Bystander Role, CNN, available at http://www.cnn.com/2009/CRIME/ 10/28/california.gang.rape.bystander/index.html ("For more than two hours on a dark Saturday night, as many as 20 people watched or took part as a 15-year-old California girl was allegedly gang raped and beaten outside a high school homecoming dance, authorities said.As hundreds of students gathered in the school gym, outside in a dimly lit alley where the victim was allegedly raped, police say witnesses took photos. Others laughed. 'As people announced over time that this was going on, more people came to see, and some actually participated," Lt. Mark Gagan of the Richmond Police Department told CNN.').

239 I debated how to counsel this student. After all, having drummed into my students the policy based justifications of deterrence, efficiency, corrective justice, and safety that the torts system functions to advance, this doctrine could hardly be justified by any of these rationales. Certainly, this nonfeasance rule did nothing to promote deterrence since it did not encourage parties to intervene or set the appropriate incentive to discourage passivity. As a matter of efficiency, who could justify not picking up a telephone to alert campus authorities about the sexual assault underway. Nor did the rule advance corrective justice for the victim or overall safety for the campus students. In another abstract scholarly context, it might have been appropriate to discuss John Austin, Jeremy Bentham, Hans Kelsen, and H.L.A. Hart's pessimism of the law on the one hand or Thomas Aquinas, Michael Moore, Philip Soper, and Ronald Dworkin positivism on the other. But in this intimately moral context, what could one say?

240 See generally John Finnis, NATURAL LAW AND NATURAL RIGHTS (Oxford: OUP 1980).

241 See, e.g., Robert P. George, Making Men Moral 41-42 (1993); Joseph Boyle, Positivism, Natural Law, and Disestablishment, 20 Valparaiso L. Rev. 55, 59 (1985): "Thomas Aquinas, a natural lawyer if ever there was one, . . . argues that the law should not seek to prohibit all vices, but only the more serious ones, and 'especially those which involve harm to others, without whose prohibition human society could not be preserved.'" (Quoting Thomas Aquinas, Summa Theologiae at First Part of the Second Part, Question 96, Article 2; emphasis added.)

242 See Michael J. Perry, Religious Freedom and Beyond; The Right to Moral Freedom, Social Science Research Network (SSRN) 19-20, available at http://ssrn.com/abstract=1446430 ("As with the right to religious freedom, so too with the right to moral freedom: All citizens of liberal democracy--Christians no less than non-Christians and

however, mean that law should not embrace a minimum morality that is necessary to the healthy functioning of a democratic republic.[243] As demonstrated above and discussed further below, it is entirely feasible that law can embrace a interrelatedness value system oriented toward individual and collective spiritual well being while fostering a moral freedom where the latter is conducive to the preservation of the former.[244] While I quickly remind my students that I do not pretend have all the answers and that there is no one size fits all for these kinds of questions, I thoughtfully provide my own approach.

A SPIRITUAL BASED LAW PRACTICE APPROACH TO RELIGIOUS BELIEFS

I advise any students who ask that I take a spiritual based approach to my religious faith. As a Christian, I take on many of these tensions which have been nicely summarized in the law and religion literature. One of the key issues relates to the legal profession's allure for status, wealth and power that seem to contradict the values of "apostolic poverty, vulnerability and humility."[245] This is often an issue for many students and practicing lawyers. For my own part, I have reconciled this tension between the material success of my practice to achieving the overall well being of my clients. In so doing, I have to come to view my efforts focus as a hired dove, a problem solver for my client as the principle objective of my efforts and that any material prosperity gained, is a justly enriched prosperity that reflects the exercise of my good conscience in action. Poverty, vulnerability and

---

non-believers--have the same basic reason to embrace the right to moral freedom: Government--a political majority--is not to be trusted (i.e., beyond a certain point) as an arbiter of moral truth; moreover, the coercive imposition of moral uniformity is (beyond a certain point) more likely to corrode than to nurture the strength of a democracy. Religious believers do not have less reason than non-believers--instead, religious believers and non-believers have the same basic reason--to insist that government not ban (or otherwise impede) a moral practice unless the ban is necessary to serve a legitimate governmental interest, the weight of which is proportionate to the weight of the burden imposed by the ban. Christians and other believers no less than non-believers--all of them have good reason, the same good reason, to affirm…that "the moral aspirations of the law [should be] minimal.").

243 Id. ("Laws [should] seek to establish and maintain only that minimum of actualized morality that is necessary for the healthy functioning of the social order.").

244 Similar pedagogical issues present themselves each year in my law teaching and in the questions at the podium following each class. Issues of acceptance, inclusion, respect and hate often predominate the themes of these discussions of legal doctrine. Whether it is recent legislation, court decisions or popular referendums banning gay marriage, a ban on marital divorce, a judge who refuses to marry an interracial couple, a European ban on wearing burkhas in France or hostility to Islamic practices in Italian law as non- hygienic, whether the first bullet or third from Bernard Goetz's gun in the infamous New York subway shooting of black youths was justified, whether an Islamic law prohibiting women to drive, or forcing them to relinquish custody of a child to the father after reaching a certain age, whether parents should face criminal liability for their child's morbid obesity, or failing to provide chemotherapy to their cancer-ridden child on religious objections all present significant questions of law, faith and morality. How is the law professor to respond to such issues while ensuring integrity and openness in class discussion in a responsible fashion? Other students feeling a comfort level with my presence approach me out of class for counseling because they find it difficult reconciling the tension between their religious beliefs with the perceived demands of the practice of law and law culture.

245 Dan Edwards, Reflections on Three Stories: "Practicing" Law and Christianity At The Same Time, 27 Tex. Tech L. Rev. 1105, 1112-1115 (1996)(: The first source of the tension is that lawyer culture is seductive in its promise of rewards for the successful. Money, power, and prestige are available in legal practice, and are commonly regarded as valuable, not only in themselves, but as indicia of professional skill and accomplishment. However, the deliberate accumulation of money, power, and prestige run counter to the Christian values of apostolic poverty, vulnerability, and humility. The adversarial process and the aggressive ethos of the profession may not be problematic in themselves; but they aggravate the drive toward success measured by victory rather than by faithfulness, integrity, and the genuine excellences of good lawyering.")

humility does not mean that one must accept a vow of poverty or that there is something innately holy in poverty or a vulnerability that would have one throw oneself at mercy in the streets begging for alms. Nor is it case that vulnerability and humility means to subjugate one self when a dove must still confront the turbulent winds of avarice, injustice and corruption. Nor does it mean one should subscribe to the view that the root of all evil is money. Instead, I come to see that it is in fact the love and pursuit of money for its own sake or its undue powerful influence to undermine justice and fairness is a root of evil in society which has corrupted and diminished public confidence in the private sector. Whether it is the Blackwaters, the Halliburtons, the Enrons, the Countrywides, the Bank of Americas, the Goldman-Sachs, the AIGs, the Silverados, the Worldcoms, the Arthur Andersons or the lawyers who failed to put the ethical breaks on them, this undue influence is the challenge of the hired dove as lawyer-advocate or lobbyist. Likewise, such undue influence of lobbyist money also threatens to undermine the legitimacy of law, politics and public government even further with the Supreme Court's recent decision in *Citizens United v. Federal Election Commission* which upheld unlimited corporate independent expenditures in political campaigning.[246] This undue influence can be overcome by leading a balanced, harmonious life which is furthered when one's principle motivation is premised on their client's good, as opposed to financial gain. I also take this time to inform my students of the comprehensive law movement which receives little exposure in the law school curriculum and the problem solving model. When students are exposed to these alternative models of lawyering and dispute resolution, they have an alternative reality to the adversarial process that promotes winning and victory over integrity and good lawyering.[247] If one subscribes to the view that the client should always be in the driver's seat in the lawyer-client relationship where the client is bent on vindictive, greedy or spiritually unhealthy actions, he or she will miss a critical opportunity to see how the lawyer can transform that relationship into a healthy, financially and spiritually prosperous outcome.[248] Such a limited view fails to see how the lawyer can facilitate a client's spiritual growth in ways that ultimately advance a client's best interest. The ability to do so, however, requires excellent communications skills, sharp powers of discernment, and the ability to consciously detach oneself from the angry client and their desired vindictive scheme.[249]

---

246 Citizens United v. Federal Election Commission, 558 U. S. ____ (2010). During the Gilded Age, historians Samuel Eliot Morison and Henry Steele Commager once wrote: "The nation was fabulously rich but its wealth was gravitating rapidly into the hands of a small portion of the population, and the power of wealth threatened to undermine the political integrity of the Republic." Justice Felix Frankfurter was to remarked that the 19th Century, had been marred by a "popular feeling that aggregated capital unduly influenced politics, an influence not stopping short of corruption." See http://www.scotuswiki.com/index.php?title=Citizens_United_v._Federal_Election_Commission#A_Few_Open.2C_or_Not_So_Open. 2C_Questions_After_the_Ruling

247 See e.g., Linda Morton, Teaching Creative Problem Solving: A Paradigmatic Approach, 34 CAL. W. L. REV. 375, 386-87 (1998)(noting that a creative problem solving paradigm can teach other methods that lawyers might use including "identifying the problem, taking into account interests and needs of those involved; the desires of the client; what the client can afford; how the client's values and interests compete with others involved; what other disciplines should be consulted; can the conflict be resolved through a negotiation, mediation; Who might be harmed; what is the best solution, etc.").

248 Dan Edwards, Reflections on Three Stories, at 1112-1115. ("The second source of tension is the desire and financial incentive to please our clients. Subservience to the client's will is a problem for several reasons. Our clients' goals are often meanspirited, vindictive, greedy, or otherwise contrary to a healthy spirituality. Moreover, the goal of pleasing the client not only separates us from a single-minded devotion to the will of God, it also impairs our ability to serve our client's interests, since client goals are often contrary to the client's interests, even when judged by objective economic criteria.").

249 Id. See also Steven Keeva, What Clients Want: People Who Come to Arnie Herz Seeking Legal Help Leave With Some Unexpected Solutions, 87 A.B.A.J. 48 (June 2001); see also Susan Daicoff, Resolution Without Litigation: Are Courtrooms Battleground For Losers?, GP SOLO, Oct./Nov. 2003 at 45-46. ("Attorney Arnie Herz, for example, represented an imposing ex-football player we shall call John Smalls, in a dispute with the new owners of the

Thus, it is possible to serve as an effective lawyer while representing a client that seeks optimal spiritual well being.[250] Indeed, perhaps the most salient issue one confronts in their practice of law is with regard to the tension it poses to one's faith. Law, as an instrument of state power involuntarily coerces resolution in a way that may be fundamentally at odds with one's beliefs that the power in truth should be the governing instrument for seeking resolution.[251] Rather than take a defeatist attitude in seeing resorting to legal action as a resort to despair, the foregoing discussion demonstrates how legal action can advance truth, faith and dignity.[252] Nor is it the case that lawyering always involves invoking the power of the state rather than the power of truth. This observation misapprehends the powerful soul force behind the Civil Rights movement. Indeed, promoting a legal conscience of a just morality means instead invoking the power of the state to recognize and uphold the power of truth. Dr. King accomplished in his buy boycott movement by invoking the power of the state to give effect to the power of truth. In speaking truth to power in

company Smalls had just sold, after ten years of successful solo ownership. Smalls was furious with the new owners' treatment of him as employee post-sale and with their mismanagement of the company. Unfortunately, he had signed a noncompete agreement as part of the sale and felt bound by it, despite his frustration. Determined to sue the new owners for mistreatment and mismanagement, he approached Herz, who opined that a lawsuit might succeed but would cost well over $100, 000 in fees and costs to litigate. Smalls was ready to move, but Herz decided to slow him down a bit and asked, "If you could have anything you wanted in your life, what would you want your life to look like six months from now?" Smalls said more than anything, he wanted to be free of the new owners and wanted to make more money. He thought he could make a lot more money without them but didn't want to "let them off the hook." Frustrated that Herz was trying to talk him out of suing, Smalls commented, "You're too nice- I need a tough litigator," packed up, and started to walk out the office. Talking a big risk, Herz responded, "I know you think I'm not tough, but in all my years of experience, I think you may be the weakest person I've worked with. You set out a vision that was to be free of these people—you didn't mention that you wanted to punish them, teach them a lesson, or spend $100,000 of your own money and five years of your life doing so. What I see is that you don't have the strength to hold on to your own vision and deal effectively with your own anger. And I'll bet you've been doing this all your life." At first Smalls flushed with anger. But something in what Herz said rang true. He sat down and began listening and discussing; together, they agreed on a plan of action that involved a more collaborative, nonlitigious approach to resolving the matter. Smalls was freed from his noncompete clause three months later. The new owners teetered on the edge of bankruptcy for years—as Herz had predicted; even had Smalls sued, he would not have been able to collect a dime. Freed of the new owners, Smalls was in fact able to make a lot more money. Financially, the plan was a huge success. Personally, Smalls later said, the process of resolving this legal matter had allowed him to learn how his anger had been controlling his life, affecting his relationship with his wife and his kids, and blocking him from his full potential. Herz's approach to representing Smalls is one illustration of how a comprehensive lawyer might conduct such a law practice. Herz went beyond the law to ask about the client's deepest needs, goals, and desires and then used that information to create, with the client, the best strategy. Admittedly, he took a major risk early in the lawyer-client relationship, and not all comprehensive lawyers would be comfortable doing so. Using excellent interpersonal skills, though, Herz assessed that Smalls was a no-nonsense person who would respond only to straight talk—which he did. Litigation in this case only would have wasted time and money and fueled the client's excessive anger. The final process and outcome were not only financially successful but also personally and emotionally beneficial for Smalls.").

250 Steven Keeva, What Clients Want: People Who Come to Arnie Herz Seeking Legal Help Leave With Some Unexpected Solutions, 87 A.B.A.J. 48 (June 2001); see also Susan Daicoff, Resolution Without Litigation: Are Courtrooms Battleground For Losers?, GP SOLO, Oct./Nov. 2003 at 45-46.

251 Dan Edwards, Reflections on Three Stories, at 1112-1115. ("The final, and perhaps most difficult source of tension, is that Christianity is often held to eschew the use of power as a way of confronting the world, even when confronting evil, in favor of the vulnerable assertion of truth. Law, on the other hand, is ultimately a power game. The judgment is ultimately enforced by uniformed people carrying guns. Lawyering is invoking the power of the state rather than trusting in the power of truth. Arguably, resort to legal action is an act of despair rather than hope.").

252 Certainly, Brown v. Board of Education, 347 U.S. 483 (1954), as a legal action became a source of hope and despite the many setbacks since then, it remains the pinnacle of legal optimism for societal change.

the prophetic Christian ethos, Dr. King was able to say true to his Christian values by imbibing legal actions with a spiritual based approach to his religious convictions.[253]

PROMOTING A LEGAL CONSCIENCE OF A JUST MORALITY

In his famous Letter from a Birmingham Jail, Dr. Martin Luther King, Jr. eloquently raised the specter of a law codified by man and a law, a moral, natural, eternal law that reflects God's law. But this dichotomy was not the distinction Dr. King sought to impress as another was eminently more important. When addressing the question of how he could advocate breaking some laws like segregation laws of the south and obeying others like the 1954 Supreme Court decision outlawing segregation in education, Dr. King observed that there are two types of laws: just and unjust.[254] In advocating a moral duty to disobey unjust laws, it is clear that King did not discard respect for the concept of law itself. "[T]he individual who disobeys the law, whose conscience tells him it is unjust and who is willing to accept the penalty by staying in jail until that law is altered," King declared, "is expressing at the moment the very highest respect for the law."[255] This conception of civil disobedience also comports with recent theorists such as John Rawls, for example, who conceives such civil disobedience as "a public, nonviolent, conscientious yet political act contrary to law usually done with the aim of bringing about a change in the law or policies of the government."[256] But this distinction between universal just law and man's unjust law is also significant for reasons other than what Dr. King articulates. Indeed, the ramifications are much larger for if a man made law is one that comports with a true sense of moral, unseen eternal and universal justice that is equally applied to all universally and rooted in uplifting the human personality and spirit, then there would seem to be a legitimate place to acknowledge the role of the laws of the universe, God or spirituality in the development and administration of legal systems predicated on achieving meaningful justice.

CONCLUSION

253 Although Dr. King was not a lawyer, it should not be forgotten that he employed lawyers to enforce his radical civil rights agenda. Further, if "lawyering" is defined more broadly as advocacy for set objectives, then there are few excellent exemplars of advocacy lawyering in history than Dr. King's Letter from a Birmingham Jail which lays forth persuasive arguments for embracing a jurisprudence grounded in Christian spiritual values of a just legal morality.

254 Martin Luther King, Jr., Letter From A Birmingham Jail, reprinted in A TESTAMENT OF HOPE: THE ESSENTIAL WRITINGS AND SPEECHES OF MARTIN LUTHER KING, JR. 49 (James M. Washington ed., 1986) "One has not only a legal but a moral responsibility to obey just laws. Conversely, one has a moral responsibility to disobey unjust laws. I would agree with St. Augustine that "an unjust law is no law at all." Now, what is the difference between the two? How does one determine whether a law is just or unjust? A just law is a man made code that squares with the moral law or the law of God. An unjust law is a code that is out of harmony with the moral law. To put it in the terms of St. Thomas Aquinas: An unjust law is a human law that is not rooted in eternal law and natural law. Any law that uplifts human personality is just. Any law that degrades human personality is unjust. An unjust law is a code that a numerical or power majority group compels a minority group to obey but does not make binding on itself. This is difference made legal. By the same token, a just law is a code that a majority compels a minority to follow and that it is willing to follow itself. This is sameness made legal. Let me give another explanation. A law is unjust if it is inflicted on a minority that, as a result of being denied the right to vote, had no part in enacting or devising the law."); Dan Edwards, Reflections on Three Stories, at 1112-1115.

255 Martin Luther King, Jr., Love, Law, and Civil Disobedience, NEW SOUTH (Dec. 1961), reprinted in A TESTAMENT OF HOPE: THE ESSENTIAL WRITINGS AND SPEECHES OF MARTIN LUTHER KING, JR. 49 (James M. Washington ed., 1986).

256 JOHN RAWLS, A THEORY OF JUSTICE 364 (1971); see also Hugo A. Bedau, On Civil Disobedience, 58 J. PHIL. 653, 661 (1961).

Thus, like the law itself, we can view spirituality, as "entail(ing) a way of defining and pursuing truth beyond oneself that is more important than the individual, giving the individual's actions meaning and purpose in a larger context."[257] Thus, if we are to overcome our collective gestalt lessons, we would do well to realize that America has much cause for optimism in positive thinking as part of its spiritual awakening to the metaphysical laws of the universe, but it should not abuse or egocentrically miss an opportunity to apply those laws in ways that enhance our spiritual growth and soul conscience rather than undermine it.[258] Likewise, law must reflect and take account for its effect, not merely abandon its moral calling by cloaking itself it an artificial ego formalism of logic if it is to continue to advance and reflect our spiritual growth as individuals and as a nation. Indeed, "entrapping the intellect into attempting logical solutions to these ultimately spiritual questions . . . reveal[s] the inherent limitations of the legalistic mind as an instrument of knowledge or justice."[259] This would mean, as Justice Holmes suggested, that the "path of the law is not logic, but indeed experience."[260] But as we have also seen, the Kantian principle that demonstrates that every rational being is an end in itself is universal and applies to all rational beings comes from reason, not from experience. Accordingly, contrary to popular conception, reason need not be the antipathy of experience with respect to determining justice under the law nor does either fall prey to mutually exclusive ends. In fact, as I have attempted to show, both reason and experience lead to the common denominator of reciprocity, interrelatedness and mutual regard that have always formed the bedrock of a soul conscience jurisprudential approach that characterized genuine transformative sociolegal reform in America. In fact, these challenges can best be met by an inclusive embrace of the values of mutuality, awakened compassion, rational duties of reciprocity, spiritual interrelatedness and its reaffirming myriad of societal experiences all of which may promote inclusiveness, reconciliation, forgiveness as well as the restoration of the individual and community relationship in the administration of policies and justice.[261]

---

257 Lucia Ann Silecchia, Integrating Spiritual Perspectives With the Law School Experience: An Essay and an Invitation, 37 San Diego L. Rev. 167, 229 (2000).

258 As I argue and attempt to show, the spiritual pitfalls that accompany the abuse of the positive thinking movement have contributed to and will only lead to the embrace of a narrow construction of a post-racial society that is acontextual and which suffers from much of its same pitfalls including denial, blame and complacency with regard to viewing racial progress in America. The result is a thought movement that justifies further de-linking of the concept of racial interrelatedness and mutuality that may ultimately exacerbate racial inequality.

259 Paul Savoy, The Spiritual Nature of Equality: Natural Principles of Constitutional Law, 28 How. L.J. 809, 812 (1985).

260 Oliver Wendell Holmes, The Path of the Law, 10 Harvard Law Review 457 (1897).

261 Kay Pranis, "From Vision to Action: Some Principles of Restorative Justice," Church & Society, March/April, 1997 at 32. ("there is an enormous gap between what we teach in our churches, mosques, temples and synagogues and what we practice in daily personal and political life about the possibilities of forgiveness and redemption and about the fundamental dignity of all human life.").

Burden of Network Neutrality Mandates on Rural Broadband Deployment

George S. The Ford, PhD†
Lawrence J. Spiwak, Esq.‡

Abstract: Policymakers are presently evaluating policies to extend high-speed Internet services to nearly all households and business. At the same time, some communications regulators are considering regulating service providers under the auspices of network neutrality regulation. We examine empirically the impact that a regulatory mandate like network neutrality would have broadband Internet network deployment, with an eye toward the relative impacts between high-cost, rural areas and lower-cost, urban areas. Using publicly available network cost models and data from the United States, we show that under plausible conditions, while network neutrality mandates negatively impact broadband deployment in all geographic areas regardless of average cost characteristics, such rules are likely to disproportionately impact broadband deployment in high-cost areas. Moreover, our analysis that suggests the differential reduction in service availability for high-cost rural areas is six times as much as in lower cost, more urbanized markets.

I. Introduction

By all accounts, the widespread deployment of broadband services is the dominant issue in the current debate over communications regulation in almost all countries. Yet, at the same time as policymakers grapple with this difficult and complex task, there is a growing movement to impose regulations aimed to restrict the business decisions of broadband service providers in a variety of ways in the name of "network neutrality". To this end, many vocal proponents of network neutrality encourage regulators to adopt and enforce limitations on broadband pricing, service offerings, network design, network management, and consumer information (Marsden 2010). Many of these mandates would, almost by definition, make broadband networks either more costly to build by limiting freedom in network design (Clarke 2009), or less valuable by limiting efforts at surplus extraction or demand enhancement (Jamison and Hauge 2009; Sidak and Teece 2010). Increasing the cost of designing and operating broadband networks or reducing their revenue potential would certainly have a negative impact on the economics of deploying broadband. At a time when expanded broadband availability is a key policy goal, the application of regulations reducing the financial success of networks seems conflicting. Nevertheless, the debate proceeds, in part because no analysis has been performed on the impact that a network neutrality regulatory mandate would have on the incentives and ability of firms to deploy broadband services, particularly in those high-cost areas where service is often absent.

We show in this paper that while network neutrality regulation that increases costs or reduces profits would reduce broadband deployment generally, such regulations could disproportionately impact broadband in areas that are, on average, high-cost areas (such as rural markets). Empirical analysis suggests the differential between rural and urban is six fold.

† Chief Economist, Phoenix Center for Advanced Legal & Economic Public Policy Studies.
‡ President, Phoenix Center for Advanced Legal & Economic Public Policy Studies. The views expressed in this paper are the authors' alone and do not represent the views of the Phoenix Center, its Adjunct Fellows, or any of its individual Editorial Advisory Board members. We are indebted to Randy Beard, Adjunct Fellow, for his assistance in formulating the economic model we present in this paper.

In Section II, we present a conceptual framework for this analysis, and Section III attempts to calculate the disproportionate impact that a network neutrality mandate will have. Using publicly available network cost models and data from the United States, we show that under plausible conditions, while cost-increasing or revenue-reducing network neutrality mandates will materially impact broadband deployment in all geographic areas, such rules can be expected to disproportionately impact broadband deployment in high-cost areas and potentially by a significant amount. Our particular analysis indicates the differential impact is about six times as much as in lower cost, more urbanized areas.

II. Conceptual Framework

We set out to explore the impact that increased costs (or reduced value) of a broadband network caused by network neutrality mandates could have on the eventual deployment of such network in certain areas, particularly high-cost areas. We demonstrate in this section how an increase in costs of building or operating a network could have a disproportionate impact on deployment decisions in particular areas even if the cost change from the regulatory mandate is identical across all areas.

Figure 1. Network Deployment

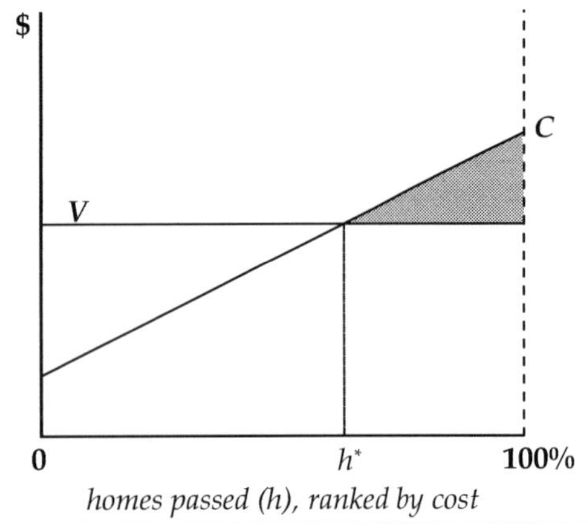

We can, in general, represent the effect an increase in costs has upon broadband deployment with some simple graphics. In Figure 1, we illustrate the economics of deployment. For the figure, we assume the broadband service provider must expend a fixed costs *C* to build network to a particular household (while *C* is incremental to each house, it is a fixed capital expense in that it is spent only once and is required to provide service). The cost of building a wireline broadband network varies widely by geography and to a large extent is driven by population density (Gasmi et al, 2002). The line labeled *C* in Figure 1 demonstrates this relationship—the vertical axis measures the costs to build out to a household and the horizontal axis is the percentage of households passed, where households are ranked by the fixed cost of constructing the network to *each* house.[1] Since the homes are sorted by *C*, the *C* curve slopes upward, with the lowest cost households on the far left and the highest cost households on the far right.

The horizontal line labeled *V* is the expected value of the household to the broadband network operator. The value might be considered the net revenues (or gross profits) that a firm expects to

[1] In other words, the curve labeled *C* is the fixed capital cost for the household *h* and not the sum of fixed capital costs at *h*. For simplicity, we illustrate the distribution of the per-household fixed capital costs as linear across all households (with total households being *H*). We have normalized households by dividing by total households *H* so that the horizontal axis is measured on the unit interval (i.e., the lowest value is 0 and the highest value is 1 or 100%).

generate from each particular household that it passes. It is important to note that V represents the "value" of the network to the network service provider—effectively the present value of gross profits that the firm can realize from building and operating the network.[2] For our purposes, we assume that the value of a broadband network for residential consumers is essentially unrelated to the underlying capital cost of constructing network. This assumption seems reasonable, since there is little reason to think that consumers in high-cost areas are willing to pay substantially more (or less) for voice, video and high-speed broadband data services than consumers in lower cost areas. As a result, the V curve is flat.

The network firm will build a network to a household as long as the expected value meets or exceeds the fixed costs of serving household i (where $V \geq C_i$). This equilibrium occurs where the C and V lines intersect, rendering the equilibrium percentage of households passed of h^*. Households to the right of h^* are too costly for the private sector to serve given expected benefits V. The shaded area in Figure 1 essentially represents a type of "gap" or "shortfall"—the portion of the service area where the cost of building a network is greater than the private value of the network that can be captured as revenues by the network provider. A subsidy of this amount would be sufficient to ensure ubiquitous coverage of the network. Policymakers that seek to promote the broadest penetration level for broadband network should favor policies that seek to minimize the size of this triangle as much as possible in economically efficient ways.

Now, consider the effect of increasing the capital cost of deploying network through, say, network neutrality regulations. An increase in costs lowers the equilibrium penetration of the broadband network. Figure 2 demonstrates this effect. If regulation increases the cost of the network deployment (by ΔC, with Δ meaning "a change in"), then the C curve shifts upward to C_R (the latter being cost with "Regulation") as illustrated in Figure 2. Now, the profit maximizing network operator builds to only h_R homes, reducing deployment by Δh homes. So, Figure 2 shows how increasing the cost of network deployment through regulation reduces the equilibrium number of homes passed.

Figure 2. Network Deployment with Cost Increase from Regulatory Mandate

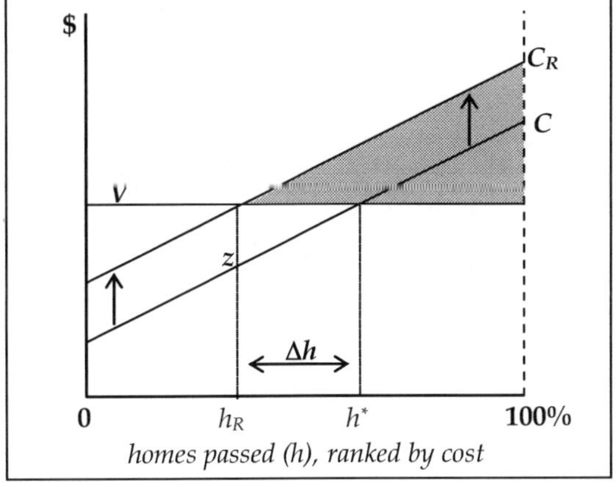

2 As a result, in this conceptual framework, V only represents the net revenues from the network that the network service provider can actually collect from users of the network. It is not a statement of the complete "social" value of the network or the value that consumers would place upon the network. In analyzing a firm's build-out decision it is, of course, obvious that only the "value captured by the firm" is relevant to the firm's decisions.

For ease of presentation, in Figure 2 we treat the effect of this regulatory mandate as an increase in capital cost to deploy network. But the same effect would be observed if the regulatory mandate effectively increased the incremental (or operating) cost of or reduced the revenue that the provider could collect from the network (by shifting the *V* curve to intersect *C* at *z*).

It is important to see that not only has the cost hike decreased broadband penetration from h^* to h_R, but the size of the shortfall shaded area has increased significantly. The "shortfall" between the cost of the network and the value of that network has increased, a development that would certainly make the goal of achieving universal access to broadband more costly to achieve.

Thus far, the conceptual argument is straightforward and intuitive, but our interest lies in the relative effect that cost increases has upon a particular category of households—those that are in high-cost areas (or areas with higher average cost of service). In particular, while our previous analysis clearly shows that a cost increase from a regulatory mandate decreases overall broadband deployment regardless of the level of cost, our focus in this paper is on whether that mandate would affect deployment disproportionately in areas that are, on average, high-cost compared to lower-cost markets.

We show now how the extent to which an increase in costs may differentially affect deployment across different areas. To do so, we turn to some simple algebra in order to demonstrate that it is not the average cost across markets that matters, but rather the slope of the cost distribution. Looking back to Figure 1, say that all customers have the same value to the broadband service provider *V*. The capital cost to serve a household is unique and when homes are ranked from lowest to highest costs, costs are distributed linearly across homes so that

$$C = a + bh \qquad (1)$$

where *a* and *b* are parameters of the capital cost function (or distribution). The marginal (or last) home passed satisfies the condition

$$V = a + bh\,, \qquad (2)$$

meaning the firm just breaks even on the last home passed. We define this last home as h^*, which is the equilibrium number of homes passed. Rearranging Equation (2), we have

$$h^* = \frac{V - a}{b}\,. \qquad (3)$$

Consider an increase in cost on network deployment as we did in Figure 1. If network neutrality regulation increases the cost of deployment, or shifts the cost distribution upward, then we have

$$\frac{\Delta h^*}{\Delta a} = -\frac{1}{b} < 0\,. \qquad (4)$$

From Equation (4), we see the change in homes passed is related to the slope of the cost distribution. The smaller is *b,* the larger the effect on homes passed. A small *b* implies a flat cost distribution so that deployment costs are similar across homes (around h^*).

If network neutrality regulation reduces the value of the network by raising incremental costs or reducing demand or revenues, the change in homes passed is measured as

$$\frac{\Delta h^*}{\Delta V} = \frac{1}{b} > 0, \qquad (5)$$

where again the change in homes passed depends only on the (inverse of the) slope of the cost distribution (*b*). Regardless of how network neutrality regulations impact profits, it is the slope of the cost distribution (around *h**, which is constant in the linear case) that determines the impact on homes passed. Further, the algebra shows that for every cost change, there is a change in gross profit that renders the same effect on homes passed.

Figure 3 illustrates the algebra by showing an increase in fixed cost in two different markets that are alike in many ways (average cost and penetration), but differ in the slopes of their *C* curves (i.e., the cost distribution). To illustrate the cost increase, the *C* curves in Figure 4 have been increased to C_R. As we illustrated in Figure 2, this increase in cost will decrease deployment in both markets, but Figure 3 shows that the market in Panel A sees a much more substantial decrease in network construction in response to an identical change in costs across markets.

Figure 3. Impact of Cost Change

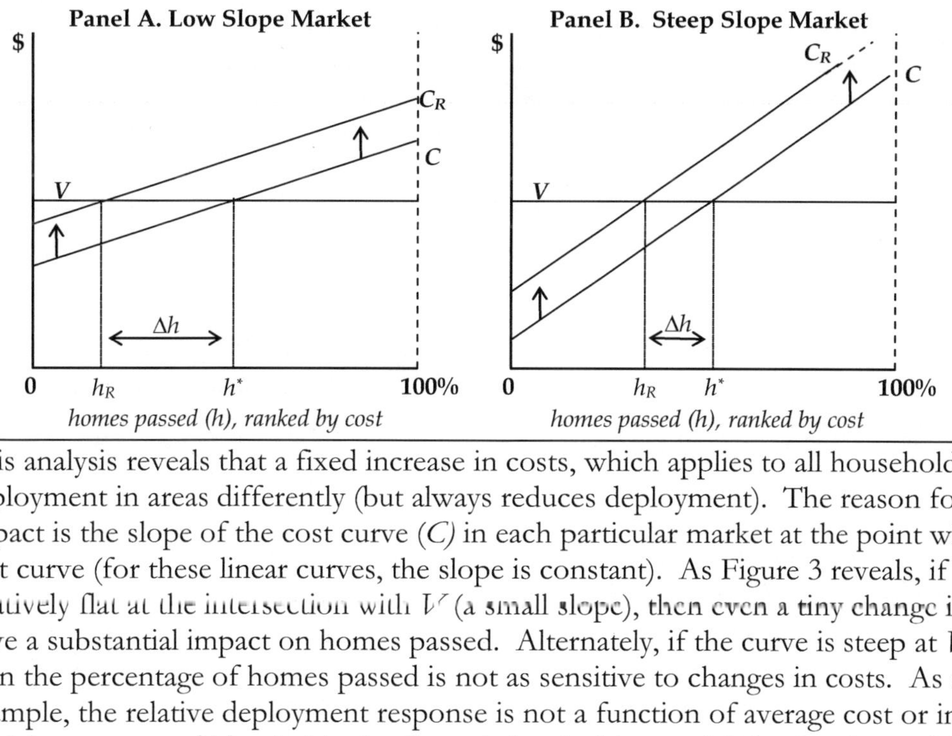

This analysis reveals that a fixed increase in costs, which applies to all households equally, can affect deployment in areas differently (but always reduces deployment). The reason for this differential impact is the slope of the cost curve (*C*) in each particular market at the point where *V* intersects that curve (for these linear curves, the slope is constant). As Figure 3 reveals, if the *C* curve is relatively flat at the intersection with *V* (a small slope), then even a tiny change in fixed costs will have a substantial impact on homes passed. Alternately, if the curve is steep at *V* (the slope is large), then the percentage of homes passed is not as sensitive to changes in costs. As shown in this example, the relative deployment response is not a function of average cost or initial penetration (which are assumed identical in the figures), but is driven solely by the slope of the *C* curve. Thus, if we know the slope of the curve at and around some point, then we can make estimates of the relative responses of network deployment to changes in costs across a variety of markets.

This linkage between response and the slope of *C* suggests a very useful tool of empirical analysis. If we can calculate these slopes for particular markets, then we can make certain predictions about the extent to which a regulatory policy might disproportionately impact deployment in that particular market and compare that impact on other markets with different characteristics. It is possible, for example, to analyze whether a regulatory mandate might disproportionately affect deployment in certain areas, such as high-cost areas, or urban areas, or states, or even by the service area of a particular local telephone company.

To develop this tool, however, we need granular, cost data that allows us to calculate the slopes of these cost curves. Complicating this analysis is the fact that, unlike our figures, the actual network cost curves in markets are highly non-linear; as a result, the slope in unique at each point along the curve. Fortunately, publicly-available network cost models have been created that do in fact estimate the fixed costs of building networks in various markets throughout the country. In Section III, we demonstrate how we can use this data to analyze and effectively calculate the slopes of these cost curves around some point V. With this data, we also calculate an index of the relative burden between low-cost and high-cost markets. While all increases in costs should be expected to reduce deployment, this analysis will show whether the burden of an increase cost would fall on high-cost areas well beyond what an equal impact on markets would render.

III. Simulation Data and Methodology

In recent years, for the purpose of distributing subsidies and setting unbundled element rates, the Federal Communications Commission and industry have developed and utilized cost models that effectively estimate the costs of building a communications network in the United States (Gasmi, et al. 2002). For some models, cost estimates provided all the way down to the "Census Block Group" level, which are relatively small geographic areas established by the United States Census. In 1990, there were about 230,000 Census Block Groups ("CBG") in the United States, so the network cost analysis is fairly granular. We can utilize this data and these models to estimate the slope of the fixed cost curves (C) that we describe in Section II above. With this information, we can determine whether or not, on average, areas with higher average costs are disproportionately and negatively affected by network neutrality rules (or any other regulatory mandate).

A. *Data*

To conduct the empirical analysis, we first collected the CBG loop cost estimates (L) for a large number of local exchange carriers using the HAI cost model.[3] Our sample was constructed by choosing states randomly and including all carriers in the state with data available. The result of this procedure is significant diversity in geography and costs. In our sample, there are about 95 million access lines and about half of all CBGs are represented.[4]

Once the data is collected, we calculate a cost index (u) for each CBG by dividing the CBG loop cost by the sample mean loop cost. The distribution of u is an index that measures the C values illustrated in Figures 1 and 2, though in reality the distribution of costs is nonlinear rather than linear as illustrated in those figures. We then use the average of this index for each carrier in each state as a measure of relative costs across markets. For each market, we have an average cost index of $\bar{u}$. In summarizing our results, we will use this cost index ($\bar{u}$) as the descriptor of each carrier/market. If the cost index $\bar{u}$ is large, then the market is considered a "high cost" market, on average. If $\bar{u}$ is low,

3 HAI Cost Model Version 5.0, which was the last version of this model to provide nationwide estimates of costs. We use the HAI model because it provides cost estimates down to the CBG level, whereas the FCC's Synthesis Model results are provided at the Wire Center level only. The two models produce highly comparable estimates of relative loop costs, with the two series having a very high correlation coefficient (Ford 2004). States included in the analysis are: AZ, CA, CO, FL, NY, GA, IA, LA, MD, MO, MS, MT, NC, NE, OH, SC, TX, VA, and WV.

4 In the 1990 Census, there were 229,466 Census Block Groups defined. Our sample includes 112,990 Census Block Groups.

then the market is a relatively "low cost" market, on average. The mean of $\bar{u}$ is 1.00 and the $\bar{u}$ series has a range of 0.46 to 2.10, so we have in our sample a wide range of average costs.

B. *Results*

As we discuss in Section II above, to assess the impact of Network Neutrality regulations on different markets, our task is to measure and compare the deployment response to a particular cost change (what is Δh in response to ΔC?). To make this calculation, we must first compute h_U, which is equilibrium number of homes passed in the Unregulated environment in each market that we study. To make this calculation, we need to assume some value (V) for the network, and V must be on the same scale as our cost index $\bar{u}$ (with the mean of $\bar{u}$ being 1.00).

We initially set V equal to 1.6 and do so because it is this value that produces an average homes passed rate of 50% (with a homes passed penetration rate ranging from a minimum of 26% to a maximum of 62%).[5] Clearly, an average penetration of 50% (and maximum of 62%) is low when discussing broadband network deployment (FCC 2010: 43), but setting V equal to 1.6 allows us to establish a *lower* bound response differential to cost changes. As shown in sensitivity analysis, larger values of V only strengthen the relationship found at $V = 1.6$. Nothing prohibits considering values of V less then 1.6, except as V gets smaller the ratio of value to costs gets so small that the network is barely deployed even in an unregulated market.

After computing h_U for the 51 markets in our sample using these inputs, we then compute homes passed in the regulated environment (h_R) by raising the capital cost of deployment in all markets by the same small, fixed amount (ΔC) as we did in the conceptual analysis in the previous section. So that ΔC is constant across markets, we set ΔC equal to 5% of V (since V is equal across and constant in all markets) and then compute h_R. (This calculation again illustrates that changes in C can be equivalent to changes in V).

With both h_U and h_R computed, we can then determine whether or not there is any relationship between the change in household penetration (Δh, or the difference between h_U and h_R) and the average cost index ($\bar{u}$). Essentially, this comparison will determine whether high-cost (often rural) markets are more or less affected by network neutrality regulations than their low-cost counterparts. We define $\Delta h = h_U - h_R$, which is always a non-negative number (h_U will equal or exceed h_R in all circumstances).[6] Higher values of Δh imply larger percentage-point reductions in the homes passed rate in a given market.

We use three different tools of statistical analysis to examine the relationship between this change in penetration (Δh) and the index of average costs ($\bar{u}$). First, Figure 4 provides the scatter plot and linear fit of the relationship between Δh and $\bar{u}$. As shown above, the plotted points are measures of the inverse slopes of the cost distributions. The figure illustrates that it is typically the case that the higher are average costs in a market ($\bar{u}$), the larger is the reduction in network deployment (that is, the smaller is h). Thus, there is reason to believe that network neutrality regulations will disproportionately harm high-cost, rural areas.

5 This assumption implies that a network company would have gross margin of about \$1.60 for \$100 in network investment. Press stories indicate that AT&T is spending about \$250 per line to upgrade to IPTV. At $V = 1.6$, this assumes that the additional margin from the upgrade will be only \$4 per month, which is probably lower than that expected by AT&T. Thus, setting V = 1.6 is conservative.

6 The calculation Δh could be zero, however, if the change leads to no reduction in homes passed because $V > u$ for all households with or without regulation.

Figure 4. Network Neutrality and Service Reduction

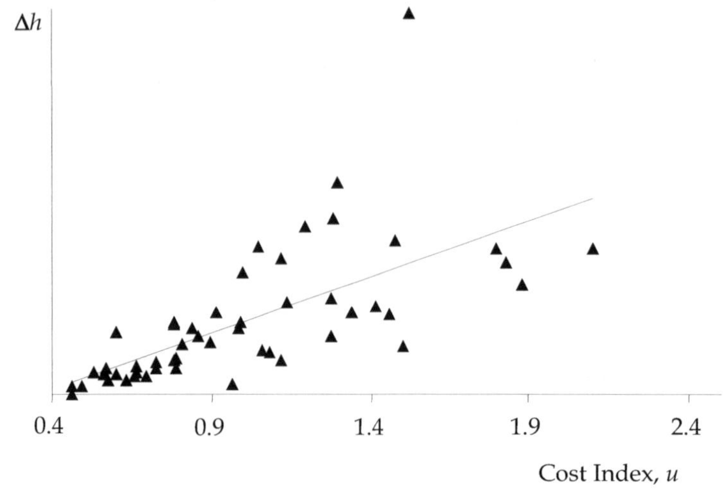

A second way to analyze this relationship is to compute the simple correlation coefficient between Δh and $\bar{u}$ (Gujarati 1995: 78). The computed correlation coefficient between the two series Δh and $\bar{u}$ is 0.66, which indicates a strong positive linear correlation. The correlation coefficient thus indicates that there is a high linear correlation between the reduction in network deployment and average costs of network, and confirms that network deployment is typically (though not always) reduced more in high-cost, rural areas.

Our findings of a strong relationship between Δh and $\bar{u}$ are again confirmed by using least squares regression (Gujarati 1995). The trend line in Figure 5 is based on least squares regression

$$\Delta h = \beta_0 + \beta_1 \bar{u} + \varepsilon, \qquad (6)$$

where the β are estimated parameters and ε is the disturbance term. As shown in Figure 5, the slope of the line estimated for this data is positive ($\beta_1 > 0$), indicating disproportionate harm in high-cost, rural areas from Network Neutrality regulations. The slope coefficient is statistically different from zero at better than the 1% level (t-stat = 6.12).

C. *The "Relative Burden" Index*

Our results establish that there is a strong relationship between the change in network penetration caused by a regulatory mandate and the average network cost index of a market. In other words, we can say that a regulatory mandate that increases the costs of building a broadband network will disproportionately and adversely affect broadband deployment in high-cost areas. It should not be a surprise to policymakers that an increase in network costs will decrease network deployment; what might be a surprise is the extent to which these increases costs will disproportionately affect high-cost areas, even if the costs of complying with the regulatory mandate do not vary by geography. Finding that high-cost areas will be disproportionately affected is important enough in itself, but "by how much" is an inevitable follow-up question to this conclusion. It is possible to provide a rough estimate the extent of this disproportionate impact on rural, high-cost areas. Our estimate of disproportionate impact, which we call the "relative burden index," is intuitive from a policy perspective. The availability of broadband service in all areas of the country is a national policy goal, so it would be reasonable to assume that policymakers would want their policies to apply with equal impact across markets. That is, if policymakers choose to impose a regulatory mandate that results in lower broadband penetration, then rural markets should not be burdened with more than their "fair share" of that burden. Stated differently, the probability that a household does not have access to a modern broadband network due to network neutrality regulations should be equal in high- and low-cost areas.[7] By comparing these probabilities across markets, we can generate a meaningful measure of disparity.

The results we calculate above can be used to compute this "relative burden index." To compute this relative burden index, we first compute the share of total homes in the sample for (particular definitions of) low-cost markets ($\bar{u} \leq 0.75$) and high-cost markets ($\bar{u} \geq 1.25$), which are labeled N_{HC} and N_{LC} (where subscripts "*HC*" and "*LC*" indicate high cost or low cost). Then, we compute the share of total homes passed lost to regulation for the high-cost and low-cost markets, which we label L_{HC} and L_{LC}. The index of relative burden is

$$BURDEN = \frac{L_{HC} / N_{HC}}{L_{LC} / N_{LC}}. \qquad (7)$$

The index *BURDEN* has an intuitive interpretation. If *BURDEN* = 4.0, for example, then high-cost markets bear four-times the burden from network neutrality regulations as do low-cost markets in terms of the reduction in homes passed. Put another way, if the index is 4.0, then a home in a high-cost market is four-times more likely not to have access to the network than if the home was in a low-cost market based on the imposition of network neutrality mandates. An index of 4.0 would be found, for example, if the percentage of total homes in high-cost markets is 10% and in low-cost markets is 40%, yet the high-cost and low-cost markets each contain 20% of the homes not passed due to network neutrality regulations [= (0.2/0.1)/(0.2/0.4)]. Thus, high-cost markets have 20% of the homes lost to regulation but only 10% of the homes, whereas the low-cost markets have only 20% of the homes lost to regulation but 40% of total homes. The impact in high-cost markets is, then, four times larger than low-cost markets.

Our calculations above permit us to calculate *BURDEN* for the network neutrality mandate as follows:

$$BURDEN = \frac{L_{HC} / N_{HC}}{L_{LC} / N_{LC}} = \frac{0.227 / 0.068}{0.382 / 0.722} = 6.31.$$

Thus, network neutrality regulation burdens high-cost markets more than low-cost markets by a factor of 6.31. Moreover, *BURDEN* rises if we use more extreme definitions of "low" and "high" cost. If we define high-cost markets as those with $\bar{u} \geq 1.5$ (markets with average cost more than 50% of the mean) and reduce the low-cost market boundary to $\bar{u} \leq 0.50$ (markets with average cost only 50% of the mean), then *BURDEN* = 16.93. *BURDEN* is consistently above 1.00 for any sensible definition of low- and high-cost. Even if we define low- and high-cost as being below or above the mean cost, then *BURDEN* = 4.47.

7 This statement is true regardless of the initial level of homes passed, since the percentage change in homes passed is computed using total homes.

The disparate burden that a network neutrality mandate would impose on high-cost markets is substantial. Even though the costs of complying with a regulatory mandate may not vary by geography, broadband deployment in high-cost areas will be disproportionately affected by that mandate. The disparate burden increases significantly in even high-cost markets.

D. *Sensitivity Analysis*

We have made a number of assumptions in our analysis, but our findings are robust to alternative assumptions.[8] One area where a sensitivity analysis is particularly warranted is the estimated value of a household in terms of gross profits, which form the basis for the *V* curve. In Table 1, we present five different values of *V* (including 1.6) to evaluate the role the selection of *V* plays in our findings. As revealed in the table, the disproportionate harm to high-cost areas rises as *V* rises.[9]

Table 1. Sensitivity Analysis

V	Correlation Coefficient	t-stat(β_1)	Relative Burden (*BURDEN*)
1.6	0.66	6.12*	6.31
1.8	0.68	6.41*	6.08
2.0	0.68	6.42*	7.66
2.2	0.83	10.28*	8.93
2.4	0.82	10.06*	9.37

* Statistically different from zero at the 5% level or better.

One interpretation of the rising burden in *V* is that the more valuable the service (or, the higher the penetration in an unregulated environment), the greater will be the relative harm to high-cost markets for some given cost change. Since broadband is considered to a high-value service (indeed, the triple play is a $100+ bundle of services), our analysis suggests that the impact on high-cost areas from network neutrality regulations could be substantial.

E. *Caveats*

As with any theoretical or empirical analysis, the conclusions reported here are based in large part on the underlying assumptions of the model. We have assumed that the cost of deploying a modern broadband network is correlated with the forward-looking cost of deploying telephone network. We believe this assumption is reasonable, particularly in the case of fiber deployment. It is certainly possible to imagine networks (particularly hypothetical networks) which do not exhibit the expected cost properties with respect to household density, and in such cases our findings may change. Nevertheless, under the plausible framework we have set forth here, the results are robust.

---

8 As long as the actual *C* curve for deployment is proportional to our variable *u*, the disproportionate impact on rural areas remains, though its size may differ.

9 Of course, as *V* gets smaller than 1.6, the relatively harm declines. When *V* is 0.8, the effect across markets is roughly equal (and inverted for values below 0.8). However, at $V = 0.8$, the average penetration of the service is only 34%, and as low as 12% in high-cost areas. It is little surprise that the deployment effect becomes small in high-cost areas when deployment is almost non-existent even in the unregulated state. As a technical matter, the relationship of *V* to Δh suggests that low-cost markets typically have very flat *C* curves in the lower cost segments of their markets with sharply rising C curves as penetration approaches 100%. In contrast, the C curves of high-cost markets typically rise even in the lower cost areas but do not rise very steeply as penetration approaches 100%.

IV. Conclusion

Increasing the costs of building or operating a broadband network by a regulatory mandate unquestionably will result in lower broadband network construction across the board. But our analysis shows that this decline in construction will not be evenly spread across the country as a whole—in fact, deployment in high-cost areas will be harmed disproportionately by any such cost-increasing mandate.

Using publicly available data and cost models, we show in this POLICY PAPER that a regulatory mandate like network neutrality could result in at least a six-fold relative reduction in broadband deployment in high-cost rural areas than in low-cost urban areas (under plausible conditions). In a very real way, the burden that a network neutrality mandate would create would be disproportionately (but not exclusively) borne on the back of rural America. These findings give credence to arguments raised by some that have warned that network neutrality mandates could "seriously delay the benefits of new broadband deployment" in rural communities.[10]

Understanding the impact that public policy will have on broadband deployment is of crucial importance. The goal of universal broadband service has been called the "primary challenge" of the nation's telecommunications policy. Given that overarching goal, it is therefore appropriate to examine closely a public policy like network neutrality that will disproportionately and adversely affect broadband deployment in rural areas before we rush to pass legislation. We encourage further research on this important topic.

[10] National Grange, *Rural Public Interest Group Concerned About Net Neutrality Debate in Light of Congressional Hearing,* (May 25, 2006) (available at: http://www.nationalgrange.org/PressRoom/pr/2006/Neutrality.htm).

REFERENCES

Clarke, Richard .N (2009) *Costs of Neutral/Unmanaged IP Networks*, REVIEW OF NETWORK ECONOMICS: Vol. 8, 61-89 .

FCC (2010) *High-Speed Services for Internet Access: Status as of December 31, 2008*, Federal Communications Commission: Washington, DC (available at: http://hraunfoss.fcc.gov/edocs_public/attachmatch/DOC-296239A1.pdf).

Ford, George S. (2004) *Federalism in Telecommunications Regulation: Effectiveness and Accuracy of State Commission Implementation of TELRIC in Local Telecoms Markets,* Phoenix Center Policy Bulletin No. 9 (available at: http://www.phoenix-center.org/PCPB9Final.pdf.

Gasmi, Farid, D. Mark Kennet, William W. Sharkey, Jean-Jacques Laffont (2002) *Cost Proxy Models and Telecommunications Policy: A New Empirical Approach to Regulation.* MIT Press: Boston, Massachusetts.

Gujarati, Damodar N. (1995) *Basic Econometrics.* McGraw Hill: New York.

Jamison, Mark A. and Janice A. Hauge (2009) *Dumbing Down the Net: A Further Look at the Net Neutrality Debate*, in *Internet Policy and Economics: Challenges and Perspectives*, W. Lehr and L. M. Pupillo eds. at 57-72: Springer: Dordrecht.

Marsden, Chris (2010). *Net Neutrality: Towards a Co-Regulatory Solution.* Bloomsbury USA.

Sidak, J. Gregory and David J. Teece (2010) *Innovation Spillovers And The "Dirt Road" Fallacy: The Intellectual Bankruptcy of Banning Optional Transactions for Enhanced Delivery Over The Internet, forthcoming in* 6 JOURNAL OF COMPETITION LAW & ECONOMICS (2010).

Made in the USA
Monee, IL
05 November 2026

67813172R00146